THE CAMBRIDGE COMPANION TO
VATICAN II

This *Companion* provides an accessible guide for those seeking to comprehend the significance of Vatican II for Catholicism today. It offers a thorough overview of the Second Vatican Council, the most significant event in the history of Roman Catholicism since the Protestant Reformation. Almost six decades since the close of the council, its teaching remains what one pope referred to as a "sure compass" for guiding today's church. The first part of the volume examines the historical, theological, and ecclesial contexts for comprehending the significance of the council. It also presents the key processes as well as the participants who were central to the actual conduct of the council. The second part identifies and explores the central themes embedded in the council documents. The volume concludes with a unique appendix intended to guide students wishing to pursue more advanced research in Vatican II studies.

RICHARD R. GAILLARDETZ is the Joseph Professor of Catholic Systematic Theology at Boston College. He has published numerous articles and authored or edited fourteen books, most recently, a newly revised and expanded edition of his popular book, *By What Authority? Foundations for Understanding Authority in the Church* (2018). He has also published *An Unfinished Council: Vatican II, Pope Francis, and the Renewal of Catholicism* (2015). Dr. Gaillardetz received the Sophia Award from the Washington Theological Union in 2000 for theological excellence in service of ministry and the Yves Congar Award for theological excellence from Barry University in 2018. He served as president of the Catholic Theological Society of America in 2013–14.

CAMBRIDGE COMPANIONS TO RELIGION
This is a series of companions to major topics and key figures in theology and religious studies. Each volume contains specially commissioned chapters by international scholars, which provide an accessible and stimulating introduction to the subject for new readers and nonspecialists.

Other Titles in the Series

AMERICAN ISLAM Edited by Juliane Hammer and Omid Safi

AMERICAN JUDAISM Edited by Dana Evan Kaplan

AMERICAN METHODISM Edited by Jason E. Vickers

ANCIENT MEDITERRANEAN RELIGIONS Edited by Barbette Stanley Spaeth

AUGUSTINE'S "CONFESSIONS" Edited by Tarmo Toom

KARL BARTH Edited by John Webster

THE BIBLE, 2nd edition Edited by Bruce Chilton

THE BIBLE AND LITERATURE Edited by Calum Carmichael

BIBLICAL INTERPRETATION Edited by John Barton

BLACK THEOLOGY Edited by Dwight N. Hopkins and Edward P. Antonio

DIETRICH BONHOEFFER Edited by John de Gruchy

JOHN CALVIN Edited by Donald K. McKim

CHRISTIAN DOCTRINE Edited by Colin Gunton

CHRISTIAN ETHICS Edited by Robin Gill

CHRISTIAN MYSTICISM Edited by Amy Hollywood and Patricia Z. Beckman

CHRISTIAN PHILOSOPHICAL THEOLOGY Edited by Charles Taliaferro
   and Chad V. Meister

CHRISTIAN POLITICAL THEOLOGY Edited by Craig Hovey and Elizabeth Phillips

THE CISTERIAN ORDER Edited by Mette Birkedal Bruun

CLASSICAL ISLAMIC THEOLOGY Edited by Tim Winter

JONATHAN EDWARDS Edited by Stephen J. Stein

EVANGELICAL THEOLOGY Edited by Timothy Larsen and Daniel J. Treier

FEMINIST THEOLOGY Edited by Susan Frank Parsons

FRANCIS OF ASSISI Edited by Michael J. P. Robson

THE GOSPELS Edited by Stephen C. Barton

THE HEBREW BIBLE/OLD TESTAMENT Edited by Stephen B. Chapman
   and Marvin A. Sweeney

THE JESUITS Edited by Thomas Worcester

JESUS Edited by Markus Bockmuehl

JUDAISM AND LAW Edited by Christine Hayes

C. S. LEWIS Edited by Robert MacSwain and Michael Ward

LIBERATION THEOLOGY Edited by Chris Rowland

(continued after index)

THE CAMBRIDGE COMPANION TO

VATICAN II

Edited by

Richard R. Gaillardetz
Boston College, Massachusetts

With the assistance of
Elyse J. Raby

CAMBRIDGE
UNIVERSITY PRESS

BX
830
1962
C484
2020

CAMBRIDGE
UNIVERSITY PRESS

University Printing House, Cambridge CB2 8BS, United Kingdom

One Liberty Plaza, 20th Floor, New York, NY 10006, USA

477 Williamstown Road, Port Melbourne, VIC 3207, Australia

314–321, 3rd Floor, Plot 3, Splendor Forum, Jasola District Centre,
New Delhi – 110025, India

79 Anson Road, #06–04/06, Singapore 079906

Cambridge University Press is part of the University of Cambridge.

It furthers the University's mission by disseminating knowledge in the pursuit of
education, learning, and research at the highest international levels of excellence.

www.cambridge.org
Information on this title: www.cambridge.org/9781108483568
DOI: 10.1017/9781108698610

First published 2020

A catalogue record for this publication is available from the British Library.

Library of Congress Cataloging-in-Publication Data
NAMES: Gaillardetz, Richard R., 1958– editor.
TITLE: The Cambridge companion to Vatican II / edited by Richard R. Gaillardet, Boston
College, Massachusetts ; with the assistance of Elyse J. Raby.
DESCRIPTION: Cambridge ; New York : Cambridge University Press, 2020. | Series:
Cambridge companions to religion | Includes bibliographical references and index.
IDENTIFIERS: LCCN 2019046133 (print) | LCCN 2019046134 (ebook) | ISBN 9781108483568
(hardback) | ISBN 9781108457637 (paperback) | ISBN 9781108698610 (epub)
SUBJECTS: LCSH: Vatican Council (2nd : 1962–1965 : Basilica di San Pietro in
Vaticano)–History. | Catholic Church–History–20th century. | Catholic Church–Doctrines.
CLASSIFICATION: LCC BX830 1962 .C484 2020 (print) | LCC BX830 1962 (ebook) |
DDC 262/.52–dc23
LC record available at https://lccn.loc.gov/2019046133
LC ebook record available at https://lccn.loc.gov/2019046134

ISBN 978-1-108-48356-8 Hardback
ISBN 978-1-108-45763-7 Paperback

In memory of Gerard Mannion,
our esteemed colleague

Contents

Abbreviations of Conciliar Documents

AA   *Apostolicam Actuositatem*. Decree on the Apostolate of the Laity.

AG   *Ad Gentes*. Decree on the Church's Missionary Activity.

CD   *Christus Dominus*. Decree on the Pastoral Office of Bishops in the Church.

DH   *Dignitatis Humanae*. Declaration on Religious Liberty.

DV   *Dei Verbum*. Dogmatic Constitution on Divine Revelation

GE   *Gravissimum Educationis*. Declaration on Christian Education.

GS   *Gaudium et Spes*. Pastoral Constitution on the Church in the Modern World.

IM   *Inter Mirifica*. Decree on the Mass Media.

LG   *Lumen Gentium*. Dogmatic Constitution on the Church.

NA   *Nostra Aetate*. Declaration on the Relation of the Church to Non-Christian Religions.

OE   *Orientalium Ecclesiarum*. Decree on the Catholic Eastern Churches.

OT   *Optatam Totius*. Decree on the Training of Priests.

PC   *Perfectae Caritatis*. Decree on the Up-to-Date Renewal of Religious Life.

PO   *Presbyterorum Ordinis*. Decree on the Ministry and Life of Priests.

SC   *Sacrosanctum Concilium*. Constitution on the Sacred Liturgy.

UR   *Unitatis Redintegratio*. Decree on Ecumenism.

Contributors

Stephen Bevans, SVD, is the Emeritus Louis J. Luzbetak, SVD Professor of Mission and Culture at Catholic Theological Union.

Catherine Clifford is Professor of Systematic and Historical Theology at Saint Paul University, Ottawa.

Edmund Kee-Fook Chia is Senior Lecturer of Theology at Australian Catholic University.

Peter De Mey is Professor of Theology and Religious Studies at KU Leuven.

Massimo Faggioli is Professor of Theology and Religious Studies at Villanova University.

Brian Flanagan is Associate Professor of Theology/Religious Studies at Marymount University.

Gabriel Flynn is Associate Professor of Theology at Dublin City University.

Mark R. Francis, CSV, is President and Professor of Liturgy at Catholic Theological Union.

Richard R. Gaillardetz is the Joseph Professor of Catholic Systematic Theology at Boston College.

James Keenan, SJ, is Canisius Professor of Theology at Boston College.

Richard Lennan is Professor of Systematic Theology at Boston College School of Theology and Ministry.

Gerard Mannion was the Joseph and Winifred Amaturo Professor in Catholic Studies at Georgetown University.

Amanda C. Osheim is Associate Professor of Practical Theology at Loras College.

Thomas P. Rausch, SJ, is the T. Marie Chilton Professor of Catholic Theology, Emeritus at Loyola Marymount.

Ormond Rush is Associate Professor of Theology at Australian Catholic University.

Karim Schelkens is Associate Professor of the History of Religion at Tilburg University.

Gemma Simmonds, CJ, is Director of the Religious Life Institute at the Institute of Theology, Cambridge, UK.

David Farina Turnbloom is Assistant Professor of Theology at the University of Portland.

Susan K. Wood, SCL, is Academic Dean and Professor of Systematic Theology at Regis College, Toronto.

Preface

RICHARD R. GAILLARDETZ

The Second Vatican Council was the most significant event in the history of Catholicism since the Protestant Reformation. Yet an accurate and comprehensive grasp of the council's abiding significance for contemporary Catholicism can be illusive. Many Catholics have only the vaguest sense of what Vatican II accomplished. For Catholic clergy, lay ministers, church activists, theologians, and church commentators, the situation may be somewhat different. They often have a working Vatican II lexicon populated by key phrases: a theology of the laity, collegiality, liturgical participation, the sense of the faithful, the church as leaven in the world. Yet too often, these phrases are wielded with little regard for their antecedents in the Catholic tradition and with little appreciation for the debates and compromises that lay behind the council's distinctive redeployment and development of these terms and concepts.

Efforts to comprehend the enduring significance of the council for the church today have been plagued by a Catholic version of the "culture wars." Those belonging to the Catholic "right" have cautiously acknowledged the council's contribution but not without considerable handwringing regarding its proper interpretation. They admit to legitimate theological developments but insist that the council effected no real change at the level of doctrine. For them, the council's primary contribution was limited to its change in pastoral tone, an emphasis on spiritual (rather than structural) renewal, and an empowerment of the laity in the secular order. Others belonging to the Catholic "left" may be tempted to simply impose on the council teaching their own agenda for church reform. They often struggle between two impulses: gratitude for the gift of the council and discouragement at the extent to which important conciliar teachings have, in their view, yet to be fully implemented.

Debates regarding Vatican II's fundamental continuity or discontinuity with the church's broader, more ancient tradition have not been particularly helpful. A living ecclesial tradition will always bear marks of both continuity and discontinuity with what came before. Without any acknowledgment of the discernible continuity of the Christian faith across time, the very notion of a "tradition" dissolves. Without the recognition of a certain discontinuity – genuine shifts and even breaks with what had come before – we cannot speak of this tradition as "living." As Pope John XXIII himself noted in his opening address at the council, there was really no need to call for an ecumenical council if such a council were to do no more than repeat what had always been taught. Yet clearly Pope John believed that the council must remain true to the church's apostolic faith. He convened Vatican II because he feared that the church's penchant for clinging to its eternal truths risked ignoring pressing challenges in both the church and the world. It was in this sense that Vatican II was to be a "pastoral" council.

The challenge of acquiring an adequate, comprehensive grasp of the council's teaching is daunting, if for no other reason than that the amount of material produced by Vatican II dwarfs that of all other councils. If one considers all twenty-one ecumenical councils together, they produced 37,727 lines of text. Vatican II alone provides 12,179 lines (approximately 32 percent), whereas the Council of Trent provided 5,637 lines. This does not include the volumes of archival material related to the council speeches, commission notes, participant memoirs, etc. Yet the difficulties attendant on the study of the council go well beyond that presented by the voluminous documentation. It has now become a commonplace to note that Vatican II represents more than a collection of sixteen documents; Vatican II was an ecclesial "event," a dramatic irruption of the Holy Spirit in the life of the church at a particular point in the church's history. To understand the full contours of this "event" one must know something about the modern history of Catholicism leading up to the council. What were some of the ordinary experiences of Catholics "on the ground" in the decades leading up to the council? What key ecclesial movements, church leaders, and influential theological voices helped pave the way for the council? And what of the council itself? To appreciate the full import of the council we must have at least a rudimentary appreciation for the rules governing the preparation for and conduct of the council and the key players who contributed to the work of the council. Finally, we must acquire an adequate hermeneutics or theory of interpretation to guide us in our study of the council's teaching.

This explains why this volume is divided into two parts. Part I includes six chapters that provide the crucial historical, pastoral, and theological context necessary for appreciating the work of the council.

Part II offers the reader a set of twelve chapters exploring themes fundamental to the council's teaching. A conscious decision was made *not* to simply offer commentaries on each of the council's documents. Rather, the chapters invite the reader to "connect the dots," identifying thematic links across the various documents. These chapters offer the reader a sense of how a particular theme was developed over the course of the council, how it was variously treated in different texts, and how that conciliar theme has been received and developed in the post-conciliar period. Each chapter ends with some limited suggestions for further reading. The volume concludes with a helpful Appendix introducing students of the council to the various scholarly instruments and resources available to them.

The volume is intended, as the title suggests, as a "companion" text. It does not substitute for the council documents themselves, but offers a set of complementary readings that can help the reader plumb the riches of the council documents more profitably. There are a number of helpful English translations to the council documents that are now available but, unless indicated otherwise, the contributors to this volume will be using the revised, inclusive-language, Flannery translation of the Vatican II documents.

I want to thank Beatrice Rehl of Cambridge University Press for initially approaching me about undertaking this project and for expertly guiding it to completion. The contributors to this volume were chosen because of their international reputation and acknowledged expertise in Vatican II studies. I have learned much from them over the years and feel fortunate that they were willing to take time from their busy schedules to participate in this project.

I have benefited from the diligence and keen eye of my research assistant, Elyse Raby, who kept track of the progress of each chapter from preliminary draft to final submission. She demonstrated extraordinary skills as a copyeditor, often bringing her own theological expertise to bear with gentle suggestions for further edits. She also undertook the difficult work of producing the index for this volume. She fulfilled these and other tasks with a grace and professionalism that marks the beginning of a promising career as a theologian.

I would like to thank my colleagues at Boston College for their support for me and my work, and my students who have shared a passion for the study of Vatican II. Finally, I want to express my immeasurable gratitude to my wife, Diana, and our sons, Andrew, David, Brian, and Greg – my most cherished companions on the journey.

Part I

Vatican II in Context

1 Church Life in the First Half of the Twentieth Century

MARK R. FRANCIS

What was the experience of being Catholic during the fifty years prior to Vatican II? How did the world appear to an average believer through a lens of faith that had not yet been refocused by the reforms wrought by the council? During these years, the demographic center of Catholicism was located in Europe and North and South America. Sub-Saharan Africa had yet to experience the amazing growth of the church it would know after 1960. Asia, with the exception of the Philippines, was still very much mission territory. For this reason, these reflections will dwell largely on life as a Catholic in Europe and North America, with some notes on Latin America.

INTRODUCTION

Sociologist of religion Peter Berger used an expression to describe how religion has traditionally served as a kind of overarching frame that gives order and meaning to the lives of believers. He coined the term "sacred canopy" to convey the way that religion can permeate practically every aspect of human life, giving meaning and coherence to one's relationship with God, other people, and the world. This is especially true for cultures characterized as "premodern" – where religious, social, and political structures are not questioned but taken as "givens" of human life ordained by God. The Catholic sacred canopy of the early twentieth century spread over an enchanted cosmos. Today its influence is different because of the challenges of globalization and our postmodern sensibilities. These tend to relativize all-encompassing narratives that explain who we are and why we are in the world. Within living memory, however, the Catholic worldview held at the beginning of the twentieth century by a majority of believers gave purpose and meaning to all aspects of life.

Prior to Vatican II there was never a doubt that everyone's actions – both good and bad – had consequences and could affect not only one's own salvation but that of others as well. A key part of the Catholic sacred canopy is the belief in the "communion of saints" that appears in the creed. It was popularly understood as defining three categories of people in the church: the church militant (the living) striving to overcome temptations to sin and live a Christian life; the church suffering (the souls in purgatory) who are being purged of sin in order to enter heaven; and the church triumphant (those in heaven) who are in the presence of God and the saints. The living, in praying for those in purgatory, could shorten "the poor souls'" time waiting to enter heaven. Those in heaven could intercede for those on earth – sometimes miraculously – to ask God to effect cures from disease and grant other favors. Everything and everyone belonged to a network of relationships.

In the eyes of most Catholics at the time, God had directly established the organization of the church. That organization was strictly hierarchical. The pope, bishops, and priests were clearly ordained by God to teach, sanctify, and rule. They, together with religious women, constituted a "spiritual elite" since, having dedicated themselves to Christ, they were considered holier than laypeople. While there were differences and even violent disagreements among national groups within the church, this hierarchy was part of the "sacred canopy," giving hope and meaning to Catholics as they faced the challenges of a changing world.

Parishes, fraternal organizations, schools, hospitals, and family traditions of piety closely linked to ethnic groups constantly reaffirmed Catholic identity during the first half of the twentieth century. In both Europe and North America, being Catholic meant participating in a web of relationships that gave each Catholic certainty about his or her place in society and successfully defended the faith from what was perceived as the hostile, secularizing voices in Europe and from the Protestant and often anti-Catholic dominant culture in the United States. A Catholic parallel universe was created that intentionally isolated and insulated the individual from a surrounding modern culture that was deemed inimical to the faith. On the eve of Vatican II, Will Herberg pointed out the omnipresence of Catholic institutions in the lives of Catholics in his now-classic work on religion in the United States, *Protestant, Catholic, Jew*. "The Catholic Church in America operates a vast network of institutions of almost every type and variety ... This immense system constitutes at one and the same time a self-contained Catholic world within its own complex interior economy and American Catholicism's resources for participation in the larger American Community."[1] How was this self-contained world maintained?

During the first half of the twentieth century in the United States this "self-contained world" has been described as the "Catholic ghetto." In this ghetto, roles were clear and shored up social and familial expectations. In the United States, Catholicism was a predominantly urban and ethnic phenomenon. After high school it was normal for young men to settle down, find a job, and marry. Young women did not aspire (or were not supposed to aspire) to work outside the home. Unless they entered the convent, they were to marry (preferably a Catholic of their ethnic group), have as many children as God sent their way, and serve as wife and mother. If at all possible, children were to attend the Catholic school attached to their parish. In many ways, the parish served as a social focus for the family, providing space and activities for old and young. It was not unusual for Catholic families to have five or six children since artificial birth control was forbidden by the church and regarded as selfish and immoral. Sometimes a family was blessed with one or more of the children choosing to become a priest or religious sister. These sons and daughters were cherished by both parents and siblings who supported their vocation.

In order to understand church life in the first half of the twentieth century, we will first examine how the nature of the church was understood and how authority was exercised. We will then see how these theological and ecclesiological positions were put into practice at the parish level. Second, it is necessary to consider how the all-important leadership of the local parish was trained. How did seminaries prepare parish priests for their key role of serving Catholics? In addition to the intellectual formation of priests, their pastoral preparation for liturgy and preaching needs to be described to understand the capacity of the clergy to deal with issues affecting their flock. How was the liturgy experienced by the people in the pews? There was no doubt that the priests were in charge of parish and sacramental life, but Catholic life was also enriched by popular devotions. These devotions were often linked to ethnic origins; they helped give voice not only to the spiritual longings of Catholic immigrants but also promoted identity and dignity in the face of a surrounding culture. Finally, we will consider the ferment in the church that led to a reconfiguration of this sacred canopy just prior to Vatican II.

---

[1] Will Herberg, *Protestant, Catholic, Jew: An Essay in American Religious Sociology* (Garden City, NY: Anchor Books, 1960), 153–54.

THE LOCAL PARISH

Historian Jay P. Dolan, in describing the US Catholic ethos of the pre–Vatican II era, identified "authority" as its first important component.[2] The Catholic Church presented itself as an international hierarchical institution and there was no doubt who held the power of governance. In 1906 Pope Pius X was unapologetic regarding the division of the church into two categories of persons whose roles were clearly delineated. "The Church is essentially an unequal society ... comprising two categories of persons, the Pastors and the flock ... The one duty of the multitude is to allow themselves to be led, and, like a docile flock, to follow the Pastors."[3] The pope is making here the classic distinction between the *"ecclesia docens"* (the teaching church – the clerics) and the *"ecclesia discens"* (the learning church – the laity). Catholics – lay and clerical alike – knew their place.

What, then, was the conception of the church held by both clergy and laypeople? Catholics before Vatican II were taught that this hierarchical arrangement came from Christ himself. Unlike the fractious Protestants, Catholics took pride in their unity of mind and heart that centered on obedience to the pope as the Vicar of Christ and to the bishops as successors to the apostles. They were also to obey their parish priests with whom they had the most dealings and who mediated the presence of Christ through the sacraments. The Catholic Church was regarded as the one, true church, founded by Christ himself when he gave the keys of the kingdom of God to the apostle Peter in Matthew 16. The unity of the church that had been centered on St. Peter as Bishop of Rome and his successors was shattered by Protestants who, in their mistaken pride, relied on their own interpretations of scripture and disdained the tradition of the church that dated from the time of the apostles. This led them into error, cut them off from the grace God made available in the sacraments, and threatened their very salvation. For that reason, Catholics were to avoid interaction with Protestants, especially religiously, lest they be swayed by their errors.

This view of the religious world and the Catholic Church's place in it was taught and professed by Catholics the world over. Confident in the church's mediating role, if individual believers followed the laws set

---

[2] Jay P. Dolan, *The American Catholic Experience: A History from the Colonial Times to the Present* (Garden City, NY: Doubleday, 1985), 221.

[3] Pope Pius X, *Vehementer Nos* (1906), 8.

down by the pope and the bishops, there was a certainty that this faithfulness and obedience would secure the salvation of their immortal souls. A prayer from the nineteenth-century *Ursuline Manual* sums up this clear vision of the reward in store for those who remain faithful to the doctrine and duties taught by the church.

> Most gracious and merciful God ... who hast made me ... a member of the one and true Catholic Church, wherein I am secured from error, and guided in the road that leads to eternal bliss. Grant, oh my God, that I may never prove so ungrateful as to waver in the faith, or to contradict it by my conduct; but that, until the end of my life, firmly believing what it teaches, and earnestly endeavoring to comply with the duties it lays down, I may merit the eternal reward thou hast promised to those who persevere to the end in the profession of Thy faith in the observance of Thy commandments.[4]

THE TERRITORIAL PARISH

Established after the Council of Trent in the sixteenth century, the territorial parish (i.e., a parish that is defined by geographical bounds) was founded by the bishop and governed by the pastor with the help of associate priests and women religious. This parish accompanied Catholics from cradle to grave through the celebration of the sacraments, the parish school, social and charitable parish organizations, and a myriad of devotional practices that had developed in the nineteenth century. The parish was such an important institution in the lives of Catholics that it served as the geographical marker for identifying neighborhoods in large cities where Catholics dominated the urban landscape. Even non-Catholics used this shorthand way to locate where they lived in a city: "I'm from Visitation" or "I live in Our Lady of Lourdes" was a common way of identifying one's neighborhood. In order to be a member in good standing of the parish it was required that parishioners do their "Easter duty," which consisted of going to confession and receiving communion during the Easter season. This minimum obligation was sometimes even monitored by cards given to the penitent at the time of their confession and then handed in when the individual went to communion.

---

[4] *The Ursuline Manual*, 139ff. Quoted in Dolan, *The American Catholic Experience*, 224.

While the pope was revered and the bishop largely respected, the average Catholic's experience of authority usually came in dealings with the local pastor. Writing to his flock in 1947, a pastor explained why it was important for lay people to heed the voice of their pastors. "Your parish is the most important society to which you as a layman can belong. Your parish speaks not only with the voice of your pastor and your Bishop, but with the voice of the Holy Father, who speaks to you the words of God."[5]

It would be difficult to underestimate the importance of the local parish priest in the lives of Catholics before Vatican II. In the United States, the pastor and his fellow priests were usually the most educated persons in parishes that were made up predominantly of working-class immigrant families. The priests' interpretation of the laws and doctrines of the Church was considered authoritative. They were also asked to help settle family disputes and serve as social workers and counselors. Much of the atmosphere of a Catholic parish prior to Vatican II was determined by the preparation of priests that took place in quasi-monastic settings, in seminaries located in the hinterlands away from the temptations of cities. Their ascetical training emphasized personal holiness and discouraged any serious engagement with the modern society lest they be corrupted by "worldliness."

THE TRAINING OF PRIESTS

Bernard Botte, a Benedictine liturgical scholar from Belgium educated before Vatican II, sketches how priests of his generation were trained in his book *From Silence to Participation*. He notes that formation for the majority of the clergy followed a classic model. In Europe, at least, "the majority of priests had six years of humanities studies in Greek and Latin before entering the seminary. Then they had two years of philosophy and at least three years of theology."[6] Most seminarians in the United States came from minor seminaries and were less prepared than their European counterparts. The historian Msgr. John Tracy Ellis offered an important critique of the intellectual life of US Catholics during this period. He decried the general low level of intellectual

---

[5] Fr. Henry Freiburg, OFM of Our Lady of the Angels in Cleveland in 1947. Cited in John T. McGreevy, *Parish Boundaries: The Catholic Encounter with Race in the Twentieth-Century Urban North* (Chicago: University of Chicago Press, 1996), 25.

[6] Bernard Botte, *From Silence to Participation: An Insider's View of Liturgical Renewal* (Washington, DC: Pastoral Press, 1988), 4.

attainment of Catholic institutions of higher learning around the country. He blamed in part anti-intellectualism in the US Catholic mentality that often passed for piety.[7] If Catholic colleges and universities suffered from this deficiency, seminaries were even more affected by this lack of concern for the intellectual life. As Bishop John Lancaster Spalding (1840–1916) lamented at the beginning of the century, "The ecclesiastical seminary is not a school of intellectual culture, either here in America or elsewhere, and to imagine that it can become the instrument of intellectual culture is to cherish a delusion."[8]

Seminarians were taught from manuals that were organized around the major themes of dogmatic theology – God, Christ, Trinity, grace. They featured short quotes from the Bible, excerpts of the writing of the fathers of the church, and theological arguments in defense of the faith based on simplified and abridged presentations of scholastic theology, especially that of St. Thomas Aquinas. Since the church was trying to defend itself against the criticism of Protestants and of intellectuals influenced by the rationalism of the Enlightenment, much of seminary education was apologetic in nature. Moral theology was taught in order to address practical issues that would arise in the confessional. New ways of evaluating human values and actions that had surfaced by new discoveries in the social or hard sciences did not usually figure in seminary curriculum.

Classes in liturgy were basically the study of rubrics – the mandatory ceremonial details required for celebrating Mass and the sacraments. The meaning behind the words and rituals, however, was not discussed. As Botte describes it,

> Liturgy ... was the ceremonial part of worship emptied of its real content. The goal was to prepare clerics for correctly carrying out ritual acts, and this was very good. Only it is regrettable that no one ever thought of explaining the liturgical texts and showing the spiritual richness they contain. From the way these texts were read it was apparent that most priests devoted only indirect attention to their meaning. The texts were neither food for clerical piety nor a source for sermons.[9]

---

[7] Thomas J. Shelley, "The Young John Tracy Ellis and American Catholic Intellectual Life," *U.S. Catholic Historian* 13, no. 1 (Winter 1995): 1–18.

[8] Bishop John Lancaster Spalding, quoted by Gary Wills, "Memories of a Catholic Boyhood," in *American Catholic History: A Documentary Reader*, ed. Mark Massa (New York: New York University Press, 2008), 263.

[9] Botte, *From Silence to Participation*, 6.

This rubricist mentality was understandable given that celebrating the liturgy was the reserve of the clerics. In order to protect this celebration from abuses the rubrics were enforced by attaching sins to noncompliance. A priest could sin in a variety of ways – even mortally – by not following the rubrics. The introductory material to the Tridentine Missal, after the exhaustive rubrics governing how the priest was to offer Mass, contained a section entitled "Concerning Defects that May Occur in the Celebration of Mass," which spelled out in great detail what needed to be done in case something unexpected should happen: for example, if a fly should fall into the chalice before or after the consecration, or if the words of consecration were changed or not pronounced in their entirety. The great worry underlying much of these cases was that the priest may do something to invalidate the consecration and thereby gravely sin. It was for this reason that rubrics were so crucial.

This extreme concern for correctly performing the rite was inculcated with seriousness when time came for a seminarian to do a "practice Mass" – usually in the presence of a canon lawyer who specialized in liturgical law. Fr. Adrien Nocent, who taught for many years at the Liturgical Institute of Sant'Anselmo in Rome, shared a story in class of a seminarian in the 1940s who was relieved when he satisfactorily completed his practice Mass. He then asked the instructor, "But Father, when is there time to pray in celebrating the Mass?" "Pray?" replied the professor – "There is no time for prayer when you are saying Mass."

While real advances had been made in the 1940s and 1950s in Catholic Biblical scholarship under Pope Pius XII, there was still a great deal of suspicion regarding scholars who employed the historical-critical method to the study of scripture.[10] Most seminary professors of scripture were ill-prepared to teach anything but a very traditional interpretation of the Bible. This largely consisted of identifying proof texts against ideas proposed by those who disagreed with the Catholic Church. Its use in preaching was not something that was emphasized. As Botte remarks,

> The Bible was regarded as a venerable but somewhat bothersome monument. It often came under attack; you did well to protect it by speaking about it as little as possible. Such was the reaction that seemed to have caused this apologetical teaching. Once in a while a

---

[10] Donald Senior, *Raymond Brown and the Catholic Biblical Renewal* (New York/Mahwah, NJ: Paulist Press, 2018), xv–xxi.

passage of Scripture would be cited to prove a point, and sermons would even begin with a biblical quotation, but these bits of isolated texts didn't have any great effect. They sounded as if they had been pulled out of some "Preachers Thesaurus" instead of the Bible itself, because the same ones always showed up – and with the same mistakes.[11]

The situation was similar in the United States. The Bible rarely was the focus of preaching before Vatican II. Few priests were able to use scripture as a basis for their sermons because they preached on what they learned in seminary. As Mary Lyons notes: "Preachers delivered for their assemblies Sunday after Sunday short courses in doctrinal or moral instruction. The focus on the perennial questions and universal concerns of Catholic life extended the formalist, didactic character of US Catholic preaching into the 1960s."[12]

The celebration of the Mass illustrated the hierarchical order by which the church was organized. The priest, standing at the altar with his back to the assembly, was the mediator of God's grace to the people. Speaking in a sacred language, trained in the prescribed gestures and by virtue of his office, it was the priest who made the presence of Christ possible during the Mass. The presence of lay people was not necessary for the celebration and, if present, they were there to assent to this presence by their silence.

THE EXPERIENCE OF THE PERSON IN THE PEW

What was it like attending mass during the first decade of the twentieth century? First, the Mass was in Latin. Unlike the practice in the 1940s and 50s, hand missals were usually not in evidence since it took time for most Catholics to get used to the idea of following the prayers of the priest because vernacular translations of the Mass had only been permitted during the later part of the nineteenth century, when Pope Pius IX removed vernacular translations of the Mass from the index of forbidden books. The architectural focus of the church building was always the high altar, attached to the back wall upon which the tabernacle containing the reserved sacrament was located.

---

[11] Botte, *From Silence to Participation*, 5–6.
[12] Mary Lyons, "Preaching, Catholic, in the United States," in *The New Dictionary of Sacramental Worship*, ed. Peter Fink (Collegeville, MN: Liturgical Press 1990), 988.

What did the person in the pew see? The priest would enter the sanctuary from the sacristy preceded by one or two altar boys who would ring a bell at the doorway to signal that all present were to rise. After placing the chalice on the altar, he would then kneel on a step before the altar with the servers and recite back and forth the "prayers at the foot of the altar" that consisted of a psalm, the *Confiteor*, and *Kyrie*. He would finally ascend to the altar for a series of prayers and then proclaim the readings (in Latin), prepare the offertory, and recite the Eucharistic Prayer. For most of the Mass the priest's back was to the gathered assembly. The only time when those assembled were invited to participate in the liturgy took place when the server rung bells during the consecration of the bread and wine when all were to look at the elevated host and chalice and adore the Body and Blood of Christ.

There was no attempt for the priest to speak loud enough for the whole church to hear what he was praying. Preaching appeared as an interruption in the Mass since it was a custom for the priest to remove chasuble and maniple and step down from the altar, mount the pulpit and begin and end the sermon with the sign of the cross. Communion was distributed at the communion rail to kneeling communicants by the priest assisted by a server with a paten at the communion rail, which separated the sanctuary from the nave. At the final blessing and dismissal, the priest would turn to the assembly. But the mass was not finished until he turned back to the altar to read "the last gospel" (the Prologue of John's Gospel) and the Leonine Prayers (prayer to St Michael the Archangel).

What were the people doing during the Mass? Most were engaged in their private devotions, such as the rosary or books of pious reflections. Botte reminds us of a curious practice that underscored the difference between what the priest was doing and what the people in attendance were doing. There was practically no connection observed between the celebration of Mass and communion of the people.

> As for communion, it was distributed before Mass, after Mass, or in the middle of Mass but never at the moment indicated in the liturgy. The schedule was the determining factor: communion was distributed every fifteen minutes. When Mass began on the hour you were sure to see, as the clock struck the quarter past, a priest in a surplice come out of the sacristy, rush to the altar, and interrupt the celebrant in order to take a ciborium out of the tabernacle. The celebrant then was allowed to continue Mass

until he was disturbed once again by the ciborium being returned to the tabernacle.[13]

Botte recalls that his sister went to her spiritual director to ask when the best practice was to receive the Eucharist – before, during, or after Mass. He happened to be a priest who held a doctorate in theology and who had even written a book on the Mass. He advised her to receive communion before Mass and then stay for Mass in thanksgiving for having received communion. For many Catholics before Vatican II, the reception of the Eucharist had become a private, personal devotion that had little direct connection with the liturgy itself.[14]

DEVOTIONAL CATHOLICISM

While it was clear that the clergy in the sanctuary were the ones who celebrated the liturgy, lay people expressed their faith in ways that were categorized as "devotional." Processions, pilgrimages, rosaries, novenas, wearing holy medals and scapulars, veneration of relics, and other special local customs developed alongside the "official" liturgy of the church from the early Middle Ages. These constituted a way that the laity could pray and celebrate their devotion to God, Christ, the Blessed Mother, and the saints in their own language and based on cultural traditions, with an emotional content lacking in the official liturgy.

A major trait of early twentieth-century devotional Catholicism was the popular belief in the miraculous.[15] The conviction that God was a personal God who could be approached though his Son and his Mother for all manner of needs was the basis for much of popular piety. The intercessory power of Our Lady of Lourdes or of one's special saint was always available for those seeking dramatic cures, safety in time of war, a promotion at work, or finding a spouse. God was not a far off, distant entity, but was present and willing to reach down and touch the lives of those who turned to him with sincerity. While God was also a judge who required penance and satisfaction for sin, popular religious belief helped soften this harsher aspect of God by invoking intermediaries, especially the Madonna, who through a mother's love was able to allay God's righteous judgment. For example, wearing the brown scapular of Our Lady of Mt. Carmel was believed to guarantee being freed

---

[13] Botte, *From Silence to Participation*, 2–3.
[14] Ibid., 3.
[15] Dolan, *The American Catholic Experience*, 233.

from the suffering of purgatory the Saturday after one's death. This aspect of traditional Catholic devotionalism sidestepped the sacramental system of the church and is illustrated in Michelangelo's fresco of the Last Judgment in the Sistine Chapel. Mary, seated next to Christ the judge, looks down to see angels pulling up two believers to heaven by means of a rosary.

But there was a challenge to such leniency that especially affected the church in Ireland and the United States, Canada, and Australia. It was characterized by the eminent Irish historian Emmet Larkin as the "devotional revolution" in the middle of the nineteenth century.[16] At a time when the church felt besieged by enemies, discipline was needed to maintain the integrity of the faith and defend the church against charges of superstition. In studying the various devotions, Ann Taves notes that in the nineteenth century the hierarchy began promoting devotions to standardize practices around the world for the first time. A key strategy for attaining this standardization was to move these practices out of the hands of the laity into the parish church and under the control of the priest. These devotions also tended to mark Catholic identity and to call for adherence to the church and the hierarchy in light of perceived threats to the faith. "In so doing, they directly and indirectly enhanced the hierarchy's control over the laity, while fostering a distinctively Catholic identity with international as opposed to national or ethnic overtones."[17]

It is important to note, though, that devotions reflecting a religious worldview rooted in ethnic identities were never fully coopted by the clergy. This was especially true with more independently-minded laity in Italian and Polish parishes. As Robert Orsi has pointed out, Italians in Harlem could consider someone religious, a good Christian, without this having anything to do with how often they darkened the door of a church.[18] Latinos had a similar relation to the laws of the church concerning Sunday Mass attendance, which was so important to Irish Americans. For historic reasons – especially owing to a chronic dearth of clergy during the colonial period in Latin America – the practice of

---

[16] Emmet Larkin, "The Devotional Revolution in Ireland," *The American Historical Review* 77, no. 3 (1972): 625–52.

[17] Ann Taves, *The Household of Faith: Roman Catholic Devotions in Mid-Nineteenth Century America* (Notre Dame, IN: University of Notre Dame Press, 1986), 111.

[18] Robert Orsi, *The Madonna of 115th Street: Faith and Community in Italian Harlem, 1880–1950* (New Haven, CT: Yale University Press, 1985), xvii.

lay-led popular religious prayer outside of the church continued and has flourished to the present day.[19]

How did devotional practices complement the official liturgy in parishes during the first part of the twentieth century? Carl Dehne describes the worship schedule for the average parish during the 1940s and 1950s. Naturally, Mass was celebrated every Sunday morning, but there was also some form of devotional service on Sunday afternoon as well as some other devotion on a weekday evening. The Sunday afternoon service, in addition to benediction of the Blessed Sacrament, would usually involve the rosary or a holy hour during most of the year, prayers to Mary during May and October, to St. Joseph in March, and to the Sacred Heart of Jesus in June. "There was little if any reference to the occurring seasons of the church year, like Lent and Eastertide. The weeknight service was often a perennial novena of some sort. The way of the cross was standard on Lenten Fridays; and once a year the forty hours prayer, a three day solemnity in honor of the Blessed Sacrament, was celebrated."[20]

ETHNIC IDENTITY

In considering the experience of Catholicism – especially in North America before Vatican II – it would be a mistake to undervalue the role that ethnicity played in forming Catholic identity. In his study of Catholicism and race in large US cities, John McGreevy described the religious landscape of the "Back of the Yards" neighborhood in Chicago:

> Residents could choose between eleven Catholic churches in the space of little more than a square mile – two Polish, one Croatian, two Irish, and one Bohemian. Together, the church buildings soared over the frame houses and muddy streets of the impoverished neighborhood in a triumphant display of architectural and theological certitude.[21]

The church played a key role in helping immigrants find their place in the new country. National parishes located in the large industrial cities were established to serve a range of European groups that had settled in

[19] See Anthony Stevens Arroyo and Ana María Díaz Stevens, eds. *An Enduring Flame: Studies on Latino Popular Religiosity*. PARAL studies series (New York: Bildner Center for Western Hemisphere Studies, 1994).

[20] Carl Dehne, "Roman Catholic Popular Devotions," *Worship* 49, no. 8 (1974): 451.

[21] McCreevy, *Parish Boundaries*, 10.

their own neighborhoods. They became the focal point for not only their faith but also for preserving their identity and language. Although the liturgy was conducted in Latin and the rubrics the priests followed were invariable from parish to parish, preaching, particular popular devotions, and social organization used the language of the national group to create a sense of home and a support for customs remembered from the old country.

A TIME OF FERMENT

While the experience of being a Catholic in the early part of the twentieth century was to live under the "sacred canopy" provided by the faith, as the century progressed there was evidence that social and religious changes were causing a reconfiguration of this canopy. While the clergy may have been in charge, during these years laypeople also became involved in movements that sowed the seeds for much of what would blossom at Vatican II.

Fr. Joseph Cardijn in Belgium (who would later become a cardinal) dedicated his ministry to the working class that seemed to be abandoned by the church. He founded the *"La Jeunesse Ouvrière Chrétienne"* (Young Christian Workers) – a movement that would grow to 500,000 members by 1938. Using the "See, Judge, Act" method, this group would eventual evolve into "Catholic Action" – a lay organization that is still active in Italy and other parts of Europe to this day. This movement was allied to what would become the modern liturgical movement that was inaugurated in 1909 by Fr. Lambert Beauduin, OSB, in a speech to a Catholic Action conference in Malines, Belgium. The overarching concern of both these movements was one of evangelizing a society becoming increasingly secularized. They also sought to promote Catholic social teaching inspired by Pope Leo XIII's encyclical *Rerum Novarum*.

The activism of the Catholic Church in Europe also affected the United States during these years. One of Beauduin's students, Virgil Michel, OSB, of the Abbey of St. John's in Collegeville, brought the liturgical movement to the United States and founded the review *Orate Fratres* in 1926 (later *Worship* magazine), which became a leading voice in promoting the liturgy as a means of social regeneration. Just as Michel saw the need to ally the worship of the church with social justice, Dorothy Day and Peter Maurin founded the Catholic Worker in 1933 during the height of the Depression. Cardijn's Catholic Action movement influenced lay people in the United States who used his

"See, Judge, Act" method to help young married couples develop a Christ-centered marriage that became the Pre-Cana Movement. Members of this same group later founded the Christian Family Movement in 1949.

In the United States, Catholics were becoming more "mainstream." After World War II, the GI Bill made it possible for Catholics to go to college in unprecedented numbers and be hired for white collar jobs in an expanding economy. There was also an exodus from the old ethnic enclaves in the cities. Catholics began to settle in the multi-ethnic and multi-religious suburbs. It was there that they began to engage with Protestant and Jewish neighbors who did not share their background. With the election of John Kennedy as President of the United States in 1960, Catholics in the United States had become an accepted part of society.

Dedicated involvement in the church's social teaching, a concern to restore the liturgy to the laity, pastoral outreach to couples and to families, all were movements promoted by both clergy and laypeople during the first part of the twentieth century. As the pastoral context evolved in Europe and North America, they helped transform Catholicism's "sacred canopy" and led to new insights into the church's engagement with the modern world that would find fuller expression in the documents of the Second Vatican Council.

FURTHER READING

Berger, Peter L. *The Sacred Canopy: Elements of a Sociological Theory of Religion*. Garden City, NY: Doubleday, 1967.

Botte, Bernard. *From Silence to Participation: An Insider's View of Liturgical Renewal*. Washington, DC: Pastoral Press, 1988.

Dehne, Carl. "Roman Catholic Popular Devotions." *Worship* 49, no. 8 (1974): 446–60.

Dolan, Jay P. *The American Catholic Experience: A History from the Colonial Times to the Present*. Garden City, NY: Doubleday, 1985.

Massa, Mark, ed. *American Catholic History: A Documentary Reader*. New York: New York University Press, 2008.

McGreevy, John T. *Parish Boundaries: The Catholic Encounter with Race in the Twentieth-Century Urban North*. Chicago: University of Chicago Press, 1996.

Orsi, Robert. *The Madonna of 115th Street: Faith and Community in Italian Harlem, 1880–1950*. New Haven, CT: Yale University Press, 1985.

Senior, Donald. *Raymond E. Brown and the Catholic Biblical Renewal*. New York/Mahwah, NJ: Paulist Press, 2018.

Shelley, Thomas J. "The Young John Tracy Ellis and American Catholic Intellectual Life." *U.S. Catholic Historian* 13, no. 1 (Winter 1995): 1–18.

Stevens, Arroyo, and Díaz Stevens, Ana María, eds. *An Enduring Flame: Studies on Latino Popular Religiosity*. PARAL studies series. New York: Bildner Center for Western Hemisphere Studies, 1994.

Taves, Ann. *The Household of Faith: Roman Catholic Devotions in Mid-Nineteenth Century America*. Notre Dame, IN: University of Notre Dame Press, 1986.

2 Theological Renewal in the First Half of the Twentieth Century

GABRIEL FLYNN

THE FLOWERING OF CATHOLIC THEOLOGICAL RENEWAL

The twentieth century, a period of unprecedented progress and development, although eclipsed by the horrors of modern war and mass genocide, was also the century of the church. In the midst of the complex crisis of atheistic secularism in Europe from approximately 1930 to 1960, Romano Guardini (1885–1968) articulated a profound desire for spiritual renewal. 'A religious process of incalculable importance has begun, the Church is coming to life in souls.'[1] As part of this process, an unexpected flowering of new ideas in the form of original initiatives in history and liturgy, scripture and patristics, ecumenism and interreligious dialogue, ministry and mission, theology of the laity, and pastoral studies emerged concurrently and swept across much of the Catholic world in the first half of the twentieth century. This broad confluence of intellectual and spiritual movements of renewal reached its zenith in the fecund reform programme of the Second Vatican Council.

The genesis of the renewal in Catholic thought lay predominantly though not exclusively in the French- and German-speaking countries but with roots in the nineteenth century, associated principally with Johann Adam Möhler (1796–1838) of the University of Tübingen and John Henry Newman (1801–90) of the University of Oxford. After the arid rationalism of the eighteenth-century Enlightenment, Europe experienced a renewal in its Christian life.[2] Möhler's highly original, patristics-based ideas on the church, with complementary pneumatological and

---

[1] Romano Guardini, *The Church and the Catholic*, trans. Ada Lane (New York: Sheed & Ward, 1935), 1.

[2] See André Haquin, "The Liturgical Movement and Catholic Ritual Revision," in *The Oxford History of Christian Worship*, ed. Geoffrey Wainwright and Karen B. Westerfield Tucker (Oxford: Oxford University Press, 2006), 696–720, at 697.

Christological elements, penetrated Catholic ecclesiology and contributed to the reforms of Vatican II. With Matthias Scheeben (1835–88),
Möhler helped to lay the foundations for the twentieth-century liturgical movement through a return to the fathers. Louis Bouyer
(1913–2004) considers the contribution of Möhler and Newman to be
equally important but questioned whether the pneumatological element had received the full place in Catholic theology that Möhler had
originally given it. Yves Congar, the eminent French Dominican
whose name is synonymous with Vatican II, lauds a distinguished
group of nineteenth-century ecclesiologists including Möhler, the
Tübingen School, along with Clemens Schrader (1820–75) and Johann
Baptist Franzelin (1816–86) – Jesuits from the *Collegio Romano* who
were among the leading theologians of the First Vatican Council
(1869–70) – for their contribution to the renewal of the mystery of
the church. By looking to Möhler and assessing his influence on
ressourcement theology, notably, the liturgy and the modern church,
we find a fresh stream of renewal that is receiving attention from a
new generation of scholars. We must also acknowledge Dom Columba
Marmion (1858–1923), the third Abbot of Maredsous Abbey, Belgium,
who helped to revitalize the church – in particular through his contribution to meditation that was popular with the youth movements and
his role in leading innumerable priests and laity to a rediscovery of the
scriptures in the period before World War II. Congar said that the most
decisive element in the ecclesiological awakening of the decades
that preceded Vatican II was a deepening in the interior life of the
church, especially with regard to the person of Christ, thanks to the
wide readership enjoyed by Marmion's deeply Christological and
liturgical works.

By the mid-twentieth century, the Catholic Church began to
emerge from the intellectual ghetto to which it had retreated in the
aftermath of the French Revolution (1789–99) to engage with a world of
myriad renewals and enlightenments where progressive Catholics could
breathe again without fear of condemnation or the imputation of heresy.
Vatican II was set to become a living testimony to what has been
appropriately called the 'epoch of movements' that flourished simultaneously with *nouvelle théologie* and *Action Catholique*.[3] Michael

---

[3] See Gilles Routhier, "Introduction," in *La Théologie Catholique entre Intransigeance
et Renouveau: La Réception des Mouvements Préconcilaires à Vatican II*, ed. Gilles
Routhier, Philippe J. Roy, and Karim Schelkens, Bibliothèque de la Revue d'Histoire
Ecclésiastique 95 (Louvain-la-Neuve/Leuven: Brepols, 2011), 5–9, at 5.

Schmaus situates this highly innovative stream of renewal at the centre of the church. 'A whole series of movements led to the new interest in ecclesiology: the biblical movement, the liturgical movement, research in patristics, the ecumenical movement, and also the question of the Church's relationship to the non-Catholic Christian Churches and of the salvation of men living outside the Catholic or Christian faith.'[4] The council quickly became the dominant instrument for renewal as a munificent series of new relationships with the world, the other Christian churches, and the major world religions began to take shape and Catholicism tentatively embraced the Augustinian-inspired *ecclesia semper reformanda* of the Reformation. Cardinal Leo Joseph Suenens (1904–96), one of the moderators of Vatican II, whose influence permeated the entire council, viewed that assembly as the rightful heir of the great movements of renewal. Along with Popes John XXIII and Paul VI, Suenens was one of the key leaders of Vatican II; his critique of the preparatory commission's proposed texts met with papal approval and contributed to an alternative agenda for the council. His 1968 book *Co-Responsibility in the Church* sought to advance the co-responsibility of all Christians in the church as the dominant pastoral theme of the council.

The poet and social critic Charles Péguy (1873–1914) coined the term *ressourcement* ('return to the sources') and exercised a profound influence on its development. The renewal was also shaped by the liturgical changes inaugurated by the popes of the period, including Pius X (1903–14), Pius XI (1922–39), and Pius XII (1939–58). Renewal of the liturgy was, in many respects, the heart of the reform movement seeking to remedy the loss of meaning, a decline dated to the beginning of the middle ages.

The emergence of a new theological system in Catholic thought during the early decades of the twentieth century, in response to the concrete needs of the time and based on a return to the sources of Christianity, led inevitably to a clash with what had gone before. Henri de Lubac provides an illuminating *précis* of events.

> The condemnation of *l'Action française* had stirred deep unrest. A certain Scholastic conservatism, which claimed in all good faith to be tradition itself, was alarmed at any appearance of novelty. A kind of so-called 'Thomist' dictatorship, which was more a

---

[4] Michael Schmaus, *The Church: Its Origin and Structure*, trans. Mary Ledderer, Dogma 4 (New York: Sheed & Ward, 1972), 75.

matter of government than intellectuality, strove to stifle any effort toward freer thought ... So, already, as in the period of 'integrism', denunciations began to pour out once again.[5]

In order to transcend the juridical idea of the church and the aridity of the manuals, Congar, together with his colleagues Marie-Dominique Chenu and Henri-Marie Féret, embarked on an enterprise to eliminate 'baroque theology', a term they coined to describe the theology of the Counter-Reformation.

The accomplishment of this goal was an important reason for the foundation, in November 1935, of the *Unam Sanctam* collection, an ecclesiological library for the renewal of the mystery of the church through a restoration of key neglected themes from the tradition. Congar directed the project under the auspices of the Dominican press, *Éditions du Cerf*. In addition to providing an extensive, university-standard theology series, *Unam Sanctam* also sought a reform of the Catholic Church and an advancement of ecumenism. The series was launched by the Dominican journal *La Vie intellectuelle* in November 1935 and became a highly influential ecclesiological and ecumenical library running to some seventy-seven volumes and is now complemented by a new *Unam Sanctam* series. It remains Congar's most significant contribution to *ressourcement*. He acknowledged that *Unam Sanctam* prepared the way for Vatican II while Chenu saw in this new collection 'one of the most beautiful fruits of our theology at Le Saulchoir'.[6] Congar, perhaps more than any other, adopted *ressourcement* as the standard of reform. 'What would a little later be called "ressourcement" was then at the heart of our efforts. It was not a matter either of mechanically replacing some theses by other theses or of creating a "revolution" but of appealing, as Péguy did, from one tradition less profound to another more profound.'[7]

A formidable coterie of opponents was ranged against the *ressourcement* project; it was severely criticized by Marie-Michel Labourdette, as well as by Réginald Garrigou-Lagrange, who seems to have borrowed the phrase *la nouvelle théologie* ('the new theology') to describe it. The controversial term was first used by Pietro Parente, then a professor of

---

[5] Henri de Lubac, *At the Service of the Church: Henri de Lubac Reflects on the Circumstances that Occasioned His Writings*, trans. Anne Elizabeth Englund (San Francisco: Ignatius Press, 1993), 47.

[6] See Yves Congar, "Reflections on Being a Theologian," trans. Marcus Lefébure, *New Blackfriars* 62 (1981): 405–9, at 405.

[7] Yves Congar, "The Brother I Have Known," trans. Boniface Ramsey, *The Thomist* 49 (1985): 495–503, at 499.

theology in Rome and later (1965) Secretary to the Congregation for the Doctrine of the Faith, in 1942. He viewed the *nouvelle théologie* as a crude attempt 'to demolish the by then classical system of the schools'.[8] The epithet *nouvelle théologie* corresponds to a theology that is concerned to know the tradition, as opposed to a purely scholastic theology. The view of tradition proposed by the *nouvelle théologie*, far from being traditionalist, in the sense of a repetition of the recent past, was concerned rather with the unity of the ever-living tradition. Nonetheless, the appellation *nouvelle théologie*, with its negative, dangerous connotations, when applied to the fledgling Catholic movement for renewal, was intensely controversial and dramatic in its consequences.

In September 1946, Pope Pius XII expressed his concerns regarding the *nouvelle théologie* to representatives of the Dominicans and Jesuits, warning against an attack on the fundamental tenets of Catholic doctrine. Then in late November 1946, an unknown group of Jesuits published an anonymous and impassioned defence of the *Sources chrétiennes* series in the Jesuit periodical *Recherches de Science Religieuse*. The project was conceived between 1932 and 1937 by Victor Fontoynont, SJ (1880–1958), professor of fundamental theology at Fourvière, with de Lubac and Jean Daniélou as directors. This highly original series of patristic texts sought, as indicated in the preface to the first volume of the 1942 edition, to provide the reader with a key to discover the treasures of the world of the fathers by means of an introduction to each work. In an atmosphere of suspicion and controversy, *Humani Generis* was published on 12 August 1950 and came as a 'lightning bolt' aimed against the new French theology. In the wake of this controversial encyclical, the leaders of *ressourcement*, astute political analysts, rejected the term 'nouvelle théologie' while their religious superiors, feeling compelled to act, initiated a series of draconian measures against them. At the Second Vatican Council, the advocates of an entrenched, defensive neo-Scholasticism, though dominant for a time, were obliged to give way to a church of the people of God, a vision championed by the *ressourcement* theologians and now renascent in the church.

What follows attempts to provide an interpretative framework for understanding the remarkable regeneration in Catholic thought that inspired a renaissance in theology and biblical studies and contributed decisively to the pivotal reforms of the council. The present chapter is in three parts and considers, first, the emergence and development of a

---

[8] Pietro Parente, "Nuove tendenze teologiche," *L'Osservatore Romano* 9–10 (February 1942): 1.

threefold stream of renewal at the centre of *ressourcement*; second, the distinctive contribution of the leading Jesuit and Dominican pioneers of *ressourcement* to theological renewal, the churches, and society; and third, the transformation of *nouvelle théologie* into a universal programme of reform.[9]

RESSOURCEMENT: STREAMS OF RENEWAL

The dominant streams of renewal at the heart of *ressourcement* are in the domains of liturgy, scripture, and patristics. Historians and exponents of renewal have documented the movement's historical evolution.[10] Roger Aubert, the distinguished Louvain historian, provides a comprehensive account of *ressourcement* in his authoritative study *La Théologie Catholique au milieu du XXe siècle*. There, he outlines the foremost trends in Catholic theology of the era that help to indicate the future orientations of religious thought. This work identifies the major preoccupations of Catholic theology as a desire for closer links with the tradition and a better adaptation to the contemporary world.

Leading members of the faculties of Le Saulchoir (Paris) and Lyon-Fourvière, respectively, guided the French *ressourcement* that also encompassed Belgium and Germany. They included the Dominicans Marie-Dominique Chenu (1895–1990), Yves Congar (1904–95), Dominique Dubarle (1907–87), and Henri-Marie Féret (1904–92), and the Jesuits Jean Daniélou (1905–74), Henri de Lubac (1896–1991), Henri Bouillard (1908–81), and Hans Urs von Balthasar (1905–88), who left the Society of Jesus in 1950. Among the new initiatives were the movement for the reform of the liturgy, *Centre de Pastorale Liturgique* (1943), followed by the launch of the journal *La Maison Dieu* (1945); the return to biblical and patristic sources, exemplified especially in the *Sources chrétiennes* series, and a second patristic series of Latin texts *Corpus Christianorum* founded by Dom Eligius Dekkers in 1947 at Turnhout (Belgium) to which was added a Greek series in 1977 with Marcel Richard as editor; the renewal of ecclesiology, demonstrated by the establishment of the *Unam Sanctam* series; the realization of the

---

[9] See Gabriel Flynn, "The Twentieth-Century Renaissance in Catholic Theology," in *Ressourcement: A Movement for Renewal in Twentieth-Century Catholic Theology*, 2nd ed., ed. Gabriel Flynn and Paul D. Murray (Oxford: Oxford University Press, 2014), 1–19.

[10] Yves Congar, "Tendances actuelles de la pensée religieuse," *Cahiers du monde nouveau* 4 (1948): 33–50; Jean Daniélou, "Les orientations présentes de la pensée religieuse," *Études* 249 (1946): 5–21.

church's missionary task exemplified in Henri Godin's famous book *La France: pays de mission?*; the encyclicals of Cardinal Emmanuel Suhard; the worker-priest movement; and new missionary strategies in France, including the Young Christian Worker / Young Christian Student movements. As Congar remarks:

> Anyone who did not live through the years 1946 and 1947 in the history of French Catholicism has missed one of the finest moments in the life of the Church. In the course of a slow emergence from privation and with the wide liberty of a fidelity as profound as life, men sought to regain evangelical contact with a world in which we had become involved to an extent unequalled in centuries.[11]

De Lubac also refers to the spirit of hope, creativity, and originality that pervaded this fertile period in the history of the French church with *Chantiers de Jeunesse*, Youth Work Camps, where de Lubac gave lectures on 'The Church in the Face of the World Crisis', and *Cahiers du Témoignage chrétien*, a weekly French newsletter founded in Lyon in 1941 by Pierre Chaillet and de Lubac, in which they presented a principled opposition to Nazism as part of a Jesuit resistance movement.

> In Lyons itself, during those same years of the 1930s, the saintly Abbé Paul Couturier enlisted me to preach during the Weeks of Unity, then a new thing: my first initiation to an 'ecumenical activity' that was going to place me in contact with two young Swiss pastors, Roger Schutz and Max Thurian, when they were laying the foundations for their Taizé monastery.[12]

Joseph Folliet (1903–72), one of the rare lay experts at Vatican II and a friend of Congar, Jacques Maritain (1882–1973), and François Mauriac (1885–1970), the 1952 Nobel Laureate and symbol of the *Résistance*, provides a contemporaneous, moving account of the period as one of 'intellectual decadence, images of what is left of a solid and brilliant past, like the works of Father de Lubac, Father Congar, Rahner, and Karl Barth'.[13]

---

[11] Yves Congar, *Dialogue between Christians: Catholic Contributions to Ecumenism*, trans. Philip Loretz (London: Geoffrey Chapman, 1966), 32.

[12] De Lubac, *At the Service of the Church*, 45.

[13] Joseph Folliet, *Le Temps de L'Angoisse et de la Recherche*, 2nd ed., Les chrétiens au Carrefour 3 (Lyon: Chronique Sociale de France, 1972), 9.

LITURGICAL RENEWAL AND THE MONASTERIES

The origins of the modern phase of the liturgical movement were both international and interdenominational, of Catholic and Protestant inspiration. Its first significant impact was in 1840 in Europe; this then spread to Britain and North America, with Catholics later assuming a pioneering role. We begin with the contribution of the Catholic monasteries of continental Europe. Bernard Botte (1883–1980), a monk of Mont César, Louvain, and a champion of the liturgical formation of priests and liturgy professors, remarks intuitively: 'In order to understand a movement, we must know its point of departure.'[14] As places of prayer and devotion, the monasteries were a natural home for liturgical renewal with the Benedictine monasteries of Belgium serving as the cradle of the modern liturgical movement.

Dom Prosper Guéranger (1805–75) played a pivotal role in the restoration of monastic life in France after the Revolution, as well as in the development of a liturgical and ecclesial spirituality. He re-founded the Abbey of Solesmes in the 1830s and became its first abbot in 1837, a position he held for twenty-eight years. His great ambition was to found a centre for the revival of the pure traditions. Solesmes was committed to the restoration of medieval ritual, its greatest achievement being the recovery and dissemination of Gregorian chant. *The Liturgical Year*, Guéranger's most successful book, provided an invaluable resource for the laity. This was complemented by *Institutions liturgiques*, where he set out the relationship between the liturgy and the unity and faith of the church. According to Guéranger, Solesmes laid the foundations for a genuine liturgical spirituality with the liturgy of the church as a model of all Christian prayer. In this way, Solesmes prefigured the modern liturgical movement and is appropriately hailed as 'the first power-house and dynamo of liturgical renewal'.[15]

The liturgical renewal is older than the biblical renewal. Its first intense period of activity from 1909 to 1945 is most closely associated with the renowned Belgian liturgist Dom Lambert Beauduin (1873–1960) and the Monastery of Mont César in Louvain. Beauduin joined Mont César in 1906 and quickly assumed leadership of the liturgical movement there, considered more pastoral and less elitist

---

[14] Bernard Botte, *Le mouvement liturgique: Témoignage et souvenirs* (Paris: Desclée, 1973), 9.

[15] Horton Davies, "The Continental Liturgical Movement in the Roman Catholic Church," *Canadian Journal of Theology* 10 (1964): 148–65, at 153.

than Solesmes. Historians view the *Congrès des Œuvres Catholiques* (Congress of Catholic Works) at Malines in 1909 as the beginning of the modern phase of the Catholic liturgical renewal, but with origins in the nineteenth century that are closely connected with monastic life.[16] It was at Malines, on 23 September 1909, that Beauduin presented the liturgy as 'The True Prayer of the Church.' He depicted the liturgy as an encounter with the God of the covenant involving the participation of all baptized Christians.[17] His bold initiative effectively launched the modern liturgical movement, not only in Belgium but also in the Netherlands and Germany. Two important objectives agreed at Malines were, first, the distribution of the French and Dutch translations of the missal and, second, that priority be given to the liturgy of the church over devotions.

Beauduin was part of a new generation of researchers that included Louis Duchesne, Fernand Cabrol, Pierre Batiffol, and Pierre de Puniet in France, and Edmund Bishop and Henry Austin Wilson in England. His principal aim was to share the treasures of the liturgy with the people and to facilitate active lay participation. He displayed a unique capacity to unite theory and practice in a successful liturgical renovation by drawing on Pius X's first *motu proprio, Tra le sollecitudini* on sacred music (1903), advocating active participation in the liturgy as the essential basis of Christian life. His most important initiative was the organization of the so-called Liturgy Weeks presented in French and Dutch at Mont César. At Beauduin's insistence, based on his desire that the liturgical renewal should reach both parties in Belgium, the periodical *Questions liturgiques*, which he founded in 1910, was also published in Flemish, *Liturgisch Tijdschrift*. In 1914, he wrote his crucial study on worship, *La piété de L'Eglise*, which became the flagship text of the liturgical renewal.

In the wake of Pius XI's letter *Equidem Verba* (1924), inviting the Benedictines to work and pray for Christian unity, Beauduin founded the Monastery of Amay-sur-Meuse, Belgium, in 1925. The monastery then transferred to Chevetogne, in the diocese of Namur, France, in 1939, where the liturgy is celebrated according to the Eastern and Western rites, as part of their efforts to establish a *rapprochement* between the churches of East and West. At Chevetogne, Beauduin

---

[16] Bernard Botte, *From Silence to Participation: An Insider's View of the Liturgical Renewal*, trans. John Sullivan (Washington, DC: The Pastoral Press, 1988), 10.

[17] Lambert Beauduin, "La vraie prière de l'Église," *Questions Liturgiques/Studies in Liturgy* 91 (2010): 37–41.

launched the ecumenical journal *Irénikon* devoted to the cause of unity; the journal has appeared continuously since 1927. Although he sought to avoid political intrigue, the clouds began to gather shortly after Cardinal Désiré-Joseph Mercier presented a paper at the Fourth of the Malines Conversations (1925) entitled *L'Église anglicane unie, non absorbée* ('the Anglican Church united to Rome, not absorbed') that had been written by Beauduin. When this controversial phrase was publicized Beauduin became the subject of considerable criticism and was condemned by a Roman tribunal in 1930 and subsequently exiled to France from 1932 to 1951. There he profoundly influenced the French liturgical renewal, sharing in the foundation of the *Centre de Pastorale Liturgique*, and also contributed to the advancement of ecumenism. Beauduin's position on reunion was later vindicated by Pope John XXIII (1958–63). In the closing years of his life, Beauduin lived in Chevetogne, where he dedicated himself to liturgy and church unity.

As the liturgical renewal spread across Europe and to the United States, the role of the Belgians receded as the movement blossomed in Germany during the inter-war period when the church was forced, especially during the Nazi era, to renounce social action and to focus instead on the lively celebration of the divine mysteries. At the famous Abbey of Maria Laach in the German Rhineland, the liturgical movement reached a high point as university students joined the community for Holy Week, 1913. Maria Laach became one of the foremost centres of liturgical scholarship, led by Abbot Ildefons Herwegen (1874–1946) and Dom Odo Casel (1886–1948), whose 'mystery theology' breathed new life into ancient concepts. Through his voluminous publications, over the period 1918–48, Casel made a unique contribution to liturgical renewal.

Beyond the monasteries, Romano Guardini (1885–1968), an Italian-born German intellectual, exercised an influential role in the formative stages of the liturgical movement.[18] He had a profound influence on Catholic culture through his writings, conferences, and engagements with his students, and is lauded as a 'Newman type of thinker in the twentieth century'.[19] His *The Spirit of the Liturgy* exhibits key themes of the liturgical renewal of the twentieth century concerning, in particular, the view of the liturgy as fellowship. The liturgical renewal

---

[18] See Robert A. Krieg, *Romano Guardini: A Precursor of Vatican II* (Notre Dame, IN: University of Notre Dame Press, 1997), 70–90.

[19] Frank O'Malley, "The Thinker in the Church II: The Urgencies of Romano Guardini," *The Review of Politics* 25 no. 4 (1963): 451–59.

could count on the active goodwill of the Holy See. This is a very important point since without the official approval of the magisterium and a true reception by the people, reform and renewal are placed in jeopardy.

CATHOLIC BIBLICAL RENEWAL: A GLOBAL *AGGIORNAMENTO*

Consideration of the origins of the Catholic biblical renewal in the twentieth century contributes to an appreciation of the remarkable opportunities that the rejuvenation in biblical scholarship engendered in research, collaboration, and dialogue. Beginning in Germany in the course of the inter-war period, it spread even to the less progressive countries. Among the signs of renewal were the prominent place given to the Bible by the Christian youth movements; the provision of highly technical works by theologians; the multiplication and vitality of various biblical collections, including *lectio divina*; works by Lucien Cerfaux and Louis Bouyer, and the vital contribution of Maria Laach and the French Dominicans in Jerusalem.

By mid-century, France and Belgium were at the centre of scientific biblical study. Catholic scholars were relative latecomers to this field, as similar work had been going on in Protestant circles for at least a century. However, the adoption of scientific methods spread rapidly once it got under way. The *École Biblique et Archéologique Française de Jérusalem*, inaugurated on 15 November 1890 as the *École Pratique d'Études Bibliques*, has had a long and distinguished tradition in the archaeology and geography of Palestine.[20] Its founder, the acclaimed Dominican exegete and historian of religions Marie-Joseph Lagrange (1855–1938), chose the title of the school in order to emphasize its unique methodology, that is, study of the Bible in the cultural, linguistic, and geographical context in which it was written. He himself taught Hebrew, Arabic, Assyrian, history, and archaeology.[21] The *Revue Biblique* was launched in January 1892 as the official organ of the *École Biblique* under the direction of the Jerusalem Dominicans of the Priory of Saint Étienne with Lagrange as its first editor, a position he held until 1923. *Revue Biblique*, the oldest biblical journal in French was followed

---

[20] A multilingual website provides an excellent introduction to the history and ongoing work of the *École Biblique*. See www.ebaf.edu/publications-2/the-etudes-bibliques/.

[21] Jean Guitton, *Portrait du Père Lagrange: Celui qui a réconcilié la science et la foi* (Paris: Robert Laffont, 1992), 46.

in 1903 by *Études Bibliques*, a major specialist series on Scripture that was reserved for over a century to works in French but is now open to other languages. The influential work of *Revue Biblique* is credited with helping to enlarge perspectives in biblical theology. In addition to the *École Biblique* in Jerusalem, Louvain merits recognition as a centre of critical biblical scholarship. Lucien Cerfaux's notable study *La Théologie de L'Église suivant S. Paul* (Paris: 1942) is recognized as marking 'a date in the history of Catholic exegesis that surpasses not only modernism but also what Wilfrid Ward called the state of siege of post-tridentine Catholic thought'.[22]

Lagrange's great ambition was to open the Bible to Catholics. A true pioneer, he launched a biblical *aggiornamento* of global proportions and is honoured as the founder of Catholic Bible study. He is credited with contributing most to the advancement of biblical scholarship and to the seismic shift in the official Catholic attitude towards critical study of the Bible, thus paving the way for Pius XII's encyclical *Divino Afflante Spiritu*. His original labours were in the domain of Old Testament study; he presented a paper entitled 'The Sources of the Pentateuch' to the Scientific Congress of Catholics in Fribourg, Switzerland, in August 1897 that was published by the *Revue Biblique* in 1898, thus precipitating a crisis in Catholic Pentateuchal scholarship. Lagrange's *Méthode Historique surtout à propos de l'Ancien Testament* (1904), which appeared in English as *Historical Criticism and the Old Testament* (1906), is culturally significant for its contribution to the knowledge of civilization. Other works included *Le Livre des Juges* (1903), *Études sur les religions sémitiques* (1903), and *La genèse* (1905). Following an interdiction of the Holy See on his Old Testament work, he turned his attention to the New Testament, producing excellent commentaries on the gospels (1911–25), as well as *Le Messianisme chez les Juifs* (1909), *Mélanges d'histoire religieuse* (1915), *La Vie de Jésus d'après Renan* (1923), and *Le Judaïsme avant Jésus-Christ*, one of his key studies published in 1931.

His study *Père Lagrange: Personal Reflections and Memoirs* (1985) is of historical importance as it documents the early history of the *École Biblique* (1889–1913) and the progress of the Catholic biblical renewal, and it provides an initial assessment of Modernism. He attributes the idea for a school of Scripture to Réginald Colchen, Provincial of the

---

[22] Louis Bouyer, "Une date dans l'histoire de l'exégèse catholique," *Dieu Vivant* 2 (1945): 137–42, at 142.

Dominican province of Toulouse. He acknowledges the support of Pope Leo XIII for his scientific study of the Bible in the form of 'a very significant letter', dated 17 September 1892, published in the *Revue Biblique* in 1893. This serendipitous papal intervention was prompted by the Dominican Cardinal T. M. Zigliara (1833–93), a distinguished Thomist expert who was appointed Prefect of the Congregation of Studies in 1888. In January 1903, Lagrange was appointed to the Biblical Commission. The zenith of achievement was reached on 20 October 1920 when the *Académie des Inscriptions et Belles-Lettres* (Academy of Inscriptions and Fine-Letters) in Paris recognized the Dominican School as the *École archéologique française de Jérusalem* (the French Archaeological School of Jerusalem) in view of its outstanding accomplishments, and thereafter it became known as the *École Biblique et archéologique française de Jérusalem* (The French Biblical and Archaeological School of Jerusalem).

While Lagrange avoided outright censure from Vatican authorities, he remained suspect and the Modernist crisis cast an ominous shadow over his life and work. His fellow countryman, Alfred Loisy (1857–1940), a secular priest, suffered a different fate and was excommunicated in 1908 at the height of the crisis. It is noteworthy that the most important factors in the rise of the Modernist movement in France were the introduction and use of the results and methods of biblical criticism, as well as new philosophical ferments. Lagrange authored a book on the affair entitled *M. Loisy et le modernisme* (1932) and in his memoirs provides an illuminating and respectful commentary on the progress of Modernism and its impact on the *École Biblique*, the *Revue Biblique*, and on himself personally. Two points may be noted. First, Lagrange extended the hand of friendship to Loisy with an offer to collaborate in the *Revue Biblique*, which, though destined to fail, shows the character of the man. Second, Lagrange continued to produce excellent work in spite of attacks on the *Revue Biblique*, the historical method, and a censure of several works by him in 1912 by a Decree of the Congregation of the Consistory. It was by showing due deference to authority, and combining 'a spirit of orthodoxy' with 'a spirit of science' that he successfully followed a middle course between the older spiritual interpretation of the biblical text and those who viewed such belief as mere superstition and myth.

The discovery of the Dead Sea Scrolls at Qumrân (1946/47–56) provided a powerful impetus to the biblical *ressourcement*. Roland de Vaux (1903–71), the Director of the *École Biblique* (1945–65), played a leading role in both the archaeological and publication aspects of this major project. He was appointed Editor-in-Chief of the fragmentary texts for Oxford University Press, a project that was completed only recently due to his untimely death in 1971. De Vaux is honoured as a brilliant academic and archaeologist, and a dynamic priest who spent himself in the service of the Word of God.[23] The single greatest achievement of the École Biblique in this era was undoubtedly the Jerusalem Bible. It was a joint collaboration between the École Biblique, also led by de Vaux with the assistance of other francophone exegetes, and the Paris-based Dominican press Éditions du Cerf. The full edition of the Bible de Jérusalem was published by Desclée de Brouwer in 1955 and subsequently in the main Western languages. The English-language edition was published in 1966, while the original French edition was fully revised in 1973. The innovative arrangement of books, with accompanying notes and scripture references, was later emulated by other editors and publishers.

There were also notable German exegetes in this period who made an important contribution to biblical renewal, including, among others, Rudolf Schnackenburg (1914–2002), Heinz Schürmann (1913–99), and Alfons Deissler (1914–2005), who helped to establish historical-critical exegesis and ecumenical dialogue. There were significant achievements like the Evangelisch-Katholischer Kommentar zum Neuen Testament (EKK), the brain child of Eduard Schweizer (1913–2006), a Zurich-based New Testament scholar. This series was launched in 1975 in collaboration with Schnackenburg, his close Catholic friend, and published jointly by Catholic (Benziger) and Protestant (Neukirchen-Vluyn) presses. Among the important and influential German Protestant scholars of the era were such figures as Ernst Käsemann (1906–98), a Lutheran historical scholar of the New Testament who was part of a generation with a vital interest in ecumenism and biblical hermeneutics, and Gerhard von Rad (1901–71), author of the seminal study *Theology of the Old Testament*.[24]

Oscar Cullmann (1902–99), the distinguished Lutheran biblical scholar and ecumenical pioneer, writing in 1964, provides an impartial assessment of the historical importance of Catholic biblical renewal. 'The biblical renewal was inaugurated especially under Pius XII. In view of the tendency to look only at the negative aspects of this pontificate,

---

[23] John Strugnell, "In Memoriam: Roland de Guérin de Vaux, OP," *Bulletin of the American Schools of Oriental Research* 207 (1972): 1, 3–5.

[24] See, Andreas Schuele, "Theology as Witness: Gerhard von Rad's Contribution to the Study of Old Testament Theology," *Interpretation* 62, no. 3 (2008): 256–67.

we should not forget one of its great merits, the promulgation of the encyclical, *De Divino Afflante Spiritu*.'[25] Cullmann offers an incisive appraisal of the remarkable advance in Catholic biblical studies as a direct result of the dialogue between biblical scholars. 'The changed orientation of the Roman Catholic Church in regard to biblical studies has fostered scholarly exchanges between Catholic and Protestant exegetes, and these exchanges, in turn, have intensified exegetical work.'[26] It is impossible to exaggerate the previously unimagined benefits of this 'fruitful collaboration' and its enhancement of Catholic biblical studies and ecumenical relations. Cullmann lists, first, the sense of liberation among biblical exegetes; second, the outstanding work of the *École Biblique* in Jerusalem and of the Biblical Institute of Rome; and third, a remarkable series of publications with the *Jerusalem Bible* receiving pride of place.

The papacy also played an important role in biblical renewal. Leo XIII (1878–1903), a diplomatic and perceptive pastor whose encyclical letter *Providentissimus Deus*, issued on 18 November 1893, provided a strong impulse to scripture study that resulted in new commentaries on the entire Bible as well as biblical periodicals, encyclopaedias, and dictionaries. He also established the Pontifical Biblical Commission in 1902 through his Apostolic Letter *Vigilantiae Studiique* with a dual mandate to promote biblical interpretation and to safeguard the Bible against false interpretation. Its mission was expanded under his successor Pius X (1903–14) to one of vigilance. The grave concern of the Catholic Church authorities regarding the scientific approach to the study of the Bible reached a climax during the pontificate of Pius when hostile winds blew fiercely on biblical and theological research. As part of a church response to the Modernist crisis and the supposed pernicious influence of rationalism on church teaching, the Pontifical Biblical Commission issued a series of decrees between 1903 and 1915 in defence of the traditional view of the Bible, including the assertion that Moses was the true author of the Pentateuch, as well as a restatement of the literal interpretation of the early chapters of Genesis, with strict binding force on Catholic scholars.[27]

---

[25] Oscar Cullmann, "The Place of the Bible at the Council," *Journal of Biblical Literature* 83 (1964): 247–52, at 247.

[26] Ibid.

[27] The texts are available online at www.vatican.va/roman_curia/congregations/cfaith/ pcb_documents/rc_con_cfaith_doc_19480116_fonti-pentateuco_fr.html. For further commentary on these documents, see Joseph A. Fitzmyer, *A Christological*

Pius X also founded the Pontifical Biblical Institute of Rome, the plans for which had been laid by his predecessor, through his apostolic letter *Vinea electa* of 7 May 1909 as a centre of advanced biblical studies run by the Jesuits. The establishment by Pius XI (1922–39) of the affiliated Biblical Institute in Jerusalem in 1927 and of a second faculty devoted to Oriental studies at the Biblical Institute of Rome in 1932 effectively realized two further elements of Leo XIII's vision for scripture study articulated in *Providentissimus Deus*.[28] But the real catalyst for change in Catholic biblical study was the encyclical *Divino Afflante Spiritu* promulgated by Pius XII (1939–58) on 30 September 1943 on the occasion of the fiftieth anniversary of *Providentissimus Deus*. The new encyclical, which owed much to the influence of the noted ecumenist Cardinal Augustin Bea, SJ (1881–1968), Rector of the Pontifical Biblical Institute in Rome, and Jacques-Marie Vosté (1883–1949), Secretary of the Pontifical Biblical Commission, quickly became the *Magna Carta* of modern Catholic biblical renewal. It called for a return to the original biblical languages rather than depending on translations and sanctioned recourse to the methods of textual criticism. The encyclical was a significant turning point in biblical scholarship and inspired a whole generation of Bible scholars. The role of the Biblical Commission continued to evolve during the papacy of Paul VI (1963–78) to that of an international body of scholars advising the pope and the Vatican on biblical matters of importance to the church. Its function was no longer that of a vigilance committee, while the binding force of its earlier decrees on biblical authorship were tacitly laid aside.

No account of Catholic biblical scholarship in the twentieth century would be complete without reference to Raymond E. Brown (1928–98), the leading American Catholic biblical scholar and one of the greatest of the era. His contribution to Johannine studies is well known. Donald Senior's masterful new biography, with its limpid account of the Catholic biblical renewal in the twentieth century, will further enhance the legacy of a great scholar. Particularly noteworthy is, first, Brown's delineation of Catholic biblical scholarship in the twentieth century in three segments: 1900–40, 1940–70, and 1970–2000. Second is his contribution to ecumenism and inter-religious dialogue, born of his deep respect for the other. 'Ecumenism was one of the most enduring interests of Raymond Brown. Along with his championing of

Catechism: New Testament Answers, New Revised and Expanded ed. (New York: Paulist Press, 1991), 119–20.
[28] See *The Catholic Biblical Quarterly*, 5 no. 2 (April 1943).

the historical-critical method, his concern for Christian unity appears in virtually all his writings.'[29]

THE PATRISTIC RENEWAL

The biblical and liturgical renewals were completed by a patristic rejuvenation, a veritable renaissance of wonder.[30] By refocusing on the vital mystery of Christianity, thus moving beyond the apologetics and polemics of Scholasticism and the Reformations as well as the harsh critique of the Enlightenments, the patristic revival facilitated a fresh reception of the fathers in their unique setting as historical witnesses to the faith of the ancients. In the apposite words of Daniélou: 'The first trait marking contemporary religious thought is renewed contact with the essential sources, namely, the Bible, the Fathers of the Church, the liturgy.'[31] Daniélou was a gifted intellectual and pastor who contributed to the founding of *Sources Chrétiennes* and exhibited a rich intuition in teaching and learning, with the *Institut Catholique* in Paris as the crucible of his research and publications. An expert in neo-Platonism and mysticism, 'Daniélou's panoramic erudition allowed him to stress that certain theological conflicts within Christianity repeated the conflicts between philosophical schools which were current at the time, which for Christians were replete with implications about faith itself.'[32] His threefold charter for renewal became the flagship for the Vatican II generation.

> First, it must treat God as God, not as an object, but as the Subject par excellence; secondly, it must respond to the experiences of the modern psyche taking account of what is new in science and history for the individual and society; and thirdly, it must become a concrete attitude before existence, to provide a unified response that engages the whole person, the interior light of a course of action that engages the whole of life.[33]

---

[29] Donald Senior, *Raymond E. Brown and the Catholic Biblical Renewal* (New York: Paulist Press, 2018), 167.

[30] See Louis Bouyer, "Le Renouveau des études patristiques," *Vie intellectuelle* 15 (1947): 6–25.

[31] Daniélou, "Les orientations présentes," 7.

[32] Bernard Pottier, "Daniélou and the Twentieth-Century Patristic Renewal," in *Ressourcement: A Movement for Renewal in Twentieth-Century Catholic Theology*, 250–62, at 262.

[33] Daniélou, "Les orientations présentes," 7.

The architects of the patristic revival revealed a hidden treasure that had been obfuscated in the neo-Thomistic hermeneutics of the seminary manuals and provided an authentic witness to the faith in a way that is sensitive to the ever-changing needs of humanity. No longer solely concerned with the study of the works of the fathers for apologetic purposes, the patristic renewal sought to recover from the fathers what had been forgotten or neglected in the course of history.

THE LEADING PIONEERS OF RESSOURCEMENT

The outstanding luminaries of *ressourcement* were Congar and de Lubac, who became synonymous with the 'new theology'. Congar is best known for his contribution to ecumenism and church reform. It was Chenu's timeless text *Une école de théologie: le Saulchoir* (1937) that influenced Congar and his *confrères* and helped to shape twentieth-century theology and Vatican II. Chenu suggested Möhler as a model for the Catholic contribution to ecumenism and, accordingly, Congar embarked on a lifelong campaign of unity. Boris Bobrinskoy, Dean of Saint-Serge, the Orthodox Theological Institute in Paris, in an address on the occasion of the launch of *Mon journal du Concile* on 27 September 2002, paid tribute to Congar's legacy and his seminal role in the genesis and realization of renewal: 'Father Congar has permanently marked this century and has inspired a theological and spiritual fermentation around the mystery of the one Church and of the division of Christians. I can say that the Orthodox theological renewal owes much to him and likewise the liturgical renewal at Solesmes or Maria-Laach, or the patristic renewal at *Sources chrétiennes*.'[34]

With de Lubac, Congar worked assiduously for a reform of the hierarchical and centralized Church that had been dominant from medieval times and, in particular, from the Council of Trent (1545–63). The most effective solution would be the revival of the 'ecclesiology of communion' as the key to renewal. Congar contributed to the formulation of an organic concept of the Church that is conciliar, collegial, Christological, pneumatological, and ecumenical, thereby restoring balance to the Church. The Second Vatican Council, called 'Congar's Council' by the American theologian Cardinal Avery Dulles

---

[34] Boris Bobrinskoy, "Le P. Yves Congar et l'orthodoxie," *Istina* 48 (2003): 20–23, at 20.

(1918–2008), became the battleground for reform, one in which he achieved unparalleled success. 'I was filled to overflowing. All the things to which I gave quite special attention issued in the Council: ecclesiology, ecumenism, reform of the Church, the lay state, mission, ministries, collegiality, return to sources and Tradition.'[35]

De Lubac's prodigious theological programme was, in many respects, a preparation for Vatican II. Joseph Ratzinger acknowledges the crucial role of his thought at the council: 'In all its comments about the Church, [Vatican II] was moving precisely in the direction of de Lubac's thought.'[36] De Lubac was instrumental, with others, in the foundation of the *Théologie* series, a project of the Fourvière Jesuits, dedicated to the 'renewal of the Church'. He launched the series before the end of World War II with Henri Bouillard, who became the project's first secretary. According to Bouillard, the twofold objective of the project was 'to go to the sources of Christian doctrine, to find in it the truth of our life'.[37] But the greatest and most enduring contribution of the Fourvière Jesuits to *ressourcement* was undoubtedly *Sources chrétiennes*, a bilingual collection of over 500 volumes to date of Greek, Latin, and occasionally Syriac and Aramaic authors, published by *Éditions du Cerf*, under the general editorship of de Lubac and Daniélou. An important aim of the series, from its inauguration, was a *rapprochement* between separated Christians of East and West.[38] De Lubac elucidates the significance of *Sources chrétiennes* for renewal as follows: 'Each time, in our West, that Christian renewal has flourished, in the order of thought as in that of life (and the two are always connected), it has flourished under the sign of the Fathers.'[39] The series has helped to make the fathers the normal spiritual *milieu* of theologians and laity. John Courtney Murray (1904–67), an expert at Vatican II, describes the success of *Sources chrétiennes* perceptively: 'We are all familiar with that definite, if undefinable reality known ... as a "climate of opinion." And we know, too, that in the patristic climate of opinion the uninitiated rather tends to gasp for breath.

---

[35] Congar, "Reflections on Being a Theologian," 405.

[36] Joseph Ratzinger, *Principles of Catholic Theology: Building Stones for a Fundamental Theology*, trans. Mary Frances McCarthy (San Francisco: Ignatius Press, 1987), 50.

[37] See de Lubac, *At the Service of the Church*, 31.

[38] Étienne Fouilloux, *La Collection 'Sources chrétiennes': éditer les Pères de l'Église au XXᵉ siècle* (Paris: Cerf, 1995), 219.

[39] De Lubac, *At the Service of the Church*, 95–96.

It is to this problem and its solution that the recently inaugurated series of patristic texts, *Sources chrétiennes*, directly addresses itself, with altogether remarkable success.'[40]

TOWARDS VATICAN II: NOUVELLE THÉOLOGIE TRANSFORMED

The movements of renewal in Catholic theology reached a dramatic high point on the eve of the Second Vatican Council when the leading *ressourcement* intellectuals were carried onto the world stage as part of the momentous agenda of renewal proposed by John XXIII. The foundations for reform had been carefully laid through the intellectual and spiritual life of the French Jesuits and Dominicans, as well as by the French- and German-speaking Benedictines and members of the Young Christian Students and the Young Christian Workers. Chenu expressed the dual rubric of the *ressourcement* theologians precisely: 'The theologian must carry his light to the heart of the world without losing the hope born of contemplation.'[41] The suspicions of doctrinal heterodoxy, neo-modernism, and relativism eventually subsided as the *nouvelle théologie* underwent a new reception in the Dutch and German contexts.[42] The unresolved tensions and antinomies at the heart of Catholic thought in the first half of the twentieth century remained dormant but unresolved only to appear again in the context of the postconciliar traumas in the Church, the repercussions of which continue to play out today. Nonetheless, for a brief period, when the spiritual and religious landscapes of mid-century were dominated by the twin edifice of the World Council of Churches and the Second Vatican Council, an era of hope and good will, based on a vibrant ecumenism and an embryonic inter-religious dialogue, illuminated both church and city. The ultimate success of the renewal movements of the first half of the twentieth century depends first on the long-term reception of Vatican II, which in turn depends on a complex series of paradigm shifts in church and society that necessitates mutuality in

---

[40] John Courtney Murray, "*Sources Chrétiennes*," *Theological Studies* 9 (1948): 250–55, at 251.

[41] Marie-Dominique Chenu, *Une école de théologie: le Saulchoir* (Paris: Cerf, 1985), 143.

[42] See Jürgen Mettepenningen, *Nouvelle Théologie – New Theology: Inheritor of Modernism, Precursor of Vatican II* (London: T&T Clark, 2010), 115–38; Loïc Figoureux, *Henri de Lubac et le Concile Vatican II (1960–1965)*, Bibliothèque de la Revue d'Histoire Ecclésiastique 102 (Louvain-La-Neuve/Leuven: Brepols, 2017).

respect for religious freedom and the dominant existentialism, neither of which is assured. And, second, it depends on the capacity of the Catholic Church to respond to the ever-expansive cultural revolution of the contemporary period, including such issues as *laïcité*, the role of women in church leadership, and the widespread indifference and/or hostility to institutional religion in secular society. Henri Bouillard articulates the perennial challenge for the present-day practitioners of renewal.

> Theology, which is a work of the reason, cannot without danger ignore the very movement of human thought; but its true refreshment comes from submersion in the Word of God, such as it is taught in the Church, ripened in a time-honored spiritual experience, developed by those Great Doctors who were at once geniuses and saints. When a theologian works, it is to this school that he returns.[43]

FURTHER READING

Daley, B. "The *Nouvelle Théologie* and the Patristic Revival: Sources, Symbols and the Science of Theology." *International Journal of Systematic Theology*, 7 (2005): 362–82.

Flynn, G. and P. D. Murray, ed. *Ressourcement: A Movement for Renewal in Twentieth-Century Catholic Theology*, 2nd ed. Oxford: Oxford University Press, 2014.

Fouilloux, É. *Les Éditions dominicaines du Cerf: 1918–1965*. Rennes: University of Rennes Press, 2018.

Kaplan, G., "The Renewal of Ecclesiastical Studies: Chenu, Tübingen, and Theological Method in *Optatam Totius*." *Theological Studies* 77 (2016): 567–91.

Lamberigts, M. "The Liturgical Movement in Germany and the Low Countries." In *La Théologie Catholique entre Intransigeance et Renouveau*, edited by Gilles Routhier, Philippe J. Roy, and Karim Schelkens. Louvain-la-Neuve / Leuven: Brepols, 2011, 91–121.

Mettepenningen, J. *Nouvelle Théologie – New Theology: Inheritor of Modernism, Precursor of Vatican II*. London: T&T Clark, 2010.

Murphy, R., ed. *Lagrange and Biblical Renewal*. Chicago: Priory Press, 1966.

Pecklers, K. F. "History of the Modern Liturgical Movement." In *Oxford Research Encyclopedias*, September 2015. DOI: 10.1093/acrefore/9780199340378.013.19.

---

[43] See de Lubac, *At the Service of the Church*, 31. The quotation is from the foreword of the fiftieth volume of the *Théologie* series.

Viviano, B. T. "The Renewal of Biblical Studies in France 1934–1954 as an Element in Theological *Ressourcement.*" In *Ressourcement: A Movement for Renewal in Twentieth-Century Catholic Theology,* 2nd ed., edited by Gabriel Flynn and Paul D. Murray, 305–17. Oxford: Oxford University Press, 2014.

3 Papal Leadership in the First Half of the Twentieth Century: Resistance and Renewal

KARIM SCHELKENS

GENERAL INTRODUCTION

When historians discuss the dawn of the twentieth century, the key moment they point to is not the year marking the turn of the century. The end of the long nineteenth century lies one-and-a-half decades later in the year 1914. The experience of World War I, which broke out in that year, caused a dramatic shift in the global landscape. Global conflict affected populations worldwide and left its mark on developments in politics, social life, culture, and, naturally, religion. Catholic Church leadership evidently did not escape from all of this. So, any attempt at describing the role of the papacy in the first half of the twentieth century needs to set out from this awareness. In this contribution, we will offer a basic survey of the role of the popes and their administrations. Historians are faced with the complexity of the period stretching between the pontificate of Leo XIII, who died in the summer of 1902, and the final years of the long pontificate of pope Pius XII, who reigned in the Catholic Church until 1958. In what follows we will start by outlining the pontificate of Pius X as that of the last nineteenth-century pope. Next we will consider the evolution of the papacy in an era marked by drastic changes: the two world wars, the global economic recession, the rise of secularism, and the threat of totalitarian regimes that shaped the papacy in the decades before Vatican II. As other contributions in this volume focus more on the description of Catholicism at a grassroots level or address the theological renewal that anticipated Vatican II, our emphasis will remain strictly on the central and universal leadership of Catholicism in its capacity as the doctrinal, pastoral, juridical, and diplomatic center of the Roman church.

THE END OF THE LONG NINETEENTH CENTURY

The Last Nineteenth Century Pope: Pius X and the Rejecting of Modernity

Early in the very last year of the nineteenth century, Leo XIII addressed a remarkable apostolic letter to the American Cardinal Gibbons under the title *Testem benevolentiae*. In this letter, the pope expressed his concerns about a growing liberalism in the Catholic Church in the United States. He stressed that Catholics could not decide doctrine for themselves and must obey the magisterial teaching authority of the church. Practices such as exposing Catholic young people to public schools were dangerous and open and public discussion of theological opinions ought to be avoided. Rome raised serious concerns around the biography of an American priest named Isaac Hecker and denounced what it called "Americanism." Any unsound beliefs in the Catholic Church in the United States were to be eradicated. In response, Cardinal Gibbons and a nearly unanimous US hierarchy strongly denied that American Catholics held any of the views condemned by the pope. While this present essay cannot treat the so-called phantom heresy of Americanism at length, this brief reference to it serves as a characteristic of the type of papal leadership that emerged in the early twentieth century. It was marked by centralism, had clear monarchic shapes, and claimed its universal role over Catholics in a church moving beyond Europe in more global dimensions.

Still, the years before 1914 cannot be neglected. In 1903, after the death of Leo XIII, a new pope was elected: Cardinal Giuseppe Melchiore Sarto was well-known to the Italian public as a pastoral and dynamic personality. Still he chose the name of Pius X, indicating his self-perception as a pope involved in a struggle with modernity. This would become apparent during the Catholic modernist crisis. Pope Leo XIII had already warned about the dangers of rationalism and "modern theology" in his treatment of the so-called *Biblical Question*. Around the turn of the century, scholars held different opinions on biblical exegesis and legitimized their own methodology based on their respective reception of Leo XIII's encyclical *Providentissimus Deus*. Basically, the modernist crisis would be seen as a clash between secular scientific progress and the church's own neoscholastic scientific model. In the nineteenth century, two paradigms for scientific research, philosophy and theology, had developed simultaneously yet separately, and the papacy would clearly stand to defend the latter. In fact, Vatican II cannot properly be understood without reference to the modernist crisis. What was at stake, then?

In the nineteenth century, scholars like Louis Duchesne and Alfred Loisy were of particular importance. They stressed the necessity of academic investigative freedom and insisted on setting aside dogmatic starting points in their research activities. Although these so-called modernists did not act as a group, did not define a clear system, and had no intention of promoting heretical opinions, their focus on secular historical research and the adoption of secular methodologies in their investigations of the sources of Christian faith (e.g. the Bible, church fathers) ended up in theological claims that ran counter to fundamental elements of late nineteenth-century neo-Thomist theology, such as the opinion that religious truth is coined in particular contexts and that dogmas are not immutable.

The idea of development, already present in nineteenth-century schools of thought such as the Tübingen School or in the thought world of John Henry Newman, when seen through Roman eyes, encouraged relativism. In fact, notions of divine inspiration, scriptural inerrancy, and God as the primary author of the Scriptures all appeared to be at stake and required a strong defense. That said, the modernist crisis was both a crisis of authority and a crisis of Catholic intellectual life. In his attempt to describe it, Thomas Michael Loome spoke about "a single intellectual *crisis* manifest in a wide variety of individual *controversies.*"[1]

Central to this, under the pontificate of Pius X, was the controversy around Alfred Loisy, a French priest-scholar and longstanding admirer of John Henry Newman. He had taught at the *Institut catholique de Paris* and published important studies in the field of biblical exegesis, on occasion in reaction to the studies of the liberal Protestant scholar Adolf von Harnack. In fact, the "first version" of what was considered Modernism was called "Loisysm."[2] Loisy's research led him to deny divine authorship of Scripture, and to question the notion of inerrancy and inspiration. Ultimately, his two "red books" were put on the Index of Prohibited Books while the Congregation of the Holy Office opened an investigation of his writings.[3] On March 7, 1908, the feast day of St. Thomas, Loisy was officially excommunicated.

---

[1] Thomas Michael Loome, *Liberal Catholicism, Reform Catholicism, Modernism: A Contribution to a New Method in Modernist Research*, Tübinger theologische Studien 14 (Mainz: Matthias-Grünewald-Verlag, 1979), 195.

[2] The term "Loisysm" was launched in 1903 by Hippolyte Gayraud, *Le Loisysme*, in *L'Univers*, November 16, 1903.

[3] *La censure d'Alfred Loisy, 1903: Les documents des congrégations de l'Index et du Saint Office*, ed. Claus Arnold and Giacomo Losito, Fontes archivi sancti officii romani 4 (Rome: Libreria Editrice Vaticana, 2009).

The aforementioned measures against Loisy were part of a much larger anti-modernist campaign that marked the era of Pius X. From the side of the Roman magisterium, any attempt at undermining neoscholasticism called for some sort of reaction. As the Loisy case shows, publications of scholars were put on the Index of Prohibited Books, often under the influence of members of *La Sapinière* – a secret network of intransigent Catholics who hounded and reported on alleged modernists. A step further was taken when Catholic scholars were excommunicated. Papal documents openly attacked and condemned Modernism, to the extent that one can easily speak of a "Document Storm,"[4] which started in 1907 with the promulgation under Pope Pius X of the Holy Office decree *Lamentabili Sane Exitu*, which condemned sixty-five propositions. This has been dubbed "the minor syllabus," connecting it directly with the Syllabus of Errors published by Pius IX in 1864. The encyclical *Pascendi Dominici Gregis* soon followed, openly condemning Modernism and urging Catholic scholars to stick with the neoscholastic paradigm. Several documents followed, the last and more moderate one being the encyclical *Spiritus Paraclitus* promulgated by Benedict XV, in 1920. All of them defended neo-Thomism, stressed a nonhistorical approach to Scripture as a source of revelation, and reiterated the necessity of safeguarding the absolute inerrancy of Sacred Scripture.

Pope Leo had already initiated his assault on modernism in 1902 by establishing the Pontifical Biblical Commission, tasked with watching over Catholic biblical scholarship. It was allowed to confer academic degrees and, from the pontificate of Pius X until the era of Vatican II, anyone who wanted to become a Catholic professor in biblical exegesis was forced to take examinations set up by the commission. In 1910, Pius X imposed on all Catholic members of clergy an oath of allegiance to Catholic doctrine and to the pope, which indicated that they refrained from any "rationalist" sympathies and would defend the Thomistic tradition.

Among Catholic intellectuals, the anti-modernist struggle caused an atmosphere of fear and distrust. On the flipside, scholarly attention to modernism has often overshadowed any interest in Pius X's pastoral commitments. Defending neo-Thomism meant defending Catholic truth and church authority and creating unity among Catholics. Although the aggressive suppression of modernism caused numerous

---

[4] See the *Enchiridion Biblicum: Documenti della Chiesa sulla Sacra Scrittura*, ed. Alfio Filippi and Erminio Lora, Collana Strumenti (Bologna: EDB, 1994).

victims, his focus on Catholic unity rendered Pius X in some ways a reform pope, as has been underlined by his twenty-first-century successor, Pope Francis.

Already in 1904, Pius X made clear that the relationship between the Vatican and nation states was still in the line of the thesis-hypothesis model that insisted on the ideal situation of state support for the privileged practice of the Catholic faith; this ran counter to democratic and modern freedoms that would be accepted at Vatican II and aimed ultimately at constructing Catholic states. Building on the heritage of Vatican I, the church's divine foundation was stressed, and consequently the position that the authority of the Roman Pontiff stood above all civil authorities was also emphasized. This organizational principle would now be fixed into juridical terms, since in 1904 Pius X commissioned Cardinal Pietro Gasparri to draft a single unified code of canon law for the Catholic Church. Up until that time, canon law had been rooted in a long tradition of jurisprudence, commentaries on the medieval Lombardian sentences, and discussions about the juridical implications of magisterial teaching.

Gasparri's work was utterly important. It would unify canon law and provide clear legal principles to be applied everywhere. It remained in vigor until 1983 and thus functioned as the juridical framework within which Vatican II would later be summoned, organized, and implemented. The *Code of Canon Law*, only promulgated in 1917, would transform Vatican I's hierarchical and institutional ecclesiology into juridical church structures. The focus on structures of universal governance was strong: A drastic reform of the Roman Curia was established in 1908, molding the ancient curial offices into a well-organized instrument of global church government. Gasparri reorganized tribunals, such as the Roman Rota, and carried through an internal reform of the Holy See's Secretariat of State. In his hands, the Roman Curia would become a powerful instrument of papal governance.

The emphasis on strengthening central governance went hand in hand with reforms in other domains. Pius X pursued Catholic unity, conceived in terms of uniformity, by way of a series of Tridentine-inspired reforms. These were oriented toward the pastoral life of the church and were reflected in a range of decisions: Daily celebration of the Latin mass and regular reception of communion immediately touched the lives of the faithful, as did the lowering of the age for children's first communion from the age of twelve or fourteen to the age of seven. The practice of catechesis thereafter focused more and more on sacramental devotion and devotional practices that encouraged a child-like piety. The reforms touched the liturgical realm: Church music moved away from Italian liturgical practice, often rooted in a rather spectacular "opera culture." The pope promoted medieval Gregorian chant. Finally, priests were made aware of their role again: Not only did they start saying mass every day; a simplification and reform of the breviary made sure they all would pray the same daily and universal prayer.

Benedict XV: The Pope and World War I

Since the nineteenth century, tensions had risen between the dual alliance set up by Bismarck (a political alliance between the German Empire and the Austro-Hungarian Empire) on the one hand, and the Russian tzarist Empire on the other hand, over the rule of the Balkan areas. In 1912 and 1913 two Balkan wars followed and led to the further destabilization of the region, until the 1914 assassination of the heir to the Austro-Hungarian throne, Franz Ferdinand of Austria, sparked the outbreak of World War I and set in motion a series of hostilities between reigning forces. The war would bring an end to the empires that had existed since the nineteenth century: the German Empire, the Austrian Empire, and the Russian Empire.

Pius X died in September 1914, months after the war had begun. The fraught political climate brought a peculiar sense of urgency to the conclave. Since Pius X's reforms had ended the ancient tradition of political interference in the conclaves, no national vetoes were possible. The climate of anxiety created by anti-modernist policies and the precarious political context resulted in the election of Cardinal Giacomo della Chiesa, who chose the name of Benedict XV. His brief pontificate would be dominated by the most devasting global conflict the modern world had experienced; he died four years after the end of the war, in 1922.[5] This pope witnessed dramatic industrial progress and the new weaponry that came with it: tanks, airplanes, submarines, and poisonous gas. All appeared in the war even as the warfare itself was carried out in the nineteenth-century tradition, with outdated strategies and mass battles. The combination of these factors, and the multitude of political alliances involved in the conflict, led to massive casualties on all sides. In January 1917, US forces entered the war and in October 1917 the Russian Revolution broke out, ending the rule of the Tzars. Members of the Romanov Dynasty were assassinated and a communist

---

[5] John Pollard, *The Unknown Pope: Benedict XV (1914–1922) and the Pursuit of Peace* (London: Geoffrey Chapman, 1999).

regime was installed in Russian-ruled territories. A new context had arisen. By the end of the war, countries like Belgium and the young state of Poland were devastated. The total number of military and civilian casualties in World War I was over 37 million, making it one of the deadliest conflicts in human history.

Throughout this conflict, Benedict XV chose never to enter into open conflict with governmental administrations, choosing to work, rather, via all diplomatic channels at his disposal. In the 1914 encyclical *Ad Beatissimi Apostolorum*, he expressed his sadness regarding the war, distressed about the end of civilized Europe. He urged all parties involved to seek and promote peace by constantly sending papal envoys. In 1915, for example, he sent Eugenio Pacelli to negotiate with the Austrian emperor Franz Joseph. However, Holy See neutrality did not have its intended effects. Germany and Austria-Hungary on the one hand, and France and Great Britain on the other, turned against the pope, accusing him of siding with the other party. In 1917, he proposed a peace treaty urging all parties involved to refrain from seeking damage compensations from the others at the end of the conflict.[6] This generated negative reactions from those countries that had suffered great losses from German and Austrian violence. On top of this, Germany promised that it would conquer the city of Rome and restore the pope's temporal powers, well aware of the fact that the papacy had basically lost all control of the Papal States at the end of the First Vatican Council. The Vatican hill had been on loan from the Italian state since the outbreak of the Franco-Prussian War of 1870.

Seven months after the victory of the Allied Forces and the Armistice of November 1918, a new world order was created with the Treaty of Versailles. The treaty did not follow the pope's proposal. Emperor Wilhelm II was charged with war crimes and a list of restrictions was imposed on the new state of Germany, restrictions which would seriously affect Germany's social and economic life in decades to come. Article 231 of the Treaty, the "War-Guilt clause," put all responsibility and accountability on Germany for the damage done to the civilian populations of the Allied Forces. This accountability, combined with severe restrictions on German military forces, led to the subsequent impoverishment of the German population. Moreover, although discrete talks were taking place in the presence of an official from the Vatican State Secretariat, Bonaventura Cerretti, the pope or his

---

[6] Francis Latour, *Le Saint-Siège et les problèmes de la paix pendant la première Guerre Mondiale* (Paris and Montréal: Persée, 1996).

ambassadors were not invited to the Versailles peace negotiations[7] and the exclusion of the Vatican created a situation in which it could not claim any compensation for church losses during the war. In the same year, 1919, the League of Nations was founded by France, Britain, Italy, and Japan. Later Belgium, Brazil, Greece, and Spain joined. United States President Woodrow Wilson had enthusiastically promoted the idea of the League as a means of avoiding any repetition of another world war, and the League was the centerpiece of Wilson's "Fourteen Points for Peace."

In this entirely new context of international alliances, the papacy came out weakened and the years after the war were spent re-establishing its international position. Benedict XV significantly expanded his diplomatic corps of nuncios, and by the end of his pontificate they were represented in twenty-seven countries. Relations with the Italian State slowly improved, as the pope abolished the nineteenth-century policy of prohibiting Catholic state leaders visiting the Italian government to also visit the Vatican. All the while, Benedict XV was among the first popes to take the harsh fate of the Eastern Catholic traditions seriously. Already before the end of the war, witnessing the communist revolution, he had established a Congregation for the Oriental Church in the Vatican, detaching it from the old *Propaganda Fide* and making clear that the Byzantine Rite churches were an integral part of the Catholic Church.

FROM THE INTERBELLUM TO THE COLD WAR: TOTALITARIANISM AND RESSOURCEMENT

The Papacy and Totalitarian Politics: From Pius XI to Pius XII

In February 1922, Benedict XV was succeeded by Cardinal Achille Ratti, who had spent much of his career as the head of the Vatican Libraries. In the years before his election, he had been a rather unsuccessful papal nuncio in Poland and Lithuania. The Warsaw political administration put so much pressure on the Vatican that Ratti was ordered to leave his post and return to Rome. He was appointed Archbishop of Milan and became a cardinal in 1921 and returned to Italy with a lifelong conviction that communism was a threat to humankind that could not be tolerated. On various occasions, he would condemn both the

---

[7] Giuseppe M. Croce, "Le Saint-Siège et la conférence de la Paix, 1919: Diplomatie de l'église et diplomaties d'état," in *Mélanges de l'école française de Rome* 109 (1997): 793–823.

communist philosophical ideology as well as those adhering to communism. But communism was not the only type of totalitarian regime that arose in the interbellum: Almost simultaneously, fascism arose. Because the pontificate of Pius XI spanned the entire interbellum, it was crucial for the Catholic Church's societal and political positioning. Vatican policies could be felt in the further expansion of the list of concordats with new nation states emerging out of the world war. When discussing the papacy and fascism, the concordat policy provides the horizon, and two of these state agreements deserve more attention.

In Italy, the Vatican benefited much from a new pact with the Italian State, led by Benito Mussolini. The concordat, signed and ratified in 1929, is known as the Lateran Treaties. This was the result of years of negotiating with the Italian government, and it led to the final settling of the "Roman Question" regarding the papal loss of territorial rulership in 1870. Italy agreed to offer independence to the Vatican State, and the grounds of the Vatican City were officially handed over to the pope. The Italian Catholic Church regained possession of lost ecclesiastical properties, such as schools and hospitals. Canon law was acknowledged as the church's proper legislation and the Italian State offered a large financial compensation for the loss of the Papal States. The Lateran Treaties also theoretically granted the Catholic Church supreme authority over Catholic education in all Italian schools, including state schools. The flipside was that the Italian fascist leader Mussolini demanded that the church cease its support for the Italian Catholic political party, the *Partito Popolare*. Pope Pius XI agreed to this, with the result that Mussolini lost all serious political opposition within Italy and Fascism gained strength in the Italian State. Mussolini rapidly dissolved several Catholic youth movements, forcing young Catholics into the Fascist youth movements.[8] Two years later Pius XI would react strongly against this move in his encyclical of 1931, *Non Abbiamo Bisogno*.

Still, two years later another concordat was signed, arranged by the former nuncio there, Eugenio Pacelli, who had been appointed Vatican Secretary of State in 1930. This so-called *Reichskonkordat* was the agreement between the Vatican and the Nazi-regime and was signed in July 1933. It sought to strengthen the position of the Catholic Church and protect the rights of Catholics under Nazi rule, but it was often

---

[8] On the clash between the Vatican and the Italian fascist regime, see the recent volume by Piero Pennacchini, *La Santa Sede e il fascismo in conflitto per l'Azione Cattolica* (Vatican City: Libreria Editrice Vaticana, 2012).

violated by the German government. From the start, the Vatican's attitude toward the Nazi Regime was two-pronged: It sympathized with Germany's situation as a buffer state against the atheistic Soviet Union, but at the same time, the Vatican carefully watched Germany's political and military evolution.[9]

In 1933, Adolf Hitler and his National Socialist German Workers Party assumed power, making Hitler the new German Chancellor, succeeding Paul von Hindenburg. Hitler's political party would openly defy the Versailles Treaty. Its impact had been devastating on Germany and it fueled the growing success of the Nazi party, which created economic growth through the re-building of infrastructure and increased military development. When Germany organized the 1936 Olympic Games, it seized the occasion to show off its new wealth and military power. At the same time, the oppression of minorities grew rapidly, and political parties other than the Nazi party were, one by one, forced to dissolve.

In 1937 Pius XI's concern led to the publication of the encyclical, in German, *Mit Brennender Sorge*, drafted by Pacelli and the German Cardinal Michael von Faulhaber. The publication of the encyclical, which openly disapproved of Nazi ideology, was prohibited by the Nazis, and many Catholics were imprisoned as a result of their secretly spreading copies of it. The encyclical was but the tip of the iceberg: In the years between 1933 and 1936 Pius XI sent over thirty letters of protest to the leaders of the Third Reich and made it clear Catholics could not be anti-Semites. After the Holocaust this intuition would only be strengthened in Vatican II's document on interreligious dialogue, which included one of the few condemnations of Vatican II: that of anti-Semitism. In the last year of his pontificate, in April 1938, Pius XI had the Congregation for the Universities and Seminaries prepare a *Syllabus against Racist Theories* to be distributed among all Catholic educational institutions. The document was never released.

And then there was another violent threat: In communist territories both Roman Catholic and Eastern Catholics faced severe suppression. Given the fact that the pope lost control over bishops and priests who were now actively persecuted and exiled, and the fact that the communist leadership forced Greek Catholics to convert to Russian Orthodoxy while it held the Russian Orthodox Church under state control, the Vatican tended to approach communism, an openly atheist ideology, as

---

[9] See the important book by Hubert Wolf, *Pope and Devil: The Vatican's Archives and the Third Reich* (Cambridge, MA: Belknap Press of Harvard University Press, 2010).

a much graver danger than fascism. At first, diplomacy was tried: In the 1920s the aforementioned papal envoy Pacelli carried on secret conversations with the Soviet Ministry of Foreign Affairs, but they ceased in 1927, although persecutions did not end. By then, Pacelli was a key figure in diplomacy: At the age of 27, he had already been appointed as a *minutante* at the Holy See's Secretariat of State. That appointment was the first step in a career under the reigns of several popes. He assisted Cardinal Gasparri in his codification of canon law, and already during World War I, he became thoroughly acquainted with Vatican diplomacy. Benedict XV sent Pacelli on a peace mission to negotiate with the Austrian emperor in 1915, and in 1917 he appointed Pacelli as nuncio in Munich, Bavaria. In this post, Pacelli was responsible both for the entire German-speaking region during the war and for conveying the pope's peace suggestions to the German emperor Wilhelm II. He witnessed the effects of the Versailles Treaty on German society and declared the treaty an international absurdity. All along, he held the opinion that the neutral position taken by Benedict XV was ultimately the best option for the Roman Catholic Church.

After the death of Pius XI in February 1939 and on the eve of World War II, there was an urgent need for a skilled diplomat as pope. On March 2, Pacelli turned out to be the major candidate. He took the name of Pius XII and remained in power until 1958, spanning World War II and the first decade of the Cold War. When Pius XII took office the world was on the brink of war: The Nazis' annexation of Austria was but the beginning of German expansion. In September of 1939 it annexed Poland. The new pope and his state secretary Cardinal Maglione had already feared this evolution and had made a radio appeal for peace in August 1939.[10]

During World War II, the results of Rome's double approach toward the Nazi regime were increasingly felt. Faced with the delicate task of positioning Catholicism against two totalitarian regimes, Pius XII adopted the diplomatic model of Benedict XV: neutrality and diplomatic action behind the scenes. Although by 1943 Pius XII was aware of the extermination policies of the Nazi regime – policies that had been officially defined as the *Endlösung* at the January 1942 Wannsee conference and would lead to a devastating situation for minorities (Jews, gypsies, homosexuals, disabled people, etc.) – he refrained from open

---

[10] On Pope Pius XII, see Philippe Chenaux, *Pie XII: Diplomate et Pasteur* [Histoire – Biographie] (Paris: Cerf, 2003); also see Margherita Marchione, *Pope Pius XII: History and Hagiography* (Vatican City: Libreria Editrice Vaticana, 2010).

condemnation. He did make allusions to the regime and criticized it strongly in his June 2, 1943, address to the College of Cardinals.

Throughout the war, Pius XII's main concern was for the safety of Catholic populations. Painful events such as the persecution of Roman Catholics after the open condemnation of Nazi rule by the Dutch episcopate had led to the awareness that diplomatic action could save lives. One of the ways of proceeding diplomatically was to support the actions of bishops in favor of peace and in support of the fate of the Jews in particular. It is no coincidence that shortly after the war, in 1946, the bishop of Münster, Clemens August Graf von Galen, was given the title of cardinal.

For the papacy, the Italian situation became complex as well. In 1939 the Italian Fascist leader Benito Mussolini signed a pact with Germany – resulting in the acceptance of the racial doctrines upheld by the Nazis within Italian Fascist circles. In 1940 Italy had declared war against France and Great Britain. In Greece and the Northern African territories occupied by Italian forces, Germany came to help out the Italians. Starting in 1943, when the Germans were losing strength as a result of Soviet attacks on its Eastern frontiers, the Allied Forces occupied parts of Italy. Italian armed forces surrendered, and a civil war broke out. The German forces reacted by conquering most of Italy, and, as a result, Vatican City State became isolated within the city of Rome. After that, Jewish deportations began in the city of Rome, lasting until June 1944, when the Allied Forces were capable of reconquering it. In April 1945, Mussolini was arrested and assassinated in Milan. As a result of the internal struggles, the monarchy was abolished after the war and Italy became a democratic republic.

After the end of World War II, the difficulties for Pius XII's pontificate were far from over. During the Conferences at Yalta and at Potsdam in 1945, the world's top political leaders – the United Kingdom Prime Minister Winston Churchill, the United States President Harry Truman, and the then Leader of the Soviet Union Joseph Stalin – reorganized the international geo-political order. Just like his predecessor, Pius XII would have to cope with a new international political landscape and the division of the world into two large spheres: one dominated by the United States and Western Europe and the other dominated by the Soviet Union and Communist China.

The Cold War began after that, and soon the nuclear arms race dominated global political relationships. From the perspective of the papacy, communism remained a central concern, as it had been since the nineteenth century; and post–World War II tensions were soon felt across the globe.[11] In the Ukraine, for example, the entire Greek Catholic episcopacy was arrested and exiled, and Greek Catholics were coerced to convert to Russian Orthodoxy; as a consequence, they were put under state control. The church behind the Iron Curtain became a "church of silence." In December 1945, Pius XII condemned communism and openly attacked the Russian Orthodox Patriarch Alexis in his encyclical *Orientales Omnes Ecclesias*, promulgated on the 350th anniversary of the Union of Brest. Pius XII would continue this policy for the rest of his pontificate with repeated condemnations of both the communist ideology as well as the people supporting it. This would be made clear on July 1, 1949, when the Holy Office (until 1968 the pope held the title of prefect) condemned communism and all who supported it. More nuance would only become possible one decade later, under John XXIII, who distinguished between the ideology and those holding it.

BETWEEN SUPPORT AND RELUCTANCE: THE PAPACY AND REFORM MOVEMENTS

However much in crisis after World War I, and however much occupied with restoring the position of Catholicism in the political realm, the papacy in the decades before Vatican II was certainly not limited to its involvement in totalitarianism and the setup of a vast network of papal ambassadors. Before the 1920s, the emphasis of Catholic thought was on the institutional, with a great deal of attention paid to papal primacy and the legal and hierarchical order of the Catholic Church; the first universal code of canon law in 1917 served as a highlight of this. The interbellum gave way to a rediscovery of ecclesiological ideas and models belonging to a time prior to the ecclesiastical centralism of Pius IX.

From the interbellum to the late 1950s, theological innovations gradually arose at the local level, although they only entered into official Roman Catholic discourse during the Second Vatican Council. A number of reform movements began to re-connect with other elements from Christian tradition. We cannot provide a full account of these movements; our focus will be on the role of the papacy in its growth and influence.[12]

---

[11] Dennis J. Dunn, *The Catholic Church and Russia: Popes, Patriarchs, Tsars and Commissars* (Burlington, VT: Ashgate, 2004), 133–52.

[12] For an overview of the liturgical and biblical renewal movements of the early twentieth century and their impact on the Second Vatican Council, see

Papal Support: Catholic Action, Liturgical Reform, and
Biblical Scholarship

The very first issue was the rediscovery of ecclesiological diversity. Where early twentieth-century ecclesiology had remained stuck in its hierarchical, juridical, and institutional perspective, clinging to the heritage of Vatican I, now, the image of the church was gradually broadened. Aware of the rise of secularism and of the need to "reconstruct" itself as a community, in the first decade after World War I, Catholicism witnessed various social-gospel-type initiatives and movements. Their common denominators consisted in uniting people, enhancing social contact, and promoting personal well-being, characteristics that were also present in the widely recognized Catholic Action movement, promoted by Pius XI.

Catholic Action emerged out of a variety of local Catholic lay organizations spread all over Europe and beyond in the early decades of the twentieth century. Many of these movements and organizations shared common features, such as their focus on the family and the conviction that family and work were closely connected, and aimed not only to strengthen society but to enhance Catholic life. In this sense, the European movements found their counterpart in the United States in the activities of the Catholic Worker Movement, led by people such as Dorothy Day.[13] French influences weighed heavily on movements in the United States, although the image of France is a contrasted one. In that same country, Pius XI had imposed himself, curtailing the extreme traditionalist movement, *Action française*, which strove toward the restoration of Catholicism and fostered monarchic and anti-democratic tendencies. The papal position confirmed that the church of the nineteenth century was gone, and resurgence of these types of integrism was becoming less and less acceptable. Catholic social movements lingered on, sometimes facing strong suspicions and doubts from Roman leadership, as was the case with the French worker-priests, some of whom were joining communist syndicates and playing a central role in helping to organize strikes.

Already Benedict XV had made efforts to unite scattered lay activities and organizations under one umbrella. Pius XI actively engaged in doing precisely this as a part of his program of "restoring everything in Christ": *instaurare omnia in Christo*. The pope described Catholic

---

"Theological Renewal in the First Half of the Twentieth Century" by Gabriel Flynn (Chapter 2 in this volume).

[13] William D. Miller, *Dorothy Day: A Biography* (San Francisco: Harper & Row, 1982).

Action as the participation of the laity in the apostolate of the Catholic hierarchy. A striking turn in this attitude was seen under Pius XII, who in his 1939 encyclical *Summi pontificatus* used the term "collaboration" to describe the *modus operandi* of the laity and the hierarchy. This illustrated how the papacy, however paternalistic its approach still was, slowly discovered the role of the laity.[14] In this sense, the Roman magisterium did not distance itself from neo-Thomist theologians, but it also started attending to other voices. Romano Guardini gave important impetus to ecclesiology in his *Vom Sinn der Kirche* of 1923. This was accompanied by a more Christocentric spirituality and a rediscovery of the diversity of biblical images for the church, particularly that of the church as the mystical body of Christ. Theologians such as Jesuit Émile Mersch elaborated on this image in the 1930s, and in the midst of World War II, in 1943, the pope followed.

Pius XII's encyclical on the church, *Mystici Corporis Christi*, emphasized the *auctoritas* of the head; the overall perspective remained quite institutional but it also offered an image of the church as consisting of a head *and* a body. In doing so, the pope created space for more attention to the laity. Throughout the 1950s then, Catholic Action gained momentum through several factors. For a start, this general sense of the emerging role of lay people came to the fore during the massive international conferences on the lay apostolate, organized in Rome in 1951 and 1957. These events helped re-position lay people within the church.[15] As a result of the 1951 meeting, the Permanent Committee of International Congresses for the Lay Apostolate (COPECIAL) was established with papal approval. It would serve as an international organism for promoting collaborative exchange between Catholic lay people, and prominent theologians such as Yves Congar and Gerard Philips would actively contribute to it.

Of particular note during this period is the rise of the biblical and liturgical reform movements. Both were connected to the aforementioned reforms of Pius X. In the case of biblical scholarship, the papal response started controversially with anti-modernism. World War I brought a tentative end to the witch hunt of the first decade of the century. A crucial catch-up took place beginning in 1943, when Pius XII

---

[14] On the growing recognition of the role of the laity during this time, see "The Christian Faithful" by Amanda Osheim (Chapter 11 in this volume).

[15] Bernard Minvielle, *L'apostolat des laïcs à la veille du Concile, 1949–1959: Histoire des Congrès mondiaux de 1951 et 1957* [Studia friburgensia: Series historica 2] (Fribourg: Éditions Universitaires, 2001).

published *Divino Afflante Spiritu*. This was a breath of fresh air for Bible scholars after a time of crisis and distrust. A revival of Catholic biblical exegesis occurred in the 1950s as practitioners began employing more historical-critical studies while collaborating with Protestant exegetes. The movement could not be stopped, but remnants of anti-modernism lived on just as well. Consequently, the second half of the 1950s saw a struggle between two Roman schools. On the one hand, faculty on the Pontifical Biblical Institute, inspired by the Dominican Marie-Joseph Lagrange, who was held suspect during the modernist crisis, had embraced new historical methodologies. On the other hand, professors at the Pontifical Lateran University defended the classical neoscholastic approach, resulting in painful clashes up to the opening of Vatican II.

The progress of historical science led not only to an interest in biblical scholarship but also to more study of early Christian sources of the liturgy. In turn, this led to a greater awareness of the importance of the entire community in the liturgical life of the church. The Benedictine order played a particularly important role in the liturgical movement. Pius X had looked to them to lead the way. Thus, it is no surprise that a Benedictine monk, Lambert Beauduin, drew from the Italian version of the 1903 motu proprio, *Tra le sollecitudini*, to promote the "active participation" of the faithful in what had become, for many, an incomprehensible Tridentine liturgy.

After the World War I, liturgical reform became a key issue and, gradually, the papacy allowed the spread of hundreds of thousands of popular missals in which the translation of the liturgy was recorded in the vernacular. Rome recognized the liturgical movement as a valid means to unite Catholics. In 1947 Pius XII, who during his German years had become well acquainted with the liturgical reform efforts rising in Northern Europe, promulgated the encyclical *Mediator Dei*. This constituted an important moment for the liturgical movement. Even if he remained vague about issues such as the common priesthood of all believers, the pope praised the active participation of the faithful, stressed the importance of the local bishop, and promoted the founding of diocesan liturgical commissions. While Pius XII made it clear that Latin, as a symbol of unity, would remain the "official" language of the Roman rite, he also recognized the value of the vernacular in parts of Catholic worship, making clear that this was to be done in agreement with Rome. The encyclical paved the way for the publication of a series of bilingual rituals approved by the Holy See, leading to the approval of a French-Latin ritual (1947), followed by the German *Collectio Rituum*

(1950) and both an English-Latin and an Italian-Latin version (1956). Also, in 1955 the rubrics of the breviary and the Roman missal were also simplified.

All of this had a broader societal relevance: In its discovery of the "church people," both Catholic Action and the liturgical movement sought the creation of a spiritually rooted Catholic elite who would help contribute to European political unification. A striking exponent was the "father of Europe," Robert Schuman, whose vision after 1950 was decisive for the interpretation of contemporary European unity. Schuman's thought was formed in the school of Guardini and by the Catholic social teachings of Leo XIII, Pius XI, and Pius XII. Encyclicals such as *Quadragesimo Anno*, which underlined the importance of subsidiarity – the responsibility at the lowest possible level of government – had their impact on Catholic thinking and filtered through the political thought of European Christian democracy. This 1931 document aimed to offer a Christian alternative to the socialist view of social justice, a fair distribution of goods and wages. That is why Pius XI emphasized that the smaller communities should remain free from an overly radical influence of powerful and bureaucratically oriented state institutions, which determine fully and from top down what an individual needs or needs to do. He was fiercely opposed to the centralist and totalitarian tendencies that, according to him, were included in the socialist human design and social idea. Over time, such encyclicals paved the way for Vatican II's reconsideration of church structures.

Papal Reluctance: Ecumenism and "New Theology"

If the picture may seem as if all Vatican II renewals were happily supported by the papacy, the reality is more complex. In fact, the responses of the popes to the renewal movements before Vatican II were never void of ambiguities. An interesting case is the ecumenical movement. This originated outside the boundaries of Catholicism and was initially viewed with suspicion by Roman officials. In 1910 an international conference on the missions took place in Edinburgh, where a large number of Protestant churches agreed with each other to put an end to competition between Christian confessions in the mission fields of Africa and Asia. The emphasis shifted from opposition to Christian cooperation. Catholicism did not heed this call. In the 1919 encyclical *Maximum Illud*, while deploring the existence of the "numberless heathen" in the world, Benedict XV devoted himself to the problems of the missionaries and promoted establishing an indigenous Catholic clergy, much in line with what had been proposed during the First Vatican Council. This missionary approach was one of evident proselytism, with a stress on converting other Christians to Catholicism. This stance was continued by Benedict XV and Pius XI, both of whom strengthened the importance of the Congregation for the Propagation of the Faith, known as the *Propaganda Fide*, an influential dicastery under the leadership of Cardinal Willem-Marinus Van Rossum. His prominent voice was already heard in the 1919 encyclical. On the one hand, many indigenous priests were made bishops as a result, leading to greater internationalization and internal diversity within the world episcopate. On the other hand, the Catholic magisterium rejected the growing ecumenical awareness that eventually gave rise in 1937 to initiatives to launch a World Council of Churches. Postponed by World War II, the council was formally established in Amsterdam in 1948. This grew in the 1950s and 1960s into one of the most important places for dialogue between the churches. Catholics were not unaware of this. From 1921 to 1926 the Malines Conversations took place, the first real dialogue between Anglicans and Catholics since the sixteenth century. In 1927, in response to the papal call expressed in *Equidem Verba*, the Center Istina was set up in Paris for dialogue with the Russian Orthodoxy, while in the same period an ecumenical abbey community was set up by Lambert Beauduin in Chevetogne.

But *Equidem Verba* did not call out for actual ecumenical relationships; in fact, Rome only fostered unionist activities and reacted negatively to attempts at dialogue without the aim of converting the others. In 1928, Pius XI forbade Catholics to take part in the ecumenical conversation. The encyclical *Mortalium Animos* insisted that Catholicism was the only true religion, and the only acceptable form of ecumenism was a return of the "dissidents" to Rome. This rejection clung to the old fears of relativism and false irenicism. Matters changed gradually under the leadership of Pius XII; on the one hand the declaration of the Dogma of the Assumption of Mary created an obstacle for dialogue, and on the other hand the 1950 decree *Ecclesia Catholica* recognized the "presence of the Holy Spirit" in the ecumenical movement. It was a reluctant openness, but Catholics like Congar, Charles Boyer, and Johannes Willebrands saw this recognition of ecclesial value outside of the confines of the Catholic Church as a sign for ecclesiological renewal. Although Rome did not engage in ecumenism, the so-called Catholic Conference for Ecumenical Questions arose in 1951.

Its activities were known in Rome, and the members held annual conferences and cooperated with the World Council of Churches. If, on the eve of Vatican II, Pius XII can hardly be said to have promoted Catholic ecumenism, he at least allowed its tacit existence below the radar.

Pius XII's approach to non-Catholic Christianity was still positive when compared to his reactions to *nouvelle théologie*. As this movement *ad fontes* wanted to tighten the bond between the life of faith and theology, it went against the narrowing of Catholic thinking reflected in nineteenth-century neoscholasticism. What the biblical movement did for a historical and critical reading of scripture, the *nouvelle théologie* did for understanding the Christian tradition, criticizing on historical grounds the illusory sense of the Catholic tradition's uniformity and immutability. A source of inspiration for these thinkers lay with John Henry Newman and the Catholic *Tübinger Schule* in the nineteenth century, both of which offered a dynamic vision of the Christian tradition. Once more, the suspect notion of "development" came to the surface. In 1935 Yves Congar published an opinion piece entitled *Déficit de la théologie*, comparing neoscholasticism to a "wax mask", a lifeless face. Theology had to become more than "hierarchology." His fellow Dominican, Marie-Dominique Chenu, also pleaded for a reform of theology, as did the Belgian Dominican Louis Charlier. Their criticism was sanctioned by Rome: In February 1942 the writings of Chenu and Charlier were placed on the ecclesiastical index of forbidden books.

When French Jesuits such as Henri Bouillard, Jean Daniélou, and Henri de Lubac took the lead, they too were soon confronted with opposition. In September 1946, Pius XII addressed the general chapters of the Jesuits and the Dominicans with a demand for a cessation of the controversy. One year later, the Roman Dominican Réginald Garrigou-Lagrange described the *nouvelle théologie* as a "new modernism wave" that warranted anti-modernist actions in the style of Pius X. His voice was not neglected: After a period in which Pius XII allowed for secret preparations for a new council to address the dangers facing the Church, he issued the 1950 encyclical *Humani Generis*, which can be regarded as the last staunch defense of neoscholasticism as a normative framework for Catholic theology.

CONCLUSIONS

In past decades, preconciliar Catholicism has been described as a monolith, an unshakable bulwark built on Tridentine and neoscholastic principles. Just as often, this widespread image is contrasted, if not opposed, to the Vatican II church, sketched as a moment of radical change and openness. The contrast is not entirely false, but its simplicity fails to do justice to both the council and the preconciliar church. Through recent scholarship that has focused increasingly on Vatican II as an agent of reception, it has become clear that many of the conciliar reforms did not fall from the sky. They were rooted not only in *ressourcement* movements but also in the substantial if at times uneven support of preconciliar popes. This requires a revision of the common perception of the pre-Vatican II era.

Yet there was more to it. The Catholic Church lived through the shocking experiences of global conflict. The interbellum and the rise of totalitarianism, World War II and the emergence of the Cold War, all marked an era of profound changes and transformations – ideologically, politically, and for church leadership. In these decades, notwithstanding the monarchic imagery of the papacy, the laity was (re)discovered, and early seeds of liberation theology were sown long before the term was coined.[16] Reforms were proposed, sometimes accepted, sometimes rejected. And above all it was during this complex period that virtually all of the bishops and theologians responsible for the conciliar reforms were educated and shaped.

FURTHER READING

Baum, Gregory. *The Twentieth Century: A Theological Overview*. Maryknoll, NY: Orbis Books, 1999.
Duffy, Eamon. *Saints and Sinners: A History of the Popes*. New Haven, CT: Yale University Press, 2002.
Flynn, Gabriel and Paul D. Murray. *Ressourcement: A Movement for Renewal in Twentieth-Century Catholic Theology*. Oxford: Oxford University Press, 2012.
Gevers, Lieve and Jan Bank. *Religion under Siege*. 2 Vols. Leuven/Dudley: Peeters, 2007.
Heynickx, Rajesh and Stéphane Symons, eds. *So What's New About Scholasticism: How Neo-Thomism Helped Shape the Twentieth Century*. Berlin: De Gruyter, 2018.
Hobsbawm, Eric J. *The Age of Extremes: The Short Twentieth Century, 1914–1991* (London: M. Joseph, 1994).
Pollard, John. *The Papacy in the Age of Totalitarianism, 1914–1958*. Oxford: Oxford University Press, 2014.

---

[16] Gerd-Rainer Horn, *Western European Liberation Theology: The First Wave (1924–1959)* (Oxford: Oxford University Press, 2008).

Radano, John A., ed. *Celebrating a Century of Ecumenism: Exploring the Achievements of International Dialogue.* Grand Rapids, MI: W.B. Eerdmans, 2012.

Schelkens, Karim, John A. Dick., and Jürgen Mettepenningen. *Aggiornamento? Catholicism from Gregory XVI to Benedict XVI.* Leiden: Brill, 2013.

Vian, Giovanni, ed. *Le pontificat romain dans l'époque contemporaine – The Papacy in the Contemporary Age.* Venice: Edizioni Ca' Foscari, 2018.

4 The Council as Ecclesial Process

MASSIMO FAGGIOLI

COUNCIL AS PROCESS FROM TRENT TO VATICAN II

The content of the teachings of the Second Vatican Council cannot be understood without locating the sixteen final documents in the context of a larger corpus of teachings for which Vatican II was the stage and the background (for example: John XXIII's opening speech of the council *Gaudet Mater Ecclesia* and the encyclical *Pacem in Terris* of April 11, 1963; Paul VI's speech to the United Nations of October 4, 1965; the "Pact of the Catacombs" of November 16, 1965). The content of the teachings of Vatican II is also inseparable from the way and the process through which the council formulated those teachings. This is one of the reasons why the diaries of the participants to the council are an integral part of the literature – not only at Vatican II but also at the most important term of comparison of Vatican II in conciliar history, that is, the Council of Trent (1545–63).[1]

The theological tradition has always been made also of conciliar *experiences* – in the age of the councils of the first millennium, in the age of the medieval councils of Christendom, and in the age of the councils of the "confessional age" from Trent to Vatican II. But all these conciliar experiences have always taken place according to a procedure that has changed during the development of the conciliar tradition and that has elements in common with previous councils (especially the voting membership and the presence of the pope or of his representatives), but also peculiarities for each particular council.

Vatican II as a process must be seen in the context of the previous councils, especially Trent and the First Vatican Council. At Trent the

---

[1] See the official edition of the documents of the council of Trent: *Concilium Tridentinum: diariorum, actorum, epistularum, tractatuum nova collectio*, ed. Görres-Gesellschaft, 13 vols. (Friburgi Brisgoviae: Herder, 1901–2001). Also *Canons and Decrees of the Council of Trent*, ed. H. J. Schroeder (Rockford, IL: Tan Books, first edition 1941, 2005).

decision of calling the council and the agenda was not set up before the beginning of the council but by the council itself after its opening – with less than thirty bishops present at Trent in December 1545, "a set of procedures did not exist, nor an agenda, and both had to be decided by the council. This was an advantage for the freedom of the council, but a problem for the progress of the work of the council."[2] The immediate predecessor of Vatican II is also important for understanding the choices made by John XXIII for the council as a process. For Vatican I, after the December 1864 decision to start the preparation of a council, in March 1865 several decisions were made by a preparatory Central Commission of five cardinals. The first decision was to not consult the Christian princes – a break from previous practice. The second decision was that only a small number of prelates were consulted, "all of whom were from Western Europe and the majority ultramontane."[3] Another decision was to create preparatory commissions ("congregations") that reflected the structure of the Roman Curia, which assumed an unprecedented role in the preparation of the council. The Central Commission took a leading role in the preparation and in the development of procedures at Vatican I.

The papacy wrestled for a long time with the issue of the unfinished Vatican I, exploring twice the idea of resuming the council: Roman commissions created by Pius XI in 1923–25 and Pius XII in 1948 studied in secrecy the feasibility of the project. Vatican I left a significant legacy about the idea of a council and its procedures. On the one hand, the centralization of the Catholic Church was a victory for the ultramontanist movement, which was the real, long-term preparation of Vatican I; on the other hand, Vatican I had shaped the conviction that after the declaration of papal primacy and infallibility another council was no longer necessary for the Catholic Church. However, at the same time, in the post–Vatican I period there was also a quiet growth of other centers of power in the new national (even though still largely informal) bishops' conferences.

---

[2] Hubert Jedin, *Il Concilio di Trento, vol. 2, Il primo periodo 1545-1547* (Brescia: Morcelliana, 1962), 23; English edition: *A History of the Council of Trent*, trans. Dom Ernest Graf, OSB, vol, 2, 154–57 (Edinburgh: Thomas Nelson and Sons, 1961). See also John W. O'Malley, *Trent: What Happened at the Council* (Cambridge, MA: Belknap Press of Harvard University Press, 2013), 77–82.

[3] John W. O'Malley, *Vatican I: The Council and the Making of the Ultramontane Church* (Cambridge, MA: Belknap Press of Harvard University Press, 2018), 108.

THE GOVERNING BODIES OF VATICAN II

Contrary to Trent or Vatican I, whose celebration had been predicted and prepared years before they were formally called by the pope, the council announced by John XXIII on January 25, 1959, was a complete surprise for the entire church, including the Vatican and the Roman Curia. This was a significant factor in the way the agenda of the council was shaped.[4] The conciliarity of Vatican II is visible from the very beginning of considerations regarding how best to build the agenda for the council. "Antepreparatory" was the neologism used on the occasion of the announcement of the institution of the "Antepreparatory Commission" on May 17, 1959. This was the commission that would determine how all subsequent preparations would proceed. Its membership included the secretaries of all the Congregations of the Roman Curia. The president was Cardinal Domenico Tardini (secretary of state and prefect of the Congregation for Extraordinary Ecclesiastical Affairs) and the secretary was Archbishop Pericle Felici, an auditor of the Roman Rota, who would play a key role during the entire council. The Antepreparatory Commission was in charge of preparing the consultation of all the bishops and Catholic universities: "this time there would be a universal consultation, unlike what Pius IX had done previously for Vatican I and what Pius XII planned to do for his council."[5] The bishops and the Catholic universities were asked for their opinions and recommendations in total freedom – thanks to John XXIII, who modified the proposal of a questionnaire focused on the "errors" with which the council should be preoccupied. The same request for proposals and recommendations was sent to the ten Congregations of the Curia. More than 2,500 future council fathers – resident bishops and abbots – were consulted. Between the summer of 1959 and the spring of 1960 the secretariat of the council received 9,438 proposals, which were condensed and organized in a two-volume *Analyticus Conspectus*. The *Conspectus* was later summarized and systematized thematically in questions [*quaestiones*] that were divided among the preparatory

---

[4] See Giuseppe Alberigo, "Passaggi cruciali della fase antepreparatoria, 1959–1960," in *Verso il concilio Vaticano II (1960–1962)*, ed. Giuseppe Alberigo and Alberto Melloni (Genova: Marietti, 1993), 15–42, now in Giuseppe Alberigo, *Transizione epocale: Studi sul Concilio Vaticano II* (Bologna: Il Mulino, 2009), 135–60; *History of Vatican II, Vol. 1: Announcing and Preparing Vatican Council II*, ed. Giuseppe Alberigo and Joseph A. Komonchak (Maryknoll, NY: Orbis, 1995), 55–59.

[5] *Vatican II: The Complete History*, ed. Alberto Melloni, Federico Ruozzi, and Enrico Galavotti (New York: Paulist Press, 2015), 48.

commissions in charge of drafting the schemata during the preparation (John XXIII, *motu proprio Superno Dei Nutu*, June 5, 1960).[6]

A Central Preparatory Commission was created in order to coordinate the work of the ten commissions, which were given the *quaestiones* on July 9, 1960 and started to work in the fall of 1960.[7] The ten preparatory commissions were created as a mirror image of the ten Congregations of the Roman Curia (doctrinal issues; bishops and dioceses; clergy; religious orders; sacraments; liturgy; studies and seminaries; Eastern Churches; missions; laity). In total the ten preparatory commissions had 846 participants: 466 members and 380 advisors. At Vatican I there had been only ninety-six advisors for five commissions. No lay person or lay woman was appointed to the commissions; 80 percent of the members were European, 25 percent Italian. The participants were supposed to keep the work of the commissions confidential.

One crucial commission that did not have an equivalent dicastery in the Roman Curia and provided a fundamental and unexpected contribution to the preparation of the council was the new "Secretariat for Christian Unity." It was created on June 5, 1960, by John XXIII, who gave it the same powers as the other commissions. The Secretariat, under the leadership of its president, Cardinal Augustin Bea, SJ, became the alternative voice to that of the Theological Commission, which was controlled by the Supreme Congregation of the Holy Office. This was the case not only on key issues such as ecumenism, non-Christian religions, and religious liberty, but on all the important theological issues discussed at the council.[8]

All the texts prepared by the commissions were sent to the Central Preparatory Commission (which met seven times between June 1961 and June 1962) and approved by it – except those schemata that were cancelled from the agenda because they dealt with matters reserved to the Holy See, were postponed to the postconciliar Code of Canon Law, or were merged with other schemata.

The number of members taking part in the work of Vatican II (voting members and non-voting experts or *periti*) was significantly larger than Vatican I: the attendance at individual general congregations was between 1,911 and 2,394 council fathers. Therefore, it needed its own set of rules. During the preparation, a sub-commission of the Central Preparatory Commission drew up the *Ordo Concilii*

---

[6] See *History of Vatican II, Vol. 1*, 140–66.
[7] See *History of Vatican II, Vol. 1*, 167–79.
[8] See *History of Vatican II, Vol. 1*, 263–72 and 318–26.

(the regulations of the council), which John XXIII approved on August 6, 1962 (*motu proprio Appropinquante Concilio*) and which was given to the council fathers on the same day as the opening of the council.[9] This first version of the *Ordo* had been prepared between June 1961 and June 1962 on the assumption that the council would last only a few weeks or months. It created a Council of Presidents consisting of ten cardinals, along with a secretary general, a secretary, and five undersecretaries. The secrecy that surrounded the preparation of the *Ordo* was one of the effects of the growth of papal power after Vatican I. This was an exception compared to previous councils in that a set of rules had been prepared before the beginning of the council itself. The first version of the *Ordo* reflected the experience and ecclesiology of Vatican I; in the summer of 1962 John XXIII amended the *Ordo* with changes directed at expanding the membership of the Council of Presidency and creating the Secretariat for Extraordinary Affairs.[10]

The Secretariat for Extraordinary Affairs was a consultative body presided over by the secretary of state, Cardinal Amleto Cicognani, and whose members were seven cardinals (one from the Roman Curia, two other Italians, three other Europeans, and Cardinal Albert Gregory Meyer of Chicago). In October 1962 John XXIII gave the Secretariat for Extraordinary Affairs the mandate to rethink the themes on the agenda of the council. The most important members of the Secretariat for Extraordinary Affairs were Cardinal Giovanni Battista Montini (elected Paul VI on June 21, 1963) and Cardinal Leo Jozef Suenens, especially for their contribution to the development of the ecclesiology that would be the main focus of Vatican II from the first intersession (January–summer 1963) on.

The first period of 1962 turned out to be a learning moment for Vatican II; beginning in early 1963 a few changes in the set of rules were introduced. In January 1963, a Coordinating Commission began its work, thanks to a decision made by John XXIII and announced on December 6, 1962.[11] The Coordinating Commission was in charge of following and coordinating the work of the eleven commissions drafting documents. It was presided over by the secretary of state, Cardinal Cicognani, and staffed by ten cardinals: three from the Roman Curia

---

[9] See *History of Vatican II, Vol. 1*, 326–35.

[10] See Giuseppe Alberigo, "La preparazione del Regolamento del Concilio Vaticano II," in *Vatican II commence... Approches francophones*, ed. Étienne Fouilloux (Leuven: Peeters, 1993), 54–72, now in Giuseppe Alberigo, *Transizione epocale*, 161–82.

[11] See Giuseppe Alberigo, "Dinamiche e procedure nel Vaticano II: Verso la revisione del Regolamento del Concilio (1962-1963)," *Cristianesimo nella Storia*, 13, no. 1 (1992): 115–64, now in Giuseppe Alberigo, *Transizione epocale*, 183–228.

and seven residential archbishops (all from Europe except Cardinal Francis Spellman, archbishop of New York); the meetings were attended by the secretary general of the council, Curia Archbishop Pericle Felici.

With the beginning of the second period in September 1963, a second set of rules (*Ordo Concilii*) was introduced in order to correct the inconsistencies of the first set of rules. This was the happy result of the proposals of the Franco-German group of experts and the Italian canon lawyer Giuseppe Dossetti, key advisor of the archbishop of Bologna, Cardinal Giacomo Lercaro. The Council of Presidents' role was now limited to resolving disputes, while "the running of the council was entrusted to a new college of four moderators with the powers of papal legates."[12] They were chosen by Paul VI: one Curia cardinal (the Armenian but born in Georgia, Grégoire-Pierre XV Agagianian) and three cardinals who were residential archbishops in Europe (Julius Döpfner from Munich, Giacomo Lercaro from Bologna, and Leo Jozef Suenens from Mechelen-Brussels). With the unfolding of the council, though, a rivalry emerged between the four moderators and the general secretary, Pericle Felici, whose control on the agenda of the council grew considerably, especially during the pontificate of Paul VI. John XXIII's prediction that Felici would be replaced because of his limited knowledge of languages other than Italian and Latin, as had happened to his predecessor at Vatican I, did not come true.[13]

DIFFERENT ROLES FOR THE PARTICIPANTS AT THE COUNCIL

In the conciliar traditions, the celebrations of councils have always been populated by a set of diverse participants. The most important difference between Vatican I and Vatican II on the one hand, and all the previous councils until Trent on the other, was the absence of a role for political authorities in the decision of calling the council, its preparation, and its development. But Vatican II remained an ecclesial event requiring different kinds of participants beyond the voting members.

In modern church history after Trent, the pope became effectively the only one with the power and authority to call a council. Unlike Pius

---

[12] *Vatican II: The Complete History*, 99; see also *History of Vatican II, Vol. 3: The Mature Council. Second Period and Intersession, September 1963–September 1964*, ed. Giuseppe Alberigo and Joseph A. Komonchak, (Maryknoll, NY: Orbis, 2000), 7–12.

[13] See *Vatican II: The Complete History*, 124.

IX for Vatican I, John XXIII's decision to call Vatican II was not preceded by discussions in the Curia or with members of the episcopate, but was a personal decision announced less than three months after his election. In the first period (October–December 1962) John XXIII had to intervene several times to resolve procedural impasses, especially in November 1962 regarding the commission's draft of the text on the "sources of revelation."[14] Pope John XXIII's contribution to the council was also evident during the first intersession with the publication of his last encyclical, *Pacem in Terris*. Paul VI was elected on June 21, 1963, in a conclave that took place during the first intersession. His role was different from that of his predecessor. His contribution to the discussions was discreet but direct, sending to the commissions on several occasions his proposals for the amendment of schemata (hence Paul VI's so-called red pencil). Neither popes participated in the works of the aula or the commissions, but both followed it closely and joined the aula in formal sessions for the promulgation of the final documents. The role of Paul VI was different from the role of John XXIII: "the papal apartment had begun to compete with the floor of St. Peter's as the council's center of gravity."[15]

The real work was done in the commissions (preparatory commissions and conciliar commissions), formed by a president, a secretary, sixteen members elected by the council, and nine members appointed by John XXIII at the beginning of the council. The president of the conciliar commission was the same as the preparatory commission in order to ensure continuity to the work – in most cases the president was the cardinal prefect of the curial congregation concerned with the same issues with which the preparatory and conciliar commission were dealing. The president had significant power on the key roles in the commission (the secretary and the speaker). A small number of additional commission members were added by Paul VI and by another election of commission members (four to eight according to the commissions) that took place on November 28, 1963. The number of commission members had been established by a special provision of the *Ordo Concilii*, but it was revised a few times by John XXIII and Paul VI.[16]

---

[14] See *History of Vatican II, Vol. 2: The Formation of the Council's Identity. First Period and Intersession, October 1962–September 1963*, ed. Giuseppe Alberigo and Joseph A. Komonchak (Maryknoll, NY: Orbis, 1997), 249–66.

[15] John W. O'Malley, *What Happened at Vatican II* (Cambridge, MA: Belknap Press of Harvard University Press, 2008), 205.

[16] For the complete list of the commissions' members (with the number of votes they received), see *Vatican II: The Complete History*, 126–33.

The major difference between the conciliar commissions of the previous councils and those of Vatican II was that at Vatican I the conciliar minority (the bishops opposed to the declaration of papal infallibility) were excluded from the commission *de fide*, the most important one. At Vatican II, the number of nine members of papal appointment (one third of the commission, plus one) was a guarantee for pluralism on the commission, given that at Vatican II a majority of two thirds was necessary to ratify the action of the commission, and not a simple majority of half plus one as was the case at Vatican I. One particularity was the Secretariat for Christian Unity: Contrary to the other commissions, some members of the Secretariat were not council fathers.

A key component of the commissions and of the council at large was the *periti*, the experts. The first list of *periti* (published on September 28, 1962) had 224 names, but by the end of the council their number had reached 480. Cultural diversity in the global Catholic Church was not really reflected in the list of *periti*: all were male and clergy who were overwhelmingly European. Many were members of the Roman Curia or professors at Roman universities. The most significant diversity pertained to their different theological orientations, their participation in different Roman factions or different Roman schools of theology. Most of them were academic theologians, and very few missionaries or pastors were among the *periti*.[17]

Together with the list of official *periti*, there was a large group of private *periti* whom the council fathers could take with them to Rome: The private *periti* did not have the right to participate in the general congregations in St. Peter's Basilica or the meeting of the commissions. Nevertheless, some of the private *periti* had a significant role. Among them were some of the most important theologians of that time, including some who had been censored, silenced, or had been under investigation by the Holy Office in the previous decades. Indeed, some of them were still under investigation during the preparation of Vatican II, like Karl Rahner, SJ. John XXIII made a point of rehabilitating this generation of theologians who had been under suspicion since the 1930s and especially since Pius XII's *Humani Generis* (1950).

Unlike at Trent and at previous councils, at Vatican II the *periti* never spoke to the assembly of council fathers, although they did often contribute in lectures or study meetings organized by bishops' conferences or informal groups and offered in Rome. The role of the *periti* grew

---

[17] See Chapter 5 of this volume for a more in-depth discussion of the various non-voting participants at the council.

significantly during the council, especially in their outreach to the media and the wider public, so much so that on September 15, 1964, Paul VI issued new norms for the *periti* that limited their ability to give interviews.[18]

Each commission was in charge of a number of schemata. The purview of each commission went through a significant reduction between the preparation period of 1960–62 and the beginning of the intersession in January 1963, when the coordinating committee decided on a reduction in the number of documents that the aula would discuss. The commissions' work had also to take into account the impact of the Roman Curia whose role at Vatican II was as influential as it was at Vatican I and more than at Trent, due to the physical proximity between the Congregations of the Curia and the conciliar event. Vatican II depended almost entirely on the organization and logistics coordinated by the Roman Curia. The council tried to debate the reform of the Roman Curia, but it was substantially prevented from doing so by Paul VI, who, in his speech opening the second period, promised the collaboration of the Curia itself in the reform of the central government of the Catholic Church. The Curia also played a key role in organizing the work of the postconciliar period concerning the application and reception of the council. This was particularly significant regarding issues that the council had decided to postpone to the postconciliar period.

As voting members, the most important figures at the council were the council fathers themselves: cardinals, patriarchs, archbishops, bishops (residential and titular [without jurisdiction of a real diocese]), abbots and *prelati nullius*, abbots superior of monastic orders, and superiors of exempt clerical orders. This membership was codified by canon law and it followed Vatican I. The total number was 2,860; between 2,400 and 2,450 attended the first session. Most of the absent were papal nuncios and apostolic delegates, but also some auxiliary bishops remained in their diocese. Residential bishops constituted the most important group. Among the nations with the highest percentage of absent bishops were Italy (42 percent), Brazil, and the United States (11 percent): most of them for ill health, but some of them prevented from attending by the political regimes of their countries (especially China, 24 absentees).

More or less one third of all council fathers came from Africa (351), Asia (408), and Australasia (74), compared to 416 from North America,

---

[18] See *Vatican II: The Complete History*, 188.

620 from Central and South America, and 1,060 from Europe. One hundred and thirty council fathers (4.6 percent) were Eastern Catholics (the most represented: 25 Melkites, 19 Ukrainians, 16 Maronites, 14 Chaldeans, 14 Armenians, and 10 Syrians). Half of the council fathers were born between 1901 and 1920; almost a thousand of them between 1871 and 1900; only twenty-four were born after 1924. There was also significant turnover: During the years of the council 296 bishops were appointed; over 250 bishops died between 1962 and 1965.[19] At the time of Vatican II there was as yet no rule requesting that bishops present their letter of resignation at the age of 75. This would be one of the fruits of the council's Decree Concerning the Pastoral Office of Bishops in the Church, Christus Dominus.

Members of religious orders played a particularly important role in the council. Canon law allowed abbots and prelati nullius, abbots superior of monastic orders, and superiors of exempt clerical orders to be present at the council. In October 1962, John XXIII also invited the superiors of some non-exempt (diocesan) religious families with more than one thousand members. Apart from the bishops who were religious (about 500), 38 percent of the assembly (940) was composed of members of religious orders who were not bishops. Friars Minors (90), Capuchins (55), Jesuits (51), Salesians (51), White Fathers (44), Congregation of the Holy Spirit (41), Benedictines (37), Dominicans (36), and Oblates of Mary Immaculate (34) were the most represented. The religious from exempt orders belonged to one of six groups: canons regular (e.g. Premonstratensians), monks (e.g. Benedictines), mendicants (e.g. Dominicans), regular clergy (e.g. Jesuits), clerical religious congregations (e.g. Redemptorists), and societies with common life without vows (e.g. Vincentians).[20]

At the time of Vatican II, only a few national conferences of bishops already existed and had a history of working together since the mid- or late-nineteenth century (for example Belgium or Germany). The Italian episcopate, by contrast, had never met in an assembly before the beginning of the council. The Ordo of Vatican II did not define the role of the bishops' conferences and continental gathering of bishops (especially the Latin American episcopal council CELAM, but also the meetings of African council fathers), but they had an important role in organizing collective vota for the preparation of the council, hosting lectures and seminars on theological issues, and gathering votes and encouraging a

[19] See Vatican II: The Complete History, 174.
[20] See Vatican II: The Complete History, 182–85.

consensus on specific proposals. From the interventions on behalf of a bishops' conference it was possible to discern the theological orientation of the majority of bishops of that country or the most pressing issues for the life of the church in that country. There was also a group coordinating the secretaries of the various bishops' conferences that met periodically at the "Domus Mariae" in Via Aurelia. Among the best organized bishops' conferences were those constituted by the Germans, the French, the Belgians, and those in the United States. Nevertheless, Vatican II was an opportunity for all bishops to work closely with their brothers in the episcopate from the same country.[21]

A wide range of informal groups, although not formally regulated, also played a significant role at the council. This was all the more significant when one recalls that "Vatican I [had] been heavily influenced by informal pressure groups" pushing for papal infallibility and its maximalist interpretation.[22] At Vatican II these informal groups gathered bishops, theologians, and lay people around a particular issue (for example, the group "The Church of the Poor") or because of a shared background (for example, the group of religious superiors or the group of missionary bishops).

Among the most significant non-voting participants at Vatican II were the ecumenical observers and guests who were invited by John XXIII through the Secretariat for Christian Unity. They constituted an informal council for Christian unity. This marked a difference from Vatican I, when the invitation from Pius IX was refused. Observers were representative of their churches, while guests technically represented only themselves. Their number grew during the council, from fifty-four in the first session to one hundred and six at the fourth session.[23] Yet another important group of non-voting participants at the council were the lay auditors, who were appointed by Paul VI beginning in the second session. Initially there were only thirteen, all of whom were male. Their number grew to forty-three; twenty-four women were named (including nine women religious) on the suggestion of Cardinal Suenens, beginning with the third session in 1964.[24]

---

[21] See *History of Vatican II*, vol. 2, 32–36 and 187–94.

[22] *Vatican II: The Complete History*, 200.

[23] See *Vatican II: The Complete History*, 192–99; *History of Vatican II, Vol. 5: The Council and the Transition. The Fourth Period and the End of the Council, September 1965–December 1965*, ed. Giuseppe Alberigo and Joseph A. Komonchak (Maryknoll, NY: Orbis, 2006), 485–539.

[24] See *Vatican II: The Complete History*, 212–15.

The media played a vital role as well. At the opening of Vatican II there were 1,200 journalists from all continents accredited to the Holy See. The secular and mainstream press had a major role, as it was impossible to limit access to the information about the council only to the media of the Holy See – the newspaper *L'Osservatore Romano* and the Jesuit-run *Vatican Radio*. The services of Italian public television (RAI) were used by another sixty-six different news organizations. The Holy See set up a press office that began operating in April 1961. Many international Catholic news agencies (Kathpress from Austria, KNA from Germany, KNP for the Netherlands) organized to gather and disseminate news about the council. Some bishops' conferences and religious orders at the council set up their own information and documentation centers.[25]

THE PROCESS OF DRAFTING, VOTING, AND APPROVING DOCUMENTS

The commissions drafted the *schemata* (drafts of the final documents) that were distributed to all council fathers for discussion in the aula. The commission presented the text in the aula and the fathers voted on the admissibility of the draft for a conciliar discussion. If approved (with a two thirds majority), the schema was discussed in the aula chapter by chapter. The fathers could vote in three ways: *placet* (approve), *non placet* (reject), *placet iuxta modum* (approve on condition of some changes). The interventions were in Latin: No translation was provided, and the interventions in French of the Patriarch of Antioch of the Melkites, Maximos IV Sayegh, were an exception. The rules gave precedence to cardinals and patriarchs, then archbishops, then bishops.

The schemata then would go back to the commissions for review of the amendments suggested by the fathers. After the schemata were amended by the commissions following the suggestions of the council fathers not members of that particular commission, they were sent back to the general congregation for approval of the changes. Those that were approved came back to the commission for their formal insertion in the schemata, and then the whole text of the schema was finally sent to the general congregation for the final approval of the conciliar text. After the final approval of the schemata by the aula, they were solemnly voted on (*placet* or *non placet*) in the presence of the pope in the "public

---

[25] See *Vatican II: The Complete History*, 208–11; *History of Vatican II*, vol. 2, 221–32, and 546–59.

sessions." The final documents were promulgated by the pope with the formula *"una cum patribus"* – the pope together with the council fathers: It was a change from Vatican I, in order to signal episcopal collegiality.[26]

The distribution among the different commissions of the themes to be discussed had been decided by the Secretariat for Extraordinary Affairs and later by the Coordinating Commission. But there were a few issues that never became part of the conciliar discussion nor were they treated in any detail in a conciliar text because of the decision of the pope to reserve those issues to subsequent papal determination. These issues were clerical celibacy, birth control, the procedure for the appointment of bishops, the reform of the Roman Curia, the Bishops' Synod, the legitimacy of nuclear deterrence, and the condemnation of Communism.

THE PROCESS OF VATICAN II: PARLIAMENTARY AND PNEUMATOLOGICAL

The procedure at Vatican II was "traditional and parliamentary in nature."[27] It was traditional because it took many features from the procedures of previous councils, especially Trent and Vatican I, in a cautious retrieval of the tradition of church governance through councils. Doing so meant treading carefully around the dangerous memory of the constitutionalist ecclesiology of conciliarism in the fourteenth through fifteenth centuries and of the different versions of Gallicanist episcopalism especially in the eighteenth century.[28] The adaptation of the tradition of previous procedures was visible in the significant updates dealing in particular with the now disappeared role for political authorities in the decision to call and lead the council, the much larger number of participants coming from all other the world, the presence of observers, auditors, and guests, and with the concern for the representation of the whole church and of world Christianity.

---

[26] See Giuseppe Alberigo, *"Una cum patribus,* la formula conclusiva delle decisioni del Vaticano II,"* in *Ecclesia a Spiritu Sancto edocta: Melanges Gerard Philips* (Gembloux: 1970), 291–319.

[27] *Vatican II: The Complete History,* 104.

[28] See Francis Oakley, *The Conciliarist Tradition: Constitutionalism in the Catholic Church 1300–1870* (New York: Oxford University Press, 2008), esp. 1–19. See also Hermann Josef Sieben, *Katholische Konzilsidee im 19. und 20. Jahrhundert* (Paderborn: Schöning, 1993).

Vatican II did not adapt the church to political customs and institutional traditions foreign to the history of Christianity; on the contrary, Vatican II cast a light on the original contribution of the ecclesiastical institutions (councils of the church but also models of governance of monastic communities and religious orders) to the history of representation in political institutions.[29] But at the same time it is undeniable that Vatican II was different from Trent and Vatican I in the sense that the governing bodies were built in order to ensure the representation of all the voting members in view of encouraging the largest possible consensus. This change certainly owed much to the theological emphasis of Vatican II on ecclesiology. But it was also due to the influence of the democratization of Western political systems and of parliaments between the nineteenth and the twentieth centuries on the culture of the organizers and participants at Vatican II. Vatican II had a "political mechanics" that had some similarities with the history of modern parliaments.[30] This helps us understand the tension between the existence of a dialectics between the majority and the minority on the one side, and on the other side the continuous effort to draft, vote, and promulgate final texts that were not texts of the majority, but which could be embraced by the entire council.

Vatican II as a process must indeed be seen not only in its institutional and "political" aspects but also in its liturgical aspect. Here we can consider Vatican II as a spiritual experience, bringing into prominence the pneumatological dimension of the conciliar event.[31] Vatican II was certainly a voting assembly, but it was also a spiritual assembly shaped by the celebration of the liturgy. The liturgy was not only one of the most important topics considered by the council members, but it shaped the council as a daily experience, a fact to which the conciliar

---

[29] See Paolo Pombeni, "La dialettica evento-decisioni nella ricostruzione delle grandi assemblee: I parlamenti e le assemblee costituenti," in L'evento e le decisioni: Studi sulle dinamiche del concilio Vaticano II, ed. Maria Teresa Fattori and Alberto Melloni (Bologna: Il Mulino, 1997), 17–49; Claire Maligot, "Vatican II au prisme des sciences politiques. Usages de la comparaison entre assemblée conciliaire et assemblée parlementaire," paper presented at the conference "Les parlements en question," Centre européen de sociologie et de science politique (Paris), 8–9 November 2018.

[30] See Philippe Levillain, La mécanique politique de Vatican II: La majorité et l'unanimité dans un Concile (Paris: Beauchesne, 1975).

[31] See Giuseppe Alberigo, "Sinodo come liturgia?" Cristianesimo nella Storia, 28 no. 1 (2007): 1–40.

diaries well attest.[32] A council, in fact, is not essentially a parliament or an academic meeting, but a religious assembly deliberating *in Spiritu Sancto* (in the Holy Spirit) and seeking its inspiration in prayer as much as in study.

In this appreciation of Vatican II as a spiritual experience lies the link between the *conciliarity* of Vatican II – expressed by the membership of bishops and council fathers – and the *synodality* of the whole Church, with whom the council was in communion also through the liturgy.[33] The most important legacy of Vatican II lay, indeed, not in its formulations, but in the very fact of its being celebrated as an ongoing process of ecclesial discernment. Seen from this perspective, the history of Christianity has always found conciliar process itself to be one of its most important moments.[34]

FURTHER READING

Alberigo, Giuseppe and Joseph A. Komonchak, eds., *History of Vatican II*. 5 vols. Maryknoll, NY: Orbis, 1995–2006.

Alberigo, Giuseppe. *Transizione epocale: Studi sul Concilio Vaticano II*. Bologna: Il Mulino, 2009.

Congar, Yves. *My Journal of the Council*. Translated by Mary John Ronaye and M. Cecily Boulding. Edited by Denis Minns. Collegeville, MN: Liturgical Press, 2012.

Faggioli, Massimo. *Il vescovo e il concilio: Modello episcopale e aggiornamento al Vaticano II*. Bologna: Il Mulino, 2005.

Faggioli, Massimo and Melloni, Alberto, eds. *Repraesentatio: Mapping a Keyword for Churches and Governance*. Berlin: LIT, 2006.

Levillain, Philippe. *La mécanique politique de Vatican II: La majorité et l'unanimité dans un concile*. Paris: Beauchesne, 1975.

Melloni, Alberto, ed. *Vatican II: The Complete History of Vatican II*. Mahwah, NJ: Paulist Press, 2015.

Oakley, Francis. *The Conciliarist Tradition: Constitutionalism in the Catholic Church, 1300–1870*. New York: Oxford University Press, 2003.

O'Malley, John W. *Vatican I: The Council and the Making of the Ultramontane Church*. Cambridge, MA: Belknap Press of Harvard University Press, 2018.

---

[32] See, for example, Yves Congar, *My Journal of the Council*, trans. Mary John Ronaye and M. Cecily Boulding, ed. Denis Minns (Collegeville, MN: Liturgical Press, 2012).

[33] About Vatican II and the synodality of the Church, see Pope Francis, Address During the Ceremony Commemorating the 50th Anniversary of the Institution of the Synod of Bishops, October 17, 2015
http://w2.vatican.va/content/francesco/en/speeches/2015/october/documents/papa-francesco_20151017_50-anniversario-sinodo.html.

[34] See Massimo Faggioli and Alberto Melloni, eds. *Repraesentatio: Mapping a Keyword for Churches and Governance* (Berlin: LIT, 2006).

O'Malley, John W. *Trent: What Happened at the Council.* Cambridge, MA: Belknap Press of Harvard University Press, 2013.

O'Malley, John W. *What Happened at Vatican II.* Cambridge, MA: Belknap Press of Harvard University Press, 2008.

Sieben, Hermann Josef. *Katholische Konzilsidee im 19. und 20. Jahrhundert.* Paderborn: Schöning, 1993.

5 The Role of Non-Voting Participants in the Preparation and Conduct of the Council

PETER DE MEY

Even if it were the council fathers who intervened during the plenary meetings in St. Peter's Basilica and also voted on the conciliar documents, the broad ecclesial event known as the Second Vatican Council included a much larger cast of characters. This chapter will focus on some of the non-voting participants who had their own important role to play, giving particular attention to the role of theological experts, or *periti*.

At the council we can identify two kinds of *periti*, those appointed as advisers to the council itself and those who accompanied individual bishops. The conciliar *periti* could attend the general congregations, that is, the general meetings in which the entire conciliar body conducted its business, but the bishops' personal *periti* could not. The *periti* could not vote and could only speak, even during the commission meetings, if directly addressed, although all but the Theological Commission generally ignored this rule. As a way of introducing the importance of these theological advisers, we will focus on three "couples" of theologians – Gérard Philips and Yves Congar, Karl Rahner and Joseph Ratzinger, and Hans Küng and Edward Schillebeeckx. The chapter ends with a brief description of the role of other non-voting participants: non-Catholic observers, male and female lay and religious auditors, and finally the journalists, with special attention to the Belgian Jan Grootaers.

THE ROLE OF THE *PERITI*

The Preconciliar Commissions

After Pope John XXIII had convened a council to allow the Catholic Church to renew itself, he remained largely dependent on the Roman Curia to prepare the documents to be discussed by the council fathers. The German Jesuit Karl Rahner was offered a seat on the commission on sacraments, but not on the Theological Commission, because the Holy

Office was investigating accusations against his work. Much to their surprise, Henri de Lubac and Yves Congar received invitations in July 1960 to become consultors of this commission. Even if rumors relate this to the explicit desire of the pope, during a preparatory meeting of the Holy Office their nomination was being proposed in order to avoid later criticism about the composition of the commission.[1] This is how Congar described their situation: "We are both *hapax* in a text whose context seems to me to be so oriented in a conservative sense! Our being named consultors is also a way of keeping us from the effective work which will be done by the members of the Commission."[2]

In March 1961 Congar met the Louvain theologian and member of the preconciliar Theological Commission Gérard Philips who told him he was asked to prepare a draft of the chapter on the laity for the next meeting of the commission. In his diary Congar expressed his frustration, since this meant that the draft he had sent to Rome at the explicit request of the secretary of the Theological Commission, Sebastian Tromp, had been ignored: "What is the meaning of all this? Had Tromp made this request *motu proprio*? Was it his intention to prepare his own redaction of *De Ecclesia*? Anyway, what I have prepared was as it were non-existent."[3]

The *'squadra belga'* (Belgian Team) and Friends: Gérard Philips and Yves Congar

After a year and a half of intensive collaboration, Congar asked in his diary what made the Belgians so successful at the council.[4] In his opinion there was a lot of truth in the expression "*Primum concilium Lovaniense, Romae habitum*" (the first Louvain council held in Rome). Unlike the bishops of France, who rarely consulted their *periti* and did not cooperate well, the Belgians formed a real team of bishops and theologians who efficiently worked together in the Belgian College. Because many of them had studied at the same *alma mater* and because the Belgian theologians were almost all secular priests, they treated each other on an equal basis. Congar especially praised the qualities of Gérard Philips. As could be expected from a member of the Belgian

---

[1] Loïc Figoureux, "Henri de Lubac et le concile Vatican II: Espoirs et inquiétudes d'un théologien," *Cristianesimo nella storia* 34 (2013): 249–71, here 251.

[2] Yves Congar, *My Journal of the Council* (Collegeville, MN: Liturgical Press, 2012), 15 (July–August 1960).

[3] Congar, *My Journal of the Council*, 40 (March 3–4, 1961).

[4] Ibid., 509 (March 13, 1964).

senate, Philips was a "conciliating" figure who knew how to reach a compromise. Within the Theological Commission he enjoyed recognition and deep respect from all sides. He was also a humble person who preferred to disappear as soon as his presence in Rome was no longer necessary. He even physically suffered from the stressful commission work and had to leave the council in the midst of the final session for medical reasons.

Philips is especially remembered by historians of the council as the architect of *Lumen Gentium*, the Dogmatic Constitution on the Church. Cardinal Suenens had asked him to rework the existing draft even before the council fathers had received it. At each step he organized meetings with colleagues such as Congar, Rahner, and Ratzinger to make the text stronger. In the spring of 1963 first a sub-commission and then the plenary commission of the Theological Commission decided to take the so-called Schema Philips as basis of the discussion because his text introduced new ideas such as the collegiality of bishops while at the same time respecting the work of the preconciliar commission. As part of the "vertical strategy"[5] of the Belgian College, Philips received the support of Bishop André Marie Charue of Namur and, as a sign of appreciation for their leadership, Philips and Charue were nominated as vice-secretary and vice-chair of the Theological Commission. During the second session the commission experienced a lot of pressure to finish the revision of the first chapter of the constitution. This chapter contains the well-known phrase that "the unique Church of Christ ... subsists in the Catholic Church." Philips wrote the official *"relatio,"* which explained a key alteration of the text. The original *"est"* was changed first to *"adest"* and then to *"subsistit,"* "so that the expression would find better accordance with the affirmation that elements of the Church are present elsewhere."[6]

Two further merits of this *"homo conciliaris"* (man of the council)[7] need to be mentioned. In June 1964, after long discussions, the Theological Commission also accepted his version of the chapter on the Mother of God as point of departure for the discussion.[8] In November

---

[5] Ibid., 368.

[6] *Acta Synodalia* III/1, 177: "Quadam verba mutantur: loco 'est', dicitur 'subsistit in', ut expressio melius concordet cum affirmatione de elementis ecclesialibus quae alibi adsunt." [my translation]

[7] Jan Grootaers, *Actes et acteurs à Vatican II* (Leuven: University Press, 1998), 412.

[8] Cesare M. Antonelli, "Le rôle de Mgr Gerard Philips dans la rédaction du chapitre VIII de *Lumen Gentium*," *Marianum* 55 (1993): 144–61.

Philips mentioned in his autobiographical notes that he was the author of the *Nota Explicativa Praevia*, the note given to the council fathers "upon higher authority," clarifying certain difficulties in the chapter dealing with the hierarchy.[9]

When looking back at the council twenty years after its opening, Congar described the exemplary cooperation of bishops and theologians as one of its highlights, especially when compared with previous councils.[10] He had become fully involved in this work after his nomination to the sub-commission on the church in the spring of 1963. Yet this work was not without its difficulties. Before the start of the third session, Congar prepared in vain a few *modi* in order to make chapter three more acceptable for the Orthodox. This led to some friction in his otherwise excellent relationship with Philips:

> NOT A SINGLE ONE of our *modi* has got through up to now. Those that seemed to us advisable, even necessary, in order to keep the text open to the Orthodox did not get through any more than the others. Philips has not enough sensitivity for this.... . I understand that Philips wants to go quickly. I understand that he was chiefly concerned with fending off the attack of the anti-collegialists.[11]

By his own account Congar had a hand in half of the council's documents.[12] Therefore, while looking back at his huge efforts during the council, only in comparison with Philips does he still hesitate to appropriate the words of Paul *"Plus omnibus laboravi"* (I worked more than all the others) to himself, but not those of Luke: *"Servi inutiles sumus"* (we are unprofitable servants).[13]

The German-speaking *Periti*: Karl Rahner and Joseph Ratzinger

The Jesuit theologian Karl Rahner was appointed by Pope John XXIII as council *peritus* and was at the same time the personal *peritus* of

[9] Karim Schelkens, *Carnets conciliaires de Mgr Gérard Philips, secrétaire adjoint de la commission doctrinale* (Leuven, 2006), 72.

[10] See the chapter on "Les théologiens: Vatican II et la théologie," in Yves Congar, *Le concile de Vatican II: Son église, peuple de Dieu et corps du Christ* (Paris: Beauchesne, 1984), 79–90.

[11] Congar, *My Journal of the Council*, 649 (October 28, 1964).

[12] Noëlle Hausman, "Le Père Yves Congar au Concile Vatican II," *Nouvelle Revue Théologique* 120 (1998): 267–81, here 274.

[13] Congar, *My Journal of the Council*, 870–71 (December 7, 1965).

Cardinal König from Vienna and of Cardinal Döpfner from Berlin. During the first year of the council the young priest Joseph Ratzinger was the personal *peritus* of Cardinal Frings from Köln, for whom he had already written a famous speech in 1961.[14] Both theologians collaborated in preparing an alternative version for the preconciliar work on the sources of Revelation. On November 13, during the first plenary meeting of the Theological Commission, Cardinal Ottaviani publicly criticized the *periti* who had dared to organize the opposition against the preconciliar schema on Revelation, even before the discussion in the council hall had started. Still, Rahner was invited to take part in the mixed commission that already met in December 1962 to revise this constitution. Together with his fellow Jesuit Otto Semmelroth, Rahner also wrote down a detailed criticism of the preconciliar constitution on the church, which served as material for the reactions of many German bishops during the debate *in aula*.[15] Both theologians also had a major role in the elaboration of the so-called German schema on the church, which was approved in early February 1963 at a meeting of the German and Austrian bishops in Munich.[16] Even if the Theological Commission eventually would opt for the "Belgian" schema, they would borrow among others the image of the church as sacrament from the German schema.[17] Rahner took part in the sub-commission and then also in the plenary meetings of the Theological Commission during the work on the new draft in the spring of 1963. His colleagues admired Rahner's many contributions but they were not uncritical. For example, Yves Congar remarked of Rahner, "Fr. Rahner monopolized the discussion once again. He is magnificent, he is brave, he is clear-sighted and deep, but, in the end, he is indiscreet. That was the end of the possibility of speaking: the opportunity, and even the taste for it, has been lost."[18]

---

[14] Joseph Ratzinger, "The World and the Church: A Contrast between Vatican I and Vatican II: Lecture-Text for Cardinal Frings (1961)," in Jared Wicks, "Six Texts by Prof. Joseph Ratzinger as Peritus before and during Vatican Council II," *Gregorianum* 89 (2008): 233–311, 253–61.

[15] Karl Rahner and Otto Semmelroth, "Animadversiones de Schemate *De Ecclesia* – Bemerkungen zum Schema *De Ecclesia*," in Karl Rahner, *Das Zweite Vatikanum: Sämtliche Werke*, 21, no. 1 (Freiburg: Herder, 2013), 298–339.

[16] See *Acta Synodalia* I/4, 601–39.

[17] Peter De Mey, "The Construction and Ongoing Modification of a Sacramental Ecclesiology: Vatican II's Relation to Aquinas' Theology of the Sacraments," in *Eine Autorität für die Dogmatik: Thomas von Aquin in der Neuzeit*, ed. Benjamin Dahlke and Bernhard Knorn (Freiburg: Herder, 2018), 208–25, especially 216–19.

[18] Congar, *My Journal of the Council*, 302 (May 28, 1963).

During the second session, Rahner and Ratzinger tried to influence the outcome of the vote on collegiality by writing a pamphlet on primacy and collegiality.[19] During this session Ratzinger also wrote the drafts of three interventions of Cardinal Frings during the plenary debate on the church, including the speech in which Frings argued for a thorough reform of the Holy Office and for a greater involvement of the college of bishops in the universal leadership of the church, which made a profound impression. In March 1964, both German theologians helped improve what would become the Dogmatic Constitution on Divine Revelation. In the spring of 1965 Congar expressed gratitude in his diary for the great help he received from Ratzinger in the sub-commission on missions, since his formulation of the theological foundation of mission found acceptance by the others. Congar characterized the later pope as "reasonable, modest, disinterested, a great help."[20]

Rahner and Ratzinger, finally, expressed a similar criticism about the final stages of the drafting process of *Gaudium et Spes*, the Pastoral Constitution on the Church in the Modern World, even if their response to the problem was different. Rahner had been involved in the consultations leading to the so-called Malines document in the fall of 1963, but *Gaudium et Spes* went through several more stages. During the third session under the guidance of Pierre Haubtmann, a draft was prepared and was presented in Ariccia in January 1965. Both Rahner and Ratzinger criticized this draft for its lack of attention to the reality of sin and its optimistic anthropology. Ratzinger's solution, however, was to reverse its inductive approach and start with Christology before turning to anthropology. Rahner proposed to stick to anthropology, but pay more attention to the transcendental orientation of humankind.[21]

Generally, one can say that the German bishops and theologians preferred the method of the "collective search for truth."[22] For this purpose, Bishop Hermann Volk of Mainz also found it useful to regularly convene a number of French and German bishops and theologians and

[19] Karl Rahner, Gustave Martelet, and Joseph Ratzinger, "De primatu et collegio episcoporum in regimine totius ecclesiae – Über den Primat und das Bischofskollegium bei der Leitung der gesamten Kirche," in Rahner, *Das Zweite Vatikanum*, 340–46.

[20] Congar, *My Journal of the Council*, 748 (May 31, 1965).

[21] Compare Brandon Peterson, "Critical Voices: The Reactions of Rahner and Ratzinger to Schema XIII (*Gaudium et Spes*)," *Modern Theology* 31 (2015): 1–26.

[22] Karl Rahner, "A Small Fragment 'On the Collective Finding of Truth'," *Theological Investigations* 6 (1969): 82–88.

Congar, Philips, Rahner, and Ratzinger were regular attendants at this meeting to determine the "conciliar strategy."

Immediately after the council Rahner and Ratzinger contributed to the collaborative project of mostly German *periti* to prepare an extensive commentary on all the documents of Vatican II that was added as a three-volume appendix to the *Lexikon für Theologie und Kirche*.[23]

The Less Successful Conciliar Experience of Hans Küng and Edward Schillebeeckx

In the preparatory stage of the council, the young Swiss priest Hans Küng was an assistant to Professor Hermann Volk in Münster. The announcement of the council inspired him to write a book titled *The Council, Reform and Reunion*. He received the imprimatur from Cardinal Franz König, who also suggested a subtitle to him: *Renewal as a Call to Unity*.[24] The Flemish Dominican Edward Schillebeeckx, who only recently had accepted the chair of dogmatic theology in Nijmegen, was asked to help prepare the letter that the Dutch episcopate intended to send to the faithful to encourage them to welcome this unprecedented event.[25] Many of the challenges mentioned by Schillebeeckx were taken up by the council. He also defended viewpoints that were too progressive for Roman ears. As his autobiographer Erik Borgman writes, Schillebeeckx offers "a picture of the Church in which the ministry emphatically took a place within and at the service of the community of faith."[26] Despite the protest of the Dutch bishops, Schillebeeckx would never obtain a nomination as council *peritus* but would still accompany his bishops to Rome as their personal advisor.[27]

As a foretaste of his critical stance during the Council, Küng visited Congar some weeks before the start of the council in order to gain sympathy for his idea to organize a "para-council of theologians, seeking

---

[23] The English translation is the five-volume *Commentary on the Documents of Vatican II*, translated by Herbert Vorgrimler and published by Herder and Herder in 1967–69.

[24] Hans Küng, *The Council, Reform and Reunion: Renewal as a Call to Unity* (New York: Sheed and Ward, 1961).

[25] "De bisschoppen van Nederland over het concilie," in *Katholiek Archief* 16 (1961): 369–84.

[26] Erik Borgman, *Edward Schillebeeckx: A Theologian in His History. Part I: A Catholic Theology of Culture (1914–1965)* (New York: Continuum, 2003), 320.

[27] Leo Kenis and J. Geldhof, "Wereld en geschiedenis als sacrament: Schillebeeckx aan de vooravond van het Tweede Vaticaans Concilie," *Tijdschrift voor Theologie* 54 (2014): 319–33, here 330.

to influence the true Council," an idea that Congar found unaccept-able.[28] When looking back to the conciliar period, in his autobiography Küng recalled that the most difficult decision he had to take was to decline the invitation from Cardinal König to serve as *peritus* on the Theological Commission. He preferred the indirect way to have an impact on the council by writing speeches for bishops such as the October 1963 speech on charisms by Cardinal Suenens[29] and publishing books and giving lectures all over the world.[30] Küng would have found it difficult to collaborate with the *periti* of the Theological Commission, since he was critical of Philips' schema. "Far from having the theological stature of a Congar, Rahner or Schillebeeckx, the short friendly prelate surpasses them all as a tactician and formulator of consensus texts." But this happens "at the expense of the truth – above all the truth of the Bible."[31] During the second session Congar used the example of Küng to make a distinction between the "revolutionary" and the more "realist" types of *periti*. Christopher Ruddy characterizes the difference between Congar and Küng well: "Congar chose the 'inside' path of an active patience and a certain incrementalism. Küng chose to remain outside, in order to avoid being compromised by collaboration with the Roman-curial system."[32]

With the strong support of the Dutch publisher Paul Brand, Küng took the lead in 1963 to start a new theological journal inspired by the council. Schillebeeckx, Rahner, and Congar accepted the invitation to join the editorial board of *Concilium*. They informed the pope about their plans and received his answer through his personal theologian, Carlo Colombo, in the spring of 1964. The ecclesiastical authorities had difficulties with the title and wanted more episcopal control, Roman theologians on the editorial board, and the removal of Küng from the board, the latter of which the other members refused since the journal was his initiative. The journal was launched one year later. Schillebeeckx and Küng got in trouble with the Holy Office due to their reports of the events of the so-called black week of the council in November 1964. During that period, several events occurred: A controversial note was attached to the chapter on the hierarchy in the draft of what would

[28] Congar, *My Journal of the Council*, 82.
[29] Hans Küng, *My Struggle for Freedom* (Grand Rapids, MI: W.B. Eerdmans, 2003), 360–62.
[30] Ibid., 303–28 and 407–11.
[31] Ibid., 350.
[32] Christopher Ruddy, "Yves Congar and Hans Küng at Vatican II," *Ecclesiology* 10 (2014): 159–85, here 180.

become the Dogmatic Constitution on the Church *Lumen Gentium;*
work on what would eventually become the Declaration on Religious
Liberty *Dignitatis Humanae* was delayed; and a number of changes
were proposed regarding what would become the Decree on Ecumenism
Unitatis Redintegratio. Schillebeeckx had agreed to publish a nuanced
article on the end of the third session in the Dominican journal *De
Bazuin* precisely to calm down the harsh criticism of Rome expressed
by Dutch progressive laity. It became necessary to write a second article
in January 1964 in response to the negative reactions to his previous
article. The inventory of the *Archivio Segreto* reveals that on March 30,
1965, an extraordinary session of the Theological Commission was
convened in order to investigate the orthodoxy of Schillebeeckx. The
case against him apparently was too light to lead to any further action.
Küng describes in his autobiography how he had to appear before Cardinal Ottaviani in October 1965 because of his publication of an article
critical of conciliar events transpiring during the third session.[33] A few
days before the end of the council the pope told him in a private
audience that he should refrain from writing anything that did not
render service to the church.

By the third session Edward Schillebeeckx was thrilled by the preparation being undertaken regarding a pastoral constitution on the
Church. In September 1964 he introduced the new draft of the so-called
Schema XIII in a lecture delivered at the opening of the Dutch documentation center on the Council.[34] He defended the notion of the
church as *sacramentum mundi* and argued that God's grace is also
revealed in the lives of nonbelievers. According to Henri de Lubac,
Schillebeeckx interpreted the genitive in *sacramentum mundi* as "the
sacrament which the world is" instead of speaking about the Church as
"the sacrament of salvation for the world." Such an interpretation in his
opinion was a betrayal of *Lumen Gentium.*[35] In the spring of 1965 Schillebeeckx finally was invited to collaborate in the sub-commission on
marriage and sexuality. Schillebeeckx defended the idea that procreation and conjugal love were equally important ends of marriage.[36]

---

[33] Küng, *My Struggle for Freedom,* 426.

[34] Edward Schillebeeckx, "Church and World," in *World and Church.* Collected
Works, vol. 4 (London: T&T Clark, 2014), 73–87.

[35] Henri De Lubac, *A Brief Catechesis on Nature and Grace* (San Francisco: Ignatius
Press, 1984), 191–234.

[36] Borgman, *Edward Schillebeeckx,* 350.

OTHER NON-VOTING PARTICIPANTS: OBSERVERS, AUDITORES LAICI, AND PRESS

Non-Catholic Observers

It was one of the tasks of the Secretariat for Christian Unity to organize the invitation of delegates and guests of other Christian churches and communities. The secretary general of the World Council of Churches, Willem Visser 't Hooft, was involved in the decision of the Secretariat to contact the great confessional federations so as to obtain a worldwide and representative group of observers.[37] The best-known observer, the Swiss Reformed theologian Lukas Vischer, had only recently been nominated secretary of the Faith and Order Commission. Forty years after the council he was the obvious candidate among the observers for the editors of the *History of Vatican II* to look back at the conciliar event.[38]

The ecumenical patriarch Athenagoras I felt bound to respect the decision by the first Pan-Orthodox Conference to refrain from accepting the invitation from Rome as long as local churches were opposed to this.[39] Unexpectedly, however, two observers of the Moscow patriarchate arrived in Rome a few days after the council had started. The ecumenical patriarch, however, still was represented by a personal delegate, the Romanian monk André Scrima. As of the second session, the World Council of Churches delegated the Orthodox theologian Nikos Nissiotis as second representative and shortly before the start of the third session the Second Pan-Orthodox Conference allowed local churches to send other observers to Rome. Other well-known guests of the Secretariat were brothers Roger Schütz and Max Thurian of Taizé, Oscar Cullmann, and the dean of St. Vladimir's Theological Seminary, Father Alexander Schmemann. The number of observers and guests was rising each year, starting with forty-six observers and eight guests attending the first session with a peak of ninety observers and sixteen guests of the Secretariat during the final session.

The observers were only allowed to attend silently the general congregations and other public events, but not to participate in the

---

[37] Mauro Velati, *Separati ma fratelli: Gli osservatori non cattolici al Vaticano II: 1962–1965* (Bologna: Il Mulino, 2014), 81–96.

[38] Lukas Vischer, "The Council as an Event in the Ecumenical Movement," in *History of Vatican II, Vol. 5: The Council and the Transition. The Fourth Period and the End of the Council, September 1965–December 1965*, ed. Giuseppe Alberigo and Joseph A. Komonchak (Maryknoll, NY: Orbis Books, 2006), 485–539.

[39] Velati, *Separati ma fratelli*, 96–112 and Radu Bordeianu, "Orthodox Observers at the Second Vatican Council and Intra-Orthodox Dynamics," *Theological Studies* 79 (2018): 86–106.

commission work. During the coffee breaks, however, they were often approached by a council father or a theological expert for a conversation. They received the same materials as the council fathers and were able to discuss these during weekly meetings organized by the Secretariat for Christian Unity. Often, one of their suggestions was taken up in an intervention made by one of the council fathers. Thus, a much-commented principle of ecumenical hermeneutics found in chapter two of the Decree on Ecumenism suggests to Catholics that they take the existence of a "'hierarchy' of truths" (UR 11) into account when engaging in dialogue with representatives of other churches. The Reformed theologian Oscar Cullmann had suggested this idea to the Swiss consultor of the Secretariat, Johannes Feiner, who inserted this concept in one of the most powerful speeches made by council fathers during the debate on ecumenism, the speech given by Archbishop Andrea Pangrazio on November 25, 1963.[40]

The black week, mentioned previously, constituted a very painful moment for the observers. This was especially the case when it became clear that Pope Paul VI had imposed some personal amendments to the final text of the Decree on Ecumenism, which could no longer be discussed in aula. This was seen by the observers as a clear sign of the persistence of Roman authoritarianism. Luckily, the observers remained convinced of the sincere intentions of the members of the Secretariat for Christian Unity:

> Bishop Willebrands' reply left us with wet eyes. He too was sorry that the change had been made ... This became suddenly a moment of rededication. We observers saw, as by a flash of light, where the knife cut deepest – in the red flesh of the Secretariat. These men, dedicated to church unity, had unexpectedly had their plans scotched by brethren of their own household.[41]

During the council the output of most observers consisted of private reports sent at a regular basis to their founding bodies. After the council the observers often contributed to the major confessional commentaries on the documents of the council.[42]

---

[40] Edward Idris Cassidy, *Ecumenism and Interreligious Dialogue: Unitatis Redintegratio – Nostra Aetate* (New York: Paulist Press, 2005), 10–11.

[41] Douglas Horton, *Vatican Diary 1964: A Protestant Observes the Third Session of Vatican Council II* (Philadelphia: United Church Press, 1965), 187.

[42] George A. Lindbeck, ed., *Dialogue on the Way: Protestants Report from Rome on the Vatican Council* (Minneapolis, 1965); Warren A. Quanbeck, ed., *Challenge ... and Response: A Protestant Perspective of the Vatican Council* (Minneapolis: Augsburg,

Male and Female Lay and Religious Auditors

The presence of Catholic laity at the council got a slow start. Before the council, Francesco Vito, who had become in 1959 the first president of the Catholic University of the Sacred Heart in Milano, was the only lay person who had been asked to become consultor for the Preparatory Commission on Studies and Seminaries. During the first session Jean Guitton, a French philosophy professor and Catholic intellectual, was the only lay person to have been invited as personal guest of the pope. During the next session he was invited to address the bishops during the debate on ecumenism, but Congar reports the criticism "that he spoke like a father of the council, not like a layperson."[43] During the first session, one of the observers also noticed the absence of women: "Up and down the nave you look and into the transepts: nothing but men. It is an abstracted body, incomplete, a torso of true catholicity, speaking more of an outmoded past than of the living present. Let us hope that the world will see something of Rome's strong women at Vatican II."[44]

When more laity were invited to attend the second session, another observer wrote in his diary that their presence "is more a symbol of the church's new concern for the laity than an actual working expression of it."[45] As part of his famous speech on the charisms on October 23, 1963, the Belgian Cardinal Suenens insisted that "women too should be invited as auditors: unless I am mistaken, they make up half of the human race."[46] This finally materialized, beginning in the third session. Twenty-three women auditors would eventually attend the council. Rosemary Goldie, an Australian lay person who was executive secretary of the Permanent Committee of International Conferences for the Lay Apostolate, and Sister Mary-Luke Tobin, the superior general of the Loretto Sisters, were *auditrices laici* who during the last intersession were nominated to take part in one of the sub-commissions of *Gaudium et Spes*.[47] The Mexican couple José and Luz-Marie Alvarez-Icaza, who

1966); Bernard Pawley, ed., *The Second Vatican Council: Studies by Eight Anglican Observers* (Oxford: Oxford University Press, 1967); Damaskinos Papandreou, ed., *Stimmen der Orthodoxie zu Grundfragen des II. Vatikanums* (Freiburg/Basel/Vienna: Herder, 1969).

43 Congar, *My Journal of the Council*, 465 (December 3, 1963).

44 Douglas Horton, *Vatican Diary 1962: A Protestant Observes the First Session of Vatican Council II* (Philadelphia: United Church Press, 1964), 63.

45 Robert McAfee Brown, *Observer in Rome: A Protestant Report on the Vatican Council* (Garden City, NY: Doubleday, 1964), 66.

46 Carmel E. McEnroy, *Guests in Their Own House: The Women of Vatican II* (New York: Crossroad, 1996), 41.

47 Congar, *My Journal of the Council*, 716 (February 4, 1965).

were the co-presidents of the Christian Family Movement, had the floor at a gathering of the mixed commission preparing the chapter on marriage and the family during the final session. Luz-Marie was successful in her request to revise a line speaking in a too negative way about human sexuality: "Since I am the only married woman here, I feel I have the responsibility of saying that when we have had intercourse, giving life to our children, it wasn't an act of concupiscence but an act of love, and I believe this is true of most Christian mothers who conceived a child."[48] As a recent study made clear, however, the input of women at Vatican II was larger than these official interventions.[49]

The Press, With Special Attention to the Belgian Journalist Jan Grootaers

The press represented a final group of council participants worthy of consideration. This was the first council conducted under the watchful eye of the modern media. There were approximately 1,000 journalists present at the opening. Pope John met with them in small groups prior to the opening and was impressive for his courtesy and general good humor. One of the interesting sub-plots at the council concerned the leaders' determination to preserve the secrecy of the sessions in the face of the media's creative attempts to get information. Since they were barred from the council meetings the press had to rely on news summaries prepared under the Secretary General's direction. Complaints were made that the bulletins sounded suspiciously as if they had been written in advance of the meetings. At the beginning of the second session the rules were changed to allow the bishops to speak of the content of the debates of the general sessions but not of the commissions.

The best-known journalist during the council wrote his contributions in *The New Yorker* under the pseudonym Xavier Rynne and later made his identity known as the Redemptorist *peritus* Francis X. Murphy.[50] Rynne's contributions are well known, so we will instead focus on the role of an important Belgian journalist. In Louvain a group of Catholic lay intellectuals had first organized a national congress of the lay apostolate in 1956 and then created in 1958 the independent

---

[48] McEnroy, *Guests in Their Own House*, 143.

[49] Gisela Muschiol and Regina Heyder, eds., *Katholikinnen und das Zweite Vatikanische Konzil: Petitionen, Berichte, Fotografien* (Münster: Aschendorff Verlag, 2018).

[50] Xavier Rynne, *Vatican Council II* (Maryknoll, NY: Orbis Books, 1999).

monthly *The Month*, which was interested in questions pertaining to religion and culture.[51] The main editor of the journal was the jurist Jan Grootaers, who was librarian at the Belgian parliament and after the council became one of the first lay professors at the Louvain faculty of theology. During the council he regularly reported about the council.

Grootaers had mixed feelings at the end of the second session, not about the improved schemata, but about the "institutional powerlessness of the council."[52] The majority at the council had not been able to push through the idea of a permanent episcopal body, a standing synod, to assist the pope in his ordinary magisterium and could not block the postponement of the discussion on religious freedom to the next session. His report at the end of the third session was a more positive one, because the council had already started to harvest great fruits, especially through the promulgation of *Lumen Gentium* and *Unitatis Redintegratio*. As to the events of the black week, he knew that the *Nota Explicativa Praevia* had been approved by the Theological Commission and understood the concern of the pope to keep the minority on board. His article ended with a subsection entitled "Conciliarity Begins at Home," in which he explained that many bishops showed one face in their conciliar interventions and another in their behavior at home.[53] He also complained that the laity at home were not well enough prepared to start practicing a stronger collaboration with the hierarchy. Finally, he recommended that the pope, the only one who was "at home" during the council, leave his home more regularly since Grootaers had observed during some of his trips that the pope was more relaxed abroad than at home. After the fourth session Grootaers published a final, exceptionally long article on the conclusion of the council since he felt the need to comment extensively on the tensions between pope and council during the final redaction of the chapter on marriage and the family in *Gaudium et Spes*.[54] After the council Grootaers would become an internationally recognized specialist on Vatican II, especially

---

[51] Lieve Gevers, "Kerkelijke ontwikkelingen in Vlaanderen in het licht van Vaticanum II: De stem van het lekenblad 'De Maand' (1958–1971) [Ecclesial developments in Flanders in the light of Vatican II: the voice of the lay journal 'The Month' (1958–1971)]," *Trajecta* 5 (1996): 275–96.

[52] Jan Grootaers, "Een sessie met gemengde gevoelens" (A session with mixed feelings) in *De Maand* 6 (1963): 590–606, here 590.

[53] Ibid., "Concilie en paus te Rome en thuis: een bewogen sessie" (Council and Pope in Rome and at home: a loaded session), in *De Maand* 8 (1965): 16–35, especially 30–35.

[54] Jan Grootaers, "Het concilie in crisis" (The Council in Crisis), in *De Maand* 9 (1966): 88–111.

through his edition of the archive materials of Msgr. Philips on the *Nota Explicativa Praevia*.[55]

CONCLUSION

Since the Council of Chalcedon, the proverb goes: *concilium episcoporum est* – the council belongs to the bishops. Even if this chapter dealt with the non-voting participants at the Second Vatican Council, observers needed a bishop to take up their ideas *in aula* and the success of the *periti* depended on their close collaboration with particular bishops. For Schillebeeckx, the Dutch bishops were "his" bishops and he was "their" theologian. The German bishops preferred to prepare drafts and reactions in common, with the help of the theologians. The best team of bishops and theologians operated from the Belgian College in Rome. Even if the postconciliar relationship of theologians and magisterium was often problematic, the council demonstrated the possibilities of a more collaborative relationship reflected in the ideal: "In maintaining, practicing and professing the faith that has been handed on there is a unique interplay between the bishops and the faithful" (DV 10).

FURTHER READING

Bordeianu, Radu. "Orthodox Observers at the Second Vatican Council and Intra-Orthodox Dynamics." *Theological Studies* 79 (2018): 86–106.

Congar, Yves. *My Journal of the Council.* Collegeville, MN: Liturgical Press, 2012.

De Mey, Peter. "Non-Catholic Observers at Vatican II." In *The Oxford Handbook on Vatican II*, edited by Catherine Clifford and Massimo Faggioli. Oxford: Oxford University Press, 2020.

Donnelly, Doris et al., eds. *The Belgian Contribution to the Second Vatican Council.* Leuven: Peeters, 2008.

Figoureux, Loïc. *Henri de Lubac et le concile Vatican II: 1960–1965.* Turnhout: Brepols, 2017.

Hensmann-Eßer, Anne, ed. *"Abenteuer in Rom." Texte aus dem Nachlass Werner Küppers am Alt-Katholischen Seminar der Universität Bonn.* Bonn: Alt-Katholischer Bistumsverlag, 2017.

Heyder, Regina and Gisela Muschiol, eds. *Katholikinnen und das Zweite Vatikanische Konzil.* Münster: Aschendorff Verlag, 2018.

Hopf, Margarethe. *Ein Osservatore Romano für die Evangelische Kirche in Deutschland: Der Konzilsbeobachter Edmund Schlink im Spannungsfeld der Interessen.* Göttingen: Vandenhoeck & Ruprecht, 2020.

---

[55] Jan Grootaers, *Primauté et collégialité. Le dossier de Gérard Philips sur la Nota Explicativa Praevia* (Leuven: University Press, 1986).

Rynne, Xavier. *Vatican Council II*. Maryknoll, NY: Orbis Books, 1999.

Scatena, Silvia. *Taizé: una parabola di unità. Storia della comunità dalle origini al concilio dei giovani*. Bologna: Il Mulino, 2018.

Velati, Mauro. *Separati ma fratelli: Gli osservatori non cattolici al Vaticano II: 1962–1965*. Bologna: Il Mulino, 2014.

6 Conciliar Hermeneutics

ORMOND RUSH

Interpreting the most significant ecclesial event in the last 150 years of the Catholic Church's history requires careful consideration. As with interpretation of the Bible, there can be specious attempts at the interpretation of the Second Vatican Council, neither grounded in what happened at the time nor faithful to the complexity of the texts it produced, let alone attentive to the diverse contexts out of which the council's final vision has to be interpreted. Some would see the council and its texts as a breach with the very identity of Catholic Christianity; others would see it as a failed attempt to fix it. Less extreme, others would claim that Vatican II wasn't really trying to change things in a fundamental way, but rather just tweak a few things; the council, they would emphasize, was thoroughly in 'continuity' with the church of the past 2,000 years. Yet again, while not rejecting the continuity argument, others would claim that the council at least wanted 'discontinuity' with certain aspects of Catholic self-understanding in the previous centuries, above all its ever-increasing emphasis on the pope as the veritable heart and centre of the church. According to the historian Massimo Faggioli, such diverse interpretive positions have been in 'battle' since the council ended.[1] Pope Benedict XVI entered into the debate over 'continuity' and 'discontinuity'.[2] He spoke, instead, of a hermeneutics of 'reform' as the best way to understand what Vatican II was on about. But this chapter proposes that a somewhat more nuanced approach is needed still.

ELEMENTS OF A COMPREHENSIVE INTERPRETATION

To arrive at that more nuanced approach, there is need to call on the assistance of a background theory called 'hermeneutics.' This discipline

---

[1] Massimo Faggioli, *Vatican II: The Battle for Meaning* (New York: Paulist Press, 2012).
[2] Benedict XVI, "Interpreting Vatican II," *Origins* 35, no. 32 (January 26, 2006): 534–39.

originated in philosophy, but was soon appropriated by other disciplines such as literary and legal studies, history and theology.[3] One of its main contributions to our subject here, the Second Vatican Council, is that understanding an event fifty or so years ago is not a simple thing. It first of all proposes that we cannot naively presume that we can enter into the minds of the bishops at the council; all we can do is reconstruct that, according to the best historical evidence. Nor are the texts the council produced totally lucid documents; there are lots of vague bits, and even contrasting elements. These aspects of uncertainty mean that we must be attentive to a theory of interpretation that is cognisant of how the interpreters of the council have a necessarily creative role in bringing the council to life fifty years on, in new circumstances.

Hermeneutics proposes that all human understanding is embedded in one's historical situation (context, culture, worldview, gender, etc). All understanding is historically conditioned in this way; we can't avoid 'history'; we are embedded in it; we always understand from a particular perspective. Hermeneutics, therefore, reminds us that whenever we comprehend (*understand*) a text, a person, or an event, we come to such understanding because we are able to make sense of it (*interpret* it) as meaningful for our particular circumstances (*apply* it). These three elements (understanding, interpretation, application), although distinct, are nevertheless intertwined. We only ever come to *understanding* because we already have a framework of *interpretation* out of which we comprehend the meaning of some text or event or person. But coming to understand the unfamiliar in terms of the familiar, if it is meaningful, is already an *application* to my present context. Understanding has taken place because I know what it means for me in my horizon of experience. Thus, understanding, interpretation and application are intertwined.

In other words, understanding always involves interpretation from a particular context and application to that context. For literary hermeneutics, this means that a work of literature, for example a novel, only comes to life when someone actually engages with it. Put simply, the novel is dead until it is read. The 'meaning' of a work is not to be restricted to the intention of the author, nor even to the work itself with its various elements; it is the reader who completes the meaning by engaging with it from a particular context. This 'reception'

---

[3] See Anthony C. Thiselton, *Hermeneutics: An Introduction* (Grand Rapids, MI: W.B. Eerdmans Pub. Co., 2009).

(understanding-interpretation-application) of a novel then becomes part of the meaning of the work, long after the author wrote it.

Hermeneutics highlights that, while the receiver's 'reception' is essential for bringing a text alive, that reception is still limited to an individual's perspective, and that fuller understanding of a historical event or a literary work's meaning is always an ongoing process. Hermeneutical theory speaks, therefore, of 'the hermeneutical circle' of understanding: my understanding of 'the whole' of a subject matter, for example, is always limited to my particular viewpoint; however, when I get more information on the details of a topic, that sense of the 'part' broadens my sense of the 'whole'. So, understanding is a back-and-forth questioning process, from not-knowing to better-knowing, from a sense of the whole to a sense of a part and then back again to the whole, in an ever-widening circle of understanding. All of these insights are relevant when understanding either events in history or textual documents, as well as their ongoing reception from diverse contexts throughout history.[4]

Accordingly, a thoroughly hermeneutical approach is needed if we are to comprehend a complex event such as Vatican II, 'quite possibly the biggest meeting in the history of the world'.[5] Over 2,000 bishops met for two months each year over four years (1962–65). There were, at times, fierce differences during debates; at other times, easy agreement. The multiple factors making up the dynamic of the council need to be investigated. Thus, the texts the bishops finally produced emerged out of a very historically conditioned event, and any attempt to understand them properly must take that complex history into account. Then, once the council ended, that historical event itself entered into 'history', along with its sixteen promulgated texts. Throughout the history of the reception of Vatican II, this complex event and its complex documents have been received from new horizons once the council was finished. Thus, modelled on the three elements of communication at play, for example, in a literary work (the writer, the written word, the reader), we could say that there are three elements that need to be

---

[4] See Ormond Rush, *The Reception of Doctrine: An Appropriation of Hans Robert Jauss' Reception Aesthetics and Literary Hermeneutics* (Rome: Gregorian University Press, 1997).

[5] John W. O'Malley, *What Happened at Vatican II* (Cambridge, MA: Belknap Press of Harvard University Press, 2008), 18.

attended to in a conciliar hermeneutics: the council meeting; the texts it produced; and the postconciliar reception.[6]

Before we go on to examine these three levels of enquiry, some preliminary points need to be made. First, a distinction can be made between 'the council' and 'the documents'. This distinction parallels the distinction between the 'spirit' and 'letter' of Vatican II, made by the Final Report of the 1985 Extraordinary Synod of Bishops marking the twentieth anniversary of Vatican II.[7] The 'spirit' of Vatican II refers to 'the mind of the council', what emerged from all the speeches, written submissions, drafting and voting, as the final 'intention' of the assembled bishops as a single but diversified conciliar body. The 'letter' refers to the final form of the sixteen documents through which they expressed their common mind. The 'spirit' of what the bishops wanted to convey in a particular document, revealed through historical studies of the drafting process, must inform the interpretation of the 'letter', i.e., the text itself. But then again, in a hermeneutical circle of understanding, the final documents should illumine reconstruction of what the bishops were intending to communicate.

Second, attention must be paid to the relationship between the 'pastoral' and the 'doctrinal' concerns of the council. The bishops wanted to address human beings in their concrete situations and to proclaim the gospel in a way that addressed those multiple and ever-changing situations in history. Therefore, what the church teaches (doctrine) should illumine and support human beings in their daily lives (pastoral); and, in turn, their experience of daily living provides an essential context for making sense out of church teaching. Embracing the direction given by Pope John XXIII in his opening address on October 11, 1962, the Second Vatican Council set out to be a 'pastoral' council. According to Christoph Theobald, this 'principle of pastorality' is *the* hermeneutical key for interpreting Vatican II.[8] The last document Vatican II promulgated is called 'The *Pastoral* Constitution on the Church in the World of Today'. A footnote to that title states a principle that well applies to all the documents; there is a close interrelationship between the pastoral and the doctrinal: 'The Constitution is called

---

[6] See Ormond Rush, *Still Interpreting Vatican II: Some Hermeneutical Principles* (New York: Paulist Press, 2004).

[7] Extraordinary Synod of Bishops, "Final Report," in *Documents of the Extraordinary Synod of Bishops November 28–December 8, 1985* (Homebush, Australia: St. Paul Publications, 1986), 17–51, at 22 (Section I, 5).

[8] Christoph Theobald, *La réception du concile Vatican II: I. Accéder à la source* (Paris: Cerf, 2009), 281–493.

"pastoral" because, while resting on doctrinal principles, it sets out the relation of the church to the world and to the people of today. In Part I, therefore, the pastoral emphasis is not overlooked, nor is the doctrinal emphasis overlooked in Part II.'[9] For Theobald, the pastorality principle which John XXIII and the council desired can be summarised in this way: 'there can be no proclamation of the gospel without taking account of its recipients'.[10]

Third, attention must be paid to the dialectic of faithful 'proclamation' and open 'dialogue' desired by the council. Vatican II wanted to proclaim the gospel fervently, but not in a monologic way. For the sake of a more effective proclamation, it also wanted to enter into dialogue: dialogue within the church (both within the Catholic Church and between it and the other Christian churches and ecclesial communities), and dialogue with other religions, with cultures, with 'history', with 'the world', even with nonbelievers and atheists. This word 'dialogue' was a leitmotif that captured a dramatic shift in the church's stance in the face of a great diversity of viewpoints and beliefs in the contemporary world.

Fourth, the principle of necessarily interrelating *ressourcement* and *aggiornamento* should be kept in mind. The Italian word *aggiornamento* ('updating') was a key concern of Pope John XXIII – the church must attend to the new circumstances and worldviews that change throughout the flow of history, in order that it might address the needs and hopes of human beings in new contexts. That God's Spirit is actively guiding the movements of human history demands that the church be attentive to 'the signs of the times' (GS, 4; cf, GS, 11). Somewhat paradoxically, this desire for *aggiornamento* at Vatican II was fed by the work of the council's *periti* (theological experts), many of whom were proponents of the *ressourcement* ('back to the sources') theology of the decades before the council. These scholars had taken on a 'historical consciousness' not only in their theologies of the nature of faith and its reception of revelation within history but also with regards to a historically critical interpretation of the biblical, patristic, ecumenical, philosophical, and theological riches of the 'living tradition'

[9] Austin Flannery, ed. *Vatican Council II: The Basic Sixteen Documents. Constitutions, Decrees, Declarations* (Collegeville, MN: Liturgical Press, 2014), 172.

[10] Christoph Theobald, "The Theological Options of Vatican II: Seeking an 'Internal' Principle of Interpretation," in *Vatican II: A Forgotten Future? Concilium* 2005/4, ed. Alberto Melloni and Christoph Theobald (London: SCM Press, 2005), 87–107, at 94.

(DV 12) of the Catholic Church, and indeed other Christian churches and ecclesial communities.[11] These two impulses of *ressourcement* and *aggiornamento* would have an impact on the rigorous debate that gave rise to many elements of the conciliar vision. Once again, the hermeneutical circle was at work: what is retrieved from the past must, however, be updated for the present, just as the present can provide new perspectives for interpreting the past.

Fifth, attention must be paid to the principle of necessarily interrelating the council's concern for both continuity and reform. The previous dialectical principle of *ressourcement* and *aggiornamento* is here treated in terms of the tensions that often arise when that principle is applied. This is the inevitable tension between constancy and change, sameness and innovation. The tension is evident throughout the drafting and final texts of Vatican II, both in terms of the preferred elements of the resourced tradition to be retrieved, and the precise way in which a particular aspect of belief or practice is to be 'updated' within new horizons of understanding.

Keeping in mind these hermeneutical insights, we can now move to examine more closely the three levels of enquiry that are needed for arriving at a comprehensive understanding of Vatican II.

THE SPIRIT: RECONSTRUCTING THE COUNCIL DEBATES AND DRAFTING

First, attention should be given to the debates and drafting process during the council's preparation, its four sessions, and the periods in between. In what could be called 'a hermeneutics of the authors', this enquiry helps the interpreter to reconstruct 'the spirit' behind the council's vision. The documents of the council have a history that needs to be investigated. How did the council come to a common mind on a particular document, such that a text could be produced that the majority of council members could vote on approvingly? Two factors in particular can be seen to be at work: an ideological tension within the conciliar body, as various groups jostle in a power play for influence; and a theological tension among the bishops regarding how to evaluate the 'old' and 'new' frameworks for presenting Christian beliefs and practice.

---

[11] Gerald O'Collins, "Ressourcement and Vatican II," in *Ressourcement: A Movement for Renewal in Twentieth-Century Catholic Theology*, ed. Gabriel Flynn and Paul D. Murray (Oxford: Oxford University Press, 2011), 372–91.

Before the council began, preparatory commissions had produced more than seventy documents for the council's consideration. The vast majority of these were judged by the bishops as inadequate for what the council was trying to achieve. Basically, only one survived their critique, the one on the liturgy. It was approved because it was thoroughly grounded in the deep research of the liturgical movement of the previous decades, and found easy resonance with the pastoral instincts of the bishops. Others found quick resistance, for example, the document on revelation, tradition and scripture, and the document on the church. The council asked that these be thoroughly revised.

Early in the proceedings, a clear division among the council members emerged; understanding this tension is important for interpreting the council and its documents. The first group was a small minority, perhaps a few hundred bishops; in a total of over 2,000, they made up basically 10 to 15 per cent. This minority, while not always getting their way, would constantly make their presence felt throughout the council. Many of these were cardinals, archbishops, and bishops who worked in the ten dicasteries (departments) of the Roman Curia. Other bishops from around the world willingly attached themselves to the position taken by this powerful group. That position generally followed the approach taken in the seventy preparatory documents, which were couched in the language and theological framework of neo-scholastic theology. It was precisely this theology that the second group, the vast majority of the council assembly, wanted to challenge. This group was open to the *ressource-ment* scholarship of the previous three decades. Many of the bishops would have been quite familiar with, and inspired by, the works of theologians like Henri de Lubac, Yves Congar and Karl Rahner. Some were now appointed to conciliar commissions, and would also give regular talks around Rome during the council sessions to help the bishops understand the issues at stake in their deliberations.

In the task of drafting and revising documents, the official *periti* had an important role assisting the bishops on the various commissions entrusted with incorporating the council's desires into each document. Their job was to sift through what each bishop or groups of bishops had said or submitted in writing on a particular matter and to come up with a fair rendition of what everyone wanted. When certain requests were not incorporated, this would be explained to the council assembly in a report (*relatio*) by one of the bishops on that commission. It was a laborious process, which required a delicate balancing of the bishops' different perspectives on the same topic. Therefore, sometimes a document might use within it different theological frameworks juxtaposed alongside one another to express the same doctrinal point. One thread might employ the language and particular theological framework of a previous church teaching, which had presupposed at the time of its original formulation a relevant background theory from a discipline such as philosophy, psychology or sociology. Another thread might presuppose a newer and different background theory, thereby presenting a shift in theological perspective, and perhaps a 'development' in the church's teaching regarding a particular truth of the faith.

Pope Paul VI was hinting at this hermeneutical problem and theological challenge when he addressed the assembled bishops on the day before Vatican II ended: '[The council] did not attempt to resolve all the urgent problems of modern life; some of these have been reserved for a further study which the Church intends to make of them, many of them were presented in very restricted and general terms, and for that reason are open to further investigation and various applications.'[12] According to Hermann Pottmeyer, the juxtaposition of different theological positions within the final texts calls for a new synthesis by theologians after the council: 'the needed synthesis is a task the Council sets for the Church and for theologians; it is a task of reception, which is far from being a merely passive process'.[13] Likewise, Walter Kasper, commenting on the final documents emerging from the long drafting process, states: 'admittedly, the harmonization between earlier and later tradition is often not completely successful; for – like most previous councils – Vatican II solved its task, not with the help of a comprehensive theory, but by pegging out the limits of the church's position. In this sense it was completely in the conciliar tradition for a juxtaposition to remain. As in the case of every council, the theoretical mediation between these positions is *a task for the theology that comes afterwards.*'[14] As Pottmeyer has stated: 'Vatican II has left us only with a building site.'[15]

---

[12] "Address of Pope Paul VI during the Last General Meeting of the Second Vatican Council, 7 December 1965." www.vatican.va/holy_father/paul_vi/speeches/1965/documents/hf_p-vi_spe_19651207_epilogo-concilio_en.html [accessed 14 February 2019].

[13] Hermann J. Pottmeyer, "A New Phase in the Reception of Vatican II: Twenty Years of Interpretation of the Council," in *The Reception of Vatican II*, ed. Giuseppe Alberigo, Jean Pierre Jossua, and Joseph A. Komonchak (Washington, DC: Catholic University of America Press, 1987), 27–43, at 38.

[14] Walter Kasper, "The Continuing Challenge of the Second Vatican Council: The Hermeneutics of the Conciliar Statements," in *Theology and Church* (New York: Crossroad, 1989), 166–76, at 171. Emphasis added.

[15] Hermann J. Pottmeyer, *Towards a Papacy in Communion: Perspectives from Vatican Councils I & II* (New York: Crossroad, 1998), 128.

Although 'a very serious attempt at integration was made at Vatican II', the council did not intend to produce systematic treatises.[16] But it did articulate trajectories from which we can reconstruct its common mind. In this sense, 'the council' is more than its final documents, and what the council communicates goes beyond the written word of those documents. The documents cannot capture the whole of what the council was and is. In this sense, the spirit is more than the letter. For example, Joseph Ratzinger wrote after the third session regarding the change that was taking place in the bishops: 'This spiritual awakening, which the bishops accomplished in full view of the Church, or, rather accomplished *as* the Church, was the great and irrevocable event of the Council. It was more important in many respects than the texts it passed, for these texts could only voice a part of the new life which had been awakened in this encounter of the Church with its inner self.'[17]

THE LETTER: READING THE FINAL TEXTS AS A CORPUS

Second, attention should be given to the final texts that these debates produced. In what could be called 'a hermeneutics of the texts', this enquiry focuses on 'the letter' of the council's teaching. If the previous level of enquiry was all about reconstructing how the texts came into being during the council, this second level forgets (for the moment) those historical questions, and looks at just the texts themselves, in their final form. While the event of the council's meeting is now a thing of the past (but still with its effects in history), the texts it produced are something 'solid' we have that endures, something fixed that lives on long after those who authored them.

There are sixteen of these texts, written in Latin, each on a particular topic, and each with a different 'grading' as a 'constitution', 'decree', or 'declaration'. No single document can be considered in isolation from the others. Certainly, each is to be taken in its own right, with its own argument and structure. But the documents are best considered ultimately as a unity. They constitute a "corpus" of texts, a body of writings that are interrelated and make up a whole, somewhat like chapters in a book. They have each received approbation from the same group of

---

[16] Yves Congar, "A Last Look at the Council," in *Vatican II: By Those Who Were There*, ed. Alberic Stacpoole (London: Geoffrey Chapman, 1986), 337–58, at 343.

[17] Joseph Ratzinger, *Theological Highlights of Vatican II* (New York: Paulist Press, 2009), 194. Original emphasis.

people, and each was intended to further the overall agenda of the council – the pastoral purification, renewal, and reform of the Catholic Church.

However, one problem is that these texts weren't intended by the bishops to be systematic treatises on the topics discussed, nor did they attempt to say everything on those topics. Also, sometimes they contain confusing inconsistencies; sometimes one document may approach a topic from one angle and another from a different angle, or use one Latin word meaning different things in different contexts. Although there is coherence to each document, the interpreter is often left with the task of putting all the pieces together into a comprehensive vision, not only of what each document is saying but also of what all the documents together as a whole are saying.

Two hermeneutical insights from literary hermeneutics are helpful here: the notion of '*intra*-textuality' and the notion of '*inter*-textuality'. *Intra-textuality* refers to the relationship of linguistic units (words, sentences, paragraphs, chapters) within a single conciliar document. The interpreter needs to see those individual units in a particular document in the light of other units within the same document. Sometimes this enquiry reveals tensions in the text. Therefore, the parts should be mutually interpretive. Another important element to note here is the *genre* of the text. With the documents of Vatican II it is immediately obvious how different these conciliar texts are from those of the twenty previous councils of the church. Here we have a different 'style' of teaching, more in the mode of persuasion than legal proclamation.[18] Furthermore, the structure of a document and the order of its chapters can be significant. For example, in *Lumen Gentium* we find a chapter on the whole people of God before a chapter on the hierarchy; in the first part of *Gaudium et Spes*, we find four chapters on the various aspects of the human condition in the world today all ending with a final article affirming Jesus Christ as the exemplar of the perfect human being in community.

Inter-textuality refers to the relationship of such linguistic units and single documents to all the other documents of Vatican II and their linguistic units. This highlights the importance of appreciating the council documents not only as discrete texts on particular topics but also as a body or 'corpus' of interrelated texts. The individual 'texts' have a broader 'con-text' – they are to be interpreted in terms of the

---

[18] See O'Malley, *What Happened at Vatican II*, 43–52; 305–8.

vision that the whole collection projects. However, that is not to lessen the integrity of each document and their own importance in a hermeneutical circle of understanding; the comprehensive vision of the council as a whole can only be reconstructed by means of evaluating the elements of the individual documents.

Within the conciliar corpus of sixteen documents, the four constitutions have a special place, in a way analogous to that of the four Gospels in the New Testament. As the 1985 Report of the Synod of Bishops put it: 'Special attention must be paid to the four major Constitutions of the Council, which are the keys to the interpretation of the other Decrees and Declarations.'[19] But, among those four, there is one that, arguably, should be the key to interpreting the others. Since *Dei Verbum* deals with the fundamental datum of the Christian faith – God's personal self-revelation to human beings in Christ through the Spirit, and its witness in scripture and tradition – it must have a hermeneutical priority over the constitutions that deal with the Christian realities emerging from that primary revelation – the church and its worship. However, even here, care must be taken. According to the principle of inter-textuality, the fact that *Dei Verbum* says nothing about divine revelation coming through other religions doesn't mean that is all the council has to say on the topic. The teaching of *Dei Verbum* must be complemented by that of *Nostra Aetate*, which affirms revelation and salvation in some way coming through other religions. Another example of the importance of inter-textuality is the relationship between the two constitutions on the church. *Lumen Gentium* and *Gaudium et Spes* are to be read as mutually interpretive. For instance, although *Lumen Gentium* does have a concern for the *ad extra* aspect of church life, those references are limited, and need to be balanced by those of the Pastoral Constitution.

These sometimes puzzling issues revealed in an enquiry into the 'letter' of the council's teachings show that a singular focus on this level of enquiry is not enough; we need to go back and look at the detailed history of debate behind those issues. There is, therefore, a necessary overlap between the two levels of enquiry. While helpfully distinguished, a focus on the 'letter' and a focus on the 'spirit' eventually need to be co-ordinated. The conciliar documents are complex texts. In places they contain passages deliberately expressed either in an open-ended way or with juxtapositions of traditional and innovative

---

[19] Extraordinary Synod of Bishops, "Final Report," 22 (section I, 5).

formulations. Interpretation of such passages requires interrelating a hermeneutics of the text with a hermeneutics of the authors.

Within the debates, bishops with different perspectives argued for their view to be included in the final documents. The drafting commissions, faithful to their responsibility, genuinely attempted to incorporate the various perspectives, as their reports (*relationes*) to the assembly reveal. The result is often a juxtaposition of different theological approaches within the same treatment of a particular subject. Some safeguard past formulations, generally couched in neo-scholastic terms; others, appropriating more recent theologies, attempt to retrieve the tradition while embracing *ressourcement* approaches. Sometimes the juxtaposition is in terms of different streams of the Catholic tradition, for example, Augustinian or Thomist.

Whatever the differentiating aspect, the juxtaposition in the final texts is not so much one of contradictory views, but rather of differing perspectives on the same mystery. However, a 'trajectory' towards a newer understanding of an issue is often evident, and this trajectory must be given weight in the interpretation of the text. As Pottmeyer proposes: 'by being complemented the older thesis is relativized as one-sided and *bearings are given for further development* in understanding of the faith'.[20] Generally, it was the majority view that indicated a 'trajectory' towards a new perspective. In these ways, either leaving open an issue or expressing it in terms of a juxtaposition of approaches, the council was able to come to a compromise and reach a 'consensus', in a form of text which the vast majority of bishops, despite their theological differences, could vote on affirmatively. Alberigo speaks of 'the recurring compromises in the development of the texts. Indeed, compromise was required for obtaining a broad consensus bordering on unanimity'.[21] Therefore, interpretation of the council and its documents should attend to both sides of the juxtaposition, while at the same time attending to the trajectory towards a new approach indicated by the view of the majority, as Pottmeyer advises:

> Fidelity to the Council requires that both juxtaposed theses be taken seriously and that an attempt be made through more penetrating theological reflection and a renewed ecclesial praxis to

[20] Pottmeyer, "A New Phase in the Reception of Vatican II," 38. Emphasis added.
[21] Giuseppe Alberigo, "Transition to a New Age," in *History of Vatican II, Vol. 5: The Council and the Transition. The Fourth Period and the End of the Council, September 1965–December 1965*, ed. Giuseppe Alberigo and Joseph A. Komonchak (Maryknoll, NY: Orbis Books, 2006), 573–644, at 628.

reconcile them in a synthesis that will allow further advances. Fidelity to the Council also requires that we pay heed to the stress that the Council itself laid on the one or the other thesis, according as a thesis was supported by the majority or the minority. The fact remains, however, that majority and minority alike agreed to both theses and in particular to their juxtaposition.[22]

The bishops were aware that after the council, theologians would need to bring such open-ended formulations and juxtapositions into a unity; it was beyond what they could achieve, and indeed it wasn't the business of councils to present systematic treatises. As Joseph Doré put it: 'The Council did not claim to be expressing the final word on the subjects it treated, only to be pointing out *the direction* in which further reflection should develop.'[23]

It is therefore the role of theologians to extrapolate these 'trajectories' indicated in the council debates and final texts, and bring them to synthesis. Out of these two levels of enquiry into the 'spirit' and 'letter', they can propose a comprehensive interpretation of all the principles making up 'the vision of Vatican II'.[24] However, a vision needs to be received and realized.

RECEIVING THE VISION FROM SHIFTING HORIZONS

Therefore, and third, what could be called 'a hermeneutics of the receivers' brings to the fore the necessity of 'reception.' Once again, hermeneutics can help us a little here.

Just as a text is dead until it is read, so too Vatican II needs its receivers to transform its vision into reality. According to literary hermeneutics, a text such as a novel imagines 'a world' (the world of the text), a way of living and interrelating (for good or bad).[25] The text projects that world, and proposes it to an implied reader and ultimately to a reader in the 'real' world, inviting the reader to imagine (or reject)

---

[22] Pottmeyer, "A New Phase in the Reception of Vatican II," 39.

[23] Joseph Doré, "Vatican II Today," in *Vatican II: A Forgotten Future?* ed. Alberto Melloni and Christoph Theobald (London: SCM Press, 2005), 137–47, at 142. Emphasis added.

[24] For one such proposal, see Ormond Rush, *The Vision of Vatican II: Its Fundamental Principles* (Collegeville, MN: Liturgical Press, 2019).

[25] On a hermeneutical discussion of 'the world behind the text', 'the world of the text', and 'the world in front of the text', see Paul Ricoeur, "Time and Narrative: Threefold Mimesis," in *Time and Narrative* (Chicago: University of Chicago Press, 1984), 1:52–87, esp. 70–87.

that proposed world in his or her own context (the world in front of the text). In the reader's application of the text to the real world, vision can become a reality, no matter how distant in time the receiver is from the production of the text. Moreover, even though the text may not address all the specific issues that are urgent in the reader's world, the world that the text imagines may indeed provide a blueprint for addressing those issues.

Similarly, together as a corpus, the sixteen documents of Vatican II project a world in front of it. That world foresees a renewed way of being Catholic. In a reconfiguring of the Catholic imagination, the vision of Vatican II imagines relationships within the church in a new way, just as it imagines the church relating in a new way to those who are outside it. A significant element of that renewed vision is the way the Catholic Church is now seen, not solely in terms of a universal church with a centre (Rome) but rather in terms of, as Karl Rahner perceived, 'a world church', a communion of local churches, but of course with a unifying role given to one of those churches, the church of Rome and its bishop.[26]

Once the simple insight of Karl Rahner regarding the council's desire for a world church is acknowledged, the future reception of the conciliar vision is wide open, because the contexts within which Vatican II's vision are received throughout the world church are now theoretically endless. After Vatican II local churches and their theologies have taken up the challenge and elucidated the ever-expanding kaleidoscope of perspectives from which 'the vision of Vatican II' has been interpreted and applied over the last half-century: class, gender, race, culture, economic-political-social conditions, geography, local history, global history, and so on. And that is to say nothing, within those manifold contexts, of the many personal factors that have conditioned each individual believer's reception of divine revelation through faith, in their 'sense of the faith' (sensus fidei), all of which contribute to the whole church's 'infallibility in believing' (see LG 12). The way Vatican II put great store in the local churches (by seeing the universal Catholic Church as a communion of churches), along with the importance it placed on the sensus fidelium, means that the multiplicity of receptions of Vatican II from all these perspectives is an intended consequence of its vision.

---

[26] Karl Rahner, "Basic Theological Interpretation of the Second Vatican Council," in *Theological Investigations*, Volume 20 (London: Darton, Longman & Todd, 1981), 77–89.

In the articulation of this vision, Vatican II didn't set out to predict all the problems that the world (and the church in that world) might encounter once the council had ended; its limited context was the 1960s. However, its open-ended vision did project into an unknown future by presenting a vision of a church that was to be ever attentive to the shifting conditions of human history. Why be attentive to history? Because the living God continues to converse with the church through that history (DV 8); God may well be saying new things (albeit in Christ through the Spirit) as history unfolds. Vatican II was the first council to ever think in this historically conscious way, not only in the way it viewed the church's past, but also in the way it viewed the world's present ambiguous situation, as well as its unknown future until the eschaton. In other words, what Vatican II interpreted as the pressing issues for the church in the 1960s may not necessarily be the pressing issues of the year 2020 and beyond. New questions will always arise in history, questions which the council itself may have left open, or not even addressed, or could not have even envisaged. But those questions may well find answers through a reception of the council's comprehensive vision. Therefore, while Vatican II may not have addressed every problem the world will ever face, it did leave a blueprint for addressing it. Lieven Boeve speaks of 'the method manifested in *Gaudium et Spes*'.[27] Here, the vision projects 'a world' in which the church is ever attentive to 'the signs of the times' (GS 4) and ever confident that the gospel, as proclaimed by Vatican II, can be a firm criterion for finding a humane and divinely endorsed solution for all unforeseen issues. Also, it is important to remember that the reception of Vatican II takes place alongside the church's ongoing reception of scripture and tradition (of which Vatican II is now an element).

Throughout this process of creative reception, what the receiver finds relevant in the conciliar vision can be unpredictable, depending on their context. One insight from literary hermeneutics has proven to be true of the reception of the council. Reception involves selection. A receiver might bring certain elements in the vision to the foreground as more important than others for a particular context. For example, while conflict between the world's religions has marked the history of Christianity's presence in the world, tensions between the world's

---

[27] Lieven Boeve, "Beyond the Modern and Anti-modern Dilemma: Theological Method in a Postmodern European Context," in *Scrutinizing the Signs of the Times in the Light of the Gospel*, ed. Johan Verstraeten, *Bibliotheca Ephemeridum Theologicarum Lovaniensium*, 208 (Leuven: Peeters Press, 2007), 151–66, at 158.

religions has been particularly fraught in the decades since Vatican II. *Nostra Aetate*, the Declaration on the Relation of the Church to Non-Christian Religions, is a brief document, a mere five articles, classified as a 'declaration', the lowest in the council's estimation of importance among its documents. However, it has assumed great significance for Catholics in understanding the mission of the church in a world where religious divisions threaten global peace.

A crucial question with regards to the reception of Vatican II is: who are the agents of reception? The council's own vision gives us guidance. Just as Vatican II emphasized that all the faithful constitute the people of God and are called to full participation in the mission of the church, so too all the faithful must be creative participants in bringing the conciliar vision to realization. According to the council's own 'principle of pastorality' (as formulated by Theobald, 'there can be no proclamation of the gospel without taking account of its recipients'[28]), it is the intended recipients of the conciliar vision who are now part of the council's history, because it is they who will live it (or resist it). Those potential recipients make up the whole people of God, who the council emphasizes are the primary recipient of divine revelation. Therefore, there is a wide circle of voices and authorities within the contemporary church who are to participate in that comprehensive reception and assessment by the whole people of God (the *sensus fidelium*, theologians, and the episcopal magisterium), as taught by *Dei Verbum* 8.[29]

These three ecclesial authorities correspond to the three levels of reception outlined by Alois Grillmeier in his classic work on the reception of councils in the early church. He highlights three levels: kerygmatic reception, spiritual reception, and theological reception.[30] Of course, within each of these levels, there can also be 'non-reception', a deliberate resistance to the conciliar vision, for various reasons.

The first of Grillmeier's levels of reception is the papal and episcopal magisterium's promotion of a council, giving their particular

---

[28] Theobald, "The Theological Options of Vatican II," 94.

[29] See Ormond Rush, *The Eyes of Faith: The Sense of the Faithful and the Church's Reception of Revelation* (Washington, DC: The Catholic University of America Press, 2009), 241–91.

[30] See Alois Grillmeier, "The Reception of Chalcedon in the Roman Catholic Church," *Ecumenical Review* 22 (1970): 383–411; Alois Grillmeier, *Christ in Christian Tradition. Volume Two: From the Council of Chalcedon (451) to Gregory the Great (590–604). Part One: Reception and Contradiction: The Development of the Discussion about Chalcedon from 451 to the Beginning of the Reign of Justinian* (Atlanta: John Knox Press, 1987), 7–10.

interpretation of the council's vision, and making it a reality in the life of the church. In terms of Vatican II, this refers to the official promotion given by a pope and the Vatican Curia, as well as the bishops of the world at the local level. At the international level, it takes effect by means of, for example, regarding the doctrine of collegiality, the way local bishops are treated by the Roman Curia and the way institutions such as the international synod of bishops are organized and structured, or the way local bishops are treated during their *ad limina* visits. At the local level, official reception takes effect by means of a range of ecclesial factors, from the personal agenda of the local bishops to the institutional structures he either passively tolerates or actively promotes. Here too further research is needed on a global history of how local bishops, over the last half-century, have personally embraced the conciliar vision and implemented it (or otherwise). Nevertheless, as Gilles Routhier emphasizes, this official dimension of reception is still 'just a little part of the story'.[31]

The second dimension, theological reception, refers to the work of academic theologians attempting to bring to synthesis the vision of the conciliar decisions and documents, whether as a whole or with regards to particular teachings.[32] This reception has taken place from multiple perspectives which are influenced by variations in geography; culture; gender; power relationships; and social, ecological, economic and political conditions. Since the council, theologians have a keener awareness of the call to help their local communities listen to, discern, and determine the *sensus fidelium*, and to offer local theologies as articulations of the lived faith of their communities.

The third dimension is spiritual reception, the appropriation by all the faithful of the council's vision into their lives and spiritualities. Given Vatican II's primarily pastoral orientation, this is the deepest level of reception desired. Leonardo Boff is referring to this dimension when he speaks of the 'spiritual meaning' of Vatican II's vision and the need for creativity in its reception in local churches, in his case in Latin America:

---

[31] Gilles Routhier, "Reception of Vatican II and Elements for Further Studies," in *The Living Legacy of Vatican II: Studies from an Indian Perspective*, ed. Paul Pulikkan (Bengaluru, India: ATC Publishers, 2017), 90–109, at 95.

[32] See the fine survey and typology of post-conciliar theologies in John A. Dick, Karim Schelkens, and Jürgen Mettepenningen, *Aggiornamento! Catholicism from Gregory XVI to Benedict XVI* (Leiden: Brill, 2013), 198–209.

The ultimate justification for creative reception in ecclesiology lies in a sane epistemology of the act of faith ... According to an intelligent epistemology, the meaning of a text (setting forth, for example, a rule or some other determination) emerges not only from the minds of the authors of the text (from the *mens patrum*, in the case of a conciliar text) – but also from the addressees, who are coauthors of the text, inasmuch as it is they who insert the message of the text into the vital contexts in which they find themselves. The addressees, too, place accents, and perceive the relevancy and pertinence of aspects of the text in question that illuminate or denounce historical situations. The original meaning of the text – the meaning contained in the 'letter' – stirs new echoes when that text is heard in determinate circumstances. The spiritual meaning becomes revealed. To read, then, is always, to *re*read. Whenever we understand, we interpret; this is how our spirit is structured. The original message does not remain a cistern of stagnant water. It becomes a font of living water, ready to generate new meanings, by prolonging and concretizing the original meaning. The latter functions as a generator of new life through the new significations it awakens.[33]

When Vatican II ended on the 8th of December 1965, it entered into 'history', the condition of human existence marked by time and place, culture and circumstance, certainty and uncertainty. And within those historical conditions, the council would itself have 'a history'. A council can have no 'effect' without 'reception'; for it to be effective, its vision must be received. Both as a historic event in the life of the church and as an authoritative collection of texts, 'Vatican II' has now undergone a history of reception for more than half a century. To varying degrees and in diverse ways, the council has been received, or not received, across the globe, in multiple geographical and cultural areas of the church. As Karl Rahner observes: 'It will certainly be a long time before the Church which has been given the Second Vatican Council will be the Church of the Second Vatican Council.'[34]

---

[33] Leonardo Boff, "Theology of Liberation: Creative Acceptance of Vatican II from the Viewpoint of the Poor," in *When Theology Listens to the Poor* (San Francisco: Harper & Row, 1988), 1–31.

[34] Karl Rahner, "The Council: A New Beginning," in *The Church after the Council* (New York: Herder and Herder, 1966), 9–33, at 28.

FURTHER READING

Faggioli, Massimo. *Vatican II: The Battle for Meaning*. New York: Paulist Press, 2012.

Lamberigts, Mathijs, Gilles Routhier, Pedro Rubens Ferreira Oliveira, Christoph Theobald, and Dries Bosschaert, eds. *50 Years after the Vatican II Council: Theologians from All over the World Deliberate*. Paris: Federatio Internationalis Universitatem Catholicarum, 2015.

Komonchak, Joseph A. "Benedict XVI and the Interpretation of Vatican II." In *The Crisis of Authority in Catholic Modernity*, edited by Michael James Lacey and Francis Oakley, 93–110. New York: Oxford University Press, 2011.

O'Malley, John W. "The Style of Vatican II: The 'How' of the Church Changed during the Council." *America* (February 24, 2003): 12–15.

Routhier, Gilles. "Reception of Vatican II and Elements for Further Studies." In *The Living Legacy of Vatican II: Studies from an Indian Perspective*, edited by Paul Pulikkan, 90–109. Bengaluru, India: ATC Publishers, 2017.

Ruggieri, Giuseppe. "Towards a Hermeneutic of Vatican II." *Concilium* 1 (1999): 1–13.

Rush, Ormond. *Still Interpreting Vatican II: Some Hermeneutical Principles*. New York: Paulist Press, 2004.

Part II

Conciliar Themes and Reception

7 The Pilgrim Church: An Ongoing Journey of Ecclesial Renewal and Reform

GERARD MANNION

VATICAN II ON THE CHURCH: HISTORICAL AND INTELLECTUAL BACKDROP

Adventures of Ideas: A Rapidly Changing Climate for Ecclesiology throughout the Long Nineteenth Century and Beyond

That the Second Vatican Council revolutionized the self-understanding (ecclesiology) of the Roman Catholic Church is now taken as a given. However, that revolution did not come about out of the blue, thanks to sudden moments of collective inspiration on the part of the council fathers. Nor is it a story that began and remains within the confines of Catholicism alone. Indeed, the journey to the understanding of the church that became the centerpiece of Vatican II's *aggiornamento* – a bringing up to date or renewal of the church in all its aspects – is one that begins much further back. The nineteenth and twentieth centuries saw enormous development and changes in the self-understanding of the Christian Church – i.e. in ecclesiology. Many of these were positive and had ecumenically positive implications as well. Some were more aimed toward further consolidation of institutional organization and power, with a concentration on central authorities.

The approach to history in the nineteenth century, which was not simply confined to historical studies, led to the emergence of ideas, theories, and systems exploring the sense of development and progress in the world (or otherwise). So, philosophical and political thought, along with the emerging social sciences, also conspicuously began to examine the direction in which history had developed and was developing, or at least could or should develop. Aspirations were built into such ideas as well as, in places, social critique. So philosophies of history that focused on the progressive march of history, such as Georg Friedrich Hegel's dialectical idealism, or political, economic, and social ideas from those who developed his work in very different ways, such as Karl

Marx's dialectical materialism, helped people to explore, explain, and understand the world and its history in very different ways – looking both forward and backward. In the case of scholars such as Marx, famously, they also encouraged and inspired people to seek to *change* that world – to help shape history, the march of time, and societal structures in ways never before envisioned.

Such developments would also have a profound effect on multiple aspects of the church and theology alike in many differing ways and eventually, therefore, the ideas and ecclesiological vision of Vatican II. Chief among those effects was the impact on the modern study of eschatology, which would prove vital to the ecclesiology of Vatican II. Previously, especially in Catholic theology and teaching, eschatology (from the Greek, *eschaton*, the "end") was understood as doctrine pertaining to "the last things" (such as death, the return of Christ, the apocalypse [revelations] concerning the end of time, and eternal life). In other words, eschatology was literally the study of the things of the "end." But in the modern period eschatology gradually (and increasingly) came to be understood less in temporal or ultimate terms and more in relation to the unfolding of history, the direction of human life – both collective and individual – and the role of God in drawing creation back toward union with Godself. And so, just as the understanding and study of history were transformed in the modern period, so also did eschatology gradually become bound up with the unfolding of *salvation* history – God's intentions for humanity and the world, and the role Christians, the church, and all of humanity have to play in this. As a result, eschatology was no longer discourse simply about the "last things," but rather was concerned with a reality unfolding each and every day as our lives – and history itself – move toward their consummation, but which is, as with creation itself, taking place in each and every moment. The modern period would see many Christian doctrines reframed, reformulated, and re-stated in diverse ways for new times and for new cultural contexts alike. Some churches, at the official level, at least, would see such developments as controversial. Catholicism, in this respect, would resist such reformulations for some time.

A second key development was the emergence of *programmatic* social visions aimed toward critiquing the failings of society and promoting radical change and social justice. It is not that the church had never given attention to such areas before, of course. But the intellectual, industrial, economic, and social developments of the eighteenth, nineteenth, and, increasingly, twentieth centuries impacted church thinking and practice in major ways. The reverse can also be said to be true. Marx's system, as with Hegel's, could rightly be described as secular forms of eschatology and, indeed, particularly in the case of Marx's work, utopian visions analogous to the culmination of traditional Christian doctrines of eschatology.

Forms of both such developments fed into the emergence of modern Catholic Social Thought and practice (even if often in a reactionary or competitive sense), as the church in the later nineteenth century increasingly addressed social injustices. The intertwining of eschatology and a firm commitment to social change and justice would be twin pillars of the ecclesiology of Vatican II.

Ecclesiology Betwixt and Between: The Preconciliar Climate

Catholicism, in this modern era, had become a decidedly centralized institution. This had been a long time coming and was set in train thanks to the outcomes of the implementation of (although, as John O'Malley shows so well, not the explicit direct intentions of) the Council of Trent.[1] Anything that seemed to stray from the path of official ideas, manuals, and teachings was frowned on at best, and ruthlessly condemned and suppressed at worst. At the official level, Catholicism had shunned modernity (while nonetheless availing itself of multiple aspects of it). Political developments in Italy and elsewhere, of course, played a major part. But this turn inward by the church, this isolationist stance, left a deep impact on ecclesiology. The Catholic Church's official self-understanding was triumphalist, self-congratulatory, and exclusivist.

This did not mean that no Catholic scholars were continuing to engage with the emerging and ongoing developments. But it did mean that they had to do so with extreme caution and that the fruits of much of their research more often than not remained unpublished. However, Catholic scholarship was never cut off completely from encounter with and influence by what was happening elsewhere. And, in some places, more pragmatic attitudes were being taken toward engagements with the works and ideas not just of fellow Christians but also, crucially, with the ideas and works of modern Catholic philosophers (who often enjoyed more leeway than their theological counterparts).

Gradually, a greater tolerance of modern biblical scholarship emerged, so that by the 1940s Pius XII endorsed certain aspects of it, alongside new translations of the Bible, in his 1943 encyclical *Divino*

---

[1] John W. O'Malley, *Trent: What Happened at the Council* (Cambridge, MA: The Belknap Press of Harvard University Press, 2013).

Afflante Spiritu. He went on to encourage Catholics to read scripture enthusiastically in their homes. At the same time, the increased availability of key works of the patristic era attracted renewed attention by a new generation of scholars weary of the strictures of the "received wisdom" of neo-scholasticism; Catholic scholarship and therefore ecclesiology were gradually transformed. The tragic political events of the twentieth century also helped to demonstrate that division and rigid boundaries between peoples, including their ideas and faiths, were not serving the human family well. Few knew this more than the vastly experienced diplomat Angelo Roncalli – the future Pope John XXIII.

Each of these developments slowly but surely sowed the seeds whereby Catholic scholars of ecclesiology gradually began to inch away from seeing the church in terms of how it had come to be perceived, and indeed actually administered, in the modern era – a "perfect [monolithic] society" (in terms borrowed from early modern political discourse) or a vast centralized institution and the sole and unique institutional means of salvation. Instead, thanks to these multiple intellectual and social developments, many began to perceive the church in differing ways.

By the 1940s and 1950s, Catholic scholars of ecclesiology and related fields were caught "between two worlds" in many ways. On the one hand, there were developments such as the emergence of the *nouvelle théologie* – a loosely associated group of scholars and methods that embraced many of the approaches listed earlier. Most particularly they utilized the method and notion of *ressourcement* – a return to the sources. Several important Catholic thinkers, including those associated with this movement but also others in Germany, Belgium, and elsewhere less associated with it, were also engaging ecumenically with other Christians in a variety of ways. Two world wars had shown this was necessary, too.

And, ecclesiologically speaking, even at the official level, there were signs of change. In 1943, Pius XII issued *Mystici Corporis Christi*, which, in several important ways, moved away from that predominant emphasis upon a "political society" understanding of the church, even returning to biblical and New Testament images as well as ecclesiological motifs from the early church. It also employed much vivid imagery and symbolism – biblical, sacramental, and otherwise – to explain what the church actually is and to explicate this understanding of the church as the "Mystical Body of Christ."

But, on the other hand, the very same encyclical continued to affirm that the church is a "perfect society" and equates the mystical body of

Christ with the institutional Roman Catholic Church itself (along with those churches in communion with it). It reiterated the sense of a hierarchical, exclusivist, and institutional ecclesiology. So, while the more novel (for its time) ecclesiological images were welcomed, such sat uncomfortably, even in a contradictory sense, with the more familiar normative modern notions of the church.

Furthermore, suspicions of new and especially Protestant ideas continued and many scholars at the forefront of moving Catholic theology forward were under heavy suspicion, with not a few being censured, removed from posts, exiled, and forbidden to publish their writings. Theologians who were deemed suspect faced continued investigation and censure. Many such theologians were leading lights in terms of contributions to ecclesiology and other branches of theology. And yet, several of these same figures would later take center stage at Vatican II, once rehabilitated, and would be highly influential on the conciliar proceedings and final documents.

WHAT CHANGED? HOW AND WHY VATICAN II TRANSFORMED THE SELF-UNDERSTANDING OF THE CHURCH

This lengthy historical prolegomenon, which briefly treads on material covered in Part One,[2] is necessary in order to appreciate the full nature and significance of some of the key changes in the self-understanding of the church that took place at Vatican II. Let us turn to consider some of the key developments and documents that helped bring about this ecclesiological transformation.

A New Pentecost

First, and perhaps foremost, the figure of John XXIII is key to so many of the major achievements of the council, being both the pope who envisioned such a monumental undertaking – the largest gathering of religious leaders of its kind in history – and its initial architect in terms of what its intentions and aims were. He was, above all, a pastorally driven pope. In his view, the church as institution exists to serve its mission and not the other way around. He was pragmatic and, through his many

---

[2] For more information on the historical and political context of the early twentieth century and its impact on the council, see "Papal Leadership in the First Half of the Twentieth Century: Resistance and Renewal," by Karim Shelkens (Chapter 3 in this volume).

encounters with and outreach to people of other churches and faiths (and those of no faith), he was a pope open to others and to the work of the Spirit wherever it might be found in the world. His diplomatic postings in Eastern Europe, Turkey, and war-time France, for example, allowed him to build and form rich relationships with Orthodox Christians, Muslims, and Jewish people (thousands of whom he helped escape the Holocaust). This would prove of considerable significance for the council. Serving as Archbishop of Venice, despite its opulent center a very poor and industrial archdiocese, gave him further insight into what the church's priorities should be for the second half of the twentieth century and beyond. He learned of the dynamics between the church and world in multiple contexts and could see that the relationship could be one of mutual learning and cooperation, as opposed to the negative one-directional dynamic (in which the church *teaches and saves* the world, while needing nothing from it in return) that had too frequently prevailed before (and, indeed, at times, since).

Pentecost was a very familiar theme in his thoughts and words. He truly believed in the work of the Spirit in the world. As a historian, he also believed that history unfolds and can move backward and forward in terms of the progress of humanity toward its goals and destiny, but nonetheless there is a divinely intended pathway and ultimate destiny for the world. In other words, he truly believed in eschatology. His stewardship of and therefore vision for the church was anything but short-termist in orientation.

For Pope John, once he had conceived of the council, he became convinced it could be a new Pentecost for the church. And this would be a theme he would return to again and again. When he announced the council to his surprised audience of cardinals on January 25, 1959, one of his revelations was that the council would reach out to other Christians – a major break with official attitudes toward ecumenism held by a majority of his post-Reformation predecessors. He gave instructions to the Antepreparatory Commission on the feast of Pentecost itself (May 17, 1959) and charged them with consulting widely with bishops, faculties of theology and canon law around the world, as well as throughout the Roman Curia itself. He wanted the commission to discern what people believed the church's, and therefore the council's, priorities should be for today.

John made clear to the central conciliar preparatory commission that, above all, the council should be more constructive and open than previous synodal and conciliar gatherings. It would positively engage the wider world. It would not be, as previous councils had most often been, about condemning doctrinal errors. His key priority, which became the council's driving priority as well, was *aggiornamento* – the renewal or bringing-up-to-date of the church. This concept, in itself, would help transform the council's ecclesiological thinking, further priorities, and eventual documents. This concept was forward-looking, acknowledging that the church was not perfect and needed change, and that this task of renewal was something, by definition, which could not be done once and for all but must be conceived of as an ongoing process—indeed, in *eschatological* terms.

So, when John opened the council on October 11, 1962, he reiterated these intentions and priorities and emphasized that the council was to be primarily *pastoral* rather than doctrinal in orientation.[3] This did not mean that it would be of any lesser significance. Quite the opposite – it was about putting the church's priorities into their correct order. He reiterated the eschatological character of the council and church alike also, stressing that the church must not only reach back across the centuries of its own experience and traditions, but must now also look toward the future, free of fear. It must engage the wider world and modernity rather than recoil from and shun both. He said we must learn the lessons of history, for it is life's great teacher. He stressed that God is at work in these times as in every time; therefore, the church should learn from its past as well as the world's present alike and see what new opportunities were being presented for the gospel in the present day. And the church has to seek to *serve* the world of contemporary times, as opposed to simply being preoccupied with preserving the things of the past. Another surprising shift was that he made clear that the practice of magisterium was to serve pastoral ends and not vice-versa – the ancient substance of the faith is *not* the same as its doctrinal forms of expression. He therefore said that the church, if it is to serve the contemporary world, has to prove the relevance and validity of its teaching, rather than simply condemning those who disagree with it. John continued by urging the church to reach out to the entire human family and to uphold the dignity of all.

The sense of a new Pentecost would filter into the conciliar deliberations and eventually find expression in a variety of ways in the final

---

[3] Pope John XXIII, "Gaudet Mater Ecclesia" – "Mother Church Rejoices," trans. as Pope John XXIII, "Pope John's Opening Speech to the Council," in *Documents of Vatican II*, ed. Walter M. Abbott (New York: America Press, 1966), 710–19. John's address speaks of Christians as pilgrims on this earth at §11. For the original text see https://w2.vatican.va/content/johnxxiii/la/speeches/1962/documents/hf_jxxiii_spe_19621011_opening-council.html.

conciliar documents. And so, among the most significant transformations in the self-understanding of the church and its mission that
would emerge from Vatican II was a shift toward perceiving of the
church and its mission in *pneumatological* terms – that is, in seeing
the Holy Spirit ever-present in and guiding the church along its way.
What was that way exactly, and how did the council understand and
express it? To that aspect of the council's ecclesiological developments
we now turn.

Transformations in Core Ecclesiological Ideas: A Church and People in Eschatological Motion, Journeying Along the Way

The draft schema on the church *De Ecclesia* was introduced at the first
session and, as the first period of Vatican II drew to a close, debates
followed concerning how the council should proceed in reflecting on the
church itself. The result was that the draft, prepared under the supervi-
sion of Cardinal Ottaviani (Prefect of the Holy Office) and featuring
much of the material left undiscussed from Vatican I (which ended
some ninety-two years previously), was rejected (albeit without a vote),
having been perceived as being utterly out of touch with the times.
Instead, key council fathers intervened to ensure a very different ecclesiological outlook would both inform and emerge from the council's
work. Pope John concurred with such interventions.

This allowed some of those leading theological lights, suspect and
banished in the 1950s and before under Pius XII (yet brought in from the
cold by John), to come into their own. An alliance formed between
several prominent cardinals and bishops began to exert more and more
influence over proceedings, draft documents, debates from the council
floor, and subsequent discussions. In this they were served well by their
theological expert advisers (*periti*), among whom those rehabilitated
theologians previously ostracized would prove to be some of the most
important voices of all. In terms of ecclesiology, such influence would
prove vital. Yet various additional alliances and factions would develop
during the council, as well, and influence its proceedings in a variety of
ways. And while no one single faction or ecclesiological standpoint
would ultimately triumph overall, Vatican II is remembered less for
the compromises and oft-time contradictory nature of some of its documents (especially in the final two periods) than for the marked shifts
in perspective, language, and therefore ecclesial climate and practice
that took place during and especially subsequent to the council's
completion.

Central to what changed was a shift away from that triumphalist, normative, exclusionary, and predominantly institutional ecclesiology that had prevailed for so long prior to 1962. There emerged a collective acknowledgment, at first on the part of significant conciliar fathers and theological advisers but then of an overwhelming majority of voting members of the council, that not only had the world changed but that the church had as well. What is more, there was eventually a collective realization and therefore conciliar documentary acknowledgment that not only was this *not* something to be resisted or shunned but that it was something divinely ordained. Indeed, such change was essential to the divine plan of salvation for the world. The eschatological backdrop to such realizations was profoundly significant. This was contrary to the turn away from modernity that had prevailed, with the occasional hiatus, since the late eighteenth century. Pius X had insisted that doctrine is not subject to the processes of evolution, historical or otherwise, and sharply condemned and rebuked any scholars who may have felt – in agreement with modern historical thinking – that such was inevitable and indeed welcome.

What helped bring about this shift in thinking? The idea that the church, and all of its members, are in motion – historically, existentially, and soteriologically (i.e. in terms of salvation and the progress toward it for the world in general and its peoples specifically): they are journeying along the way. The Bible is replete with such journey and movement-oriented metaphors and analogies to describe the journey of humanity toward God's ultimate purpose for them. For example, the Hebrew Bible tells of the journey of the Israelites out of Egypt and their path to the promised land; in the New Testament, the Gospels (alongside other texts) constantly speak of "the way," something at one and the same time conveying a sense of missionary activity, but also existential and soteriological progression.

In many respects, coupled with the key developments in modern intellectual and social life, what helped transform the self-understanding of the church was a return to this sense of the *provisionality* of what the church is and is experiencing as it seeks to fulfil the gospel and fulfil its mission for new times and contexts. So, also, there emerged at Vatican II an acknowledgment of how change and new directions, as well as setbacks and disappointments and failure, are only to be expected and are part and parcel of the journey. Such does not necessarily mean the church is no longer moving, in the wider picture, toward what God has ordained for it. But nor should such experiences be dressed up as anything other than the realities of human existence that they are.

All in all, then, what changed during Vatican II is that a sense of ecclesiological *realism* came into conciliar deliberations, along with the constructive resources and evocative theological discernment offered by framing all this in *eschatological* terms. History and soteriology entwined in the service of the world and, above all else, in the service of promoting justice in that world, in collaboration with others beyond the church. At the core of this eschatological turn was the notion of the church as *pilgrim*.

This emphasis on pilgrimage cannot be unrelated to Rome's ancient reputation as one of Christianity's most sacred centers of pilgrimage, as well as the fact that Vatican II was the most wide-reaching gathering of its kind in history, with many of the conciliar fathers, expert advisers (*periti*), and observers – over two and a half thousand attending the first session and close to that number at the final session – having made enormously lengthy journeys to the eternal city to be present. At times, they must indeed have felt as if their trips to Rome were very intentional acts of pilgrimage. The sense of the church, itself, as pilgrim that emerged at Vatican II had a twofold emphasis: first, the foundational ecclesiological sense of the church as pilgrim itself; second, the expanded and qualified sense of the church as the *pilgrim people of God*. We turn to explore both these ecclesiological emphases, beginning with the latter.

A CHURCH WITHOUT BOUNDARIES?
THE PEOPLE OF GOD

In terms of (formal) ecclesiology *per se*, many believe that neither Trent nor Vatican I, the two great post-Reformation councils of the Roman Catholic Church, satisfactorily dealt with the nature, role, and self-understanding of the church itself in any fulsome or systematic fashion. Vatican II's *Lumen Gentium* (The Dogmatic Constitution on the Church) would reflect those key developments in the self-understanding of the church in the 1940s and 1950s, yet also inspire a further wealth of ecclesiological visions, debates, and interpretations.

Lumen Gentium offered an ecclesiology rich in biblical imagery alongside many other theologically evocative images and unfolded rich new ways of understanding the church as a community. In addition to that core ecclesiological notion of the church as people of God, also central to its imagery was the *pilgrim* nature of the church as it goes about fulfilling its mission. This was also vital to that shift from an institutional ecclesiology to one where the church is understood in more open, universal, and egalitarian terms.

While the document is not as anti-hierarchical or quite so radical as many have subsequently believed it to be, it nonetheless affirms the priesthood and apostolate of all believers, focuses upon a model of the hierarchy viewed in terms of its *service* to the church, and pushes back the boundaries, somewhat, of who constitutes the "people of God." It further offers a positive and enabling interpretation of the place and role of the laity. The text betrays the tensions of the council factions, but nonetheless is often masterful in its energizing treatment of fundamental ecclesiological questions. On the whole, its ecclesiology laid the foundations for a more *open* and *dialogical* church, as well as a more *collaborative* and wide-reaching definition of ministry and a truly *ministerial* (as opposed to authoritarian) understanding of leadership and authority.

This ecclesiological notion of the church as the "people of God," therefore, can be said to constitute Vatican II's core ecclesiological concept. It is a guiding theme throughout many conciliar documents and, in particular, was the core focus of much of *Lumen Gentium*, in which the specific chapter dedicated to the image itself (chapter 2) was placed ahead of the chapter on the hierarchy. The latter achievement, not without resistance, controversy, and compromise, was arguably another of the most significant ecclesiological breakthroughs of the council. The document acknowledged the fullness of lay participation in the mission of the church.

The notion of the "people of God" was so important because it helped introduce a way of looking at the church for new times that was, first, grounded in biblical and ancient ecclesial traditions. In particular, it was a theme that bridged the sense of the covenant in the Hebrew Bible and the notion of a new covenant with the gentiles, which also developed in the early church. But it was also a notion that spoke to the contemporary world in a way that was much less patronising or alienating than much of the official discourse of recent centuries. It especially marked a clear departure from the juridical and institutional-dominated character of ecclesiological discourse since the late eighteenth and especially nineteenth and early–mid-twentieth centuries.

"People of God" was an image of the church that was less exclusivist and less affirmative of those perceived boundaries that had hitherto defined the church at many times throughout history. It also helped overcome the overt emphasis in older official teachings and ecclesiological treatises on the sense of the church as a divinely ordained hierarchy, and it helped the church to focus on factors other than its institutional structures (although the notion of hierarchy did not disappear from the conciliar deliberations and remained in many of the final documents, e.g. *Lumen Gentium*, Chapter 3).

The concept also challenged any *rigid* sense of the church as the mystical body of Christ, which had become popular in the 1940s, particularly the forms of mystical body ecclesiology that identified that mystical body with the institutional (Roman) Catholic Church itself. The notion of the people of God also had profound implications for ecumenical and interfaith relations. This was because the people of God was a more fluid and engaging sense of the church as a community that traversed specific communities. This was especially significant in terms of the church's affirmation of the universal salvation of all, which was given greater emphasis. It was also a notion with greater historical implications (locating the church as an ongoing entity across both time and space), existential implications, and sociological implications in a world so recently ravaged by national and ethnic self-interest during World War II. The church was a fluid community in the midst of other wider communities and in the midst of the ongoing story of the collective human race. Again, eschatology was at the forefront. History was understood in the context of *salvation* history.

Such developments were vital in ensuring the council consciously and deliberately moved away from the notion of the church as a perfect society or as an exclusive body of salvation beyond which salvation/grace did not exist. Instead, with the church now being understood as the pilgrim people of God, this was a people whose limits were known to God alone and not determined by the institutional church. Having considered, then, the notion of the church as people of God, what of the ecclesiological significance of the notion of *pilgrim*?

A Pilgrim People, a Pilgrim Church

While Pope John's opening address to the council had spoken of Christians as pilgrims on this earth,[4] the tone was set for the ecclesiological motif of the church, itself, as pilgrim in the very first document promulgated at the council, *Sacrosanctum Concilium* (Constitution on the Sacred Liturgy). At its very outset, in *Sacrosanctum Concilium* 2, the church is described as both holy and sinful at the same time, already and

---

[4] Pope John XXIII, "Gaudet Mater Ecclesia," §11.

not yet along its rightful way. The beginnings of an ecclesiological humility largely absent from modern church teachings are there also:

> The Church is both human and divine, visible but endowed with invisible realities, zealous in action and dedicated to contemplation, present in the world, yet a migrant (*peregrinam*), so constituted that in it the human is directed toward and subordinated to the divine, the visible to the invisible, action to contemplation, and this present world to that city yet to come, the object of our quest. (SC 2)

Then we find the *membership* of the church described as pilgrims journeying toward the heavenly Jerusalem in article 8. The eschatological orientation of the conciliar ecclesiological thinking, then, was present from this very first document onward. Indeed, the council, by the close of its second period, had already embraced so many of the key ecclesiological themes that would come to help ensure its legacy would prove truly transformative for the church. Again, such would contrast in a quite marked fashion from the prevailing ecclesiologies in the decades and earlier immediate eras prior to the council.

And, of course, thanks to this first document, Vatican II also eventually initiated a revolution in the understanding of and celebration of the liturgy. This liturgical *ressourcement* and *aggiornamento* was also influenced by the eschatological language and sense that the church is never once and for all complete: for if it be so, neither can the church's forms and styles of worship and mission be fixed and complete, or beyond change and reform, either. Overall, *Sacrosanctum Concilium* reflects those significantly transformative developments that had emerged from the debates about the nature and understanding of the church and its purpose in general during the first two conciliar periods.

As with the notion of people of God, the sense of the church and its members as pilgrims along the way was central to *Lumen Gentium*. In its very first chapter on "The Mystery of the Church," the document employs a number of the rich variety of biblical images to help explain the sacramental nature and mission of the church. The document opens with a clear declaration of the sacramental nature of the church – which, in itself, is an eschatologically charged ecclesiological motif – framing the church's mission in an open-ended, ongoing fashion and declaring the council's intention to offer a new articulation of how the church understood itself in these times:

> Christ is the light of the nations and consequently this holy synod, gathered together in the holy Spirit, ardently desires to bring to all

humanity that light of Christ which is resplendent on the face of the church, by proclaiming his Gospel to every creature. Since the church, in Christ, is a sacrament – a sign and instrument, that is, of communion with God and of the unity of the entire human race – it here proposes, for the benefit of the faithful and of the entire world, to describe more clearly, and in the tradition laid down by earlier councils, its own nature and universal mission. (LG 1)

The pilgrim and (semi-realized) eschatological nature of the church is further underlined in a passage in *Lumen Gentium* 8 in which the constitution speaks of the church as "at once holy and always in need of purification, [which] follows constantly the path of penance and renewal." Citing Augustine's *City of God* (and echoing article 7, which cites Rom 8:17), the first chapter closes by speaking of the church continuing on its pilgrimage.[5] This passage also draws together many of Pope John's priorities and core aspects of his vision for the council and his ecclesiological vision for renewal and reform alike. Moreover, in chapter III, the document refers to Christ guiding the people of the New Testament "on their journey towards eternal happiness" (LG 21). Thus *Lumen Gentium* draws together eschatology, provisionality, ecclesial humility, and the need for ongoing renewal and reform, that is, for ecclesial change and transformation.

Chapter VII of *Lumen Gentium* further explicates this core ecclesiological theme, elaborating in an explicit fashion upon the eschatological nature of "The Pilgrim Church" and its union with the "Church in Heaven." Here more traditional themes in theological discussions of eschatology become blended with newer and more modern developments. This chapter opens by drawing on scripture to point toward the destiny intended for the whole human race, i.e. salvation, and by stating that the church is called in its mission to facilitate that. The church is then described in a phrase that would become very famous in subsequent ecclesiological discussions and research: The church, which is also the body of Christ, through the Holy Spirit, constitutes the "universal sacrament of salvation" (LG 48). This illustrates key aspects of Vatican II's ecclesiology that are also made evident throughout the conciliar documents as a whole. The sense of the church as pilgrim, this notion of a semi-realized eschatology, was bound up with a firm belief that God has a definite purpose for the world and therefore for the

---

[5] Flannery's edition has "pressing forward," as does the translation on the Vatican's own website.

church. The phrase "universal sacrament of salvation" is repeated with direct reference to the coming of the kingdom of God in *Gaudium et Spes* 45, again directly linking this to the efficacy of "the pilgrimage of the People of God" (the latter again tying together these two fundamental ecclesiological metaphors).

Indeed, through such ecclesiological imagery evoking the church as *sacrament* – that is, as both sign and instrument of God's purpose and destiny for the world – Vatican II was communicating that the church's mission is to both bear witness to and be an active means of helping to bring about God's will for the world. And when the council fathers reflected on just how God's will is made known in this world and in what ways God sustains and guides the church in its mission, of course, it turned to the ever-present work of the Holy Spirit, yet another theme expanding on conciliar ecclesiology's eschatological emphasis. Throughout the first chapter of *Lumen Gentium*, we see that the church is infused with, as well as inspired, unified, guided, renewed, and sustained by, the presence of the Spirit. The Spirit pours out its gifts or charisms on the church, manifesting themselves in multiple differing ministries.

Lumen Gentium 4, in particular, expands on several different images and pneumatological themes applied to the church. Invoking the story of the original Pentecost, the document cites or alludes to various biblical passages and early church fathers in relation to the Spirit. Among the most evocative images is the allusion to 1 Cor 3:16 and 6:19: "The Spirit dwells in the Church and in the hearts of the faithful, as in a temple." This theme is seen again in article 17, where the document states that the church "prays and works so that the fullness of the whole world may move into the people of God, the body of the Lord and the temple of the holy Spirit and that in Christ, the head of all things, all honor and glory may be rendered to the Creator, the Father of the universe."[6] This continual attention to the work of the Spirit in the church also helped articulate the council's notion of the entire faithful's discernment of the faith – the *sensus fidei* (i.e., "sense of the faith" [LG 12, 35]). Pneumatology had previously been an oft-neglected theme in much Catholic theology. The council rectified this and led to an outpouring of pneumatological studies and themes for many decades to come, down to the present day.

---

[6] The Vatican online translation reads more evocatively, still: "that the entire world may become the People of God, the Body of the Lord and the Temple of the Holy Spirit."

Therefore, at Vatican II the church itself was also very much explained and interpreted in *pneumatological* terms. And in the sense of the church as pilgrim, eschatology and pneumatology combine. For God guides the pilgrim church on its way, toward its ultimate end and destiny. As *pilgrim* this church works toward the enhancement of justice throughout the world. The eighth chapter of *Lumen Gentium* illustrates very well how eschatology, pneumatology, and social justice become entwined, as elsewhere in the conciliar corpus. Already we have seen how the church is the body of Christ and constitutes the sacrament of universal salvation "*through* the Holy Spirit" (my emphasis). The document continues to demonstrate the intertwining of these themes in the following fashion, which again shows the "already but not yet" semi-realized eschatological emphasis once more.

> Already the final age of the world is with us and the renewal of the world is irrevocably under way; it is even now anticipated in a certain real way, for the church on earth is endowed already with a sanctity that is true though imperfect. However, until the arrival of the new heavens and the new earth in which justice dwells the pilgrim church, in its sacraments and institutions, which belong to this present age, carries the mark of this world which will pass, and it takes its place among the creatures which groan and until now suffer the pains of childbirth and await the revelation of the children of God. (LG 48)

The text then turns to more familiar eschatological language drawn from scriptural, theological, and patristic sources, speaking of church members on earth as "wayfarers," united with those passed and gone before us (LG 49), "pilgrim members" (LG 50), joined inseparably with the dead who inspire the living on their journey toward union with God. The remainder of chapter 8 gives further attention to the relationship of those living pilgrims and the communion of saints, i.e. those who have gone before us, are further along their journey, or, indeed, have reached its beatific end.

In fact, this chapter had originally been drafted to be a separate document but was brought into *Lumen Gentium* at the request of Paul VI in May 1964. Its earlier, more traditionally eschatological language was given a comprehensive reworking, breathing new ecclesiological life into the theme of eschatology in general by the theological adviser whose hand can be seen on every aspect of the council's key ecclesiological themes discussed in this chapter, the French Dominican Yves

Congar. He was likewise influential in advancing the pneumatological aspects of the conciliar texts, as well as *Lumen Gentium* in general and the notions of the church as pilgrim and as people of God.

Alongside *Lumen Gentium* and *Orientalium Ecclesiarum*, the Decree on the Eastern Catholic Churches, the third period of the council ended with another highly significant document being promulgated – *Unitatis Redintegratio*, the Decree on Ecumenism, which incorporates the pilgrim theme at its outset: "The Church, then, God's only flock, like a standard lifted on high for the nations to see, ministers the Gospel of peace to all humankind, as it makes its pilgrim way in hope toward its goal, the homeland above" (UR 2).

This decree also spoke of the need for continual reformation in the church as well as the necessity of righting historical ecclesial wrongs, stating that if, in the past, there may have been "deficiencies in moral conduct or in church discipline, or even in the way that church teaching has been formulated – to be carefully distinguished from the deposit of faith itself – these should be set right at the opportune moment and in the proper way" (UR 6).

The decree further emphasises the twofold nature of the church as holy and sinful simultaneously, stating that "during its pilgrimage on earth, this people, though still in its members liable to sin, is growing in Christ and is guided by God's gentle wisdom, according to God's hidden designs, until it shall happily arrive at the fullness of eternal glory in the heavenly Jerusalem" (UR 3). Again, the underlining emphasis here is eschatological.

Although its subject matter was among the very first issues to be debated at the council, *Dei Verbum*, the Dogmatic Constitution on Divine Revelation, was so contested by council fathers that it was among the final ones to be promulgated. The sense of the church as pilgrim finds its way into that final text as well. In setting out the inseparability of tradition and scripture, the two are described as being "like a mirror, in which the church, during its pilgrim journey here on earth, contemplates God, from whom it receives everything, until such time as it is brought to see him face to face as he really is" (DV 7). The eschatological and provisional nature of the church's journey is further confirmed in *Dei Verbum* 8: "As the centuries go by, the church is always advancing towards the plenitude of divine truth, until eventually the words of God are fulfilled in it."

Dei Verbum would soon be followed in promulgation by another controversial document, *Dignitatis Humanae*, the Declaration on Religious Liberty, widely regarded as effecting a sea change in official Catholic attitudes toward the question of religious freedom and furthering the developments introduced by John XXIII with regard to the priority of human dignity and conscience. In article 12, we are told that affirming religious liberty is being "faithful to the truth of the Gospel," despite the "vicissitudes of human history" that have sometimes led the "people of God in its pilgrimage" astray in thinking otherwise. This document, in turn, was followed by *Ad Gentes*, The Decree on the Missionary Activity of the Church, which also reflected the eschatological and pneumatological nature of the council's ecclesiological thinking when it asserted clearly from the outset that "the Church during her pilgrimage on earth is missionary in nature, because it is from the mission of the Son and from the mission of the Holy Spirit, in accordance with the plan of God the Father" (AG 2).[7] With these lines it set down a renewed theology of mission for the times and offered reflections on how missionary activity should interact with and respect the specific cultures of each context where missionary activity is carried out; in effect, inculturation was not only encouraged but recommended. In *Ad Gentes* 2, pneumatology also returns to the fore, with a trinitarian rendering of the church's missionary efforts articulated there as well.

But perhaps the conciliar document that really blends all the key ecclesiological themes outlined above together the most – eschatology, pneumatology, the church as pilgrim and as the people of God, the church as sacrament, the church requiring humility, and the church's missiological priority to work unswervingly for justice *in* history (not simply waiting for the kingdom but making it present here and now) – was the final and arguably most controversial and most contested conciliar document of all, *Gaudium et Spes*, The Pastoral Constitution on the Church in the Modern World. Throughout this document we find the church as journeying along the way, committed to playing a fundamental role in history in working for the good, in working with and learning from others beyond the church. Ultimately, the document offers a programmatic ecclesiology that must result in concrete action. So, in *Gaudium et Spes* 45, we read that

---

[7] My translation (Flannery's edition states, "The Church on earth is by its very nature missionary since, according to the plan of the Father, it has its origin in the mission of the Son and the holy Spirit").

whether it aids the world or whether it benefits from it, the church has but one sole purpose – that the kingdom of God may come and the salvation of the human race may be accomplished. Every benefit the people of God can confer on humanity during its earthly pilgrimage is rooted in the church's being "the universal sacrament of salvation" at once manifesting and actualizing the mystery of God's love for humanity.

The eschatological emphasis is made explicitly clear as the chapter echoes Christ's words as recorded in the Book of Revelation that he is the "alpha and the omega, the first and the last, the beginning and the end" (Rev 2: 12–13). The document goes on to state that a commitment to the faith should entail that Christians, "in their pilgrimage to the heavenly city," should keep in mind the things that pertain to the beyond *in order that* this should inspire them to be more committed to working with others "for the establishment of a more human world" and, indeed, to realize that work and culture play a vital role in such work (GS 57). This, in turn, leads to an appreciation that no single culture offers the sole key to working toward such ends (GS 58).

Therefore, all the ecclesiological themes introduced earlier in our chapter come together in the mature and hard-fought-for final form of *Gaudium et Spes*. It was certainly the most significant conciliar document in terms of its impact on social ethics and on the transformation of the church's relationship with the wider world and in its proactive approach to carrying out the gospel mission. Furthermore, it helped completely transform the church's practice with regard to acting in that world and collaborating with others beyond the church. This stance stood also in contrast to the siege mentality that had developed earlier in the church, especially at the official level, throughout the late-eighteenth century onward. Indeed, it could be argued that the pastoral constitution was the most important council document of all because it further articulated not only a radically altered understanding of the church but also of the church's very *raison d'etre*, its mission. The document inspired so many subsequent initiatives, practices, and collaborations throughout the church and between Catholicism and partners from other churches, faiths, and people of no declared religious persuasion. So also did it influence the development of theology in general, especially moral theology and social ethics in multiple constructive directions. In doing all of this, it ensured that ecclesiology itself would never be the same again.

Indeed, thanks to the broad ecclesiological developments outlined in this chapter, ecclesiology witnessed the opening up of so many new frontiers in the field across widely differing global contexts, forever changing how the church would be understood and how the church would go about collectively living out its missionary calling as the pilgrim people of God. The church would no longer see itself as aloof from change or the need for constant renewal and reform. It had transformed the sense of its own nature and purpose alike, as well as its relation to other Christians, to people of other faiths, and to the life of broader societies and the world in general. The council's "eschatological turn" breathed vibrant energy and new life into the ecclesial journey and the journey of all Christians, offering a vision of a church sacramental and missionary in character, always at one and the same time already and "not yet" in its collective building of the kingdom.

FURTHER READING

Aubert, Roger. *The Church in a Secular Society*. New York: Paulist Press, 1978.

Comblin, José. *People of God*. Maryknoll, NY: Orbis, 2004.

Congar, Yves. "The Church: The People of God." *The Church and Mankind: Concilium* 1, no. 1, 7–19. New York: Paulist Press, 1965.

Congar, Yves. "The Pneumatology of Vatican II." In *I Believe in the Holy Spirit*, vol. 1, 167–73. New York: Seabury Press, 1983.

Häring, Bernard. *Road to Renewal: Perspectives of Vatican II*. New York: Alba House, 1966. Italian original: *Il Concilio Comincia Adesso*. Rome: Edizione Paulo, 1966.

Hughson, Thomas SJ. "Interpreting Vatican II: A New Pentecost." *Theological Studies* 69 (2008): 3–37.

Komonchak, Joseph A. "Towards an Ecclesiology of Communion." In *Church as Communion: Third Period and Intersession, September 1964–September 1965*, edited by Giuseppe Alberigo and Joseph A. Komonchak, 1–93. Vol. 4 of *History of Vatican II*. Maryknoll, NY: Orbis Books, 2004.

McCool, Gerald A. *Catholic Theology in the Nineteenth Century: The Quest for a Unitary Method*. New York: Seabury, 1977.

Melloni, Alberto. "The Beginning of the Second Period: The Great Debate on the Church." In *The Mature Council: Second Period and Intersession, September 1963–September 1964*, ed. Giuseppe Alberigo and Joseph A. Komonchak, 1–115. Vol. 3 of *History of Vatican II*. Maryknoll, NY: Orbis Books, 2000.

Melloni, Alberto, Federico Ruozzi, and Enrico Galavotti, eds. *Vatican II: The Complete History*. Mahwah, NJ: Paulist Press, 2015.

O'Malley, John W. *What Happened at Vatican II*. Cambridge, MA: Harvard University Press, 2008.

Ruggieri, Giuseppe. "Beyond an Ecclesiology of Polemics: The Debate on the Church." In *The Formation of the Council's Identity: First Period and Intersession, October 1962–September 1963*, edited by Giuseppe Alberigo and Joseph A. Komonchak, 281–357. Vol. 2 of *History of Vatican II*. Maryknoll, NY: Orbis Books, 2006.

8 The Church in Mission

STEPHEN BEVANS

This chapter will propose that the ecclesiology of the Second Vatican Council might best be characterized as a "communion-in-mission." In this it differs from a more standard interpretation that the council's ecclesiology is based on an understanding of the church as communion or as community. A first section will show how the council should be regarded as a "missionary council" from start to finish. A second section will reflect on the fact that Vatican II worked out of a renewed understanding of mission, rooted in the mission of God as such, and constituted not only by the witness and proclamation of the gospel but also by commitment as well to inculturation, justice, and dialogue. A final section will point to a growing reception of the council's missionary ecclesiology beyond communion ecclesiology and the New Evangelization. Such a reception is marked by Pope Francis's understanding of the church as a "community of missionary disciples."[1]

A MISSIONARY COUNCIL

In his 1964 encyclical *Ecclesiam Suam*, Pope Paul VI noted that the doctrine of the church was "the principal topic engaging the attention" of the council.[2] Indeed, Vatican II could well be called the council of the church, for in many ways it attempted to balance the rather incomplete ecclesiology presented at Vatican I.[3] The council spoke of the church in terms of a communion anchored in the fundamental equality bestowed by baptism on all the people of God. It saw itself as the "universal

---

[1] Pope Francis, apostolic exhortation *Evangelii Gaudium* (Washington, DC: United States Conference of Catholic Bishops, 2013), 24.
[2] Paul VI, encyclical letter *Ecclesiam Suam*, August 6, 1964, 31.
[3] See John W. O'Malley, *Vatican I: The Council and the Making of the Ultramontane Church* (Cambridge, MA: The Belknap Press of Harvard University Press, 2018), esp. 184–88, and Kristin M. Colberg, *Vatican I and Vatican II* (Collegeville, MN: Liturgical Press, 2016).

sacrament of salvation," a sign and instrument of God's grace in the world (LG 48). As Patrick Granfield has pointed out, ecclesiology at Vatican II "shifted dramatically from the sociological to the biblical, from the jurisdictional to the sacramental, from the sectarian to the ecumenical, from the papal to the episcopal, from the hierarchical to the collegial."[4]

During the council itself, and in its aftermath, these dramatic shifts have certainly been highlighted and emphasized by both academic and pastoral theologians. It is a commonplace to say that the major shift in ecclesiology at the council was one from understanding the church as institution to seeing it as a community, or from understanding the church as essentially monarchical and hierarchical to seeing it as the people of God. This was the story behind the revision of the schema on the church presented to the bishops at the first session of the council, when a more juridical, clerical, and triumphalistic ecclesiology was replaced by one that was more biblical and patristic. In that revision, and in the final document itself, the church was described not in abstract principles but in terms of mystery, "a reality imbued with the presence of God."[5] In 1985, at the Extraordinary Synod of Bishops, which was called to assess the council after twenty years, the bishops determined that "the ecclesiology of communion is the central and fundamental idea of the council's documents."[6]

There is no doubt that "communion" is central to the basic ecclesiology developed – or retrieved through the method of *ressourcement* – by the council. However, a closer reading of the event of the council and of its documents reveals that perhaps a better way to speak of the council's "fundamental idea" might be to speak of the church as a "communion-in-mission." The church's mission, not only its inner reality, was very much at the heart of everything the council did and taught; in fact, it might even be said that in its deepest intuitions, Vatican II was a "missionary council."[7] Consequently, its ecclesiology

---

[4] Patrick Granfield, "The Church as Societas Perfecta in the Schemata of Vatican I," *Church History* 48 (1979): 446, quoted in O'Malley, *Vatican I*, 246, 283, note 12.

[5] Paul VI, "Opening Allocution of the Second Session of the Council," in *Enchiridion Vaticanum: Documenti Il Concilio Vaticano Secondo*, Seventh Edition (Bologna: EDB, 1968), 96.

[6] Final Report of the 1985 Extraordinary Synod, www.ewtn.com/library/CURIA/ SYNFINAL.HTM.

[7] Johannes Schütte, "Ce que la mission attendait du Concile," in *Vatican II: l'Activité missionaire de l'église*, Unam Sanctam 67, ed. Johannes Schütte (Paris: Éditions du Cerf, 1967), 120.

might be best summarized in two phrases that appear in paragraphs in the Dogmatic Constitution on the Church *Lumen Gentium* and its Decree on Missionary Activity *Ad Gentes*. In *Lumen Gentium* 4 we read from St. Cyprian that the church is "a people made one by the unity of the Father, the Son and the holy Spirit" (communion); in *Ad Gentes* 2 we read that "the church on earth is by its very nature missionary since, according to the plan of the Father, it has its origin in the mission of the Son and the holy Spirit" (mission).

John XXIII's Vision: A Church More Equipped to Preach the Gospel

Pope John XXIII's intuitions in calling for the council developed from 1959 through 1962. Church historian Giuseppe Alberigo writes that it became clear that the pope "wanted a council that would mark a transition between two eras, that is, that would bring the Church out of the post-tridentine period and ... into a new phase of witness and proclamation." In this way, "the Church would then be able to present the gospel message to the world and explain it to human beings with the same power and immediacy that marked the first Pentecost."[8] In his opening speech to the council on October 11, 1962, Pope John admitted that a council was not necessary at that point to clarify or defend doctrine. The world did need, however, a deeper understanding of the church's teachings that "should be studied and expounded through the methods of research and through the literary forms of modern thought." *Aggiornamento*, in other words, was not about change for change's sake, but finding ways by which the church's teaching "should be guarded and taught more efficaciously," thus equipping the church to better preach the gospel.[9] Updating (*aggiornamento*), renewal/reform (*ressourcement*), and development were ultimately about enhancing and strengthening the church's mission.[10]

John's vision was helped greatly by a memo submitted to him by Cardinal Léon-Josef Suenens, the primate of Belgium. Kristin Colberg relates that during the preparatory period of the council, Suenens sought

---

[8] Giuseppe Alberigo, "The Announcement of the Council from the Security of the Fortress to the Lure of the Quest," in *History of Vatican II, Vol. 1: Announcing and Preparing Vatican Council II*, ed. Giuseppe Alberigo and Joseph A. Komonchak (Maryknoll, NY: Orbis Books, 1995), 42–43.

[9] John XXIII, "Pope John's Opening Speech to the Council," in *The Documents of Vatican II*, ed. Walter M. Abbot (New York: Herder and Herder, 1966), 715, 713.

[10] See John W. O'Malley, *What Happened at Vatican II* (Cambridge, MA: The Belknap Press of Harvard University Press, 2008), 36–43.

an audience with Pope John to express his concern for an overall plan for the council, lest it get lost in too many schemata and too many details. John asked Suenens to devise that plan – which the cardinal did about a month later. Suenens' memo suggested that the council focus on one question: "How is the Church of the twentieth century measuring up to the Master's last command: Go, therefore, make disciples of all nations (Matt 28:19)."[11] The "basic idea" was that the council should focus, on the one hand, on its internal life (*ad intra*), and then focus on its relation to the world (*ad extra*). The *ad intra* aspect would focus on the church as evangelizer, teacher, sanctifier, and community at prayer. The *ad extra* aspect would focus on questions around the family, contraception, religious freedom, and relations between church and state. Both aspects, it is clear, would be about mission.[12]

Suenens proposed this plan in a speech to the council toward the end of the first session. His intervention was met with warm applause and basically adopted as a kind of roadmap for the council. His memo undoubtedly influenced Pope John in the months before the council as his goals for it gained more and more clarity, and was perhaps reflected in his important radio address in September 1962, just a month before the council's opening.[13]

The Council's Documents: Missionary Orientations

A reading of the council's documents reveals that every one has some reference to the church's mission, and that there are well over one hundred references in all sixteen. These references range from only one in the document on the Eastern Churches to more than twenty-five in the Dogmatic Constitution on the Church.[14] Even in the decree on non-Christian religions, where the council admits that the church rejects nothing of the truth and holiness in the world's religions, and so is a charter for interreligious dialogue, it also admits that Christians are duty-bound to proclaim Christ, in whom women and men find "the fullness of their religious life" (NA 2). Other documents, like those on

---

[11] Kristin Colberg, *Vatican I and Vatican II*, quoting Léon-Josef Suenens, "A Plan for the Whole Council," in *Vatican II Revisited: By Those Who Were There*, ed. Alberic Stacpoole (Minneapolis: Winston Press, 1986), 97.

[12] See Colberg, *Vatican I and Vatican II*, 101–12.

[13] O'Malley, *What Happened at Vatican II*, 157–58. On Pope John's radio address see *Enchiridion Vaticanum*, 24–31. On the *ad intra/ad extra* dynamic, see 26.

[14] See Vatican Council II, Decree on the Catholic Eastern Churches, *Orientalium Ecclesiarum* 3; LG 1–13, 16–20, 23–24, 27, 30–31, 33–38; 43–44, 65.

ecumenism, bishops, laity, and religious freedom, all take on their fullest meaning in the light of the church's mission.[15]

The Extraordinary Synod of 1985 ruled that of the sixteen documents, the four Constitutions on the Liturgy, the Church, Revelation, and the Church in the Modern World are their "interpretative key."[16] In each of these constitutions the church's mission plays an important role – especially in their introductory paragraphs but also in other significant ways.

The Constitution on the Sacred Liturgy *Sacrosanctum Concilium*, the first document to be promulgated by the council, begins by summarizing the goals that Pope John had articulated during the council's preparatory period: growth in the Christian life, becoming responsive to the present time, seeking the unity of Christians, and strengthening "whatever serves to call all of humanity into the church's fold" (1). The church's mission is alluded to in the constitution's famous paragraph 10, in which the liturgy is described as the summit of the church's activity and the source of its evangelizing power. Paragraphs 37–40 show an attentiveness to culture in "mission lands," but it is an attentiveness that obviously needs to be shown in every context in which the church lives. Massimo Faggioli argues that the council understood that the liturgy could be "a powerful tool for the Church's missionary identity and activities."[17]

In his commentary on *Lumen Gentium*, chapter I, Aloys Grillmeier reflects on the first two words of the constitution and its title: *Lumen Gentium*. The phrase goes back to Augustine, but was also used by Pope John in his radio message of September 1962. As Grillmeier comments, the phrase is "in itself a sketch of the programme of reform envisioned by the Council for the missionary effort of the Church": the light of Christ, reflected in the Church, shining and illuminating all the peoples of the world.[18] This is why the church "is a sacrament – a sign and

---

[15] Vatican Council II, Decree on Ecumenism, *Unitatis Redintegratio*; Decree on the Pastoral Office of Bishops in the Church, *Christus Dominus*; Decree on the Apostolate of Lay People, *Apostolicam Actuositatem*; Declaration on Religious Liberty, *Dignitatis Humanae*.

[16] See Ormond Rush, "Toward a Comprehensive Interpretation of the Council and Its Documents," in *50 Years on: Probing the Riches of Vatican II*, ed. David G. Schultenover (Collegeville, MN: Liturgical Press, 2015), 38.

[17] Massimo Faggioli, *True Reform: Liturgy and Ecclesiology in Sacrosanctum Concilium* (Collegeville, MN: Liturgical Press, 2012), 38.

[18] Aloys Grillmeier, "Chapter I: The Mystery of the Church," in *Commentary on the Documents of Vatican II*, ed. Herbert Vorgrimler (New York: Herder and Herder, 1967), 139. The reference to Augustine is found in note 3.

instrument, that is, of communion with God and of the unity of the entire human race" (LG 1). The first paragraphs of the document (1–5) go on to trace the history of salvation as the work of the Trinity, culminating in the Holy Spirit being poured out on Jesus' disciples, so that they receive "the mission of proclaiming and establishing among all peoples the kingdom of Christ and of God," of which the church is the "seed and the beginning" (LG 5). The phrase in *Ad Gentes* 2 about the essential missionary nature of the church refers back to *Lumen Gentium* 1, signaling the bishops' understanding of the church as missionary. Matijs Lamberigts relates how, when the council's statement on mission was in danger of being reduced to a handful of propositions in the third session, a number of bishops in the course of the debate reminded the bishops that *Lumen Gentium* had already stated how mission is central to the church, and so mission deserved its own proper document.[19] A powerful summary of the church's mission is given in LG 16–17 – to give just one more example of many references to mission that appear in the constitution.

The first paragraphs of the Constitution on Divine Revelation *Dei Verbum* speak, first, of the reason for a document on revelation and tradition: so that the entire world will hear the good news of salvation, and so may believe, hope, and love (1). Then the document rehearses the history of salvation, in which God speaks to men and women as "friends ... and lives among them" in order to enter into relationship with them (2). This trinitarian action in the world demands "the obedience of faith" (5; Rom 16:26), the summons to which is accomplished by the apostolic mission that continues in the church (7).

The Pastoral Constitution on the Church in the Modern World *Gaudium et Spes* opens with the famous words about the joys, hopes, grief, and anguish of the world being those as well "of the followers of Christ" (1). Through this document the council addresses all of humanity, offering its service to human beings and to the world, never motivated by anything but to continue the work of Christ in the power of the Spirit (3). From beginning to end, this lengthy document expresses in more accessible language that the church's mission in the world is to call humanity to its deepest self (see 11). Cardinal Suenens' landmark speech in the last days of the first session proposed that the council take Pope John's words about "the church of Christ, the light of the world,"

---

[19] Mathijs Lamberigts, "Vatican II, Non-Christian Religions and the Challenges for (New) Evangelization," in *The New Evangelization: Faith, People, Context and Practice*, ed. Paul Grogan and Kirsteen Kim (London: Bloomsbury, 2015), 20–22.

as its basic theme. This would mean thinking of the church in two ways: first, with reference to itself, second, with reference to its dialogue with the world. Although *Lumen Gentium* makes it clear that it is not possible to speak of the church as such without somehow speaking of its mission, we have here also the seeds of what became the great missionary constitution of *Gaudium et Spes*.[20]

The Turn to the World

Cardinal Suenens' suggestion of a double focus for the council turned the church from concentrating exclusively on itself and enabled it to turn definitively toward the world. A century before, the church saw the world as an enemy of the church, threatening its legitimacy and teaching authority. In 1864 Pius IX issued the *Syllabus of Errors*, eighty propositions that condemned many of the basic tenets of modernity. The final proposition, "the most global and revealing," condemned the proposition that the pope "should adapt himself to progress, liberalism, and the modern culture." As John O'Malley comments: "Popes had issued condemnations many times before, but never with such a sweeping rejection of the reality of the world in which they lived."[21]

In stark contrast to this position, in a very different context, *Gaudium et Spes* takes a basically positive attitude to the dignity of the human person, to human equality, and human autonomy, all key values of the modern world. Particularly in chapter IV part one, *Gaudium et Spes* reflects on the "Role of the Church" – in other words, its mission – "in the Modern World." To individuals in the world, the church offers its solidarity with the contemporary commitment to human rights (41). Although it does not have a political, economic, or social mission, the gospel message "can be the source of commitment, direction, and vigor" for human communities (42). Although it recognizes the passing nature of human life, it values human activity and promotes active and responsible citizenship (43). The church also is enriched from its dialogue with secular society, learning from past history, from science, culture, and the arts. Openness to such riches only enhances the church's missionary efforts to witness to and preach the gospel worthily (44). These attitudes of openness, though always critical of reducing

---

[20] O'Malley, *What Happened at Vatican II*, 157–58.

[21] O'Malley, *Vatican I*, 105. The quotation from the *Syllabus* is from ed. Heinrich Denzinger, *Enchiridion symbolorum definitionum et declarationum de rebus fidei et morum/Compendium of Creeds, Definitions, and Declarations on Matters of Faith and Morals*, 43rd edition in Latin and English, ed. Robert Fastiggi and Anne Englund Nash (San Francisco, 2012), #2980 (p. 598).

Christianity to humanism or rationalism, are seen in other documents: on religious liberty, on missionary activity, on non-Christian religions, on education, and on the laity, to give a few examples.[22] Reading through the documents, it is striking how often a phrase like "in our times" appears.[23] The vision of Vatican II is clearly of a church whose mission embraces the world.

The Turn to Culture

Another indication of the missionary nature of the council is its turn to culture. A sensitivity to culture had always been part of the church's missionary activity, as attested by the work of Justin Martyr, the East Syrian missionaries in China, Cyril and Methodius, and Matteo Ricci.[24] Nevertheless, critics of Christian mission are more than justified in accusing missionaries of importing a Western religion and Western culture and disparaging the culture of the local peoples.[25] In the same way, as John XXIII realized, Christian practice and teaching in the twentieth century, even in the West, was in need of renewal and updating (aggiornamento). In his great opening speech of the council, John insisted that the church should always remain faithful to the received tradition. Nevertheless, he said, the church must always look at new ways of expressing these age-old and ever-valid treasures of the past. "The substance of the ancient doctrine of the deposit of faith is one thing, and the way in which it is presented is another."[26] New times, new situations, demand new ways of presenting the gospel – a truly missionary attitude.

John's missionary concerns for communicating the gospel were expressed early in the council in the document on the liturgy. The liturgy, it said, is made up of divinely instituted unchangeable elements but also elements that are subject to change. As time passes and circumstances change, these changeable elements *need* to be changed, so

---

[22] For example, DH 5–6; AG 11–12; NA 2; AA 7; Vatican Council II, Declaration on Christian Education *Gravissimum Educationis*, 1.

[23] For example, Vatican Council II, Decree on the Ministry and Life of Priests *Presbyerorum Ordinis*, 7, 16, 19.

[24] See, for example, Stephen B. Bevans and Roger P. Schroeder, *Constants in Context: A Theology of Mission for Today* (Maryknoll, NY: Orbis Books, 2004).

[25] To give one example of such critique, see Amos Yong and Barbara Brown Zikmund, eds., *Remembering Jamestown: Hard Questions about Christian Mission* (Eugene, OR: Wipf and Stock, 2010).

[26] John XXIII, "Pope John's Opening Speech," in *The Documents of Vatican II*, ed. Walter M. Abbott (New York: Guild Press/America Press, 1966), 715.

that the faithful can better understand the liturgical rites and participate more fully (SC 21). It is in this context that the constitution admitted the use of vernacular languages while keeping Latin as the norm (36), and in this context as well that it called for the adaptation of the liturgy "to the temperament and traditions of peoples" (37). Rather than imposing "a rigid uniformity" on every culture, the aim of the liturgy is to "cultivate and foster the qualities and talents of the various races and nations" (37). The council had in mind here the situation in "mission lands," but it implicitly recognized the importance of adaptation in every cultural situation.

Ad Gentes is paradigmatic in terms of its appreciation and sensitivity to local cultures and situations, even beyond the liturgy. Paragraph 11, for example, emphasizes the importance of the church's rootedness in particular cultural and social contexts. Christians should identify themselves with the people among whom they live, and participate in "their national and religious traditions," respecting "the seeds of the word which lie hidden among them." In this way, "through sincere and patient dialogue they themselves might learn the riches which a generous God has distributed among the nations." Paragraph 22 calls for the development of a theology that would be sensitive to local cultures, one that would be firmly rooted both in Christ and in the indigenous soil. In this way the faith can be explained in terms of local wisdom, customs, and philosophy. As *Gaudium et Spes* expresses it: "Indeed, this kind of adaptation and preaching of the revealed word must ever be the law of all evangelization" (44).

The council's most extensive reflection on culture takes place in this document on the church's mission in the modern world. While the document sometimes speaks of a "higher" kind of culture – philosophy, history, mathematics, science, and the arts (GS 57, 59), it clearly acknowledges the "plurality of cultures" recognized by the social sciences (53). The church, the document insists, is not tied to any one culture, but has received the mission to go to every people and every culture, "enriching both itself and the cultures themselves" (58). The council's turn to culture points to a church that finds its essence in communicating the gospel in ways that the peoples of the world can understand.

The Turn to Persuasion

Although he admits that it is a "problematic concept," John W. O'Malley argues that the "spirit" of Vatican II may well be found more in its "style" or *how* it teaches rather than in the content or *what* it teaches.[27] Previous councils – from Nicea to Vatican I – made use of two basic elements, both of which were rather juridical and polemical. The first was the "canon," a proposition that usually began as "who ever says ... " and ended with "*anathema sit*," or a sentence of condemnation or excommunication. The second element was a particular vocabulary that was appropriate to such a juridical and polemical literary genre. This vocabulary consisted of "words of threat and intimidation, words of surveillance and punishment, words of a superior speaking to an inferior – or an enemy. It consisted of power words."[28]

The style or literary genre of Vatican II, in contrast, was more pastoral or missionary. The inspiration for it might be traced to Pope John's seminal opening speech, in which he said that in opposing errors, the church has "frequently ... condemned them with the greatest severity." Today, however, the pope added, "the Spouse of Christ prefers to make use of the medicine of mercy rather than that of severity."[29] Instead of the rhetoric of threat and condemnation, therefore, what the council chose to do was to aim at inspiration and conversion of heart in an effort to communicate the good news that is the gospel. Its rhetoric was what O'Malley calls "epideictic," an "instrument of persuasion, not coercion."[30] Instead of a church caught up in its own righteousness, the council chose to portray the church as eager to share God's grace and graciousness with the entire world. As O'Malley puts it: "The council is speaking for the church and thus manifests what it holds to be the church's inner reality ... The council is speaking about the very identity of the church. It *teaches* by means of its style."[31]

Vatican II's style can be expressed in several categories. First, there are "horizontal-words" or "equality-words" like people of God, brothers and sisters, the priesthood of all believers, and collegiality. Second are words of "reciprocity" like cooperation, partnership, and collaboration. Words like pilgrim and servant are "humility words." Words that admit change like development, progress, and even evolution O'Malley calls words of "change." Finally, O'Malley says, there are "interiority-words" like consciousness and holiness.[32]

---

[27] John W. O'Malley, "Vatican II: Did Anything Happen?" in *Vatican II: Did Anything Happen?*, ed. David Schultenover (New York: Continuum, 2007), 81.

[28] O'Malley, *What Happened at Vatican II*, 45.

[29] John XXIII, "Pope John's Opening Speech," 718.

[30] O'Malley, *What Happened at Vatican II*, 47.

[31] Ibid., 49.

[32] See Ibid., 49–51.

These are words of mission. There is a confidence in what the church and the gospel is, and an urgency that that gospel be proclaimed to all peoples. At the same time, the council speaks to the world with gentleness and respect, ready to listen and dialogue with everyone, even enemies and unbelievers (see GS 44; 19–21).

The Turn to Baptism

A final indication that Vatican II proposes a missionary vision of the church is its turn to baptism as the fundamental sacrament of discipleship. Vatican II is rightly acclaimed for its move from imagining the church as an institution to imagining it as a community, the people of God. One of the most important moments at the council took place in the second session when Bishop Giuseppe Gargitter of Bolzano-Bressanone proposed to the council the idea – originated by Cardinal Suenens – that a new chapter be added to the revised schema, to be called "The People of God." Uncoupling this theme from the proposed chapter on the laity and placing it before chapters on both laity and hierarchy had the effect of emphasizing that before any distinction in the church there is a fundamental unity and equality. As O'Malley comments, "the first reality of the church is horizontal and consists of all the baptized, without distinction of rank. Only then comes the vertical reality, hierarchy."[33] Or, as *Lumen Gentium* 32 expresses it: "The chosen people of God, is, therefore, one: ... there is a common dignity of members deriving from their rebirth in Christ, a common grace as sons and daughters, a common vocation to perfection ... there is, then, no inequality arising from race or nationality, social condition or sex."

Although the council's theology of the laity may be somewhat ambiguous and inconsistent,[34] the turn to baptismal equality had profound effects on it. Through baptism, the laity share "in their own way" in the threefold office of Christ as priest, prophet, and king (servant) (LG 30). What this means is that they participate directly, not as "helpers" of the clergy, in the mission of the church – "it is by the Lord himself that they are assigned to the apostolate" (AA 3); "there is no such thing as a member who does not have a share in the mission of the whole body" (PO 2). All members of the people of God, and so lay women and men, participate in the priesthood of Christ, a priesthood they hold in

---

[33] O'Malley, *What Happened at Vatican II*, 178.
[34] See Richard R. Gaillardetz, *An Unfinished Council: Vatican II, Pope Francis, and the Renewal of Catholicism* (Collegeville, MN: Liturgical Press, 2015), 110–12.

common. As Richard Gaillardetz expresses it, "the substance of this common priesthood is the life of discipleship, following Christ in such a way that one's entire life becomes an offering to God." They exercise this priesthood particularly by participation in the liturgy, "because it sends believers forth into the world ... in order that they might serve the coming reign of God."[35] In fact, it is the particular responsibility of those who are ordained, as Pope John Paul II put it several decades later, to "help the People of God to exercise faithfully and fully the common priesthood which it has received."[36] In the same way the laity participate in Christ's prophetic office (LG 35). This entails not only Christian witness in their daily lives but also, "whenever God opens a door for the word" to proclaim it "confidently and perseveringly" according to their ability (AG 13). Finally, lay people share in Christ's kingly/servant office on account of the charisms with which each is endowed, and these are to be used to build up the church community and the reign of God in the world (LG 12; AA 7). Lay people also have some voice in the governance of the church. Not only are they encouraged to share their wants and needs with the clergy. According to their own professional competence or authority in certain areas, they are "entitled, and indeed sometimes duty-bound, to express their opinion on matters which concern the good of the church" (LG 37).

Baptism implies mission. There can be no passive members in the church, since the church is missionary by its very nature. As Gaillardetz notes, "the implications of the council's theology of baptism and discipleship can be properly grasped only in the context of its theology of mission."[37] Its priority of mission reflected a way of thinking about the church.

The council was indeed a "missionary council." Its vision of the church was to be people in mission, a communion-in-mission, called together for the life of the world.

A RENEWED UNDERSTANDING OF MISSION

When the council speaks of mission, however, it reflects an understanding that is very different from the one that is often understood. The

---

[35] Richard R. Gaillardetz, *Ecclesiology for a Global Church: A People Called and Sent* (Maryknoll, NY: Orbis Books, 2008), 189.

[36] Pope John Paul II, apostolic exhortation *Pastores Dabo Vobis* (Washington, DC: United States Catholic Conference, 1992), 17.

[37] Gaillardetz, *Ecclesiology for a Global Church*, 189.

council's renewed understanding of mission, in which the entire church is engaged, is one that goes beyond "foreign missions." It is an understanding that goes beyond efforts that result only in conversion to the church. Indeed, it is an understanding of mission that goes beyond only conversion to Christianity. Mission is the church's participation in the mission of the Triune God, and so is about the well-being and flourishing of all humanity and all creation.

Beyond Foreign Missions

There is certainly ample evidence that mission refers to "the missions" in exotic locations where the gospel had not been preached sufficiently or the church had not been sufficiently established. This understanding is present especially in *Ad Gentes* (see 6 particularly), but it is also present in *Sacrosanctum Concilium* (e.g. 39, 65, 68, 119), in *Lumen Gentium* (16–17), and in *Unitatis Redintegratio* (10). It is implied in the Decree on the Ministry and Life of Priests *Presbyterorum Ordinis* in the context of the distribution of priests throughout the world (PO 10).

Nevertheless, much more evident in the council's documents is a more general understanding of mission as a commitment to preach the gospel faithfully at all times and in all places. This commitment is undertaken in obedience to Christ's command, originally given to the disciples and the twelve apostles (e.g. CD 3; NA 2, 4; DH 14; AG 3, 5, 7). It is also, however, something that is incumbent on the church as it understands the truth that God has revealed to all humanity. "Christ is the light of nations," *Lumen Gentium* proclaims, and the church "ardently desires to bring to all humanity that light of Christ which is resplendent on the face of the church" (1). Such motivation is expressed implicitly in the first paragraphs of *Lumen Gentium*, but quite explicitly in the statement in *Ad Gentes* that the church is missionary by its very nature because it participates in the life of the Trinity (AG 2). This phrase also points to the fact that mission is constitutive of the church, that it is not simply one thing the church does, but that which gives it existence. *Ad Gentes* emphasizes that mission is first and foremost about preaching the gospel to unbelievers but it also acknowledges that the church's missionary identity is lived out in its ordinary pastoral activity and its work for Christian unity (6). Mission includes "missions," but goes far beyond such a restricted understanding. It is everything the church does.

Beyond Conversion to the Church

Mission in the council documents seems sometimes to be quite ecclesiocentric. The documents often give the impression that mission exists to bring all peoples into the church – the Catholic Church. The last of the four goals of the council articulated in *Sacrosanctum Concilium* is to help the church more effectively call all humanity into its fold (SC 1). It is implied in the conviction that "all are called to this catholic unity of the people of God" (LG 13). It is expressed as well in the opening paragraph of the Declaration on Religious Liberty *Dignitatis Humanae*, speaking of the "Catholic and Apostolic Church, to which the Lord Jesus entrusted the task of spreading it among all peoples" (DH 1).

There are other passages, however, which speak of the church's mission in a less ecclesiocentric way – as one of preaching the gospel and its promise of salvation. The document on the liturgy describes the church's mission as announcing the good news of salvation to unbelievers, calling them to repentance and thus salvation (SC 9). The introduction to the Declaration on Christian Education *Gravissimum Educationis* points to the fact that the way the church fulfills Christ's command to mission is to promote human welfare throughout peoples' lives (Introduction). In *Lumen Gentium*, the laity should act in a way that the church's mission should be relevant in today's world (36). *Ad Gentes* proclaims that missionary activity is nothing more and nothing less "than the manifestation of God's plan, its epiphany and realization in the world and in history; that by which God, through mission, clearly brings to its conclusion the history of salvation" (AG 9).

This wider and more eschatological understanding of mission is expressed in the council's rather hesitant and yet hugely significant statement that "church" and "kingdom" are not the same reality. Although Pope John does make this equation in his September 1962 radio address,[38] *Lumen Gentium* 5 breaks with this theological tradition. It speaks of the church's mission as "proclaiming and establishing among all peoples the kingdom of Christ and of God, and is, on earth, the seed and the beginning of that kingdom." This is a move, Gaillardetz notes, that will be developed by theologians and the magisterium in future decades.[39]

More than Conversion to Christianity

It is in the Constitution on the Church in the Modern World, however – one of the very last to be promulgated by the council – that many of the ambiguities of its understanding of mission are resolved. *Gaudium et Spes* begins with the famous proclamation that the "joys and hopes, the

---

[38] Pope John XXIII, Radio Address, *Enchiridion Vaticanum*, 25.
[39] Gaillardetz, *Ecclesiology for a Global Church*, 190.

grief and anguish of the people of our time" are the same as that of the church (1). The church therefore desires to be of service to humanity (3). It is clear in its conviction and duty to proclaim the truth of Christ, but it does so aware of the deep changes that have taken place in the world (5–7), of the imbalances among the peoples of the world (8), and the reasons for unbelief – often due to Christians' betrayal of the gospel (19–21). The church's role (that is, mission) is to uphold the dignity of human nature (41) and work for the flourishing of the economic and political order (42–43). But its role is also to acknowledge that grace is at work in the world and that it has profited from the advances of science and the beauty of artists. The document goes on to discuss issues regarding the family, culture, justice, and world peace (46–90). Mission is more than efforts of conversion to Christianity and efforts of getting people to join the church. *Gaudium et Spes* makes clear that it is working with God to make God's world a more just and liveable place, where women and men can live as sisters and brothers together. The document's conclusion emphasizes the importance of dialogue – both within the church and with the world (92). In *Gaudium et Spes* we find the key to the renewed understanding of mission on which the council built its ecclesiology of communion-in-mission.

Other documents complete and enrich this missionary ecclesiology. *Dignitatis Humanae* insists, on the one hand, on the church's right to exist and on Christians' right to practice their religion freely and openly (4). On the other hand, the freedom of religion taught by the council is a freedom for *everyone* from any kind of coercion by anyone or any institution in matters of religious conviction (1). This latter concern, of course, has great implications for mission, since mission is always about the free invitation to respond to God's grace and never about the manipulation or coercion involved in proselytism (see AG 13).

The acknowledgment of the importance of religious freedom forms the basis for the acknowledgment of grace outside the boundaries of the church, and offers a foundation for the importance of dialogue with other Christians and members of other religions as an essential and constitutive dimension of Christian mission. The council never used the phrase "outside the church there is no salvation." Rather, it spoke of how other Christians are "joined" to the Catholic Church by baptism (LG 15), with the result that working for the church's unity is part of the church's mission (AG 6). Non-Christians are "related" to God's people in a variety of ways (LG 16). Most closely related are members of the Jewish people, but any people who believe in God the Creator are included here, first of whom are Muslims (LG 16). Even those who do not believe in God but who sincerely seek God and/or follow their consciences are embraced by God's grace (LG 16). The Declaration on the Relation of the Church to Non-Christian Religions *Nostra Aetate* insists that Christians are bound to preach the gospel, but acknowledges nonetheless that the church does not reject anything that is good in other religions, because they "often reflect a ray of that truth that enlightens all men and women" (2). Dialogue, therefore, is a basic way of engaging in mission. Anne Hunt connects the practice of dialogue with the church's trinitarian nature: "To recognize that the church is missionary by her very nature, with her mission deriving from the Trinity, is also to recognize that she is dialogical by nature, both *ad intra* and *ad extra*."[40]

Sacrosanctum Concilium and *Ad Gentes* emphasize the "turn to culture" in the church's commitment to evangelization. Mission recognizes that culture is an ally rather than an enemy, and that the church's evangelizing work can only be enhanced if it recognizes the "seeds of the word" present even before the missionaries' arrival (AG 11).

The church envisioned in the council documents is a missionary church, a communion-in-mission. It is a church that is not afraid to witness to and preach Christ to the world, and it understands itself as the place where the reign of God is most fully inaugurated in this world. It is the universal sacrament of salvation (LG 48), the kingdom's sign and instrument (LG 1). As a *sacrament*, however, it also points to grace beyond its boundaries: grace in the world, grace in the world's religions, grace in the world's cultures, grace in human searching, and grace in the struggle for peace and justice in the world. The church envisioned by the council documents is a church that is called to be itself, in the words of Yves Congar, with its whole heart.[41]

A GROWING RECEPTION

As noted in the beginning of this chapter, the standard reception of the ecclesiology of Vatican II has been the recognition of the move from visible society to communion, from institution to people of God, an interpretation confirmed by the 1985 Synod of Bishops. In 1975, however, Paul VI had alluded to *Ad Gentes'* description of the church's essential missionary nature in his Apostolic Exhortation

---

[40] Anne Hunt, "The Trinitarian Depths of Vatican II," in *50 Years on*, 149.
[41] Yves Congar, *Power and Poverty in the Church* (Baltimore: Helicon, 1964), 131.

Evangelii Nuntiandi by speaking of the church as "linked to evangelization" in its "most intimate being."[42] In 1990, John Paul II once more emphasized this essential missionary nature, and even though his encyclical *Redemptoris Missio* was focused mostly on the mission *ad gentes*, he also spoke of the church's mission in terms of the church's pastoral work and its need to engage in a "new evangelization" with those peoples and parts of the world who had drifted from the practice of faith, or who had become indifferent to it.[43] In an intriguing section, John Paul moves mission beyond territorial limits to speak of "modern forms of the Aereopagus" in terms of the world of communications, commitment to peace and justice, safeguarding the integrity of the created world, the world of art, science, and the world's cities (RM 37). Although he was strong in his understanding of the church as communion, *Redemptoris Missio* seems to press beyond to a more missionary perspective of the church as communion-in-mission.

John Paul II's call for a "new evangelization" emerged more and more clearly in his pontificate. It was a call that he described as "new in its ardour, methods, and expression."[44] Increasingly, although it was not confined to the West, this was a way of speaking about the church's mission in countries that had abandoned or become caught up in secular values. Implied by the "new evangelization" was that the church was in a missionary situation everywhere it found itself. There was still need for a first witness to and proclamation of the gospel in traditionally "mission lands" and among peoples who had not heard the gospel, but there was also a need to think missiologically in places that had long thought of themselves as mission-sending churches.

Unfortunately, however, the "new evangelization" focused increasingly on the "re-evangelization" of the West. This was the task uppermost in the mind of Pope Benedict XVI, who in 2010 established the Pontifical Council for Promoting the New Evangelization, and called for the 2012 Synod of Bishops to take the new evangelization as its theme. The result of the synod, however, was to reconnect the new

---

[42] Paul VI, *apostolic exhortation Evangelii Nuntiandi* (Washington, DC: United States Catholic Conference, 1966), 15.

[43] John Paul II, *encyclical letter Redemptoris Missio* (Washington, DC: United States Catholic Conference, 1991), 1, 34.

[44] John Paul II, Discourse to the XIX Assembly of CELAM (March 9, 1983), *L'Osservatore Romano: Weekly Edition in English* (April 18, 1983), 9; *Acta Apostolicae Sedis* 75 (1983): 778.

evangelization with the church's worldwide mission, and to once more emphasize the essential missionary nature of the church as a communion-in-mission.[45]

Significantly, Pope Francis's lengthy post-synodal apostolic exhortation *Evangelii Gaudium* mentions the new evangelization only twelve times. As Francis's biographer Austen Ivereigh comments, "Francis paid only lip service to Benedict XVI's synod on the new evangelization the year before," but he demonstrated "in every paragraph what it means to evangelize."[46] In this powerful and eminently readable document, Francis speaks of the church as a "community of missionary disciples" (EG 24), dreaming he says "of a 'missionary option,' . . . a missionary impulse capable of transforming everything," so that the church "can be suitably channeled for the evangelization of today's world rather than for her self-preservation" (EG 27). Perhaps more than any other document since Vatican II, *Evangelii Gaudium* recognizes the council's missionary ecclesiology as a communion-in-mission.

Catholic ecclesiology in the last several years has also slowly begun to recognize the dynamic, missionary nature of the church that Vatican II inspired. Scholars such as Richard R. Gaillardetz and Neil Ormerod have published major works in ecclesiology that point to the essential missionary nature of the church. Stephen Bevans and Roger Schroeder have emphasized the rich ecclesial nature of missiology, and emphasize a theology of mission that is inclusive of witness and proclamation, working for justice, inculturation, reconciliation, and dialogue. Patrick J. Brennan has recognized the important implications of mission for ordinary pastoral work.[47] One can only hope that, in a globalized world that is experiencing unparalleled migration, poverty, and ecological fragility, and in a rapidly secularizing world in so many places (including urban areas in Asia, Africa, and Latin America), the reception of Vatican II's missionary ecclesiology will continue to gain ground.

---

[45] See Stephen Bevans, SVD, "Beyond the New Evangelization: Toward a Missionary Ecclesiology for the Twenty-First Century," in *A Church with Open Doors: Catholic Ecclesiology for the Third Millennium*, ed. Richard R. Gaillardetz and Edward P. Hahnenberg (Collegeville, MN: Liturgical Press, 2015), 3–22.

[46] Austen Ivereigh, *The Great Reformer: Pope Francis and the Making of a Radical Pope* (New York: Macmillan, 2014), 210.

[47] Gaillardetz, *Ecclesiology for a Global Church*; Neil Ormerod, *Re-Visioning the Church: An Experiment in Systematic-Historical Ecclesiology* (Minneapolis: Fortress Press, 2014); Bevans and Schroeder, *Constants in Context*; Patrick J. Brennan, *The Mission-Driven Parish* (Maryknoll, NY: Orbis Books, 2007).

FURTHER READING

Bevans, Stephen. "Beyond the New Evangelization: Toward a Missionary Theology for the Twenty-First Century." In *A Church with Open Doors: Catholic Ecclesiology for the Third Millennium*, edited by Richard R. Gaillardetz and Edward P. Hahnenberg. Collegeville, MN: The Liturgical Press, 2015.

Bevans, Stephen. "Revisiting Mission at Vatican II: Theology and Practice for Today's Missionary Church." In *50 Years On: Probling the Riches of Vatican II*, edited by David G. Scholtenover. Collegeville, MN: Liturgical Press, 2015.

Bevans, Stephen and Jeffrey Gros. *Evangelization and Religious Freedom: Ad Gentes, Dignitatis Humanae.* Mahwah, NJ: Paulist Press, 2009.

Gaillardetz, Richard R. *An Unfinished Council: Vatican II, Pope Francis, and the Renewal of Catholicism.* Collegeville, MN: The Liturgical Press, a Michael Glazier Book, 2015.

Gaillardetz, Richard R. *Ecclesiology for a Global Church: A People Called and Sent.* Maryknoll, NY: Orbis Books, 2008.

Gaillardetz, Richard R. *The Church in the Making: Lumen Gentium, Christus Dominus, Orientalium Ecclesiarum.* Mahwah, NJ and New York: Paulist Press, 2006.

Ormerod, Neil. *Re-Visioning the Church: An Experiment in Systematic-Historical Ecclesiology.* Minneapolis: Fortress Press, 2014.

Pope Francis. Apostolic Exhortation *Evangelii Gaudium*. Washington, DC: United States Conference of Catholic Bishops, 2013.

9 Revelation

RICHARD R. GAILLARDETZ

The church is not its own lord. It is the *congregatio fidelium*, the gathering of the Christian faithful, called into being by the Divine One who addresses us as friends and invites us into God's own company (DV 2). This invitation warrants a certain hermeneutical priority for the council's teaching on divine revelation,[1] a priority explicitly acknowledged by the Doctrine Commission.[2] The council's theology of revelation represents one of its most dramatic theological transpositions. It is in evidence throughout the entire conciliar corpus, as we will see, but the key text remains the Dogmatic Constitution on Divine Revelation, *Dei Verbum*.

THE LONG JOURNEY TO *DEI VERBUM*

On the eve of Vatican II, the dominant theology of revelation was still largely indebted to the teaching of Vatican I's dogmatic constitution, *Dei Filius*, as it found its way into the dogmatic manuals that were used for the training of clerics. Vatican I's teaching had focused on the proper relationship between faith and reason. Its presentation was quite balanced for the time, trying as it was to steer between the nineteenth-century Scylla of rationalism and Charybdis of fideism. Yet the document was less concerned with the actual content of God's saving offer than with the more formal aspects of revelation, namely the objective certitude it offered and its accessibility by faith. This tendency would

---

[1] This argument has been proposed by several theologians: Jared Wicks, SJ, *Investigating Vatican II* (Washington, DC: Catholic University of America Press, 2018), 84; Gerald O'Collins, SJ, *"Dei Verbum* and Revelation," in *God's Word and the Church's Council*, ed. Mark O'Brien, OP, and Christopher Monaghan, CP (Adelaide: ATF Theology, 2014), 2; Christoph Theobald, SJ, *La reception du concile Vatican II, I. Accéder à la source* (Paris: Éditions du Cerf, 2009), 769; Ormond Rush, *Still Interpreting Vatican II* (Mahwah, NJ: Paulist Press, 2004), 42–43.
[2] *Acta Synodalia* 4/1: 341.

continue in the dogmatic manuals of the late nineteenth and early twentieth centuries. The manualists' treatment of revelation was also crafted in reaction to the perceived threat of the modernists who, it was thought, gave excessive emphasis to the subjective and experiential character of revelation. For Vatican I and the manualists, revelation was comprehended according to the model of divine "speech" (locutio) and presented as a set of clearly articulated, propositional truth-claims that would then be defended with prooftexts from Scripture, church fathers, and prior magisterial pronouncements.

During the council's preparatory period, two draft texts had been prepared by the Theological Preparatory Commission, "The Sources of Revelation" and "Guarding the Purity of the Deposit of Faith." Both were heavily indebted to the propositional model of revelation. Alternative texts were in circulation during the preparatory period, including a more biblically grounded text authored by the Secretariat for Promoting Christian Unity; a Christologically oriented text produced by two influential German periti, Karl Rahner, SJ and Joseph Ratzinger; and a third by the noted French peritus, Yves Congar, OP, on the relationship between Scripture and tradition. Unfortunately, the commission ignored these entirely.[3]

The bishops debated the draft "The Sources of Revelation" during the first session. The draft text on the deposit of faith never made it to the council floor, though select elements were eventually incorporated into the main text on revelation. Almost immediately on being introduced to the council bishops, the draft on revelation was subjected to harsh criticism. Many noted that its treatment of Scripture drew little on Pope Pius XII's 1943 encyclical, Divino Afflante Spiritu, in which the pope had encouraged Catholic biblical scholars to make prudent use of the modern tools of historical biblical criticism. Others complained that the text's dependence on the disputed "two-source theory" (the theory that Scripture and tradition represented two independent sources of revelation) was foreign to the ancient tradition and was deeply anti-ecumenical.

After a number of often heated exchanges, the council leadership conducted a straw vote regarding the status of the draft. Surprisingly, the vote was framed not as a vote on the approval of the draft but as a vote to end debate on the schema (a vote which would necessitate it being set aside in favor of the production of a fresh text). This led to the

---

[3] See Wicks, Investigating Vatican II, 80–97.

odd situation of bishops being asked to vote in the affirmative if they wished to reject the text, and in the negative if they wished to retain it. In spite of the confusion with the ballot formulation, a clear majority voted in favor of ending the debate and removing the text, but the vote came just short of the required two-thirds majority. The next day, in a rare case of Pope John intervening in the affairs of the council, the pope called for the removal of the text on his own authority and mandated the creation of a new mixed commission to draft an alternative text. This text would have the longest history of any council document, spanning all four sessions. Over the course of its documentary history, some of the most influential council *periti* would contribute to the text: Umberto Betti, OFM; Congar; Jean Daniélou, SJ; Alois Grillmeier, SJ; Piet Smulders, SJ; Rahner; Ratzinger; Heribert Schauf; and Otto Semmelroth, SJ.

CENTRAL THEMES

Given the decisive significance of the council's treatment of revelation for almost every topic the council considered, it will be helpful to identify and explore six distinct features of the council's theology of revelation. Our focus will be on *Dei Verbum* while also considering the treatment of these themes in other documents.

Revelation as God's Self-Communication in Love

The opening sentence of *Dei Verbum* describes the task of the council: "Hearing the Word of God reverently and proclaiming it confidently, this holy synod makes its own the words of St. John" (DV 1). With these words the council announced a renewed theology of revelation closely related to the emerging ecclesiology of the council. The church is not a self-contained institution with divine truth as its private possession. Rather, it transcends itself in a posture of openness and receptivity to divine revelation, a revelation which it receives as servant rather than as master.

Chapter 1 of *Dei Verbum* begins with an account of revelation that stands in stark contrast to the neo-scholastic presentation found in the preparatory draft. This chapter was not present, in any form, in the preparatory text provided for the bishops. That draft had turned immediately to the question of the sources of revelation. Here, by contrast, we begin with the presentation of the primacy of the living Word of God, spoken from the beginning of creation, incarnate in Jesus of Nazareth, and proclaimed in the life of the church. The inclusion of this theme gives early evidence of the fruit of ecumenical conversation for the council's work, as some scholars have detected here the influence of the Protestant theologian Karl Barth.[4]

This opening chapter attends not to the communication of discrete truths but to the trinitarian dynamism by which God shares God's very self in a communicative event, an eternal act of divine self-disclosure that invites its recipients into relationship.

> By this revelation, then, the invisible God, from the fullness of his love, addresses men and women as his friends, and lives among them, in order to invite and receive them into his own company. The pattern of this revelation unfolds through deeds and words which are intrinsically connected: the works performed by God in the history of salvation show forth and confirm the doctrine and realities signified by the words; the words, for their part, proclaim the works, and bring to light the mystery they contain. The most intimate truth thus revealed about God and human salvation shines forth for us in Christ, who is himself both the mediator and the sum total of revelation. (DV 2)

This rich text includes several key features that deserve our attention. We begin with its strikingly personalist tone. Revelation in its primary modality comes to us as an invitation into relationship. The Father addresses us not by way of a text or proposition but as a divine person, Jesus Christ, who is "both the mediator and the sum total of revelation."

Numerous commentators have noted the significance of this passage for Catholic theology. Joseph Ratzinger, in his authoritative commentary, notes:

> We can see again here how little intellectualism and doctrinalism are able to comprehend the nature of revelation, which is not concerned with talking *about* something that is quite external to the person, but with the realization of the existence of man, with the relation of the human "I" to the divine "thou," so that the purpose of this dialogue is ultimately not information, but unity and transformation.[5]

---

[4] Joseph Ratzinger, "Chapter 1: Revelation Itself," in *Commentary on the Documents of Vatican II*, 5 vols., ed. Herbert Vorgrimler (New York: Herder and Herder, 1989, originally published, 1969), 3: 170.

[5] Ibid., 175.

Dermot Lane contends that what we have here "is a clear movement . . . away from revelation as simply *revelata* (truths disclosed) to *revelatio* (personal disclosure)."[6] In a similar vein, Gerald O'Collins highlights the use of "mystery" in the singular. This is not unique to this passage, he notes, calling our attention to the fact that the council documents appeal to "mystery" in the singular 106 times, and to "mysteries" only 22 times.[7] The use of mystery in the singular recalls for us the sense of revelation, not as a communication of truths or mysteries, but of God's eternal self-communication. Article 5 draws to completion the trinitarian grammar of this revelation that comes to us from the Father in Christ, affirming that it is the Holy Spirit "who moves the heart and converts it to God, and opens the eyes of the mind and 'makes it easy for all to accept and believe the truth'." As addressed to humanity, revelation is fully realized, it becomes fully "word," only when it is received. It is the Holy Spirit who makes this reception effective.

The personalist and trinitarian account of God's revelation is by no means limited to *Dei Verbum*. In *Lumen Gentium* it is Christ, "the light of nations," before whom the church wishes to bring all humanity (LG 1). The church is called into existence by God who sends Christ to the world to make us, by the power of the Holy Spirit, adopted sons and daughters (LG 3). In the Constitution on the Sacred Liturgy, *Sacrosanctum Concilium*, we are told that our divine worship represents our graced response to God who "when the fullness of time had come, sent his Son, the Word made flesh, anointed by the Holy Spirit, to preach the Gospel to the poor, to soothe the broken hearted, to be a bodily and spiritual physician, the mediator between God and humanity" (SC 5). The Pastoral Constitution on the Church in the Modern World, *Gaudium et Spes*, positions the church in radical solidarity with humankind as a community "united in Christ and guided by the holy Spirit in their pilgrimage towards the Father's kingdom, bearers of a message of salvation for all of humanity" (GS 1). The Decree on the Church's Missionary Activity, *Ad Gentes*, invokes the trinitarian shape of God's invitation to humanity to share in the divine life (AG 2–3).

The Soteriological Character of Revelation

Dei Verbum 2 tells us that revelation comes not only in words but in "deeds," that is, God's action in salvation history. God's self-communicative "word" cannot be separated from God's saving agency

---

[6] Dermot Lane, *The Experience of God* (New York: Veritas, 1981), 56–57.
[7] O'Collins, "*Dei Verbum* and Revelation," 4.

in human history. Articles 3–4 narrate the unfolding of this divine action in history. Revelation does not offer a collection of fun facts to know about God; it has as its goal the salvation of the world. God reveals to us the offer of saving love in Christ "to deliver us from the darkness of sin and death, and to raise us up to eternal life" (DV 4). The Christocentrism of the council's theology of revelation stands in contrast to Vatican I's own account of revelation in which, according to René Latourelle, it was the church and not Christ that stood at the center.[8] This emphasis on the soteriological character of divine revelation and the inseparability of "word" and "deed" was introduced into the text, directly or indirectly, by theologians Piet Smulders and Jean Daniélou. It may also have been encouraged by the widely distributed Ratzinger/Rahner text mentioned previously.[9]

According to Vatican II, revelation comes to its term in the paschal mystery: "Everything to do with his presence and his manifestation of himself was involved in achieving this: his words and works, signs and miracles, but above all his death and glorious resurrection from the dead, and finally his sending of the Spirit of truth" (DV 4). This revelation of God's saving love is mediated, and not only through God's deeds in human history; it is also mediated sacramentally through the church, which is "the universal sacrament of salvation" (LG 48, AG 1).

A Dynamic Theology of Tradition

One of the most problematic features of the preparatory schema was its articulation of the relationship between Scripture and tradition. Through most of the first thousand years of Christianity, few conceived of tradition as something completely separate from Scripture. Tradition was the faith of the church testified to in Scripture and now preserved and developed through the example of martyrs, the witness of ordinary believers, the celebration of the liturgy and sacraments, daily practices of Christian discipleship, theological reflection, and Christian art. Only in the Middle Ages does tradition begin to acquire a more independent status as a collection both of church teachings and customs distinct from Scripture.

The question of the proper theological relationship between Scripture and tradition did not arise in a formal sense until the Protestant Reformation and the Reformers' espousal of the *sola scriptura* doctrine.

---

[8] René Latourelle, "Le Christ signe de la révélation selon la constitution 'Dei Verbum'," *Gregorianum* 46 (1966): 658–709, at 686–88.

[9] Wicks, *Investigating Vatican II*, 85–94.

The Reformers objected to the haze of accumulated customs, practices, and speculative propositions that had proliferated in late medieval Catholicism, all of which, in their view, obscured the evangelical message of the Bible. The first formal Catholic articulation of the church's own understanding of the relationship between Scripture and tradition came at the Council of Trent, largely in response to the Reformers. In one of its decrees the council tried to articulate the proper relationship between Scripture and the various traditions of the church (Trent did not refer to "tradition" in the singular). An early draft proposed that divine truths were contained "partly" in the "written books" and "partly" in unwritten traditions. The final text, however, was revised to read that truth was found "*both* in the written books *and* in unwritten traditions."[10] The preliminary formulation suggested that these were two distinct sources of divine truth while the final formulation was at least open to the interpretation that there were not different *sources* of truth at all but only different *modes of expression*. Unfortunately, many theologians and clerics would, after the Reformation, maintain a position more reflective of the first formulation. In other words, with important exceptions (e.g., Bossuet, Möhler, Newman), many would continue to hold the view that Scripture and tradition were distinct sources of revelation. This tendency would continue in the nineteenth- and twentieth-century manualist tradition and it appeared in the council's preparatory draft on the sources of revelation. That draft also suffered from a pronounced subordination of Scripture to tradition.

The final text of *Dei Verbum* is noteworthy for its reconsideration of the relationship between Scripture and tradition. The reworked text drew on a trinitarian theology of revelation and affirmed that the living Word, incarnate in Jesus Christ, is the one source of revelation. Scripture and tradition "make up a single sacred deposit of the word of God, which is entrusted to the church" (DV 10). Here the council restores the ancient unity of Scripture and tradition. Scripture and tradition were distinct but interrelated modalities of God's one self-communication in "Christ the Lord, in whom the entire revelation of the most high God is summed up" (DV 7). The good news of Jesus Christ, the fullness of divine revelation, was proclaimed by the whole Christian community under the leadership of the apostles. The apostolic witness was preserved in both biblical canon and the ongoing *paradosis* or "handing on" of the apostolic faith in the Christian community. The council

---

[10] Norman Tanner, ed., *Decrees of Ecumenical Councils* (Washington, DC: Georgetown University Press, 1990), 2: 663. The emphasis is mine.

established the unity of Scripture and tradition in the one Word whose presence in human history comes to its unsurpassable actualization in Jesus Christ. The unity of Scripture, tradition, and the living communion of the church itself is fundamental.

In contrast to Trent, Vatican II chose to consider tradition in the singular rather than the plural; tradition was a living, dynamic reality. Rather than delineate, materially, the content of tradition, the council offered a more formal definition, asserting that tradition "comprises everything handed on by the apostles that serves to make the people of God live their lives in holiness and increase their faith" (DV 8). This was followed by one of the most important theological passages in all the council documents:

> The tradition that comes from the apostles makes progress in the church, with the help of the holy Spirit. There is a growth in insight into the realities and words that are being passed on. This comes about through the contemplation and study of believers who ponder these things in their hearts. It comes from the intimate sense of spiritual realities which they experience. And it comes from the preaching of those who, on succeeding to the office of bishop, have received the sure charism of truth. Thus, as the centuries go by, the church is always advancing towards the plenitude of divine truth, until eventually the words of God are fulfilled in it. (DV 8)

Congar, among others, clearly played a hand in the drafting of this text. The passage draws inspiration from the thought of nineteenth-century figures like Newman and Möhler. A number of specific contributions in this passage to a renewed theology of tradition are worthy of further reflection.

First, the text no longer singles out the magisterium as the sole agent for the development of tradition. Rather, the text identifies three overlapping created agencies, two explicitly and one implicitly. The text explicitly mentions the sure preaching of the bishops but, provocatively, precedes this reference by first affirming the contemplation and spiritual experience of ordinary believers. Tradition develops because of the contributions of all God's people. This claim is reinforced in *Lumen Gentium*'s assertion that the whole people of God possess by baptism a supernatural instinct for the faith (*sensus fidei*) that allows them to receive the faith of the apostles, to penetrate its meaning, and to apply it more profoundly in their lives (LG 12). It occurs whenever a parent catechizes their child, whenever the liturgy is celebrated and the gospel proclaimed, whenever the values of the gospel are testified to in the work habits and attitudes of Christians in the marketplace and their daily advocacy for peace and justice.

Scholars and theologians represent the implicit third agent in the development of tradition. Their role is suggested indirectly in the phrase, "the contemplation *and study* by believers." According to Umberto Betti, OFM, secretary of the sub-commission that drafted this text, the words *"et studio,"* were inserted after *"contemplatione"* in the third draft as a response to several requests from bishops, who asked for some reference to the work of scholars and theologians in the development of tradition.[11]

Second, we see in this text a wonderful example of the council's recovery of pneumatology. The Holy Spirit is the transcendent agent of tradition's growth and development. It is the Holy Spirit who confers on believers the supernatural instinct for the faith, and it is the Holy Spirit who empowers the teaching ministry of the magisterium. It is precisely because both the *sensus fidei* and the magisterium are both empowered by the same Spirit that they cannot be placed in a competitive relationship with one another.[12]

Third, *Dei Verbum* 8 testifies to the eschatological character of revelation. As befits a "pilgrim church," the council modestly acknowledged only that the church was "advancing towards the plenitude of divine truth, until eventually the words of God are fulfilled in it." This passage reflects an eschatological humility that was typical of the council.[13] It is one thing to say that the church possesses the fullness of truth, as would have been common in the decades prior to the council. It is altogether something different to say that the church is moving *toward* the fullness of divine truth.

The council also departed from the preconciliar tendency to grant the magisterium authority over Scripture and tradition. The council's treatment of the magisterium is consistent with *Dei Verbum's* opening lines which began with *hearing* God's Word. The magisterium must first listen and learn before it can teach. The bishops' teaching is not a *determinatio fidei*, an independent determination of the faith of the church, but a *testificatio fidei*, an authoritative witness to that which the bishops have received, to that which they have heard.

---

[11] Umberto Betti, OFM, *La dottrina del concilio Vaticano II sulla trasmissione della Rivelazione* (Rome: Pontificium Athenaeum Antonianum, 1985), 152n75.

[12] For an exploration of Vatican II's non-competitive ecclesiology see Richard R. Gaillardetz, *An Unfinished Council* (Collegeville, MN: Liturgical Press, 2015), 91–113.

[13] Ibid., 73–89.

This Magisterium is not superior to the word of God, but is rather its servant. It teaches only what has been handed on to it. At the divine command and with the help of the Holy Spirit, it listens to this devoutly, guards it reverently and expounds it faithfully. All that it proposes for belief as being divinely revealed it draws from this sole deposit of faith. (DV 10)

Finally, although the council made considerable contributions toward a renewed theology of tradition, we must point out the failure of the council to explicitly acknowledge the necessary distinction between tradition and traditions as Congar had done in his own work.[14] Explicitly acknowledging this distinction would have allowed the council to affirm that not every aspect of tradition is necessarily positive or has enduring value.

The Circumscribed Role of Doctrine and the Hierarchy of Truths

We have noted here the council's consistent efforts to shift away from a strictly propositional theology of revelation. It would be wrong to assume, however, that the council wished to reject the necessary role of propositional truths communicated through church doctrine. Nevertheless, the council was unquestionably concerned to avoid the harsh dogmatism that was so often evident in magisterial pronouncements in the century prior to the council. In many ways, the council was guided by Pope John XXIII's treatment of the topic in his remarkable opening address, *Gaudet Mater Ecclesia*. In that address he offered an unambiguous affirmation of the church's fidelity to its doctrinal heritage. However, he also insisted that fidelity to the church's doctrinal heritage means more than the rote repetition of doctrinal formulas.

The Christian, Catholic and apostolic spirit of the whole world expects a step forward toward a doctrinal penetration and a formation of consciousness in faithful and perfect conformity to the authentic doctrine, which, however, should be studied and expounded through the methods of research and through the literary forms of modern thought. The substance of the ancient doctrine of the deposit of faith is one thing, and the way in which it is presented is another.[15]

---

[14] Yves Congar, OP, *Tradition and Traditions* (New York: Macmillan, 1967).

[15] Pope John XXIII, "Pope John's Opening Speech to the Council" (*Gaudet Mater Ecclesia*), English translation taken from Walter M. Abbott, SJ, ed., *The Documents of Vatican II* (New York: Herder and Herder,1989), 1: 710–19, at 715.

The pope exhibited an understanding of doctrine quite different from what was found in the manual tradition. According to Pope John, doctrine is rooted in particular historical contexts and has to be studied "through the methods of research and through the literary forms of modern thought." Most doctrinal teachings emerged in the church not as theoretical proposals but as determinate responses to particular church crises or challenges. The appropriate pastoral application of a church doctrine requires that one knows something of the historical and pastoral context in which a teaching first emerged. In addition, as the pope insisted, the church must always be open to the possibility that a doctrine may need to be reformulated in ways that better express its deep meaning and which are more conducive to its proper communication in the modern age.

From this more sophisticated appeal to church doctrine Pope John then offered a critical assessment of the way in which church teaching authority had been exercised in the past. An emphasis on the vigorous condemnation of error must be replaced, he insisted, by the "medicine of mercy" and by persuasively demonstrating the truth of church teaching. This requires a teaching magisterium "which is predominantly pastoral in character."[16] The church must not be content with offering a mere repetition of doctrinal formulations; what is demanded is a penetration of church doctrine in view of the pressing questions of our age.

The council's consideration of the role of doctrine is marked by many of the pope's concerns. We see a pronounced humility regarding the claims of church doctrine.

> The Church is guardian of the deposit of God's word and draws religious and moral principles from it, but it does not always have a ready answer to every question. Still, it is eager to associate the light of revelation with the experience of humanity in trying to clarify the course upon which it has recently entered. (GS 33)

This more measured appraisal of the place of church doctrine is also evident in the council's teaching on the "hierarchy of truths" found in the Decree on Ecumenism, *Unitatis Redintegratio*.

The term was first brought into the council's deliberations by Archbishop Andrea Pangrazio in November of 1963.[17] He wished to

---

[16] Ibid., 715.
[17] See Catherine Clifford, "L'herméneutique d'un principe herméneutique: La hiérarchie des vérités," in *L'Autorité et les autorités: L'herméneutique théologique*

emphasize the substantial agreement among all Christians on many matters central to the faith. In his intervention he distinguished between truths of the faith directly concerned with the goal of our salvation, such as the Trinity and the incarnation, and those truths that are more concerned with the means toward our salvation, such as the sacraments and the hierarchical structure of the church.[18] In a similar manner, Cardinal Franz König complained of the Catholic tendency to simply list the truths of the faith. He contended that it was necessary to make a qualitative distinction between teachings that were in close proximity to the core of the Christian message and those that were more peripheral.[19]

These concerns found their way into the final text. There the council encourages ecumenists to begin from a robust Christocentrism. Thus, the council encouraged Catholic ecumenists:

> When comparing doctrines with one another, they should remember that in catholic doctrine there exists an order or "hierarchy" of truths, since they vary in their relation to the foundation of the Christian faith. Thus the way will be opened whereby this kind of friendly rivalry will incite all to a deeper realization and a clearer expression of the unfathomable riches of Christ. (UR11)

In this brief passage, not only does the council suggest that there is a qualitative distinction among the church's dogmatic teachings but it also introduced a crucial distinction between the substance of divine revelation ("foundation of the Christian faith"), understood as God's self-communication in Christ by the power of the Spirit, and those church doctrines that, in varying degrees, symbolically mediate that revelation. When the council first articulated this teaching in *Unitatis Redintegratio*, Oscar Cullmann, noted Protestant theologian and observer at the council, remarked that this teaching was "the most revolutionary ... not only in the schema *De Oecumenismo*, but in all

de Vatican II, ed. Gilles Routhier and Guy Jobin (Paris: Éditions du Cerf, 2010), 69–91.

[18] An English translation of the text of his speech can be found in Andrea Pangrazio, "The Mystery of the History of the Church," in *Council Speeches of Vatican II*, ed., Hans Küng, Yves Congar, OP, and Daniel O'Hanlon (Glen Rock, NJ: Paulist Press, 1964), 188–92.

[19] For a summary treatment of König's views on the hierarchy of truths, see George Tavard, "Hierarchia Veritatum: A Preliminary Investigation," *Theological Studies* 32 (September, 1971): 279–80.

the schemas of the council."[20] In the Decree on Ecumenism, the council appreciates the role of doctrine in symbolically mediating a reality that is, nevertheless, more "foundational" than the doctrinal expressions themselves.[21]

This conciliar commitment to the hierarchy of truths and, more generally, to what Christoph Theobald, SJ has termed, "the pastorality of doctrine,"[22] would largely be ignored in the postconciliar period until the election of Pope Francis. In his address at the plenary session of the Congregation for the Doctrine of the Faith in January 2014, Pope Francis distilled his understanding of doctrine into one sentence: "In reality, doctrine has the sole purpose of serving the life of the People of God and it seeks to assure our faith of a sure foundation."[23] Doctrine plays a necessary role in the life of the church but it should not be used as an excuse for suppressing disagreement and doubt. Pope Francis has insisted, moreover, that doctrine be comprehended in relation to this more basic Christian message. This conviction is evident in his return to the council's teaching on the hierarchy of truths.[24] For Francis too, doctrine is always at the service of the fundamental Christian message. This is because doctrine employs a kind of second-order language that expresses in precise propositional terms the central convictions of the Christian faith. This more formal, propositional language inevitably puts doctrine at several degrees of abstraction from the gospel as it is experienced concretely in the life of discipleship. The pope writes:

> Pastoral ministry in a missionary style is not obsessed with the disjointed transmission of a multitude of doctrines to be insistently imposed. When we adopt a pastoral goal and a missionary style which would actually reach everyone without exception or exclusion, the message has to concentrate on the essentials, on what is most beautiful, most grand, most appealing and at the same

---

[20] Oscar Cullmann, "Comments on the Decree on Ecumenism," *Ecumenical Review* 17 (1965): 93.

[21] For more on the "symbolic mediation" of revelation in church doctrine see Avery Dulles, SJ, *Models of Revelation* (Garden City, NY: Doubleday, 1983), 131–73.

[22] Christoph Theobald, SJ, "The Principle of Pastorality at Vatican II: Challenges of a Prospective Interpretation of the Council," in *The Legacy of Vatican II*, ed. Massimo Faggioli and Andrea Vicini, SJ (New York: Paulist Press, 2015), 26–37, at 28.

[23] Pope Francis, "Address to the Congregation for the Doctrine of the Faith" (January 31, 2014). The text can be accessed online at www.zenit.org/en/articles/pope-francis-address-to-congregation-for-the-doctrine-of-the-faith.

[24] Pope Francis, *Evangelii Gaudium*, 36. This document can be accessed on-line at: http://w2.vatican.va/content/francesco/en/apost_exhortations/documents/papa-francesco_esortazione-ap_20131124_evangelii-gaudium.html.

time most necessary. The message is simplified, while losing none of its depth and truth, and thus becomes all the more forceful and convincing . (EG 35)

Francis is not afraid to affirm the necessary place of doctrine in the church, but he consistently orients that doctrine toward the core Christian *kerygma* and situates it within the pastoral life of the church.

The Authority of Scripture

The third chapter of *Dei Verbum* addresses three thorny issues regarding the authority of Scripture: biblical inspiration, biblical inerrancy, and biblical interpretation. Prior to Vatican II most theories of biblical inspiration were heavily influenced by the analogy of prophetic utterance and various notions of instrumental causality. At times, inspiration was even conceived as a form of divine dictation. In the nineteenth century, Catholic scholars like Newman and Johann Baptist Franzelin grappled with how to best to recognize the Bible's inspiration while allowing some room for non-revelatory error. However, Pope Leo XIII's encyclical, *Providentissimus Deus* (1893), while offering a modest encouragement for contemporary biblical scholarship, appeared to put an end to such theories with its unambiguous assertion that the Bible was without error in all matters. The climate for biblical scholarship improved considerably when Pope Pius XII published his encyclical, *Divino Afflante Spiritu* in 1943. Pope Pius reasserted Pope Leo's conviction regarding the total inerrancy of Scripture yet he also took the important step of permitting Catholic biblical scholars to make full use modern historical-critical methods.

The final version of *Dei Verbum* offered a rather modest and even cautious re-consideration of biblical inspiration and inerrancy. Its most significant advance was the consequence of its situating the revelatory character of Scripture within its richer, trinitarian theology of revelation. As Denis Farkasfalvy O. Cist. notes, this emphasis on God as revealed in salvation history "did not allow the notion of 'revealed truth' to be reduced or restricted to propositional statements."[25] It also allowed for a broader notion of divine inspiration, one that moved away from a theory of verbal inspiration and assigned a greater role to human agency in the authorship of Scripture. Article 11 holds that the

---

[25] Denis Farkasfalvy, O. Cist., "Inspiration and Interpretation," in *Vatican II: Renewal within Tradition*, ed. Matthew L. Lamb and Matthew Levering (New York: Oxford University Press, 2008), 77–100, at 79.

Scriptures were written under the inspiration of the Holy Spirit, but it refrains from developing any particular theory regarding that inspiration. The final version of article 11, while calling God the author of Scripture, refrains from calling God the *principal* author. In response to views of inspiration which treated the human authors as automatons, the council insisted that the human authors made full use of their own powers and abilities such that they also may be called "true authors."

As regards the tricky question of biblical inerrancy, the preparatory draft had asserted that Scripture was without error "in any matter, religious or profane."[26] This claim was seen as increasingly problematic in the face of modern biblical scholarship. On October 2, 1964, Cardinal König of Vienna gave a provocative speech in which he warned the bishops not to ignore what many biblical scholars already knew, namely that certain scientific and historical claims and/or assumptions in the Bible were "deficient."[27] The classic example often cited was Mark 2:26 in which Jesus mentions David's entering the house of God under the high priest Abiathar to eat the "bread of the presence" with his soldiers. This conflicted with the account in 1 Samuel 21:1–6, which said that David did so, not under Abiathar, but under his father Ahimelech. In this instance clearly someone was mistaken, either the Gospel writer or Jesus! One could also list inconsistencies in the Gospels regarding the timing of the so called cleansing of the temple (at the beginning or the end of Christ's ministry), geographic inaccuracies in the Gospel of Mark, or the disagreement among the Gospels regarding whether Christ's last supper occurred on Passover or not.

The drafters of a statement on biblical inerrancy faced a considerable challenge: they were determined, on the one hand, to avoid any sense that only "parts" of Scripture were inspired while, on the other hand, allowing for the reality of certain "deficiencies" in the biblical text. The official formulation of the council's teaching was arrived at only after tortuous negotiation in which even the pope weighed in with his views on the matter. In article 11 the council insisted that Scripture was indeed without error in teaching "that truth which God, for the sake of our salvation, wished to see confided in the sacred scriptures." The key phrase here was "for the sake of our salvation." This formulation subtly shifted the emphasis from the content of Scripture, that is, the biblical text itself, to the divine intention. Rather than risk dividing

---

[26] For the Latin text of the preparatory draft presented to the council see, *Acta Synodalia*, 1/3: 14–26.

[27] *Acta Synodalia* 3/3: 275.

Scripture into religious and profane truths, or inspired and non-inspired passages, the council held that inspiration and inerrancy be viewed from the perspective of God's salvific intention. *All* Scripture was inspired, but inspired with a view to communicate God's saving offer, not necessarily with a view to communicating accurate historical, geographic, or scientific facts. The scientific and historical frameworks of biblical texts are to be read as a medium for the communication of God's offer of salvation.

Equally important was the council's presentation of some hermeneutical rules intended to guide the task of biblical interpretation in *Dei Verbum* 12. These rules were largely drawn from Pius XII's encyclical *Divino Afflante Spiritu*, but in subtle ways they advanced the topic further. Because the biblical authors wrote out of their knowledge and abilities, proper interpretation of a biblical text requires retrieving the author's understanding of the text. The intention of the author is the *primary* referent in determining a text's meaning. The council acknowledged, following Pius XII, the legitimacy of attending to the diversity of literary genres in the Bible as well as the historical and cultural context of the biblical authors themselves. Alongside these historical and literary-critical guidelines for interpretation, the council also insisted on a second set of guidelines, drawn more from dogmatic theology. Scholars must pursue the meaning of a given text in the light of the entire biblical canon. In this pursuit, other forms of biblical interpretation preserved in the tradition continue to have value.

The postconciliar period has seen considerable movement beyond the council's rather cautious approach to the authority of Scripture. Broader considerations of the authority of Scripture have often drawn on modern hermeneutical theory, particularly in the work of figures like Paul Ricoeur.[28] Sandra Schneiders, IHM, for example, draws considerably on Ricoeur's understanding of *testimony*.[29] For Schneiders and others, testimony is a fundamental category for grasping the character of Scripture. She notes that the very category of testimony presupposes "limits" since testimony, however much inspired by God, still draws from the particular witness/witnessing community's perspective and experience. And all human perspectives, however inspired, are necessarily limited. The Pontifical Biblical Commission has issued several

---

[28] Paul Ricoeur, "The Hermeneutics of Testimony," in *Essays on Biblical Interpretation* (Philadelphia: Fortress Press, 1980), 119–54.

[29] Sandra Schneiders, IHM, "Scripture as the Word of God," *Princeton Seminary Bulletin* (1993): 18–35.

texts that have affirmed the fruits of the modern tools of biblical criticism and have offered more nuanced positions on biblical inspiration and inerrancy.[30]

Some contemporary scholars have challenged fundamental claims regarding the authority of Scripture. Whereas the council was grappling with the possibility of errors within the biblical text of a historical, geographical, and scientific nature, now questions are being raised regarding deeper problems with the text. What does the reader do with texts that appear to be anti-Semitic or misogynist in their treatment of women? How is the reader to come to terms with the Bible's attitude toward slavery? These problems have given rise to the application of a "hermeneutic of suspicion." By "hermeneutic of suspicion" is meant a critical criterion that requires the biblical interpreter to adopt a stance of deliberate "suspicion" toward the possibility of bias in a given text. Feminist theologians, in particular, have employed this hermeneutic with respect to the appearance of patriarchal and androcentric bias. Such a bias is reflected in biblical assumptions, whether implicit or explicit, that maleness is somehow the norm for understanding human experience and, to that extent, also for understanding God. For many feminist scholars, the pervasive presence of such bias in the Bible raises particular difficulties for claims to biblical inspiration. At the minimum, it suggests that the acknowledgment of human deficiencies in biblical texts must go beyond the spheres of science and history to include systemic cultural bias.

From a quite different perspective, we also find scholars who, while affirming the continued necessity of historical criticism, also complain that the dominance of modern historical-critical methods has led to a disparagement of patristic and medieval exegesis, which, according to the council, must continue to play a role in biblical interpretation.[31] Pope Benedict XVI reminded us in his apostolic exhortation *Verbum Domini* that the interpretation of the Bible as Scripture is ultimately, "a theological and ecclesial practice."[32] He also warned that Scripture

---

[30] Pontifical Biblical Commission, *The Interpretation of the Bible in the Church* (Washington, DC: United States Catholic Conference, 1995); *The Inspiration and Truth of Sacred Scripture* (Collegeville, MN: Liturgical Press, 2014).

[31] See Denis Farkasfalvy O. Cist., *Inspiration and Interpretation* (Washington, DC: Catholic University of America Press, 2010); William M. Wright IV, "*Dei Verbum*," in *The Reception of Vatican II*, ed. Matthew L. Lamb and Matthew Levering (New York: Oxford University Press, 2017), 61–112.

[32] Pope Benedict XVI, *Verbum Domini* (2010), no. 25. This document can be accessed online at: http://w2.vatican.va/content/benedict-xvi/en/apost_exhortations/documents/hf_ben-xvi_exh_20100930_verbum-domini.html .

can only be called the Word of God by way of analogy. For Christians, God's Word comes to us not initially as a text but as a Person, the divine *Logos*, who in the fullness of time was incarnate in Jesus of Nazareth. Christianity is not, properly speaking, "a religion of the book," the pope asserted. Why? Because the Word of God does not reside exclusively in a written text: "the Scripture is to be proclaimed, heard, read, received and experienced as the word of God, in the stream of the apostolic Tradition from which it is inseparable" (VD 7).

Scripture in the Life of the Church

One of the great, underappreciated contributions of the council was its reconsideration of the place of Scripture in the pastoral life of the church. The constitution on the liturgy recalled this in its guidelines for the renewal of the liturgy, calling for the faithful to have much greater exposure to Scripture through an expanded lectionary (SC 35). Massimo Faggioli has pointed out that over half of the footnotes in the liturgy constitution refer to biblical texts.[33] Article 35 of *Sacrosanctum Concilium* explicitly called for the restoration of a "more ample, more varied, and more suitable selection of reading from sacred scripture." *Optatam Totius*, the Decree on the Training of Priests, called for a renewed emphasis on Biblical studies in the formation of priests, noting that Scripture ought to be "the very soul of all theology" (OT 16). The council emphasized the need for seminarians to be trained well in Biblical studies (OT 4). In *Presbyterorum Ordinis*, The Decree on Priestly Ministry and Life, priests are reminded that proclaiming the gospel represents one of their primary ministries. The faithful are to be nourished at the two tables of "holy scripture and the Eucharist" (PO 18). Biblical preaching requires that the homilist explain God's Word not in an abstract or didactic fashion but so as to speak to the particular circumstances and conditions of people's daily lives (PO 4). In the council texts Scripture is encouraged for the spiritual nourishment of both consecrated religious (PC 6) and the laity (AA 4).

No document, however, paid as much attention to the renewal of Scripture in the life of the church as did the final chapter of *Dei Verbum*. The chapter emphasized the need for Scripture to be made more widely available to ordinary Christians (DV 22). This will require, the council

---

[33] Massimo Faggioli, *True Reform: Liturgy and Ecclesiology in* Sacrosanctum Concilium (Collegeville, MN: Liturgical Press, 2012), 50.

insisted, both vernacular translations and study editions that provide helpful notes and commentary (DV 25).

Relative to the period immediately prior to the council, one must acknowledge the extent to which the church has responded to these challenges. The ordinary Catholic today has access to considerable biblical resources including vernacular translations and biblical commentaries. Parish-based Bible studies like the Little Rock Bible Study program have proliferated in local churches. At the same time, many ordinary Catholics in the pew continue to complain about the poor quality of biblical preaching that they experience in the pews. Both parish-based and Catholic school-based catechetical resources have done a much better job of introducing young Catholics to the riches of the Bible. Although there is much more work to be done, the gains that have been made in biblical literacy among ordinary Catholics are undeniable.

CONCLUSION

The Second Vatican Council was a momentous event in the life of the Roman Catholic Church going back at least to the Protestant Reformation. Its many contributions are documented throughout this volume. It re-centered Catholic ecclesiology on the sacraments of baptism and Eucharist and brought to the foreground of the church's consciousness a sense of the church as the pilgrim people of God sent forth in mission. It followed the lead of Pope Paul VI in emphasizing the priority of dialogue within the church, in the church's engagement with other Christians, in its engagement with other world religions, and with the world itself. It articulated a more robust account of the contributions of the laity and placed ordained ministry in service of the fulfillment of the baptismal priesthood of all believers. It called for a comprehensive reform of the liturgy. The council established a new foundation for moral theology based on human freedom, the dignity of human conscience, and a life of virtue.

Yet all of these advances depend on the council's most fundamental contribution, its account of a God who comes to us in Christ as vulnerable, redeeming love and through the Spirit makes possible friendship with God. It is the revelation of this God that establishes us as God's people made one in Christ by the power of the Holy Spirit. It is this God who sends us forth in mission as a sacrament of God's saving love that we might care for the least, preach a message of justice and reconciliation, and serve the coming of God's reign.

FURTHER READING

Congar, Yves, OP. *Tradition and Traditions: An Historical and Theological Essay*. New York: Macmillan, 1966.

Dulles, Avery, SJ. *Models of Revelation*. Garden City, NY: Doubleday, 1983.

Espin, Orlando. *The Faith of the People: Theological Reflections on Popular Catholicism*. Maryknoll, NY: Orbis Books, 1997.

Farkasfalvy, Denis, O. Cist. *Inspiration and Interpretation: A Theological Interpretation to Sacred Scripture*. Washington, DC: Catholic University of America Press, 2010.

Fiorenza, Elizabeth Schüssler. *Bread not Stone: The Challenge of Feminist Biblical Interpretation*. Boston: Beacon Press, 1984.

Gaillardetz, Richard R. *By What Authority: Foundations for Understanding Authority in the Church*. Revised and expanded edition. Collegeville, MN: Liturgical Press, 2018.

Gnuse, Robert. *The Authority of the Bible: Theories of Inspiration, Revelation and the Canon of Scripture*. Mahwah, NJ: Paulist, 1985.

O'Brien, Mark, OP, and Christopher Monaghan, CP, eds. *God's Word and the Church's Council*. Adelaide: ATF Theology, 2014.

O'Collins, Gerald, SJ. *Rethinking Fundamental Theology: Toward a New Fundamental Theology*. Oxford: Oxford University Press, 2011.

Rush, Ormond. *The Eyes of Faith: The Sense of the Faithful and the Church's Reception of Revelation*. Washington, DC: Catholic University of America Press, 2009.

Schneiders, Sandra M., IHM. *The Revelatory Text: Interpreting the New Testament as Sacred Scripture*. New York: HarperCollins, 1991.

Segundo, Juan Luis, SJ. *The Liberation of Dogma*. Maryknoll, NY: Orbis, 1992.

Thiel, John E. *Senses of Tradition: Continuity and Development in Catholic Faith*. New York: Oxford University Press, 2000.

Wicks, Jared, SJ. *Investigating Vatican II*. Washington, DC: Catholic University of America Press, 2018.

Witherup, Ronald D., PSS. *Scripture: Dei Verbum. Rediscovering Vatican II*. Mahwah, NJ: Paulist, 2006.

10 Liturgy

DAVID FARINA TURNBLOOM

On December 4, 1963, the day that the Constitution on the Sacred Liturgy *Sacrosanctum Concilium* was promulgated, Pope Paul VI gave an address in which he described the liturgy as God's "primary invitation to the human race."[1] This phrase is a beautiful summary of the Second Vatican Council's vision of the liturgy: Through the liturgical life of the Church, divine life is graciously offered to humankind. As we will see, the council documents display a steadfast preoccupation with the personal relationship between God and humankind. Deeply pastoral in their foundations, the documents of the Second Vatican Council provide a consistent vision of the liturgy as the summit and source (*culmen et fons*) of a living, dynamic, and diverse Christian faith.

For this reason, the council repeatedly described the liturgical life of the church in terms of participation. In particular, the council was greatly concerned with the renewal of the Christian faithful's participation *in* the liturgy. By examining the way the liturgy is treated throughout the documents of the council, the primary goal of this chapter is to help contextualize what it means to "participate in the liturgy." In the end, the council documents appear less concerned with individuals participating *in* the liturgy and more concerned with the church participating in God *through* the liturgy. Only after understanding this broader vision of liturgical participation can a student of the conciliar documents adequately appreciate the reforms that followed and the reforms that are still needed.

THE LITURGICAL MOVEMENT: FOUNDING THE CONCILIAR VISION

It is important to note that the council's treatment of the liturgy was far from an unanticipated innovation. The Benedictine monk and liturgical

---

[1] Anscar Chupungco, OSB, "The Vision of the Constitution on the Liturgy," *T&T Clark Companion to Liturgy*, ed. Alcuin Reid (New York: Bloomsbury T&T Clark, 2016), 265.

scholar Anscar Chupungco has noted that *Sacrosanctum Concilium* was the result of a liturgical movement that had its beginnings in Europe.[2] While much can and has been said regarding the history of this movement, for our purposes it will suffice to briefly highlight the liturgical movement's focus on renewing participation in the liturgy.

Building on the nineteenth-century work accomplished by Benedictine monks, like Dom Prosper Guèranger, Pope Pius X issued the *motu proprio* on the use of sacred music, *Tra le Sollecitudini*.[3] In this 1903 letter, the pope upholds the faithful's "active participation" in the liturgy as the primary means by which the Holy Spirit takes root in the life of the church. "Our people assemble for the purpose of acquiring the true Christian spirit from its first and indispensable source, namely, active participation in the most sacred mysteries."[4] This focus on participation in the liturgy for the sake of greater life in the Spirit would continue to be the focus of the liturgical movement as it moved into the twentieth century.

In 1909, a Benedictine monk from Belgium named Dom Lambert Beauduin gave a paper at the National Congress of Catholic Action in Malines, entitled "The True Prayer of the Church," which stands as a turning point for the liturgical movement's support of greater participation in the liturgy. In this paper, Beauduin saw the need to help the Christian faithful come to a deeper understanding of the liturgical texts by translating them into vernacular languages. As a result, bilingual translations of the missal began to appear.[5] Beauduin's call to translate these texts was one way of taking up Pope Pius X's exhortation to increase active participation in the liturgy. Further, Beauduin saw the diversity of liturgical traditions as a gift to be celebrated. Beauduin spent his life supporting the ecumenical movement through the study and promotion of Eastern and Western liturgical traditions. Rather than insisting on uniformity, supporting liturgical diversity was a way to simultaneously increase participation in the liturgy and encourage the unity of different Christian churches.

Then, during the papacy of Pius XII, the liturgical movement enjoyed considerable affirmation. Of note was Pius XII's 1947 encyclical *Mediator Dei*. In this letter, the pope explicitly praised the work of the

---

[2] Ibid., 263.

[3] Rita Ferrone, *Liturgy:* Sacrosanctum Concilium (Mahwah, NJ: Paulist Press, 2007), 5–8.

[4] *Tra le Sollecitudini*, translation taken from Ferrone, *Liturgy*, 6.

[5] Catherine Vincie, "The RCIA and the Liturgical Movement," *Liturgy* 31, no. 2 (2016): 3–10.

liturgical movement, encouraged the work of liturgical reform, and reaffirmed Pope Pius X's focus on the intimate connection between liturgical participation and the vitality of the church: "Through this active and individual participation, the members of the Mystical Body not only become daily more like to their divine Head, but the life flowing from the Head is imparted to the members."[6] Hence, when his successor Pope John XXIII announced plans for an ecumenical council, a preparatory commission on the liturgy was among the first commissions established. While the preparation for the council was not free from controversy regarding the trajectory of liturgical reform, the preparatory commission continued the trajectory of the liturgical movement. In the end, the conciliar documents would put forth a liturgical vision rooted in a pastoral concern for the dynamic lives of the Christian faithful.

THE LITURGY IN THE CONCILIAR TEXTS

As the first document of the council, *Sacrosanctum Concilium*'s influence is clearly seen throughout the rest of the conciliar documents. Hence, when examining the Second Vatican Council's treatment of the liturgy, one must give special attention to the Constitution on the Sacred Liturgy. However, this document is by no means the only document that addresses the liturgical life of the church. In this section, we will focus on the broader liturgical vision articulated throughout the documents.

Participating in God through the Liturgy

Given the liturgical movement's vision for liturgy's role in the life of the church, it should be of little surprise that the opening paragraph of *Sacrosanctum Concilium* focuses on the relationship between liturgical renewal and the lives of the faithful. The "vigor" of the faithful, the unity of the church, and the church's evangelical mission are all meant to be supported by the renewal (*aggiornamento*) of the church's practices and institutions, foremost of which is the liturgy (SC 1). Any liturgical reforms proposed by the council need to be understood in relation to these goals. Hence, liturgical reform is not an attempt to be more traditional for the sake of historical continuity. Rather, the council shows a clear preoccupation with the church's participation in the

---

[6] Pope Pius XII, *Mediator Dei*, November 20, 1947, §78.

life of God. Put differently, the goals of liturgical renewal are concerned with the future of the church's everyday life. Hence, the first chapter of *Sacrosanctum Concilium* begins with a consideration of the liturgy's "importance in the life of the Church."

The liturgy is revered as central to the Christian faith because of its relationship to the incarnation. Quoting the ancient Verona Sacramentary, the council emphasizes that the incarnation (especially its culmination in the paschal mystery) is the "perfect achievement of our reconciliation" and the "fullness of divine worship" (SC 5). This is to say that God's activity in history has a two-fold character. First, as the incarnate Word of God, Jesus is the *source* of our salvation. Through the life, death, and resurrection of Jesus, God's Word calls us from death to life, reconciling humanity to divinity. Second, Jesus is the fullness of worship *because* Jesus is perfect (i.e. sinless) humanity. Through his life, death, and resurrection, Jesus shows us the way to *become* true worship. As St. Irenaeus of Lyon wrote, "the Glory of God is a human being fully alive."[7] As such, Jesus Christ is also the *summit* of the Christian faith.

After receiving the Holy Spirit on Pentecost, the community of disciples is sent to be the presence of Christ. Or, in the words of *Lumen Gentium*, "By communicating his Spirit, Christ mystically constitutes as his body his brothers and sisters who are called together from every nation" (LG 7). The life of the church is the life of Christ in the world. Hence, the salvation accomplished through Jesus Christ is an ongoing historical event. By bringing a community of disciples to himself and sending those disciples into the world, Jesus continues to reconcile humankind to God and continues to offer worship. This vision of salvation history provides the backdrop for understanding the importance of the liturgy. Rather than a mere repetition of Jesus's past activity, the liturgy is the ongoing communication of God. "For in the liturgy, God speaks to his people, [and] Christ is still proclaiming his Gospel" (SC 33). Through liturgical participation, the faithful are listening to the Word of God that is made present and communicated through their worship. That is to say, liturgical participation is the *source* of Christian life because it moves the hearts and minds of the faithful.

However, the first chapter of the Dogmatic Constitution on the Church *Lumen Gentium* also clearly describes the liturgy as the *summit* of the Christian faith. In this ecclesiological document, the church is repeatedly described as the Body of Christ united in

---

[7] St. Irenaeus of Lyon, *Irenaeus on the Christian Faith: A Condensation of against Heresies*, ed. James R. Payton Jr. (Cambridge: James Clarke & Co, 2012), 116.

communion: "Really sharing in the body of the Lord in the breaking of the Eucharistic bread, we are taken up into communion with Him and with one another" (LG 7). This communion ecclesiology tends to describe the church primarily in terms of the church's identity with Jesus Christ. This identity is most fully manifested in the celebration of the Eucharist, "especially in the same eucharist, in one prayer, at one altar, at which the bishop presides, surrounded by his college of priests and by his ministers" (SC 41). In this Eucharistic celebration, the Body of Christ offers its divine life of communion as a sacrifice of praise to God the Father (LG 11). Hence, the celebration of the Eucharist is the *summit* of the Christian faith.

However, to avoid degenerating into triumphalist self-idolatry, it is of paramount importance to note that the communion ecclesiology found in *Lumen Gentium* is heavily rooted in St. Paul's epistles. Citing the Letters to the Ephesians and the Colossians, Article 7 of *Lumen Gentium* describes the church as an imperfect and growing body. Through communion with Jesus, the church receives the gifts of the Spirit so that "we might through all things grow into Him who is our head." Even when seen as a communion, the church on earth still exists "as pilgrims in a strange land, following in trial and in oppression the paths [Christ] trod" (LG 7). When the liturgy is described as the summit of the Christian faith, it is always an *eschatological* summit that necessarily implies an unrealized culmination. Hence, the Pastoral Constitution on the Church in the Modern World *Gaudium et Spes* describes the liturgy as a "supper of brotherly and sisterly communion and a foretaste of the heavenly banquet" (GS 38).

The salvation of the world, then, is an ongoing history that could be described as a dynamic cycle that begins and ends with the celebration of the liturgy. In celebrating the liturgy, the Christian faithful are moved by the incarnate Word of God to "carry out the truth in love" (Eph 4:15). The provocative love of Jesus Christ is proclaimed and heard in every liturgical celebration. Moved by this salvific Word, the faithful are sent to live their lives as images of Christ in the world. Returning, then, to the Eucharist, the faithful offer their lives (i.e. their communion) as a sacrifice of praise. Every liturgical celebration (especially the celebration of the Eucharist) makes present the incarnate Word of God who is at once the source and summit of the Christian faith. The church is always being sent from the liturgy and it is always moving toward the liturgy. Simply put, the church participates in Jesus Christ through participation in the liturgy. So, while the council emphasizes the importance of participating *in* the liturgy, it is arguably more accurate to say that the council provides a theological framework through which participation in the liturgy is the height of the church's participation in God.

Given this importance of the liturgy in the church's life, *Sacrosanctum Concilium* adopts the concerns of the liturgical movement and makes the faithful's participation in the liturgy its foundational theme. As Pope Pius X stated in *Tra le Sollecitudini*, the font of the Christian spirit is not the sacred mysteries, but "active participation in the sacred mysteries." *Sacrosanctum Concilium* reiterates Pius X's point: "[participation in the liturgy] is the primary, indeed the indispensable source from which the faithful are to derive the true Christian spirit" (SC 14). The liturgy is not an entity that enjoys existence apart from its celebration. The liturgy is neither a text nor a rubric. The Christian faithful do not participate in the source of the Christian faith. Rather, the Christian faithful's act of participation liturgically manifests the source of the faith: Jesus Christ.

Because participation in the liturgy is the process by which the church comes to more fully participate in God, the council provided principles for liturgical reform in service of liturgical participation: "In this renewal [of the liturgy], both texts and rites should be ordered so as to express more clearly the holy things which they signify. The christian people, as far as is possible, should be able to understand them easily and take part in them in a celebration which is full, active, and the community's own" (SC 21). The constitution explicitly encouraged that reforms seek to multiply the number of ways the faithful could participate in the liturgy: "The people should be encouraged to take part by means of acclamations, responses, psalms, antiphons, hymns, as well as by actions, gestures and bodily attitudes. And at the proper time a reverent silence should be observed" (SC 30). Further, liturgical language was to be reformed to foment understanding and efficacy: "The rites should radiate a noble simplicity. They should be short, clear, and free from useless repetitions. They should be within the people's powers of comprehension, and normally should not require much explanation" (SC 34). Lastly, following the insights of the liturgical movement, the constitution opened the way for widespread use of vernacular languages while also maintaining a place of primacy for Latin in the Latin Rites (SC 36).

While these are just a few of the liturgical reforms outlined by the constitution, it must be reiterated that the liturgical life of the church is always being considered with regard to its effect on the life of the faithful. Changes to the liturgy were being prescribed in a way that laid the groundwork for a church with a diverse and dynamic liturgical life. As we will see, liturgical diversity was not an accidental result of liturgical reform. Rather, it was an essential component of the council's liturgical vision.

Liturgical Diversity and Culture

Before turning our attention to the council's emphasis on liturgical and cultural diversity, it will be beneficial to briefly cast our eyes a little further back to appreciate traditional Roman Catholic approaches to this issue. Nearly 350 years before the drafting of *Sacrosanctum Concilium* there were important liturgical debates surrounding the work of missionaries in China. In 1615, a group of Jesuit theologians argued that the sacred Scriptures and the liturgy should be translated into Chinese to help support the missionary work of the church, and these requests were granted in a decree known as "the privilege of Paul V" that allowed for such translations.[8] In addition to debates over translating the liturgy and scriptures into Chinese, there was much disagreement over whether Chinese Catholics should participate in rituals that honored Confucius and their ancestors. This debate became known as the Chinese Rites controversy. In short, Jesuit missionaries argued that Chinese Catholics should be allowed to participate in these rites, while Dominican and Franciscan missionaries saw the rituals as a threat to the Christian faith. In 1659, the Congregation for the Propagation of Faith put forth an instruction to guide missionary activity in China. This instruction took the side of the Jesuits, warning against cultural imperialism and advocating for appreciation of Chinese culture.

> Make no endeavor and in no way persuade these people to change their rites, habits, and mores as long as they are not very manifestly contrary to religion and good mores. Indeed what would be more absurd than to introduce Gaul, Spain, Italy or some other part of Europe to China? Bring not these things but the Faith, which neither rejects nor harms the rites, nor customs of any nation provided they are not perverse, but which rather desires them to remain intact ... Therefore, never interchange the practices of these

---

[8] For an excellent survey of the Chinese Rites controversy see Audrey Seah, "The 1670 Chinese Missal: A Struggle for Indigenization Amidst the Chinese Rites Controversy," in *China's Christianity: From Missionary to Indigenous Church*, ed. Anthony E. Clark (Boston: Brill, 2017), 86–120.

people with European practices; rather with great diligence become accustomed to their practices.[9]

However, after forty-five years, this receptive disposition toward Chinese culture was eventually reversed, and the prohibition against participating in these rites was held in place until 1939 when Pope Pius XII issued a decree declaring the Chinese Rites to be an acceptable and honorable practice. As we will now see, Pius XII's approval of the Chinese Rites was indicative of how the council would envision the relationship between liturgical participation and culture.

Because the liturgical reform was focused on full, active participation, it was necessary for the council to carefully consider the role of cultural diversity in liturgical participation. Articles 37–40 of the constitution treat the cultural "adaptations" that are necessary for encouraging full participation in the liturgy. The constitution reiterates that the Church "does not wish to impose a rigid uniformity in matters which do not affect the faith or the well-being of the entire community. Rather does it cultivate and foster the qualities and talents of the various races and nations" (SC 37). Article 40 provides a process for "radical" adaptions in which non-Christian elements of a culture or tradition are added to the liturgy. However, these adaptations are to be carried out in a way that carefully preserves "the substantial unity of the Roman rite." Without offering any specific descriptions, the council appeals to "unchangeable elements divinely instituted" of the Roman Rite's "inner nature" that are not to be altered (SC 21). Of course, these assertions about the immutable core of the Roman Rite would have benefited from some specific descriptions. However, the council does not provide these details, and, as we will see, this ambiguity has had some unfortunate consequences in the history of liturgical reform. Rather, the documents are content to say that reforms and adaptations should harmonize with the "true and authentic spirit" of the liturgy. These changes should be done "to express more clearly the holy things they signify." Despite the ambiguous language regarding the immutability of the liturgy, the personal relationship between the faithful and God remains the fundamental criterion for the cultural adaptation so necessary for the council's vision of liturgical reform. Hence, the documents establish processes for patiently attending to the dynamic relationship between liturgy and culture. With the approval of the Holy See, these cultural adaptations are tested through periods of

---

[9] Ibid., 102–3.

experimentation. Again, the focus is on how these adaptations will affect the life of the faithful who participate in these liturgies. All reform, including cultural adaptation, is to be evaluated on the degree to which it facilitates full, active participation and its effect on the vigor of Christian life.

While *Sacrosanctum Concilium* emphasizes respect for culture, this respect is largely for the purpose of helping the people of that culture participate more fully in the liturgy: "to strengthen whatever serves to call all of humanity into the church's fold" (SC 1). Simply put, the church appreciates cultural diversity for the sake of its evangelical mission to the world. This mission-focused appreciation for culture is also present in other conciliar documents. Here, it will be beneficial to quote *Gaudium et Spes* at length.

> There are many links between the message of salvation and culture. In his self-revelation to his people, fully manifesting himself in his incarnate Son, God spoke in the context of the culture proper to each age. Similarly the church has existed through the centuries in varying circumstances and has utilized the resources of different cultures to spread and explain the message of Christ in its preaching, to examine and understand it more deeply, and to express it more perfectly in the liturgy. (GS 58)

There is a clear need for the church to embrace cultural diversity so that it might more fully preach the gospel and be "the universal sacrament of salvation" (GS 45).

However, the preceding passage's appreciation for cultural diversity seems to go beyond concern for the church's mission. Rather than seeing itself as the instrument through which God saves the world, *Gaudium et Spes* details the benefits the church receives from culture. In fact, the cautious appreciation for culture present in *Sacrosanctum Concilium* finds a fuller expression in *Gaudium et Spes*. The "discoveries of different cultures" allow the church to more fully examine the gospel and come to new understandings. Further, these cultures perfect the liturgical expressions of the church. Hence, cultural adaption of the liturgy is a process of perfecting liturgical participation through which the church grows closer to God. Put differently, the pilgrim church walks toward God through the cultural adaptation of the liturgy.

In its consideration of newly established churches, the Decree on the Church's Missionary Activity *Ad Gentes* also uses strikingly powerful language to uphold the genius of the cultures in which the liturgy is celebrated: "The communion of the young churches with the whole

church should remain intimate, they should graft elements of its tradition on to their own culture and thus, by a mutual outpouring of energy
[*virium*], increase the life of the mystical body" (AG 19). The human
culture into which God's Word is spoken is a salvific force by which the
church finds its life increased. Far from being a guideline for reform,
adherence to liturgical uniformity is a stumbling block that inhibits the
mission of the church *and* inhibits the pilgrim journey of the church.
When the church isolates itself from cultural diversity, it not only
jeopardizes its salvific mission but it also jeopardizes its own salvation.

Hence, there must be practical ways for going about this necessary
process of cultural adaptation. Paramount among these processes are
the empowerment of episcopal conferences and the requirement of local
liturgical committees (SC 22.2, 44–46). The cultural competence necessary for supporting full, active participation in the liturgy is not something that can be satisfied by the mind of a single bishop, much less a
group of bishops living across the globe, removed from the culture in
which the liturgy will be celebrated. Cultural competence is of such
importance that *Sacrosanctum Concilium* explicitly instructs bishops
to humbly and regularly avail themselves of these liturgical commissions. In fact, one might argue that a good way to evaluate a bishop's
commitment to the council is to examine the activity of these councils
within his diocese. Cultural diversity in liturgical participation is
worked into the institutional structure of the church. Liturgical and
cultural diversity are intended goals of liturgical reform because they
are the manner in which the church continually deepens its participation in God.

Liturgical Diversity and Ecumenism[10]

Beyond cultural diversity in the Roman Liturgy, the council also
addresses liturgical diversity as it is found in other Christian churches
and communities. While the council was clearly able to see the Roman
Church's need to learn from other cultures, it was also able to affirm the
salvific efficacy of the liturgical life of other Christian churches.
Recalling the opening lines of *Sacrosanctum Concilium*, the goal of
the council was that the entire Christian church should grow in unity
and vitality. Hence, throughout the conciliar documents we can see a
clear desire to recognize and uphold the salvific nature of Christian life
wherever it might be found. To this end, the council promulgated two

---

[10] For further reading on ecumenism and Vatican II, see Susan K. Wood, "Ecumenism"
(Chapter 16 in this volume).

documents that explicitly address the Roman Catholic Church's relationship to other Christian churches. The Decree on Ecumenism *Unitatis Redintegratio* takes up the council's focus on the restoration of Christian unity, and the Decree on the Catholic Eastern Churches *Orientalium Ecclesiarum* takes up those Catholic traditions with whom the Roman Church shares full communion. Both of these documents put forth a vision of diversity that adds depth to the council's vision of participation in God through the liturgy.

Beginning with Eastern Catholic churches with whom the Roman Church shares full communion, we see that *Orientalium Ecclesiarum* affirms the importance of ecclesial diversity by clearly stating that the unity and catholicity of the church is manifested through diverse and dynamic traditions:

> Between those churches there is such a wonderful communion that this variety, so far from diminishing the Church's unity, rather serves to emphasize it. For the Catholic Church wishes the traditions of each particular church or rite to remain whole and entire, and it likewise wishes to adapt its own way of life to the various needs of time and place. (OE 2)

The unity of the church is manifested *in the variety* of ecclesial activity. This vision of manifesting ecclesial unity adds depth to the description found in article 41 of *Sacrosanctum Concilium*. There, it states that "the pre-eminent manifestation of the Church consists in the full active participation of all God's holy people in these liturgical celebrations especially in the same eucharist, in one prayer, at one altar, at which there presides the bishop surrounded by his college of priests and by his ministers" (SC 41). Again, this emphasis on the eucharistic celebration of a single local church can be misunderstood when examined exclusively through an ecclesiology that solely sees communion as the *summit* of the faith. Reiterating the more fundamental vision of the liturgy as source *and* summit allows us to see that the "active participation of all God's holy people in the same liturgical celebrations" occurs in the ongoing eucharistic celebrations of these diverse liturgical traditions. The unity of the church is a diverse reality.

Shifting attention to *Unitatis Redintegratio*, this decree addresses the liturgical life of "separated" churches and communities with whom the Roman Catholic Church shares a real but imperfect communion.

> Our separated brothers and sisters also carry out many liturgical actions of the christian religion. In ways that vary according to the

condition of each church or community, these liturgical actions most certainly can truly engender a life of grace, and, one must say, are capable of giving access to that communion in which is salvation. (UR 3)

Here, the council affirms the salvific nature of the liturgical life of non-Catholic churches. In their unique forms and traditions, these acts of liturgical participation are acts of participation in God. Stating the case strongly, the council says that "the Spirit of Christ has not refrained from using [other Christian churches and communities] as means of salvation which derive their efficacy from the very fullness of grace and truth entrusted to the Catholic Church" (UR 3). Put differently, the liturgical participation of these Christian churches is also the source and the summit of the Christian faith. That is to say, the salvation history that manifests the salvific life of the Spirit is being played out through these diverse Christian liturgies. Further, when addressing the separated churches of the East, the council acknowledges that the liturgy of the Western church has "drawn extensively" from these diverse liturgical traditions (UR 14). Therefore, these liturgical celebrations, although marked by important differences that should not be ignored, have clearly functioned as direct sources of the Roman Catholic Church's liturgical life. Ecumenically speaking, liturgical diversity was and continues to be a source of unity and vitality in the life of the Christian church. Hence, while the council refers to these churches as "separated brothers and sisters," it is important to reiterate the more fundamental communion we do share. Any proper evaluation of ecumenical difference must begin with a firm affirmation of the communion from which the one Church of Christ derives its existence. Through participation in the liturgy (especially our shared baptism), the entire Christian community participates in God and manifests divine, salvific presence.

Throughout the council documents, a clear vision of the liturgy is provided in which salvation history is played out in a symphony of diverse liturgical expression. The salvific Word of God is heard ever more deeply and proclaimed ever more fruitfully through the full, active liturgical participation of the faithful.

POSTCONCILIAR LITURGY: REFORMS AND CRITIQUES

Reforms

With this liturgical vision laid out by the council, the decades that immediately followed were filled with the work of reform. However, the implementation of the reform began even prior to the promulgation of the Constitution on the Sacred Liturgy. In the middle of October, 1963, Pope Paul VI asked Cardinal Giacomo Lercaro, the Archbishop of Bologna who had been an important member of the preparatory commission that developed the initial draft of *Sacrosanctum Concilium*, to assemble a group of liturgical experts. Relying on the suggestions of another important member of the preparatory commission, Father Annibale Bugnini, Lercaro assembled the group, and the pope tasked these *periti* (theological experts) with drafting a document that outlined proposals for liturgical reform.[11] Before the end of November, the group produced an instruction document that proposed a wide array of reforms to be tested in various monasteries prior to being implemented throughout the world. However, this hastily drafted instruction was not published. According to Marini, the process of drafting this first attempt at reform made it clear that implementing the liturgical vision of the council demanded more time and more people.

On January 25, 1964, less than two months after the promulgation of *Sacrosanctum Concilium*, Pope Paul VI issued the motu proprio, *Sacram Liturgiam*. Out of desire that "the souls of the faithful may not be further deprived of the fruits of the grace which are hoped for from them," the pope called for the immediate establishment of the diocesan liturgical commissions prescribed in articles 45–46 of *Sacrosanctum Concilium*. As mentioned earlier, these diocesan commissions are one of the primary ways in which full, active participation is encouraged. These commissions allow local bishops to robustly attend to the particular demands of the cultures of their local churches. Further, all seminaries were to immediately develop and implement programs in liturgical theology so that all clergy would be properly trained in the liturgy.

Most importantly, however, *Sacram Liturgiam* established the *Consilium ad exsequendam Constitutionem de sacra Liturgia*. Made up of scholars and pastors, many of whom had been involved in the drafting of *Sacrosanctum Concilium*, this group was charged with the wise and prudent implementation of the Liturgy Constitution's liturgical reforms. Cardinal Lercaro was appointed as the *Consilium*'s president, and Father Bugnini was appointed the secretary. Initially, the group intentionally minimized the number of members who held any other curial office. This allowed the *Consilium* to protect its autonomy

---

[11] Piero Marini, *A Challenging Reform: Realizing the Vision of the Liturgical Renewal* (Collegeville, MN: Liturgical Press, 2007), 9–10.

and maintain focus on its task of reform. Further, the group was intentionally staffed with international representation, a decision that was obviously in line with the spirit of the council's vision for liturgical diversity.

The first months of the *Consilium*'s work were marked by tension regarding authority. The relationship between the curial Congregation of Rites and the *Consilium* was unclear. While Lercaro and Bugnini wanted the *Consilium* to carry out the work of reform autonomously, members of the Congregation of Rites sought to reassert their authority over the liturgy of the church. Generally speaking, the *Consilium* was zealous for the council's renewed vision for the liturgical life of the church. The Congregation for Rites, on the other hand, was resistant to the conciliar vision, preferring to minimize the reforms and maintain complete curial control over the process of reform. These power struggles would prove to be an ongoing tension undergirding the work of the reform.

From March of 1964 to March of 1965, the bulk of the *Consilium*'s work was carried out by a series of study groups, with each group being assigned a different area of the liturgy. These groups focused their work on researching and proposing the various reforms named by *Sacrosanctum Concilium*. Revisions of the Liturgical Calendar, the Divine Office, the *Ordo Missae* (Order of the Mass), the Lectionary, Sacred Music, the Chrism Mass, the Roman Pontifical, the Roman Ritual, and the Martyrology (to name a few) were all addressed by the *Consilium*'s thirty study groups.[12]

In September of 1964, the instruction *Inter Oecumenici* was published and then implemented in March of 1965. This document put forward specific liturgical reforms such as naming parts of the Mass during which vernacular may be used (IO 57) and expressing the preference that altars should be "freestanding, to permit walking around it and celebration facing the people" (IO 92).[13] In addition to these material reforms, the instruction also reiterated the fundamental principles of the postconciliar reform: "to bring life to the kind of formation of the faithful and ministry of pastors that will have their summit and source in the liturgy" (IO 5). Following the publication of *Inter Oecumenici*, the *Consilium* began quickly producing documents that addressed all areas of the Church's liturgical life, including Communion under both

[12] Marini, *A Challenging Reform*, 117–32.
[13] Anscar Chupungco, OSB, "The Implementation of *Sacrosanctum Concilium*," in *T&T Clark Companion to Liturgy*, ed. Alcuin Reid (New York, 2016), 287.

species, concelebration of Mass, Gregorian chant, and revisions of the
Ordo Missae. Through all of these reforms, the *Consilium* was guided
by careful historical study and the work of *ressourcement* theologians.
For example, when the Congregation for Rites challenged the revised
Rites of Concelebration, the *Consilium* pointed out that their criticisms
had no basis in the church's liturgical history.[14] As Marini points out,
the considerable historical knowledge of the *Consilium*'s membership
gained a great deal of credibility for the group, while the considerable
lack of historical knowledge displayed by the curial Congregation
of Rites weakened its criticisms and its influence. As we will see in
our discussion of *Liturgiam Authenticam*, this lack of historical knowledge of the liturgy has not been a short-lived problem for curial
congregations.

In 1968, Cardinal Lercaro stepped down as the president of *Consilium* and was replaced by Cardinal Benno Gut, who was also named the
prefect of the Congregation of Rites. Then, in 1969, the Congregation of
Rites was divided into two curial congregations: the Congregation for
Divine Worship and the Congregation for the Causes of Saints. Cardinal
Gut was named the prefect of the Congregation for Divine Worship and
Bugnini was named the secretary. The responsibilities of the *Consilium*
were transferred over to the Congregation for Divine Worship, and the
last meeting of the *Consilium* took place in April of 1970.

Between the years of 1968 and 1973, a steady stream of revised
liturgical books was published. Notable among these publications were
the *Ordo Missae*, new Eucharistic Prayers, the Rite of Holy Orders, the
Rite of Marriage, the General Roman Calendar, the Rite of Infant Baptism, The Rite of Confirmation, the Funeral Rite, the Divine Office, the
Lectionary for the Roman Missal, the Rite of Christian Initiation for
Adults (RCIA), the Rite of Anointing of the Sick and Pastoral Care, and
the Rite of Penance. Throughout all the reforms implemented by the
Consilium and the Congregation for Divine Worship, the principle of
full, active participation was constantly upheld while also maintaining
great care for the liturgical history of the Church.

However, unlike the reforms of the Mass, which were rapidly implemented and embraced throughout the church, other revisions were
translated at varying speeds and implemented to varying degrees. For
example, Rita Ferrone has pointed out that, while the revised RCIA
enjoyed sweeping success, the revisions in the Rite of Penance have

---

[14] Marini, *A Challenging Reform*, 104.
[15] Ferrone, *Liturgy*, 62–63.

largely been ignored.[15] Form Three of the Rite of Penance allows for a general absolution of penitents, but this form has since been restricted to extremely rare circumstances, resulting in a *de facto* suppression of the rite. Rather, in Catholic parishes throughout the world, penitents continue to "celebrate" the Sacrament of Penance in an individual, preconciliar manner. The one large difference is that the option for face-to-face confession has become more popular.

Before turning to the criticisms that have been made of the reform, it is important to note that the liturgical vision of the council had a further reach than the Roman Catholic Church. As the constitution desired, the unity of entire Christian church was indeed built up by liturgical reform. For example, the development of the Revised Common Lectionary currently shared by various Protestant churches was based on the 1969 revision of the Lectionary for Mass.[16] Further, one of the great results of the postconciliar liturgical reforms has been the deepening of the ecumenical spirit that was often at the heart of the preconciliar liturgical movements. For example, in a striking affirmation of the liturgical life of Protestant congregations, then Prefect for the Congregation of the Doctrine of Faith Joseph Cardinal Ratzinger stated:

> I count among the most important results of the ecumenical dialogues the insight that the issue of the Eucharist cannot be narrowed to the problem of 'validity.' Even a theology oriented to the concept of succession, such as that which holds in the Catholic and in the Orthodox church, need not in any way deny the salvation-granting presence of the Lord [Heilschaffende Gegenwart des Herrn] in a Lutheran [evangelische] Lord's Supper.[17]

In this excerpt taken from a letter to the Bavarian Lutheran bishop Johannes Hanselmann, Ratzinger clearly affirms the *salvific* presence of Christ in a Lutheran celebration of the Eucharist. Ecumenical relationships like these have continued to bear fruit in the years since the council. A steady stream of ecumenical documents has been generated, not least of which is the World Council of Churches 1982 document, *Baptism, Eucharist, and Ministry*.

---

[16] Frank Quinn, O.P., "Forty Years and Counting," *Liturgy* 19, no. 2 (2004): 5.

[17] Joseph Ratzinger, "Briefwechsel von Landesbischof Johannes Hanselmann und Joseph Kardinal Ratzinger über das Communio-Schreiben der Römischen Glaubenskongregation," *Una Sancta* 48 (1993): 348.

In what Marini has called the "curialization of the reform," Pope Paul VI suppressed the Congregation for Divine Worship in 1975. Three years after ordaining him to the order of bishops, Pope Paul VI removed Annibale Bugnini from his role as guide of the reform. In a farewell letter written to his colleagues, Bishop Bugnini said, "There remains the most difficult task: to see to it that the celebration of the 'work of salvation,' which we humbly served, fully inspires the life of the faithful and of the Church, which is so many-sided because of the number of peoples making it up and so varied in its expressions."[18]

Critiques

Leading into the council and lasting ever since, there has been resistance to the implementation of the council's vision for liturgical renewal. For a thoughtful analysis of the postconciliar reform of the liturgy, John F. Baldovin's study, *Reforming the Liturgy: A Response to the Critics*, is an authoritative appraisal of the various critiques that have arisen since the reform began.[19] While a survey of these critiques is beyond the scope of this chapter, it will be beneficial to focus on two interrelated issues that continue to arise in the ongoing reform of the liturgy: translating liturgical texts and the authority of episcopal conferences. Tracing the relationship between issues will allow us to highlight the resistance that has accompanied the implementation of *Sacrosanctum Concilium*.

In 1969, the *Consilium* published the instruction, *Comme le prévoit*. This document put forth principles that were to guide the translation of liturgical books into vernacular languages. According to the instruction, "a faithful translation cannot be judged on the basis of individual words: the total context of this specific act of communication must be kept in mind, as well as the literary form proper to the respective language."[20] According to Anscar Chupungco, "formal correspondence" is an inadequate principle for guiding translation because "it does not take into account the culture represented by the source and the receptor languages."[21] Translation that seeks to facilitate full, active participation in the liturgy must be supported by a knowledge of and appreciation for cultural diversity. At its best, the task of liturgical

---

[18] Annibale Bugnini, *The Reform of the Liturgy: 1948–1975* (Collegeville, MN: Liturgical Press, 1990), 934.

[19] John F. Baldovin, *Reforming the Liturgy: A Response to the Critics* (Collegeville, MN: Liturgical Press, 2008), 134–35.

[20] Chupungco, "The Implementation," 288.

[21] Ibid.

translation would adopt the appreciation for culture so beautifully described in *Ad Gentes*. The process of translation, then, would be seen as a "mutual outpouring of energy" through which the church comes to more fully participate in the liturgy.

In March of 2001, the Congregation for Divine Worship and the Discipline of the Sacraments published the instruction, *Liturgiam Authenticam*. This document addressed the translation of liturgical texts into vernacular languages, and it was largely an explicit negation of *Comme le prévoit*. In Article 20, *Liturgiam Authenticam* describes liturgical translation as a work "of rendering the original texts faithfully and accurately into the vernacular language ... [T]he original text, insofar as possible, must be translated integrally and in the most exact manner, without omissions or additions in terms of their content, and without paraphrases or glosses." Under the translation principle known as "formal correspondence," translators are to render *texts* faithfully, whereas under the principle of "dynamic equivalence," translators are to communicate *messages* faithfully.

On its publication, there was no shortage of criticism for this document. As Anscar Chupungco puts it: "*Liturgiam authenticam* replaced *Comme le prévoit*. Formal correspondence replaced dynamic equivalence."[22] Emphasis on the unity of Roman Rite became the primary criterion for adapting the liturgy to various cultures. Addressing the problematic stances forwarded by *Liturgiam Authenticam*, Frank C. Quinn notes that, like the documents produced by the Congregation for Rites, this document suffers from a lack of historical scholarship: "It has to be stated that many of its assumptions and claims are not born out by any kind of scholarly study. In fact it does not demonstrate an appreciation for the mountains of research done in the past several centuries by liturgical scholars."[23] As a result of this document, many local episcopal conferences (e.g. Italy, Spain, Germany, France, and Japan) who had been developing vernacular translations began seeing their work rejected by the Congregation for Divine Worship and the Discipline of the Sacraments. Preoccupation with bolstering participation in the liturgy had given way to preoccupation with fidelity to Latin texts.

---

[22] Ibid., 291.
[23] Frank Quinn, O.P., "Forty Years and Counting," *Liturgy* 19, no. 2 (2004): 8. Quinn goes on to cite Peter Jeffery's extensive criticisms found in his work *Translating Tradition: A Chant Historian Reads* Liturgiam Authenticam (Collegeville, MN: Liturgical Press, 2005).

Then, in 2007, Pope Benedict XVI issued the apostolic letter *Summorum pontificum*. Since the beginning of the postconciliar reforms, there has always been a number of the faithful who remain "attached to the previous liturgical tradition" (SP 5). Often born of suspicion for the council's vision of the liturgy, these groups have sought to maintain the celebration of the preconciliar liturgy in order to counter-balance (or negate) the reform's emphasis on cultural and liturgical diversity. In *Summorum pontificum*, the pope authorizes the widespread use of the preconciliar Latin Mass, warning priests not to deny this liturgy to any who might request it. For some this was seen as an affirmation of the church's tradition; for others this document validated and encouraged those who have been resisting the trajectory of the reform since it began. Again, the council's emphasis on appreciation for cultural diversity was giving way to a preference for the uniformity of the "Latinized" Mass.

However, in December of 2016, Pope Francis formed an international commission to review *Liturgiam Authenticam*. The result was *Magnum Principium*, published in September of 2017. This document accomplished two important things. First, it reiterated the principle of dynamic equivalence in translation. Further, the document expressed a desire for a church in which "vernacular languages themselves ... would be able to become liturgical languages, standing out in a not dissimilar way to liturgical Latin for their elegance of style and the profundity of their concepts with the aim of nourishing the faith." Second, the document shifted the responsibility and the authority for translation from the curial Congregation for Worship to the local episcopal conferences. By revising the Code of Canon Law, *Magnum Principium* reestablished the *Sacrosanctum Concilium*'s emphasis on the authority of the episcopal conferences, an authority that greatly serves the necessary diversity of the church in its pilgrim journey. It is worth noting that *Magnum Principium*'s changes to Canon 838 are a near verbatim restatement of *Comme le prévoit*'s second article. Having died in 2013, Anscar Chupungco was not alive to see the publication of *Magnum Principium*. However, we can imagine him saying with satisfaction: "*Magnum principium* replaced *Liturgiam authenticam*. Dynamic equivalence replaced formal correspondence."

As Chupungco has forcefully pointed out, many critics of the liturgical reforms suffer from an isolated perspective. Speaking especially of those critics who would see a return to a Latinized rite that more closely resembles the pre-Vatican II rites, Chupungco says: "It is desirable that the critics of the liturgical reform of Vatican II take time and effort to experience the global Church, especially outside the northern hemisphere, and realize thereby that the Church is indeed Catholic and embraces a variety of approved forms for celebrating the liturgy."[24] Notice that Chupungco encourages anyone who would wish to evaluate liturgical reform to *participate* in the liturgy. As the council reiterated time and again, if a person does not have competence of a particular culture, then that person lacks the ability to adequately assess the adaptations of that liturgy.

CONCLUSION

As noted previously, the council's vision of the liturgy and the liturgical reforms that followed did not appear suddenly. The Second Vatican Council did not inaugurate this liturgical reform with an authoritative and hierarchical decree. Quite the opposite is true. By listening to the liturgical life of the church, the fathers of the council recognized and affirmed the Word of God that was speaking through the lives of the Christian faithful. Nearly every liturgical reform that would take hold over the decades following the council's conclusion had been discussed and tried in the years leading up to the council. In a very real way, the Second Vatican Council's vision of the liturgy was an exercise in mystagogy. In vigorously studying the richly diverse liturgical history of the church, and in reflecting on the liturgical life of the church that had been growing in fervor through the liturgical movement, the Second Vatican Council was able to humbly recognize and amplify the communication of God that had been present long before conciliar documents began being drafted. Decades after the council has closed, the church must continue to hear the dynamic and diverse liturgy of the Christian church as the visible words of a verbose God.

According to the council, the liturgy is the heart of the living Christian faith. It is right, then, that the Christian faithful should attend passionately to the liturgical life through which we live and move and have our being. The liturgy has been and will continue to be a source of much disagreement and division. However, this fact need not lead to despair. Debates and arguments over the liturgy are proof that our communities recognize its import. As *Sacrosanctum Concilium* states: "Enthusiasm for the promotion and restoration of the sacred liturgy is rightly held to be a sign of the providential dispositions of God in our time, and as a movement of the holy Spirit in his Church" (SC 43).

---

[24] Chupungco, "Implementation," 282.

In the end, an examination of the council's effect on the liturgy cannot be reduced to a consideration of liturgical reform. What I have tried to provide in these pages is a distillation of the council's vision of the liturgical nature of the Christian way of being in the world. The Body of Christ walks toward its beatific end with ever changing liturgical footsteps. Through those steps, the church learns to more perfectly hear the Divine Word it is striving to be.

FURTHER READING

Balasuriya, Tissa. *The Eucharist and Human Liberation*. Eugene, OR: Wipf and Stock Publishers, 1977.

Baldovin, John F., SJ. *Reforming the Liturgy: A Response to the Critics*. Collegeville, MN: Liturgical Press, 2008.

Berger, Teresa. *Women's Ways of Worship: Gender Analysis and Liturgical History*. Collegeville, MN: Liturgical Press, 1999.

Bugnini, Annibale. *The Reform of the Liturgy: 1948–1975*. Collegeville, MN: Liturgical Press, 1990.

Chauvet, Louis-Marie. *Symbol and Sacrament*. Collegeville, MN: Liturgical Press, 1983.

Chupungco, Anscar. *Liturgical Inculturation: Sacramentals, Religiosity, and Catechesis*. Collegeville, MN: Liturgical Press, 1992.

Faggioli, Massimo. *True Reform: Liturgy and Ecclesiology in* Sacrosanctum Concilium. Collegeville, MN: Liturgical Press, 2012.

Ferrone, Rita. *Liturgy:* Sacrosanctum Concilium. Mahwah, NJ: Paulist Press, 2007.

Harmon, Katharine E. *There Were Also Many Women There: Lay Women in the Liturgical Movement in the United States, 1926–1959*. Collegeville, MN: Liturgical Press, 2012.

Marini, Piero. *A Challenging Reform: Realizing the Vision of the Liturgical Renewal*. Collegeville, MN: Liturgical Press, 2007.

Vincie, Catherine. *Celebrating Divine Mystery: A Primer in Liturgical Theology*. Collegeville, MN: Liturgical Press, 2009.

11 The Word and Spirit Co-instituting the Church

BRIAN FLANAGAN

In the Apostolic Constitution *Humanae Salutis* by which he formally convoked the Second Vatican Council, Pope John XXIII opens with a reference to Jesus's ascension and concludes with a prayer to the Holy Spirit that the Spirit might "renew your wonders in our time, as though in a new Pentecost."[1] In this structure, we can see two aspects of the trinitarian ecclesiology of the Second Vatican Council: a robust invocation of the presence of Christ in the church, and an awareness of the role of the Holy Spirit in salvation history and in the church that grew even as the council proceeded. The first aspect, the rich invocation of Christ that is found throughout the documents of the Second Vatican Council, was the product of a remarkable century of ecclesiological thought, in which the church was viewed not only as an institution or quasi-political society – what Yves Congar famously named ecclesiology as "hierarchology"[2] – but as the mystical body of Christ and as "a sacrament – a sign and instrument, that is, of communion with God and of the unity of the entire human race" (LG 1). Vatican II's statements on the church built on that achievement, claiming this more deeply theological understanding of the church's relation to Christ. This Christocentric understanding of the church was the crucial starting point in the council's ecclesiological reflections, and remains so in our attempts to interpret it today.

John XXIII's prayer at the end of *Humanae Salutis*, however, and its reference to the Council as a New Pentecost, as a new outpouring of the Holy Spirit, also quickly became a dominant way of analyzing and remembering the Second Vatican Council.[3] But this explicit invocation

---

[1] https://w2.vatican.va/content/john-xxiii/la/apost_constitutions/1961/documents/hf_j-xxiii_apc_19611225_humanae-salutis.html.

[2] Yves Congar, *Lay People in the Church*, trans. Donald Attwater (Westminster, MD: Newman, 1965), 35.

[3] See Thomas Hughson, SJ, "Interpreting Vatican II: A New Pentecost," *Theological Studies* 69 (2008): 3–37.

of the Holy Spirit was, if not entirely surprising, somewhat unusual for mid-twentieth-century Catholic theology, and in particular for mid-century theologies of the church. Even as John XXIII called for a new Pentecost, that paragraph was the only place in the entire text where the Holy Spirit was mentioned, in comparison to its frequent reference to the presence of Christ in and through the church. This contrast between a strongly Christological understanding of the church and a relatively weak pneumatological awareness reflects the state of preconciliar ecclesiology and the starting horizon within which the ecclesiology of the Second Vatican Council developed.

Nevertheless, the starting point was not the ending point; a more balanced understanding of the church as rooted in the divine missions of the Word *and* the Spirit developed in, through, and because of the council. While retaining much of the Christological understanding of preconciliar ecclesiology, Vatican II provides a complementary pneumatological framework that more adequately situates the church in a trinitarian framework and a starting point for the more robust pneumatological ecclesiology that developed in the following decades. This was true for the text of the conciliar constitutions, especially as the council fathers adapted their own approaches to ecclesiology in conversation with theological experts and observers from the other Christian churches. But, perhaps more importantly, it was true of the overall framework in which the church was defined as a pilgrim people of God, located within history, and not only looking back to Jesus Christ as the origin of its journey but also looking forward to its future, guided by the Holy Spirit. By the end of the Council, the documents could begin to explore the idea of the church as not only the Body of Christ, but even as a distant echo of the Trinity itself. In this rebalancing, Catholic ecclesiology can more clearly, in the words of Yves Congar, identify the church as co-instituted by the Word and the Spirit.[4]

This chapter begins by outlining some of preconciliar ecclesiology's characteristic Christocentrism. It looks both at the importance of the reintegration of Christology in nineteenth- and twentieth-century theology and at some of the ways in which preconciliar Catholic theology tended to forget the Holy Spirit, often by subsuming the Holy Spirit under its statements about the church, or even by substituting other realities for the Holy Spirit in its conception of the divine economy. Second, it looks more explicitly at the place of Christ and the Holy

---

[4] See Yves Congar, "The Two Missions: The Spirit as the Co-instituting Principle of the Church," in *I Believe in the Holy Spirit* (New York: Crossroad, 1997), II: 7.

Spirit in the texts of the council, and in particular at the complementarity established between them, even if the Christological focus remains dominant in some ways. Third, it looks at two broader ecclesiological trends that the council's documents embodied and promoted, namely, the broader eschatological framework that the council renewed within its trinitarian framework, and the comparison made between the unity of the church and the *koinonia* or communion between the trinitarian persons. Finally, it will look briefly at the reception of this renewed ecclesiology of Word and Spirit.

PRECONCILIAR CHRISTOCENTRIC ECCLESIOLOGY

Catholic ecclesiology before the Second Vatican Council was marked by much of the history of the post-Reformation era; its focus on hierarchical structures of authority, its use of the marks of the church as "proofs" of the Catholic Church as the one true church, and especially its nineteenth-century ultramontanist emphasis on the papacy as the cornerstone of Catholic life all form some of the context in which the ecclesiologies of the twentieth century grew and developed. For the purposes of understanding the trinitarian origins of the church, two preconciliar ecclesiological trends are particularly significant. The first was the growth of new forms of ecclesiological reflection that drew attention not only to the visible structures of the church but to the invisible, spiritual reality of the church; this new perspective often used the image of the "mystical body of Christ" as its key metaphor for understanding that reality. A second related trend was the relative absence of the Holy Spirit in ecclesiology, either through too close an identification between the Holy Spirit and the church, or through a replacement of the functions of the Holy Spirit by other ecclesial entities, or both.

The first development can be seen as rooted most firmly in the new style of ecclesiology pioneered by the theologians of the Tübingen School of the early nineteenth century, and especially in the work of Johann Adam Möhler.[5] In both of Möhler's major works, the Spirit-centered *Unity in the Church* and the later, Christ-centered *Symbolism*, Möhler outlines a theology of the church focused neither on structures and institution nor primarily on polemicized "proofs" in support of Catholicism over Protestantism, but instead on the inner nature of

---

[5] See Johann Adam Möhler, *Unity in the Church*, trans. Peter C. Erb (Washington, DC: Catholic University of America Press, 1996); and Möhler, *Symbolism*, trans. James Burton Robinson (New York: Crossroad: 1997).

the church as the starting point for understanding its reality and that of its structures. Deeply influenced by German Romanticism, Möhler's work, and that of later nineteenth-century theologians like Matthias Scheeben, Giovanni Perrone, Carlo Passaglia, and Johann Baptist Franzelin, made ecclesiology less of an apologetic exercise in relation to Protestantism, or an adjunct to canon law that limited itself to outlining ecclesial structures in scholastic treatises *De Ecclesia*. Instead, they treated the church as an object of faith itself and as an aspect of the mystery of salvation history.

In doing so, while the Holy Spirit was almost never absent, these theologies, beginning with Möhler's *Symbolism*, were deeply Christo-centric. The church was conceived in some of these ecclesiologies almost as a form of an "ongoing incarnation" of Christ. This trajectory culminated in the theologies of the church as the "mystical body of Christ" and in the official endorsement of this theology, especially as formulated in the early twentieth century by Sebastian Tromp, in Pope Pius XII's 1943 encyclical *Mystici Corporis Christi*. This landmark encyclical, by affirming the church as an integral part of the mystery of salvation, consolidated the ecclesiological developments of the previous decades and moved away from ecclesiology as "hierarchology." Such a viewpoint set the stage for the further reflections at the Second Vatican Council on the nature and structures of the church as the expression of a theology of the church's role in salvation – in this sense, Vatican II's ecclesiology was not *sui generis*, but built on this earlier trajectory of scholarship and official teaching. With the primary metaphor of the church as the mystical body of Christ, this ecclesiology was dominated by attention to Christ's founding of the church; to the close, intimate connection between the church and Christ; and to the role of the church in continuing Christ's presence, especially through the Eucharist. This approach was not mistaken, in that many of these ideas *are* crucial to ecclesiology and were taken up by the documents of Vatican II—but it was one-sided.

Within these ecclesiologies, however, the Holy Spirit and the pneumatological foundations of the church were never so much denied as often neglected. In ecclesiology and Catholic theology more widely, there was a general "forgetting" of the Holy Spirit. Despite the consistency of trinitarian formulas throughout Christian history, and some significant thinkers and movements that emphasized the role of the Holy Spirit, Karl Rahner famously asked in his work *On the Trinity* whether the doctrine of the Trinity made any difference at all in the spiritual life of most Christians, or whether they would have any difficulty if the church were suddenly to drop or change the dogma.[6] Part of that problem, especially in the early twentieth century, involved a lack of understanding of where the Holy Spirit fits within the economy of salvation. As in some artistic depictions of the Trinity, a "two blokes and a bird" image of the Trinity, in which the clear personhood of the Father and the Son is complemented, awkwardly, by a dove representing the Holy Spirit, contributed to a practical theology in which the Holy Spirit seemed to be an unnecessary addendum to Christian faith.

In theology, this absence of awareness of the mission of the Spirit often led to the substitution of other entities in its place – usually the church. Yves Congar, in his classic treatment of this phenomenon, quotes the early twentieth-century theologian Karl Adam's elision of the church and the Holy Spirit in *The Spirit of Catholicism*: "So we see the certitude of the Catholic faith rests on the sacred triad: God, Christ, Church."[7] Congar goes on to discuss what one missionary praised as the "three white things" – "the Host, the Virgin Mary, and the Pope" – that functioned as substitutes for the Holy Spirit in some preconciliar theology and devotion; these "three white things" made Christ present, guaranteed the continuing of Christ's mission, or advocated on our behalf to God. Congar quotes Matthias Scheeben's statement that "the Eucharist, Mary, and the Holy See are the most important links by which the Church is established, maintained, and shown to be true, total, firm and living communion with Christ."[8] Many of the traditional attributes of the Holy Spirit, as enabling Christians to receive Christ, as guaranteeing the unity and indefectibility of the church, or as co-instituting the church with Christ, are attributed to Eucharist, Pope, and/or Mary, rather than to the Holy Spirit. Given such a theological environment, the Holy Spirit tended to be verbally and technically present, but functionally ignored, in much Catholic ecclesiology. One can begin to see why at the convocation of John XXIII's hoped-for New Pentecost, the Holy Spirit received but one explicit mention. And yet, as the council continued, awareness of the Holy Spirit's role in the church and attention to that fact in its documents grew into a more complete theology of the church as co-instituted by Christ *and* by the Holy Spirit.

---

[6] Karl Rahner, *The Trinity* (New York: Crossroad, 1997).
[7] See Yves Congar, "Forgetting the Holy Spirit," in *I Believe in the Holy Spirit*, 1: 159.
[8] Ibid., 161.

THE CONCILIAR TEXTS

While there are two constitutions from the Second Vatican Council that focus explicitly on the church – *Lumen Gentium*, the Dogmatic Constitution on the Church, and *Gaudium et Spes*, the Pastoral Constitution on the Church in the Modern World – arguably almost all of the council and its documents make major contributions to Catholic ecclesiology and contribute to our overall understanding of the church. Most important are the other two constitutions, *Sacrosanctum Concilium*, the Constitution on the Sacred Liturgy, and *Dei Verbum*, the Dogmatic Constitution on Divine Revelation. But many of the other decrees and declarations, such as those on bishops, on priests, on religious, on laity, and on mission, have major ecclesiological implications. Looking at some of these texts, not only in terms of their final content but also in terms of the process by which they came to be, can be helpful in understanding the overall trinitarian ecclesiology of the council, as well as the growth in that understanding over the four-year period in which the council met.

The rich Christological foundations of the Council are immediately apparent in the documents. Contrary to some initial impressions, the *lumen gentium*, the "light of the nations" to which the Dogmatic Constitution on the Church makes reference, is not the church, but Jesus Christ. Throughout that text, and indeed throughout all of the conciliar texts, Christ is named in almost every chapter and nearly every page. *Lumen Gentium* provides a good example of this dynamic. In its first chapter on the mystery of the church, we find reflections on Jesus' founding of the church (LG 3), an extended recapitulation of the ecclesiology of the Mystical Body of Christ (LG 7), a comparison of the church's divine and human elements to the hypostatic union of the incarnation (LG 8), and a claiming of Christ's mission as the church's mission (LG 8). Later chapters explore the more traditional questions of the hierarchical structures instituted by Christ and the ways in which the ordained, laity, and religious are universally called to holiness and participate in differentiated ways in Christ's mission.

Beyond the sheer number of mentions of Jesus Christ, however, the document draws on and reflects the accomplishments of preconciliar ecclesiology in pointing to the church not as a neutral institution for the transmission of information or grace, but as itself an aspect of the mystery of our salvation. We get some clue of this by comparing the draft schemas of the document on the church with what became the final text of *Lumen Gentium*.[9] As opposed to earlier versions, which began their treatment of the church with a consideration of the origins of the church's institutions and the powers and duties of hierarchy, *Lumen Gentium* begins with a reflection on the "mystery" of the church; it is empowered by Christ to "reveal in the world, faithfully, although with shadows, the mystery of its Lord until, in the end, it [the mystery of Christ] shall be manifested in full light" (LG 8). This participation of the church in the very mystery of Christ led the Fathers to start with the mystery of the trinitarian God, and to begin their treatment with scriptural images and metaphors, including that of the Mystical Body, that shed light on the nature of the church. Its second chapter on the church as a people of God, "established by Christ as a communion of life, love, and truth" and "as the instrument for the salvation of all" (LG 9) further locates the council's teaching on the church as teaching fundamentally on the nature and history of salvation. Only after these two remarkable chapters – chapters absent from the earliest schemas on the church – does *Lumen Gentium* begin to address the particular institutional and hierarchical structures of the church.

At the same time, *Lumen Gentium* goes further in complementing this focus on the church as the presence of Christ with an expansive account of the operation of the Holy Spirit in the life and witness of the church. To understand the pneumatological perspective of Vatican II, *Lumen Gentium* is our best starting point. Nearly a third of all of the explicit references to the Holy Spirit in all of the conciliar documents occur in *Lumen Gentium*; more importantly, *Lumen Gentium* establishes the complementarity of Christ and the Spirit in a programmatic way that is taken over in most, though not all, of the further documents that draw on it. Unlike past ecclesial statements in which the Trinity is invoked at the end of a long discourse on God and Christ, almost as an addendum, *Lumen Gentium* provides evidence of the trinitarian structure of Vatican II's ecclesiology.

This occurs first in a remarkable section of the first chapter of *Lumen Gentium* on the mystery of the church (LG 4). Following its discussion of the Father's and Son's roles in the origins and nature of the church, *Lumen Gentium* outlines a wide-ranging vision of the role of the Spirit in the church. As one theologian summarizes, in this one dense text the Holy Spirit "continually sanctifies, gives access to the

---

[9] See Richard Gaillardetz, *The Church in the Making* (New York: Paulist Press, 2006), 8–25.

Father, is a foundation of water springing up to life everlasting, gives life to sinners, raises up mortal bodies, dwells in the church and in the hearts of the faithful, prays in them, bears witness to their adoptive sonship, guides into all truth, unifies in communion, directs, bestows various gifts, adorns with fruits, rejuvenates, renews, and leads into perfect union with God."[10] That is quite the job description, and the remainder of *Lumen Gentium*, especially in the chapters on the people of God, the charisms of the laity and religious, the universal call to holiness, and the pilgrim nature of the church, is replete with further indications of the Holy Spirit's presence and work as the sanctifier of the church, playing a role in relation to the structures of the church similar to that of the Word in relation to the humanity of Jesus Christ. One exception to this pattern is in chapter three, on the hierarchical nature of the church, which, as the most traditional topic of preconciliar ecclesiology, retains a more exclusively Christocentric focus, leading at least one theologian to identify the "pneumatological renewal" of *Lumen Gentium* and of the council as a whole less as a completed assimilation of a fully mature theology of the Spirit, and more as a "work in progress."[11]

That progress, in the drafts of *Lumen Gentium* and in the other documents of the council, also helps us understand the Second Vatican Council as an "event" in its own right, and as a pivot or transitional point of theological development. One point of contrasting reference is the text of *Sacrosanctum Concilium*, the Constitution on the Sacred Liturgy. This document was both one of the earliest promulgated by the council, in late 1963, and also focused on one of the topics that the council fathers were most prepared to discuss when they arrived at the council, thanks to the liturgical movement of the previous decades and the maturity of theological thought on the liturgy. It is not surprising, therefore, that *Sacrosanctum Concilium* has the least developed pneumatology of any of the four major constitutions; the Holy Spirit is mentioned only five times in the entire document, and even then in a relatively formulaic and perfunctory way. Beyond a numerical comparison, the dominance of a Christological vision of the liturgy and of the church is even more clearly shown by the powerful understanding of the liturgy's ability to make Christ present in the world. *Sacrosanctum*

---

[10] Mary Cecily Boulding, OP, "The Doctrine of the Holy Spirit in the Documents of Vatican II," *Irish Theological Quarterly* 51 (1985): 259.

[11] See Jos Moons, SJ, "*Lumen Gentium*'s Pneumatological Renewal: A 'Work in Progress,'" *Ecclesiology* 12 (2016): 147–64.

Concilium describes the fourfold presence of Christ in the assembly, the presider, the word, and the eucharistic elements (SC 7), identifies the liturgy as "an exercise of the priestly office of Jesus Christ," and identifies every liturgical celebration as "an action of Christ the priest and of his body, which is the church" (SC 7). In the overall theology of the liturgy as directed toward "our sanctification in Christ and the glorification of God to which all other activities of the church are directed" (SC 10), the Holy Spirit is as forgotten or absent as in much preconciliar ecclesiology. While drawing on the richness of the church as the Body of Christ, as in preconciliar ecclesiology, *Sacrosanctum Concilium* reflects a Christocentric imbalance just as John XXIII's convocation of the council did.

By contrast, the constitutions and decrees that were developed in dialogue with or on the basis of *Lumen Gentium* reflect the trinitarian and pneumatological turn that occurred over the course of the meeting of the council. In the Dogmatic Constitution on Divine Revelation *Dei Verbum*, the complementary missions of the Word and the Spirit are invoked in explaining revelation and the transmission of God's communication through scripture and the tradition of the church; in its key paragraph on scripture and tradition, *Dei Verbum* states that

> sacred scripture is the utterance of God put down as it is in writing under the inspiration of the holy Spirit. And tradition transmits in its entirety the word of God which has been entrusted to the apostles by Christ the Lord and the holy Spirit; it transmits it to the successors of the apostles so that, enlightened by the Spirit of truth, they may faithfully preserve, expound and disseminate it by their preaching (DV 9).

In the Pastoral Constitution on the Church in the Modern World *Gaudium et Spes*, the Holy Spirit is present along with Christ from the opening paragraph of the document, and expounds its theology of the church in relation to the world by stating that "the people of God believes that it is led by the Spirit of the Lord who fills the whole world," opening the council to reflection on where that Spirit might be found outside of the explicit boundaries of the church (GS 11). Further, before its reflections on particular ethical and political issues, *Gaudium et Spes* invokes the paschal mystery of Christ as the mystery of humanity, and highlights both the Holy Spirit's role in conforming Christians to the "image of the Son" as well as the more expansive idea "that the Holy Spirit offers to all," including non-Christians, "the possibility of being made partners, in a way known to God, in the paschal mystery" (GS 22).

In the decrees focused on the institutions of the church and the different forms of life and office that constitute the Christian faithful, the council continues to invoke the Christ whom the church makes present through the guidance and inspiration of the Holy Spirit. The integration of a thoroughly trinitarian viewpoint is, as in *Lumen Gentium* itself, sometimes uneven; the decrees on bishops, priests, and religious, like chapter three of *Lumen Gentium* on the hierarchical church, focus primarily on the Christological foundations of ecclesial hierarchy without much continuing reflection on the role of the Spirit. Two of the texts that address some of the most modern issues on which the council spoke – religious liberty, in the Declaration on Religious Liberty *Dignitatis Humanae,* and other religions, in the Declaration on the Relation of the Church to Non-Christian Religions *Nostra Aetate* – barely mention the Holy Spirit.

By contrast, the Decree on the Apostolate of Lay People *Apostolicam Actuositatem,* the Decree on the Church's Missionary Activity *Ad Gentes,* and the Decree on Ecumenism *Unitatis Redintegratio* all evidence greater integration of a trinitarian theology in which the church and its activities are co-instituted by the working together of Christ and the Holy Spirit. In *Apostolicam Actuositatem,* the council outlines a potent theology of ecclesial charisms, such that lay Christians' bearing witness to Christ in the world is empowered by the special gifts of the Holy Spirit (AA 3). In *Ad Gentes,* the Holy Spirit is viewed as a principle of unity and of mission, "inspiring in the hearts of the faithful that same spirit of mission which impelled Christ himself" (AG 4). Finally, and most powerfully, in *Unitatis Redintegratio,* the council names the activity of the Holy Spirit and its charisms in and among the separated Christian churches and ecclesial communities, teaching that "the Spirit of Christ has not refrained from using them as means of salvation" (UR 3). This is particularly significant in that one of the factors that stimulated wider treatment of the joint missions of Christ and the Spirit in the church was the feedback of invited ecumenical observers critical of the exclusively Christocentric nature of the earliest texts.[12]

In summary, then, while there was a learning process that can be observed between the largely "Christocentrism-as-usual" perspective of *Sacrosanctum Concilium* and the more self-consciously trinitarian focus of *Lumen Gentium, Dei Verbum,* and *Gaudium et Spes,* as well as the supplementary declarations, Vatican II clearly identified the church as

---

[12] See Yves Congar, "The Pneumatology of Vatican II," in *I Believe in the Holy Spirit* (New York: Crossroad, 1997), 1: 167.

the joint creation of the Word and the Spirit. As in St. Irenaeus' famous analogy of the Son and Spirit as the "two hands" of the Father by which he acts in the world, the Second Vatican Council drew on a rich theology of the church as the Body of Christ, which emphasized the church's connection to Jesus, and recovered and renewed a pneumatological perspective in which the church, the Temple of the Holy Spirit, is sanctified and empowered by the Holy Spirit in its mission to the world.

TWO KEY PERSPECTIVES FOR POSTCONCILIAR ECCLESIOLOGY

The previous section focused on the explicit ways in which the conciliar texts provided a more balanced ecclesiology in which both Christ and the Holy Spirit co-instituted the church. This section stands back from that survey to look more broadly at two aspects of conciliar ecclesiology that reflect that trinitarian framework and that have had a lasting effect on postconciliar ecclesiology.

The first is the recovery of an eschatological, reign-of-God-focused worldview in ecclesiology that is found most clearly in chapter seven of *Lumen Gentium* on the pilgrim church. This chapter more than any other gives evidence of the recovery and renewal in ecclesiology of the eschatological tension between the "already" and "not yet" that is characteristic of the path of the church in history. That pilgrimage, which began with the life, death, resurrection, and ascension of Jesus Christ, continues, under the guidance of the Holy Spirit, until the fulfillment of Christ's victory in the reign of God. Recovering this way of envisioning the church in time, as a community both looking back to the events of Jesus' life as its source as well as forward to the reign of God that has not yet fully arrived, was a major accomplishment of twentieth-century theology. The council fathers noted the existence of the church in the midst of this tension:

> "Already the final age of the world is with us and the renewal of the world is irrevocably under way; it is even now anticipated in a certain real way, for the church on earth is endowed already with a sanctity that is true though imperfect. However, until the arrival of the new heavens and the new earth in which justice dwells the pilgrim church, in its sacraments and institutions, which belong to this present age, carries the mark of this world which will pass" (LG 48).

These two aspects of this ecclesiological viewpoint – looking back to the church's origins and looking forward to the church's destiny – point back to the trinitarian nature of the church. It would be wrong to draw too tight a connection between the Divine Persons and these two temporal viewpoints – the Holy Spirit enabled Jesus' conception and descended on him at the start of his ministry, and the eschatological fulfillment of the reign of God is connected with the return of Christ as Lord and Judge. But it may be suggestive to explore how preconciliar Catholic ecclesiology, with its primarily Christocentric focus, was also focused primarily on the past, on the revelation of God in Christ and the institutions and tradition that preserved and handed on that revelation. It seems no coincidence that the sections of *Lumen Gentium* and the other documents most concerned with the hierarchical structures of the church and the guarantees that allow its pastors to conserve and hand on the faith are some of the most Christocentric texts of the council.

At the same time, the new forward-looking aspects of conciliar ecclesiology invoke the Holy Spirit as a principle of their growth and guidance. A more pneumatological ecclesiology speaks about the present and future mission of the church, for, as the council teaches, "the church is driven by the holy Spirit to play its part in bringing to completion the plan of God" (LG 17). In its invocation of a universal call to holiness, of Mary and the communion of saints, of the diverse charisms of lay people and religious communities, and of the activity of the Holy Spirit outside of the visible boundaries of the Catholic Church, the Second Vatican Council's more balanced trinitarian outlook provides an ecclesiology that looks forward and outward, as well as backward. The church expects, under the guidance of the Spirit of Christ, to both carry forward what it has learned and experienced from its past but also to be empowered for, and even surprised by, its future.

A second broader concept in Vatican II's trinitarian ecclesiology that would go on to have a major effect on Catholic ecclesiology more broadly is the comparison made between the relation of the trinitarian persons in the life of God and the *koinonia*, the communion, between Christians in the church. This comparison is made explicitly in *Unitatis Redintegratio*, where the hoped-for unity between currently divided Christians as well as the already-existing unity within the Catholic Church is lauded as an image of the Trinity. This decree teaches that "this is the sacred mystery of the unity of the church, in Christ and through Christ, with the holy Spirit energizing its various functions. The highest exemplar and source of this mystery is the unity, in the Trinity of Persons, of one God, the Father and the Son in the holy Spirit" (UR 2). This theme of ecclesial unity-in-diversity is expressed differently in *Lumen Gentium*, as this document praises the unity of the church in trinitarian terms, writing that "this, too, is why God sent the Spirit of his Son, the Lord and giver of life, who for the church and for each and every believer is the principle of their union" (LG 13). It did so, however, without making a direct trinitarian analogy to ecclesial unity beyond quoting St. Cyprian's words that "the universal church is seen to be 'a people made one by the unity of the Father, the Son and the holy Spirit'" (LG 4).

Nevertheless, in a broad swath of theologies labeled "communion ecclesiologies" these related understandings of ecclesial unity as communion became a dominant trend in late twentieth-century theology, and the seeds of these ideas in the conciliar documents were identified as the foundation for these further ecclesiological developments. The Final Report of the 1985 Extraordinary Synod of Bishops, convened to mark the twentieth anniversary of the end of Vatican II, stated that "the ecclesiology of communion is the central and fundamental idea of the Council's documents," despite the relative paucity of explicit discussion of communion in the conciliar texts itself.[13] And, while it is critical to see this development as part of the history of interpretation of the council rather than part of the original intent of the council fathers, the rapid growth of various "visions and versions" of communion ecclesiology in postconciliar ecclesiology points to a change that Vatican II made in renewing an understanding of the unity of the church as something different than ecclesial uniformity.[14]

We would do well to be suspicious of theologies that too easily or lightly draw conclusions for ecclesiology based on trinitarian perichoresis – the difference between the nature of humans and human communities, on one hand, and that of the Divine Persons is too great, and in our limited, creaturely perspective we can know more about humans and human communities through our direct experience than we will know about the Trinity. But at the same time, the trinitarian analogy, and the wider trinitarian outlook that *Lumen Gentium* opened for thinking about unity and diversity within the church, demonstrates another way in which Vatican II's ecclesiology balanced the missions of the Word and the Spirit, and in so doing opened up more space for thinking about the church as a communion of diverse charisms and

---

[13] "The Church, in the Word of God, Celebrates the Mysteries of Christ for the Salvation of the World," The Final Report of the 1985 Extraordinary Synod of Bishops, II.C.1.

[14] See Dennis Doyle, *Communion Ecclesiology: Visions and Versions* (Maryknoll, NY: Orbis, 2000).

communities, rather than as a monolithic, pyramidal institution. As with its relocation of the church within time, this relocation of the church within space – geographical space and the spaces of human culture and difference – allowed ecclesiology to explore both the Christological principle of shared origin in the life and work of Jesus Christ, as well as the varied and diverse ways in which the church exists, guided by a Spirit that "blows where it wills."

THE RECEPTION OF CONCILIAR ECCLESIOLOGY

Exploration of the continued development and growth of communion ecclesiologies leads immediately to a wider exploration of the further effects of Vatican II's trinitarian ecclesiology on the church and its theology. At a minimum, one can observe in continuing Catholic theology how more attention to pneumatology and the relation of the Holy Spirit to the church has made awareness of the trinitarian co-institution of the church a standard aspect of Catholic ecclesiology. One highly visible practical effect of the renewal of a more robust theology of the Holy Spirit in the church was the Catholic Charismatic Renewal. This movement began in the United States shortly after the end of the Second Vatican Council, and in it Catholics experienced the immediate presence of the Holy Spirit and of charismatic gifts in ways similar to that in the Pentecostal movement and churches of the twentieth century. A less dramatic but perhaps more long-lasting result was the effect on all Catholics, but especially lay people, of the conciliar theology of charisms as gifts for mission and of the universal call to holiness. Lay-led apostolates, ministries, and new religious communities, building on preconciliar foundations, rapidly grew and diversified in the postconciliar church, even as vocations to ordination and to religious life simultaneously declined. The discovery of the possibility of lay vocation, of being called by baptism in Christ and empowered by the Holy Spirit to participate in the mission of the church, had perhaps the greatest impact on the life of the Catholic Church throughout the world.

Much of this occurred with a sense of upheaval, as older forms of religious life and vocational discernment were challenged in a new environment; in places like North America and Europe, the coincidence of the postconciliar period with the dramatic cultural and political upheavals of the late 1960s intensified this sense of rapid change. But in that sense of change, one can see the wider Catholic embrace of the idea of a trinitarian church rooted both in the handing on of the past action of Christ and in looking forward to the further working of the Holy Spirit in and through the communion of churches. In that, the church took to heart the Council's teaching in *Lumen Gentium* on the pilgrim people of God: "For if we continue to love one another and to join in praising the most holy Trinity – all of us who are children of God and form one family in Christ – we will be faithful to the deepest vocation of the church and will share in a foretaste of the liturgy of perfect glory" (LG 51).

FURTHER READING

The Church: Towards a Common Vision. Faith and Order Paper No. 214. Geneva: World Council of Churches, 2013.

Doyle, Denis. *Communion Ecclesiology: Visions and Versions.* Maryknoll, NY: Orbis, 2000.

Gaillardetz, Richard R. *The Church in the Making.* New York: Paulist, 2006.

Healy, Nicholas M. "The Church in Modern Theology." In *The Routledge Companion to the Christian Church*, edited by Gerard Mannion and Lewis S. Mudge, 106–26. New York: Routledge, 2008.

Imbelli, Robert. *Rekindling the Christic Imagination.* Collegeville, MN: Liturgical Press, 2014.

Komonchak, Joseph. "The Significance of Vatican Council II for Ecclesiology." In *The Gift of the Church*, edited by Peter C. Phan, 69–92. Collegeville, MN: Liturgical Press, 2000.

Markey, John. *Creating Communion: The Theology of the Constitutions of the Church.* Hyde Park, NY: New City Press, 2003.

Rush, Ormond. "Roman Catholic Ecclesiology from the Council of Trent to Vatican II and Beyond." In *The Oxford Handbook of Ecclesiology*, edited by Paul Avis, 263–92. Oxford: Oxford University Press, 2018

12 The Christian Faithful

AMANDA C. OSHEIM

In 1859, John Henry Newman, an English Roman Catholic priest, wrote an article entitled "On Consulting the Faithful in Matters of Doctrine" in the periodical he edited, the *Rambler*. It was a further reply to those who protested a previous article, in which Newman had supported the position of a lay writer for the *Rambler* and expert on Catholic schools, Nasmyth Scott Stokes, who critically, but respectfully, encouraged the bishops to be proactive in cooperating with a public commission on elementary education.[1] When his articles came under criticism from Bishop Ullathorne of Birmingham for contradicting the bishops after they had reached a formal decision, Newman penned a first reply as editor. In it he apologized that Scott Stokes's articles had been published before Newman became aware of the bishops' decision. Yet he also wrote:

> If even in the preparation of a dogmatic definition the faithful are consulted, as lately in the instance of the Immaculate Conception, it is at least as natural to anticipate such an act of kind feeling and sympathy in great practical questions, out of the condescension of those who are *forma facti gregis ex animo*.
> ["examples to their flock," 1 Peter 5:3][2]

Rather than tamping down the embers, this affirmation proved to be fuel for a firestorm of criticism. Newman records that in a subsequent conversation Bishop Ullathorne asked him, "Who are the laity?" and that the gist of his reply was, "The church would look foolish without them."[3] The conclusion of their conversation was that Newman would edit one last issue before resigning his post.

---

[1] John Coulson, "Introduction," in John Henry Newman, *On Consulting the Faithful in Matters of Doctrine*, ed. John Coulson (New York: Sheed and Ward, 1961), 10–11.

[2] Ibid., 13.

[3] Ibid., 19.

In his final issue, Newman published "On Consulting the Faithful in Matters of Doctrine," and defended his proposition at length. He insisted the laity ought to be consulted "because the body of the faithful is one of the witnesses to the fact of the tradition of revealed doctrine, and because their *consensus* through Christendom is the voice of the Infallible Church."[4] This assertion, that the laity are a source of knowing the tradition Christ entrusted to the apostles and passed down through the centuries of the church, inspired some responses that revealed a quite different estimation of the role of the laity. For instance, Monsignor George Talbot offered this retort to Newman's lay supporters: "What is the province of the laity? To hunt, to shoot, to entertain. These matters they understand, but to meddle with ecclesiastical matters they have no right at all, and this affair of Newman is purely ecclesiastical."[5]

Those who rejected Newman's claims about the laity did not arrive at their conclusions without cause. Rather, they inherited an understanding of the church that had been dominant within Roman Catholicism for several centuries. The hierarchical aspect of the church was emphasized, and the church itself was envisioned as a pyramid.[6] The pope was the pyramid's apex, and in this top position, he was closest in relationship to God. Next down were bishops, clergy, religious, and finally the laity. In keeping with a focus on the role of the hierarchy in the church, thinking of the church as a pyramid not only linked teaching authority in the church with closeness to God but also made learning in the church an attribute of the pyramid's base.

Given this way of thinking about the church, the negative responses to Newman's assertions are not surprising. Yet, a little over 100 years later, Vatican II embraced an understanding of the laity that received and developed Newman's insights as well as those of other theologians, such as Yves Congar, a French Dominican whose work challenged, though did not simply supplant, the dominant ecclesial paradigm.[7] Another vision of the church emerged within the council documents, that of an apostolic communion in which all the members of the church are sacramentally united with God and each other, with all sharing

---

[4] Newman, *On Consulting the Faithful in Matters of Doctrine,* §2.

[5] Coulson, "Introduction," 41.

[6] Ormond Rush, "Inverting the Pyramid: The *Sensus Fidelium* in a Synodal Church," *Theological Studies* 28, no. 2 (2017): 300–1.

[7] Yves Congar, *Lay People in the Church,* trans. Donald Attwater (London: Chapman, 1965).

responsibility for God's salvific mission.[8] Angel Antón notes this eccle-siology was "juxtaposed" within conciliar documents with the pyram-idal ecclesiology, leaving postconciliar theologians to work through "ambiguities" borne of the need for the texts to gain approval from the majority of the council fathers.[9]

Describing the church as an apostolic communion involved two theological shifts. The first was the recovery of baptism as the sacra-ment that constitutes the church (e.g. SC 6, LG 9, 14). The council understood baptism to create a common identity among church members. The second was the council's recovery of a more robust theology of the Holy Spirit (LG 4).[10] In baptism, the one Spirit of God unites the faithful with Christ, and so works to bring about the church's communion. The indwelling of the Spirit, which allows the Christian faithful to live in ways that are responsive to their baptismal relation-ships, means all the faithful have knowledge of God. Rather than divide the church between those who teach and those who learn, the church as a whole both learns and teaches. The different forms this learning and teaching takes are also the work of the Spirit who is not only the principle of unity within the church but also of its diversity. The Spirit's charisms, or gifts for building up the church, are received at baptism; the vocations to which the Spirit calls the faithful, even those of the church's hierarchy for authoritative teaching, arise from Christians' shared life in Christ.

Based on its understanding of baptism and the Holy Spirit, Vatican II offers a different way of thinking about Bishop Ullathorne's question, "Who are the laity?" as well as Monsignor Talbot's query into their areas of competence. It addresses these questions by responding to a related, more fundamental one: "Who is the church?" The council's reply is "the Christian faithful" (*Christifideles*). The following sections of this chapter examine theological foundations for the council's answer. First, two primary metaphors to describe the Christian faithful: the body of Christ and the people of God. These metaphors speak to both unity and diversity among the Christian faithful predicated on a baptismal identity. Second, the Christian faithful participate in the

---

[8] Amanda C. Osheim, *A Ministry of Discernment: The Bishop and the Sense of the Faithful* (Collegeville, MN: Liturgical Press, 2016), 25.

[9] Angel Antón, "Postconciliar Ecclesiology: Expectations, Results, and Prospects for the Future," in *Vatican II: Assessment and Perspectives: Twenty-Five Years After*, vol. 1, ed. René Latourelle (Mahwah, NJ: Paulist Press, 1988), 421–22.

[10] Yves Congar, *I Believe in the Holy Spirit*, vol. 1, trans. David Smith (New York: The Crossroad Publishing Company, 2001), 167–72.

mystery of the incarnation and the paschal mystery. Through these mysteries, the faithful share Christ's work both within and beyond the church. Finally, the Christian faithful are called to the immanent and eschatological work of building God's kingdom. By entering into the divine life, they are collaborators in enacting God's will for salvation.

BODY OF CHRIST AND PEOPLE OF GOD

In *Lumen Gentium*, the Dogmatic Constitution on the Church, the council describes the church as rooted in God, a mystery beyond human comprehension. In order to describe the mystery of the church, the council recalls many scriptural metaphors such as a sheepfold and flock, a farm and vineyard, and the house and household of God (LG 6). The council highlights in a special way two metaphors for the church: the body of Christ and the people of God. Examining these two metaphors brings to light how the council understands the Christian faithful's identity.

Body of Christ

The Christian faithful are the baptized, the body of Christ. This metaphor has scriptural roots, yet its influence on ecclesial imagination has waxed and waned. For instance, the pyramidal ecclesiology discussed previously underscored the church's visible structures, and accentuated the church's relationship to Christ as its founder without reflecting adequately on the church as an existential union with Christ through the Spirit. In contrast, the early work of Johann Adam Möhler, a nineteenth-century Tübingen scholar, emphasized the Holy Spirit's ongoing role as the principle of the church's unity.[11] The influence of Möhler's thought on the Holy Spirit, as well as others such as Belgian theologian Émile Mersch, may be seen partly in Pius XII's encyclical *Mystici Corporis Christi*.[12] Pius identified the mystical body of Christ solely with the Roman Catholic church; however, Vatican II's use of the body of Christ metaphor demonstrates the reception of other ideas from Pius's teaching, such as the Spirit as the "divine principle of life and power" given by Christ to all the faithful who share responsibility for

---

[11] Johann Adam Möhler, *Unity in the Church or The Principle of Catholicism: Presented in the Spirit of the Church Fathers of the First Three Centuries*, trans. Peter C. Erb (Washington, DC: Catholic University of America Press, 1996).

[12] Émile Mersch, *The Whole Christ: The Historical Development of the Doctrine of the Mystical Body in Scripture and Tradition*, trans. John R. Kelly (Eugene, OR: Wipf and Stock Publishers, 2011).

the well-being of the mystical body.[13] By receiving this teaching, the council acknowledged the church as both human and divine. Therefore, when the council describes the Christian faithful as the body of Christ, it reflects on both Christ and the Holy Spirit as the principles of the church's life. The Spirit, who brings about life through Christ's incarnation and restores life through the resurrection, brings Christians to birth by uniting them with Christ's life, death, and resurrection. Baptism is the beginning of the faithful's growth into Christ; the Spirit continually vivifies and fosters the faithful as brothers and sisters of Christ, daughters and sons of God (LG 7).

This metaphor of the body also means the Christian faithful are mutually dependent and responsible. *Apostolicam Actuositatem*, the Decree on the Apostolate of Lay People, indicates: "Between the members of this body there exists, further, such a unity and solidarity (see Eph 4:16) that members who fail to do their best to promote the growth of the body must be considered unhelpful both to the church and to themselves" (AA 2). A baptized person develops into greater likeness to Christ both in and through the body; the body's imitation of Christ is dependent on each individual member.

The council differentiates between the Roman Catholic Church and other Christian churches and communities. Yet the council's emphasis on baptism into Christ through the Holy Spirit means the Christian faithful are not limited to those within the visible structures of the Roman Catholic Church, but rather include all those who through baptism are part of the Church of Christ. Indeed, the incorporation of the Christian faithful into Christ through baptism is an impetus for seeking Christian unity (LG 8).

The Christian faithful are nourished as Christ's body through the Eucharist. The council points to eucharistic reception as a way of receiving Christ's presence. Yet just as the parts of a physical body do not relate only to the body's head but to each other as well, so through the Eucharist the faithful receive not only Christ but each other. This transformative reception of other members of Christ's body leads the faithful to such a high degree of union that they are to share in one another's joy and pain. The radical solidarity within the body of Christ is itself a mirror of the incarnation: as the Word enters into the world through the incarnation, taking on the fullness of human experience, so

[13] Pius XII, *Mystici Corporis Christi*, June 29, 1943, Accessed March 6, 2019, http://w2 .vatican.va/content/pius-xii/en/encyclicals/documents/hf_p-xii_enc_29061943_mystici-corporis-christi.html, 56.

do the faithful enter into Christ's eternal, divine life, as well as his human, temporal way of life. In other words, through growth in union with Christ, the Christian faithful are those who learn to see, think, and act as Christ. The council draws a strong connection between being members of a body who share in Christ's suffering and the faithful's ability to recognize Christ in all poor and suffering persons (LG 8).

People of God

The council's most fully developed ecclesial metaphor is the people of God. It is given a full chapter in *Lumen Gentium*; is the basis on which the document considers the roles of ordained, lay, and religious men and women in the life of the church; is further expanded by a chapter on the pilgrim church later in *Lumen Gentium*; and is referred to in other documents. While Catherine Clifford rightly describes resistance – both hierarchical and theological – to receiving this metaphor after the council, other theologians such as Anastasia Wendlinder underscore the strong impact of the people of God metaphor for describing Christian identity and the role of the laity both within council documents and in the years following the council.[14] In *Lumen Gentium*, the chapter on the people of God precedes those on the hierarchy and laity, suggesting that this metaphor's concepts are foundational for understanding the roles of both laity and hierarchy. The metaphor reflects several characteristics of those who make up the Christian faithful. They are (1) called by God to freedom and worship; (2) drawn from within and across geographies and cultures; (3) represent the local and universal church; (4) in process of conversion to God; and (5) related to other faith traditions.

First, the metaphor recalls the Old Testament description of God calling forth the Hebrew people from slavery to liberation. This liberation is tied to worship and living in a covenant relationship with God, as well as with a journey into a promised land. When this covenant, with its implications for living in right relationship with God and one another, flourishes, the people are witnesses to the world of God's goodness (LG 9, cf. SC 10). Second, the council sees the Christian faithful as called together for salvation. It strongly emphasizes that the people of God are drawn together from across time, geography, history,

---

[14] Catherine Clifford, "Reflections on 'Peoplehood' and the Church," *Theoforum* 46 (2015): 275–78. Anastasia Wendlinder, "Empowered as King, Priest and Prophet: The Identity of Roman Catholic Laity in the People of God," *New Blackfriars* 95 (May 2013): 106–7.

ethnicity, and culture (LG 9). Thus, the Christian faithful are not to be equated with one particular group of people who are bonded together by factors such as culture or geography; their unity is formed through God's call to salvation and the people's response (cf. AG 8). Nevertheless, the cultures, histories, and geographies of the Christian faithful are not disregarded in this metaphor, but are rather incorporated into the church (cf. GS 38). In other words, to be part of the Christian faithful is not a calling to live above culture or outside of history. Just as God is at work within history to bring about salvation, so are God's people called to receive and respond to God's work within their own contexts. The people of God are one, and this unity includes the diversity not only of individuals but also of communities and their cultures and histories in which the Christian faithful hear and respond to God's call. The council leaves unaddressed how the Christian faithful might discern together unity in faith within the diversity of cultures and histories making up the church.

Third, recognition of the people of God's temporal context is not only important for the Christian faithful's mission. It also means the church is catholic, or universal, through the communion of the local churches (or dioceses). According to the Constitution on the Sacred Liturgy *Sacrosanctum Concilium*, the church is fully present in local churches when the Christian faithful are gathered together with their bishop around the eucharistic altar (SC 41). The local bishop symbolizes both the unity in faith of those in the local church and the communion of all local churches throughout the world under the pope's ministry (CD 11). In keeping with the people of God metaphor, the Christian faithful are brought into unity beyond the boundaries of any one time and place; yet the particularities of their times and places are also where they enter into the shared worship of covenantal life. *Sacrosanctum Concilium* affirms that the Christian faithful's ways of life can be brought into liturgy if they genuinely complement the liturgy, and that liturgy may reflect the cultures of particular peoples and places (SC 37). The eucharistic liturgy unites the people of God universally, and here the council acknowledges that the particular and local may be part of, rather than antithetical to, the church's catholicity.

Vatican II gives attention to universality through the communion of local churches; however, Antón observes that this catholicity is accompanied by serious practical questions touching on matters ranging from whether canon law can be applied across diverse cultures to how local churches communicate to each another, as well as to Rome, the

particularities of their contexts.[15] These issues were not addressed by
the council, and remain questions for the church today. Further, the
council did not adequately consider or exemplify representation of the
diverse personal experiences and states of life within local churches.
This criticism can be raised generally about the laity's representation,
and is exemplified with regard to women. Ivy Helman indicates that
while *Apostolicam Actuositatem* acknowledges the expanding role of
women in many societies and advocates for women's active participation in the church's mission, the council does not detail what such
participation means for the church as an institution.[16] Even within
the council, women's absence was noted as problematic. While *periti*
(experts such as theologians and canon lawyers) played a large role in
advising bishops and shaping conciliar documents, the norm was for
periti to be priests.[17] Helen Graham reports on the diary of Protestant
peritus Douglas Horton, who held that the lack of women resulted in an
incomplete catholicity, as well as Cardinal Suenens's statement that as
women make up half of humanity they ought to be present as council
auditors. Yet, of the twenty-three women eventually named as auditors,
only three were allowed to speak at the commissions that developed
conciliar texts.[18] This raises concerns about the degree to which council
texts reflect the church's catholicity, and also points to the work needed
after the council to ensure representation of the diverse forms of particularity that make up the church.

Fourth, the council unites its understanding of the people of God
with the metaphor of the body of Christ when it reflects on the Christian faithful as a pilgrim and eschatological people who are Christ's
mystical body. *Sacrosanctum Concilium* explains: "The church is both
human and divine, visible but endowed with invisible realities, zealous
in action and dedicated to contemplation, present in the world, yet a
migrant, so constituted that in it the human is directed toward and
subordinated to the divine, the visible to the invisible, action to contemplation, and this present world to the city yet to come, the object of our
quest (see Heb 13:14)" (SC 2). The Christian faithful are called together

[15] Antón, "Postconciliar Ecclesiology," 414.
[16] Ivy A. Helman, *Women and the Vatican: An Exploration of Official Documents*
(Maryknoll, NY: Orbis Books, 2012), 24.
[17] Karl Heinz Neufeld, "In the Service of the Council: Bishops and Theologians at the
Second Vatican Council (for Cardinal Henri de Lubac on His Ninetieth Birthday)," in
Vatican II: Assessment and Perspectives: Twenty-Five Years After, vol. 1, ed. René
Latourelle (Mahwah, NJ: Paulist Press, 1988), 78.
[18] Helen R. Graham, "Vatican II and Women," *Landas* 26 (2012): 81–83.

by God for salvation, and their communion with God and each other admits of growth and development (LG 7). To say that the people of God are on pilgrimage implies not only that there is a destination to be reached but also that the Christian faithful must journey toward that destination. God's salvation is offered and received, and yet this salvation is not an object to be grasped, but rather a gift the people of God continually learn to receive and understand through reflection and conversion (DV 8). The Christian faithful on earth, as *Lumen Gentium* indicates, are "endowed already with a sanctity that is true though imperfect" (LG 48). Therefore, the people of God, while called to holiness, are not without sin, nor are they unaffected by the temporal world in which they live (LG 48). Rather, the faithful are those who are called to "live more for him who died for us and who rose again," to be attentive and aware of the passing nature of their own lives, and to remain faithful to God in the face of temptation (LG 48).

The people of God who continue in their pilgrimage on earth have as their destination the kingdom of God, present already in Christ and yet awaiting fulfillment in the eschaton when God will be all in all. *Lumen Gentium* recalls the words of Paul: the faithful are still working out their salvation, not in the sense of earning it, but rather learning and living out what it means to be counted among God's people, to live in covenant (LG 48). This pilgrim people of God is part of the mystical body of Christ (LG 50), a body that includes the pilgrim church on earth, those in purgatory, as well as those who participate fully in the divine life in heaven (LG 49). What unites the pilgrim people of God with others in the mystical body of Christ is love. As *Lumen Gentium* states: "All of us, however, in varying degrees and in different ways share in the same love of God and our neighbor, and we all sing the same hymn of glory to our God. All, indeed, who are of Christ and who have his Spirit form one church and in Christ are joined together (Eph 4:16)" (LG 49). Conversely, the baptized who do not maintain the bond of love merely appear to be part of the Christian faithful, and do not participate in saving union with Christ (LG 14).

Fifth, the council's thinking about the church as people of God has implications for the church's relationship to the Jewish people as well as for Christian unity. Not without opposition from some council fathers, the Declaration on the Relation of the Church to Non-Christian Religions *Nostra Aetate* incorporated statements about the Jewish people that affirm their relationship with God and attempt to counteract dangerous falsehoods about the Jewish people (NA 4). Nevertheless, Elizabeth Groppe, describing Yves Congar's development of the people of

God metaphor in *Lumen Gentium*, argues that his "theological framework accounts for the relation between biblical Israel and the church
but leaves limited place for recognition of the contributions of postbi-
blical rabbinic Judaism to the living history of the people of God."[19] Her
observation underscores the council's failure to consider contemporary
Jews as the people of God, and the church's need to develop its understanding of Roman Catholicism's relationship with the Jewish people
through dialogue and study following the council.

Lumen Gentium describes various people's relationship to the
people of God by emphasizing God's plan and work for salvation. Drawing on language rooted in a more pyramidal view of the church, it states
that this plan for salvation is at work within the Roman Catholic
Church:

> Fully incorporated into the society of the church are those who,
> possessing the Spirit of Christ, accept its entire structure and all the
> means of salvation established within it, and who in its visible
> structures are united with Christ, who rules it through the
> Supreme Pontiff and the bishops, by the bonds of profession of
> faith, the sacraments, ecclesiastical government, and communion.
> (LG 14)

A catechumen who wants to be part of the church is considered to
already be a member, on the basis of their sincere desire in response to
the Holy Spirit, even though catechumens have not yet received the
sacrament of baptism; this pushes beyond baptism as the sacramental
source of Christian identity. Yet without naming other Christian traditions as "churches," the council also recognizes the Roman Catholic
church is "joined to the baptized who are honored by the name of
Christian, but do not profess the faith in its entirety or have not preserved unity of communion under the successor of Peter" (LG 15).
While here *Lumen Gentium* describes a lack of full communion, it does
also highlight the significance of the sacrament of baptism, shared
among all Christians, as a point of union between the Roman Catholic
Church and other Christian traditions.

Rather than stating directly that members of these Christian traditions are part of the people of God, the council indicates ambiguously
that the Roman Catholic Church is "joined" to these Christians (LG 15,
cf. UR 3). *Lumen Gentium* favorably acknowledges the presence of

---

[19] Elizabeth T. Groppe, "Revisiting Vatican II's Theology of the People of God after
Forty-Five Years of Catholic-Jewish Dialogue," *Theological Studies* 72 (2011): 600.

sacraments, creedal statements, and institutional structures in other Christian ecclesial traditions as well. This suggests that while the council perceives the people of God primarily in terms of those in full communion with the Roman Catholic Church, it does not deny the authenticity of Christian faith found in those traditions with which it is not in full, visible communion. Francis Sullivan argues communion between the Catholic church and other ecclesial communities and churches should be understood as having "various degrees of density or fullness," as opposed to thinking of communion as being either totally present or entirely absent.[20] Baptism provides a foundation for building unity between the Christian faithful of the Roman Catholic Church and other Christian traditions; shared aspects of ecclesial life, such as sacraments and scripture, are potential bridges for dialogue between Christians who seek greater unity in Christ.

THE CHRISTIAN FAITHFUL PARTICIPATE IN THE MYSTERY OF THE INCARNATION AND THE PASCHAL MYSTERY

The Christian faithful exist in and through three mysteries: the Trinity, the incarnation, and the paschal mystery. As will be discussed in the next section, Christians are constituted through the missions of the Trinity and called to participate in the divine life. Since the life and ministry of Christ is the communal and personal pattern for the Christian faithful, this section focuses on the mystery of the incarnation and the paschal mystery.

Vatican II describes the church's origin in Christ, whose very person announces the kingdom (LG 5). Through the incarnation, Christ, the kingdom, and the church are intertwined intimately. The kingdom of God is the "word, works, and presence of Christ"; the Christian faithful are both those who are redeemed through Christ and those who continue to make Christ present through their existence, words, and actions (LG 5). The incarnated union of the human and divine in Christ mediates salvation (SC 5). Received into this mystery through baptism, the Christian faithful become mediators of salvation such that the

<hr>

[20] Francis A. Sullivan, "The Significance of the Vatican II Declaration that the Church of Christ 'Subsists in' the Roman Catholic Church," in *Vatican II: Assessment and Perspectives: Twenty-Five Years After*, vol. 2, ed. René Latourelle (Mahwah, NJ: Paulist Press, 1989), 283.

church is also a sacrament of salvation whose mission is to unite all people with God (LG 1).

Through baptism, the Christian faithful not only are united with the incarnation, but enter as well into the paschal mystery – the passion, death, resurrection, and ascension of Christ – which is the fullness of salvation (SC 5). In their baptism, the faithful join Christ in his death as well as his resurrection; they are "implanted" in the paschal mystery, which is celebrated in each eucharistic liturgy as the "source" and "summit" of the church's common life (SC 6,10). The eucharistic liturgy both nourishes the faithful for loving mission in imitation of Christ, and points to the fulfilment of their labors in shared praise and thanksgiving to God (SC 6, 10). Through the liturgy, the faithful rejoice in the kingdom even as they continue their pilgrimage to its eschatological completion (SC 8).

Sharing Christ's Work as Priests, Prophets, and Kings

By living out the paschal mystery the Christian faithful are united with one another and Christ as his mystical body, continually incarnating Christ in the world. It is this union with Christ that makes the church both a witness to redemption in Christ as well as mediator of Christ's redemption. Through their participation in the incarnation and paschal mystery, the Christian faithful are not passive mediators of union with Christ. Rather, as the people of God they are conformed to Christ and empowered by the Spirit to share in Christ's three offices of priest, prophet, and king. These offices are the integral vocation of all the baptized. In other words, they are responses to God's call that are essential to the identity of the Christian faithful.

Apostolicam Actuositatem comments on these three offices:

> Lay people's right and duty to be apostles derives from their union with Christ their head. Inserted as they are in the mystical body of Christ by baptism and strengthened by the power of the holy Spirit in confirmation, it is by the Lord himself that they are consecrated a royal priesthood and a holy nation (see 1 Pet 2:4-10), this is so that in all their actions they may offer spiritual sacrifices and bear witness to Christ all the world over. (AA 3)

Thus, the apostolic quality of the church is not to be narrowly construed as only relating to apostolic succession within the episcopacy. Rather, all the baptized are implicated in the apostolic nature of the church; they share in Christ's mission to build the kingdom of God so all may participate in Christ's salvation and live in just relationship with God (AA 2).

In their priestly ministry, the Christian faithful unite their own lives with God's divine life, thus living out God's call to holiness and acting as witnesses to hope in Christ. The faithful fulfill their priestly ministry through active participation in liturgy and the sacraments, as well as through daily acts in which they "present themselves as a sacrifice, living, holy and pleasing to God (see Rom 12:1)" (LG 10). *Gaudium et Spes*, the Pastoral Constitution on the Church in the Modern World, states that through daily actions of sacrifice, the faithful live out the paschal mystery and express their hope in the resurrection:

> Christ's example in dying for us sinners teaches us that we must carry the cross, which the flesh and the world inflict on the shoulders of any who seek after peace and justice. Constituted Lord by his resurrection and given all authority in heaven and on earth, Christ is now at work in human hearts by the power of his Spirit; not only does he arouse in them a desire for the world to come but he quickens, purifies, and strengthens the generous aspirations of humanity to make life more humane and conquer the earth for this purpose. (GS 38)

In these sacrificial actions, the faithful are following the example of Christ and responding to the Spirit's impetus to fulfill the kingdom of God.

Their intimate union with Christ as members of his mystical body means the church as a whole is prophetic. All the Christian faithful receive Christ's teaching and in turn bear witness to it. It is not only through the bishops that the Christian faithful receive and understand the revelation of Christ but also through the faith of all the baptized. In consequence, the very life of the church embodies the apostolic tradition on which the church's formal teaching is predicated:

> By this sense of the faith, aroused and sustained by the Spirit of truth, the people of God, guided by the sacred magisterium which it faithfully obeys, receives not the word of human beings, but truly the word of God (see 1 Th 2:13), "the faith once for all delivered to the saints" (Jude 3). The people unfailingly adheres to this faith, penetrates it more deeply through right judgment, and applies it more fully in daily life. (LG 12)

Thus the laity are the Christian faithful not simply because of their *fides qua* (the act of personal faith) but also because of their recognition of the *fides quae* (the substance of what is believed). This shared sense of the faith, or *sensus fidelium*, is complemented by diverse gifts the faithful receive from the Spirit for the "renewal and building up" of the people of God (LG 12).

In sharing Christ's kingly office, the Christian faithful are charged with building the kingdom of God within the world, a mission considered in greater detail in the chapter's next section. However, it is important to note that this kingly work is lived out within the church as well. Not only clergy and religious but all the baptized have responsibility for nurturing the life of the kingdom within the church. This kingly ministry touches on the church's unity in diversity. The baptismal vocation is the common foundation for ministry within the church; it unites the various particular vocations of the Christian faithful such as family life and marriage, religious life, and consecration to holy orders. The council both affirms the responsibility of each of the Christian faithful for the church's shared life and mission, and distinguishes ways the faithful fulfill their responsibilities according to their roles within the church (LG 13). For instance, the council declares the need for laity to actively, freely, and obediently contribute to the church's apostolate according to the charisms given them by the Spirit, and the need for bishops to welcome dialogue and collaboration with laity while discerning the best ordering of the church's mission (AA 3, 23, 25).

Acting in the Church and World

The Christian faithful's vocation to be priests, prophets, and kings is manifested as they fulfill their Christic work within the church as well as through their activities in the larger world. The equality of baptism is the foundation for distinctions among the Christian faithful, which arise from the particular charisms distributed by the one Spirit and participation in states of life beyond baptism. The council views the faithful who are ordained, as well as the members of religious orders, as having an orientation to the building up of the people of God. From this perspective, their role is to nurture the seed of the kingdom itself so the laity are strengthened in what the council sees as their primary vocation, to build the kingdom in the secular world (cf. CD 2, OT 1, PC 1, AA 2).

As Giovanni Magnani argues in his careful exegesis of the council's description of the laity, while these orientations, to building the church or to the secular world, are seen as being primary, they are not exclusive

(LG 31).[21] It is not as though the ordained and religious are somehow abstracted from the larger world in which the church exists, nor is it the case that priests and religious ought to lack concern for and engagement with the secular world (GS 43). Similarly, while the laity are primarily seen as fulfilling their purpose by developing the kingdom in the secular world, they are also called to active participation within the church. As *Apostolicam Actuositatem* expresses: "Sharing in the function of Christ, priest, prophet and king, the laity have an active part of their own in the life and activity of the church. Their activity within church communities is so necessary that without it the apostolate of the pastors will frequently be unable to obtain its full effect" (AA 10).

The council notes a variety of ways the laity in particular fulfill their Christic offices within the church's interior life and in the larger world. For instance, the family fulfills its purpose as "the primary vital cell of society" when it is "the domestic church" in which love, prayer, hospitality, justice, and care for all in need is practiced (AA 11). Further, with great optimism, the council encourages laity to share with "the ecclesial community their own problems, world problems, and questions regarding humanity's salvation, to examine them together and solve them by general discussion" (AA 10). And in a statement that recalls the origin of Newman's dispute with Ullathorne and Talbot, the council declares, "To the extent of their knowledge, competence or authority the laity are entitled, and indeed sometimes duty-bound, to express their opinion on matters which concern the good of the church" (LG 37). Laity should make their representations through appropriate ecclesial structures, though conciliar documents do not clearly outline such structures. Without these structures, laity are hindered in fulfilling their responsibility to be collaborators with their bishops within the local church. While some structures, such as parish pastoral councils, were canonically required following Vatican II, diocesan pastoral councils exist at the discretion of the bishop, and other structures, such as diocesan synods or parish visitations, are occasional rather than regular means for the laity to consult on the needs of the church. Further, as Antón writes, though Vatican II stressed the equality of baptism, it limits the laity's participation in ecclesial structures to consultation rather than deliberation.[22]

---

[21] Giovanni Magnani, "Does the So-Called Theology of the Laity Possess a Theological Status?" in *Vatican II: Assessment and Perspectives: Twenty-Five Years After*, vol. 1, ed. René Latourelle (Mahwah, NJ: Paulist Press, 1988), 621–22.

[22] Antón, "Postconciliar Ecclesiology," 428–29.

THE CHRISTIAN FAITHFUL ARE CALLED TO BUILD GOD'S KINGDOM

The Christian faithful have a common vocation to share in the divine life. The Decree on the Church's Missionary Activity, *Ad Gentes*, views this vocation as missionary because it originates in the missions of Christ and the Holy Spirit (AG 2). The Christian faithful exist through the creative and salvific work of the Trinity, and in turn their purpose reflects the trinitarian missions.

The council describes distinct, though interrelated, roles for the divine persons. *Lumen Gentium* understands humans to be created by the Father to participate in the divine life (LG 2). This speaks both to humans' capacity for eternal life, as well as their ability to live and act as God does. God's constancy of purpose in creating human beings for this end remains despite humanity's sin, and thus the Father sends Christ to restore unity between all people and God. Christ is the first born of the family of God, whose faithfulness contrasts with fallen humanity's disobedience and is the source of redemption. The church originates in this source, and the Christian faithful both live through Christ and order their lives to Christ (LG 3). The Holy Spirit gives life through unity with Christ, and thus with the Father (LG 4). Through the Spirit the faithful are God's adopted children, gifted with charisms and guided continually in truth and love. Hence the universal church is the people of God united through the Trinity (LG 4).

Immanent and Eschatological

To participate in the divine life of the Trinity is to enter into the kingdom of God, and to bear responsibility for building the kingdom by continuing the trinitarian missions. Through the Holy Spirit, the kingdom is both the Christian faithful's inheritance as daughters and sons of God and their ongoing mission as members of Christ. This means the kingdom is immanent, or already present, and eschatological, awaiting its full completion in God. These two aspects of the Christian faithful's purpose are held together in conciliar documents.

For example, *Sacrosanctum Concilium* calls for the Christian faithful to participate fully, actively, and consciously in liturgy, and this reflects the council's emphasis on the eucharistic liturgy itself as a participation in the kingdom's eschatological completion. This is a real though anticipatory participation, for through the liturgy the faithful also learn how to live out the paschal mystery by making offerings of themselves and growing into complete union with God and one another

(SC 8; 48). Thus, participation in the church's liturgical life not only nurtures the Christian faithful in their hope for the kingdom but also forms them as living witnesses to this hope as they work for the kingdom in their daily lives. Similarly, *Gaudium et Spes* contends that while the church awaits the eschatological fulfillment of the kingdom of God, the mission of the church to build the kingdom is itself a participation in this fulfillment: "When we have spread on earth the fruits of our nature and our enterprise – human dignity, sisterly and brotherly communion, and freedom – according to the command of the Lord and in his Spirit, we will find them once again, cleansed this time from the stain of sin, illuminated and transfigured, when Christ presents to his Father an eternal and universal kingdom 'of truth and life, a kingdom of holiness and grace, a kingdom of justice, love and peace'" (GS 39). Here the council neither equates the mission of the church with the kingdom's completion, nor is the work of the Christian faithful a mere stopgap until the parousia. Rather, the church's temporal mission is eternally caught up in and transformed by Christ's eschatological completion of the kingdom.

From its opening lines, *Gaudium et Spes* announces the Christian faithful have a radical solidarity with the concrete experiences of all people, particularly the poor and vulnerable (GS 1). The body of Christ, whose members share in each other's suffering and joy, ought not be turned inward on itself. As the people of God, the church is Christ's body in pilgrimage. The church's internal commitment to union with one another in Christ and the church's external mission to share the good news of salvation are mutually dependent. Therefore, the church cannot be a sacrament of unity without acting for the restoration of justice and peace, which are the signs of right relationship between God and all people; conversely, justice and peace are not only humanistic goals but reflect God's will.

Dialogue, Conscience, and Discovery

The Christian faithful are to engage in dialogue about those elements within the world that threaten human dignity and contradict the common good (GS 3). By emphasizing dialogue, the council implicitly cautions against viewing "the world" as an object of Christian ministry, and instead advances a more interdependent understanding of the relationship between the faithful and the larger world (GS 3). In their conversation with the world, the Christian faithful contribute their discernment of the ways the gospel sheds light on the present context (GS 2; 4). This includes interpreting the good to be found in social, scientific, political, economic, and religious developments as well as identifying disparities and threats to human dignity. While *Gaudium et Spes* focuses on laying out the church's vision of these realities, it also indicates that the church both learns and benefits from the modern world, including developments in science and cultural exchanges. Contributions of all people to upholding human dignity are valued (GS 44; 40). The laity in particular are described as mediating Christian truth both nationally and internationally, and are encouraged to collaborate with others to promote the common good (AA 14). Thus, while the faithful may well join in associations with one another to promote and protect human dignity, their collaborations rightly include ecumenical, interfaith, and secular initiatives.

The council exhorts the Christian faithful to integrate their religious commitments with their daily lives so there may be "no pernicious opposition between professional and social activity on the one hand and religious life on the other" (GS 43). Through their consciences, the Christian faithful discover the call to love God as well as their neighbor, and learn to see the needs of the world as well as to judge and act rightly in response (GS 16). These dictates of conscience are not limited to the Christian faithful, but according to the council's theological anthropology are present in all people, providing a means for the faithful to work with others to discover truth and solutions in keeping with this law of love (GS 16).

The Declaration on Religious Liberty, *Dignitatis Humanae*, describes Christ as the model for noncoercive communication of divine truth, and indicates "His Kingdom does not establish its claims by force, but is established by bearing witness to hearing the truth and it grows by the love with which Christ, lifted up on the cross, draws people to himself" (DH 11). While the document briefly reaffirms past magisterial teaching about the truth of the Roman Catholic Church, it substantially develops the church's articulation of religious liberty by characterizing truth less as a deposit of objective knowledge and more as a discovery that must be undertaken with respect to human dignity.

The council's vision of this search for truth is both inherently social and personal: it requires that people join together in order to share what they have come to understand in the process of discovering truth, and that acceptance of truth be personal (DH 3). This means the Christian faithful's mission of building the kingdom must be relational and dialogical both within the church and within the larger world. The faithful engage in dialogue and discovery of truth through the loving relationships they establish within the larger world, and through their presence and active participation in the structures of society and engagement with culture (AG 11). Without denying the need to be critical of society and culture, the faithful are not to construct a Christian society parallel to the world, but instead are to enter into the world's peoples and cultures, engaging in the discovery of truth that identifies and lifts up those aspects of social life that reflect God's kingdom (AG 9).

WHO ARE THE LAITY?

The reception of Vatican II's teaching about the Christian faithful, particularly the role of the laity, impacted ecclesial practice and theory in complex and incomplete ways. For instance, in the United States, the council's teaching on the laity had a direct correlation to the exponential rise in the number of lay ecclesial ministers exercising their Christic ministries within the church. Evidence of the council's reception can be seen both in how lay ministers describe their vocations, and in bishops' articulation of lay ministry.[23] Yet the relationship between lay and ordained ministers, while often fruitful, can also be fraught by questions of authority and power, and parishioners themselves may be unwilling to accept leadership from another lay person.[24] Clericalism, which thrives under a more pyramidal vision of the church with its focus on ecclesial institutions, was challenged by Vatican II's emphasis on the Christian faithful's common identity in baptism, as well as the collaborative and dialogical relationships between laity and clergy the council encouraged. Yet bishops' decisions to cover-up sexual abuse by clergy are devastating evidence that the culture of clericalism is still strong within the church. The sense of the faithful was frequently invoked following the council as a reason to listen and learn from all within the church, and yet ecclesial structures and formation programs that allow for ongoing discernment of the sense of the faithful were not universally created. The council's emphasis on conscience not only impacted how the Christian faithful collaborate with others for the common good but also their own discernment of the meaning, relevance, and application of magisterial teaching in their own lives. Positively, this means

---

[23] Zeni Fox, *New Ecclesial Ministry* (Kansas City, MO: Sheed and Ward, 2002), 70. United States Conference of Catholic Bishops, *Co-Workers in the Vineyard of the Lord. A Resource for Guiding the Development of Lay Ecclesial Ministry*, December 2005, 17–18, accessed December 31, 2018 www.usccb.org/upload/co-workers-vineyard-lay-ecclesial-ministry-2005.pdf.

[24] Marti R. Jewell and David A. Ramey, *The Changing Face of the Church: Emerging Models of Parish Leadership* (Chicago, IL: Loyola Press, 2010), 21–22.

reception of magisterial teaching by the Christian faithful may not simply be an external obedience but rather an internalized assent to the truth proposed in the teaching; practically, it raises questions of authority and obedience which are not easily resolved as seen in questions surrounding the development and reception of Paul VI's teaching on contraception in *Humanae Vitae*.[25]

The varying impacts of Vatican II's teachings on the Christian faithful call the church to acknowledge and respond to two realities. First, the emergence within council documents of a vision of the church as an apostolic communion did not simply replace the older pyramidal ecclesiology in the council documents, and nor has it within the church. Rather, understanding and enacting the church as an apostolic communion inclusive of the laity requires a collective change in ecclesial imagination and structures. Second, in practice, an apostolic communion is a complex way for the Christian faithful to live together as the body of Christ and people of God. Collaboration with the Holy Spirit fueled by perseverance and hope will be necessary for Vatican II's teaching on the Christian faithful to be more fully embodied in the daily life of the church and to evolve further.

FURTHER READING

Anameje, Humphrey Chinedu. "Contemporary Theological Reflection on the Laity: Towards a More Active Participation in the Mission of the Church." *Ephemerides Theologicae Lovanienses* 83, no. 4 (2007): 445–70.

Clifford, Catherine. "Reflections on 'Peoplehood' and the Church." *Theoforum* 46 (2015): 271–92.

Comblin, José. *People of God*. Maryknoll, NY: Orbis Books, 2004.

Congar, Yves. *Lay People in the Church*. London: Chapman, 1965.

De Mesa, José M. "Vatican II on the Laity: 'Limen' or 'Lumen'?" *Landas* 2, no. 2 (1988): 238–45.

Dulles, Avery. *Models of the Church*. Garden City, NY: Image Classics, 1991.

Flanagan, Brian. "The Universal Call to Holiness and Laity in the Church." *Toronto Journal of Theology* 32 no. 2 (2016): 219–32.

Goldie, Rosemary. *From a Roman Window: Five Decades of the World, the Church, and the Catholic Laity*. Victoria, Australia: HarperCollins Religious, 1998.

John Paul II. *Christifideles Laici*. December 30, 1988. Accessed December 28, 2018. http://w2.vatican.va/content/john-paul-ii/en/apost_exhortations/documents/hf_jp-ii_exh_30121988_christifideles-laici.html.

---

[25] Joseph A. Komonchak, "*Humanae Vitae* and Its Reception: Ecclesiological Reflections," *Theological Studies* 39, no. 2 (June 1978): 229, 232–33.

Lakeland, Paul. *The Liberation of the Laity: In Search of an Accountable Church*. New York: Bloomsbury, 2003.

Leckey, Dolores. *The Laity and Christian Education:* Apostolicam Actuositatem, Gravissimum Educationis. Re-Discovering Vatican II Series. New York: Paulist Press, 2007.

Rush, Ormond. *The Eyes of Faith: The Sense of the Faithful and the Church's Reception of Revelation*. Washington, DC: The Catholic University of America Press, 2009.

Schillebeeckx, Edward. *Church: The Human Story of God*. New York: The Crossroad Publishing Company, 1994.

13 Leadership and Governance in the Church

THOMAS P. RAUSCH

During the debate at the Second Vatican Council on the schema that became the Dogmatic Constitution on the Church *Lumen Gentium*, an intervention of Cardinal Bernard Alfrink of Utrecht in Holland during the second session made a deep impression. While the schema referred frequently to "Peter and the Apostles," the cardinal observed that it would be better to use the phrase, "Peter and the *other* Apostles," not out of any wish to deny or lessen the primacy of Peter, but rather "to restore the pope to his place in the apostolic college."[1] This simple remark of the Dutch cardinal symbolizes in a few words the lengthy and sometimes bitter debate on collegiality.

The First Vatican Council (1869–70) had affirmed authoritatively the primacy and infallibility of the Bishop of Rome. The Dogmatic Constitution on the Church of Christ *Pastor Aeternus* declared that "when the Roman pontiff speaks *ex cathedra* ... in the exercise of his office as shepherd and teacher of all Christians ... he possesses, by the divine assistance promised to him in blessed Peter, that infallibility which the divine Redeemer willed his church to enjoy in defining doctrine concerning faith or morals" (4).

While a careful reading shows that the constitution assigns the charism of infallibility to the church, too many have seen it as an exclusive prerogative of the pope, a view that centers all authority in the Bishop of Rome. The Dominican Yves Congar captured this vision perfectly when he observed during the second session that the papal tiara, "rising from a wide base to a single point at the top, was an apt expression of the idea of pontifical monarchy and a quasi-pyramidal concept of the Church."[2] To counter this monarchical understanding of church governance, the

---

[1] See Xavier Rynne, *Vatican Council II* (New York: Farrar, Straus and Giroux, 1968), 166.

[2] Yves Congar, *Power and Poverty in the Church* (New York: Paulist Press, 2016), 69; first published in French in 1963.

reforming majority of the council fathers sought to describe the relationship of the bishops to the pope in terms of collegiality; both belonged to a corporate body or "college." Defining the collegial nature of the episcopal office was to represent the council's most significant theological advance, one that developed through several stages.

In this essay, we will consider first the drama that took place on the council floor in the process of the debate on collegiality. Then we will look at how the council's teaching on collegiality moved Catholic theology forward on several significant issues. We will then turn to the post-conciliar church to consider two "instruments of collegiality," to use the language of Pope John Paul II, episcopal conferences and the synod of bishops. Finally, we will consider some recent developments relating to collegiality during the pontificate of Pope Francis.

THE DEBATE ON COLLEGIALITY

The council's first session in 1962 saw considerable dissatisfaction with the initial draft of the schema on the church, *De Ecclesia*. A powerful intervention by Bishop Emile de Smedt of Bruges on December 1 critiqued the draft for its "triumphalism, clericalism, and juridical spirit."[3] On December 4, Cardinal Suenens, archbishop of Malines-Brussels, called for a complete redrafting of the schema. After other critical interventions, Pope John XXIII called for a revision of the entire text, to bring it more in line with the goals of the council.

When the council resumed for the second session on September 30, 1963, the fathers had a new draft to consider. Gone was the more juridical language of the first draft. The language was now more biblical, less focused on the hierarchy, more concerned with the actual life of grace. Even before the second session began, the Coordinating Commission had recommended moving the portion of chapter III relating to the church as the people of God into second place. It would eventually be chapter II, stressing the fundamental equality of all the baptized. This would be followed by the treatment of the episcopal office in chapter III and the development of a theology of the laity in chapter IV, extending to all the baptized a share in Christ's threefold office as prophet, priest, and king (LG 31).

Most important was the week and a half devoted to collegiality. While most recognized that the bishops together constituted a body or

---

[3] The text appears in *Acta Synodalia Sacrosancti Concilii Oecumenici Vaticani II*, vol. 1, part 4 (Vatican City: Typis Polygottis, 1971), 142–44.; see also Avery Dulles, *Models of the Church* (Garden City, NY: Doubleday, 1974), 35–36.

order in the church, the debate was over whether or not this "collegiality" was merely of human origin or belonged to the fundamental
structure of the church, thus of divine origin. In an important intervention, Cardinal Siri argued that the practice of ecumenical councils
showed that the bishops acting together with the pope constituted a
true college. However, he insisted that there was no genuine episcopal
collegiality without union with the pope. What remained was to harmonize collegiality with Vatican I's teaching on the primacy.

In spite of opposition from some of the more conservative bishops,
successive speakers argued that collegiality was "not new teaching," but
found in various sources – tradition, the Eastern churches, the theological manuals, and the practice of the ecumenical councils (König).
The New Testament showed Christ entrusting the church to the college
of the twelve (Meyer). The practice of the early church witnesses the
collegial nature of the episcopal office, holding local synods, bishops
exchanging letters, the practice of at least three bishops participating in
the ordination of a new bishop (Gouyon).[4] An important vote on October
30 showed a strong majority (between 74 and 98 percent) in favor of
teaching that the college of bishops succeeds to that of the apostles and
that the bishops exercised full and supreme power by divine right.[5] The
voices of opposition continued. Nevertheless, as Melloni writes, "After
October 30, collegiality and Vatican II were synonymous."[6]

As the third session opened on September 14, 1964, a minority
continued to oppose the teaching of chapter III. Late in the evening of
September 13, Pope Paul VI received an eleven-page typescript, a "note
personally reserved to the Holy Father" eventually signed by twenty-
five cardinals, sixteen of them from the Roman Curia as well as a
patriarch, and sixteen of the 103 superiors of religious congregations.
The note charged that chapter III's argument was weak, fallacious,
incoherent, and dangerous to the unity of the church. Clearly, the note
represented a critique of Pope Paul's leadership.[7] However, by now a

---

[4] Rynne, *Vatican Council II*, 178–79.

[5] Alberto Melloni, "The Beginning of the Second Period: The Great Debate on the
Church," in *History of Vatican II, vol. 3, Second Period and Intersession,
September 1963–September 1964*, ed. Giuseppe Alberigo and Joseph A. Komonchak
(Maryknoll, NY: Orbis Books, 2000), 105.

[6] Ibid., 108.

[7] See Joseph A. Komonchak, "Toward an Ecclesiology of Communion," in *History of
Vatican II, vol. 4, Church as Communion Third Period and Intersession September
1964–September 1965*, ed. Guiseppe Alberigo and Joseph A. Komonchak (Maryknoll,
NY: Orbis Books, 2003), 66–72.

strong majority was clearly in favor of the proposed teaching. On September 21, even Italian Archbishop Pietro Parente, assessor of the Holy Office, previously an outspoken conservative, came out in support of the present text.

On November 14, the fathers received a *Nota Explicativa Praevia* or Explanatory Note outlining the sense in which collegiality was to be understood. Presented as though coming from the Doctrinal Commission, it was obvious that it had come from the pope himself in an effort to gain the support of the opposing minority. The Explanatory Note insisted on four points. First, the word "college" should not be understood in the juridical sense of a body of equals who delegated their power to a president, i.e. the pope. Second, it made a distinction between the powers that came from episcopal ordination and the exercise of those powers, which always had to be in "hierarchical communion" – a term especially important to Eastern theology – with the head and members of the church. Third, the college could not exist without the pope, though as head of the college the pope could exercise his role personally. Fourth, though the college continues to exist, it exercises its authority only occasionally, and never without its head.

Many members of the majority were uncomfortable with the intervention represented by the Note, with its addition to the text without a separate vote. However, the purpose of the Note was to reassure the minority that the text did not in any way compromise papal authority, and indeed the opposition to collegiality began to fade away, as was obvious from votes on additions to chapters III and IV of the text. The vote on the entire constitution in November showed that 2,151 fathers had accepted the constitution with its teaching on collegiality; only five continued their opposition. The council had endorsed the doctrine of collegiality with virtual unanimity.

THEOLOGICAL DEVELOPMENTS

The teaching on collegiality in *Lumen Gentium* led to several developments in Roman Catholic theology; they included a clarification on the source of episcopal authority, the doctrine of collegiality itself, the concept of hierarchical communion, and the doctrine of infallibility. We will consider briefly each of these developments.

The Source of Episcopal Authority

Whether the episcopal consecration conferred a sacramental grace or merely provided greater jurisdiction to one who already had the fullness of the sacrament through presbyteral ordination had been debated since at least the Middle Ages. *Lumen Gentium* closed this debate: "The holy synod teaches, moreover, that the fullness of the sacrament of Orders is conferred by episcopal consecration, and both in the liturgical tradition of the church and in the language of the Fathers of the church it is called the high priesthood, the summit of the sacred ministry" (LG 21). In his commentary on article 21, Karl Rahner writes: "The episcopate is not regarded in the light of (simple) priesthood but envisaged in itself as the full priesthood in all regards, while the ordinary priesthood is to be explained as a limited share of the full priesthood: episcopal consecration is the primary and comprehensive instance of sacramental ordination to office."[8]

Thus, the source of the bishop's authority is his episcopal ordination; it is sacramental, though to be properly exercised it must be in union with the Bishop of Rome. "The bishops, as vicars and legates of Christ govern by their counsels, persuasion and example the particular churches assigned to them ... nor are they to be regarded as vicars of the Roman Pontiff; for they exercise a power which they possess in their own right and are most truly said to be at the head of the people whom they govern" (LG 27). In adopting this language, the council was reclaiming the theology of the early church that saw the bishop as the head of the local church and guardian of its apostolic faith. The installation of someone into the episcopal office required the approval of the community. According to Pope Celestine I (d. 432), "No bishop is to be imposed on the people whom they do not want."[9] Pope Leo I (d. 461) stated, "He who has to preside over all must be elected by all."[10]

Doctrine of Collegiality

Lumen Gentium teaches formally that the episcopal college succeeded the college of the apostles; thus, its teaching represents a development of doctrine.[11] Rahner calls the college "a juridical personality, sacramentally based." Referring to *Lumen Gentium* 21, Rahner argues that "the power of the individual bishop as an individual – the threefold office – is to be regarded as coming to him insofar as he is a member

---

[8] Karl Rahner, "The Hierarchical Structure of the Church with Special Reference to the Episcopate," in *Commentary on the Documents of Vatican II*, vol. 1, ed. Herbert Vorgrimler (New York: Herder and Herder, 1967), 193.

[9] J. Migne, PL 50, 434.

[10] Ibid., 54, 634.

[11] Melloni, "The Beginning of the Second Period," 65.

of the college and sharer in the power of the college as such."[12] The order of bishops together with its head, the Roman Pontiff and never apart from him, "is the subject of supreme and full authority over the universal church," while the individual bishops, placed in charge of particular churches, exercise their pastoral care over the portion of the People of God committed to their care (LG 22). They are the visible principle and foundation of unity in their particular churches, fashioned after the model of the universal Church: "it is in and from these that the one and unique catholic church exists" (LG 23). Thus, the church is a communion of churches.

Some theologians push the concept of collegiality beyond its more limited sense in the text of *Lumen Gentium*. For example, Charles Murphy says that collegiality has meaning for the whole church, for the church itself is "a communion of persons united in a reciprocity of gifts in the same Spirit." Thus collegiality becomes a model for all those living together and interacting in the church.[13]

Hierarchical Communion

Extremely important to chapter III is the notion of "hierarchical communion," the bond that unites the bishops with each other and with the Bishop of Rome, with Peter as the permanent and visible source and foundation of the unity of faith and communion (LG 18). Hierarchical communion means that the communion of the church is structured. Sacramental consecration and hierarchical communion with the head and members of the body constitutes one a member of the episcopal body (LG 22). Richard Gaillardetz has described the retrieval of this notion of communion (*koinonia*) as among the most influential developments at the council. He cites Pope John Paul II, who in his *Christifideles Laici* referred to the notion of communion as the central and fundamental idea of Vatican II.[14] The notion quickly became foundational to both ecclesiology and ecumenism.

The council speaks of the Spirit unifying the church (LG 4), bringing the believers into communion through sharing in the Eucharist (LG 7), uniting the church as a visible society governed by the successor of Peter and the bishops in communion with him (LG 8). It joins all the

[12] Rahner, "The Hierarchical Structure of the Church," 198.
[13] Charles M. Murphy, "Collegiality: An Essay Toward Better Understanding," *Theological Studies* 46 (1985): 39.
[14] Richard R. Gaillardetz, *Teaching with Authority: A Theology of the Magisterium in the Church* (Collegeville, MN: Liturgical Press, 1997), 8; see *Christifideles laici* §19, *Origins* 18 (February 9, 1989): 570.

faithful scattered throughout the world in communion with each other
(LG 13). Chapter III describes Peter as the permanent source and foundation of the unity of faith and communion, with the successors of the
apostles (LG 18) who exercise the threefold office of sanctifying, teaching, and governing only in hierarchical communion with the head and
members of the college (LG 21). The Decree on Ecumenism, *Unitatis
Redintegratio*, extends the concept of communion to other Christians,
separated from full communion with the Catholic Church: "For those
who believe in Christ and have been properly baptized are put in some,
though imperfect, communion with the Catholic Church" (UR 3). The
report of the 1985 Extraordinary Synod of Bishops states that the Catholic Church has fully assumed its ecumenical responsibility based on
the ecclesiology of communion.[15]

Infalllibility

When the council included the bishops with the pope in the exercise
of the church's charism of infallibility, it significantly reinterpreted
Vatican I's teaching. The constitution *Pastor Aeternus* pointed to the
pope as the one through whom "that infallibility which the divine
Redeemer willed his church to enjoy" comes to expression (4). Developing its teaching on collegiality, Vatican II included the bishops when
united with the pope in the exercise of the church's charism of infallibility: "The infallibility promised to the church is also present in
the body of bishops when, together with Peter's successor, they exercise
the supreme teaching office" (LG 25). In doing so, the fathers of the
council were not "reforming" Vatican I's teaching, but they were
reinterpreting it.

According to Rahner, the text states explicitly that when the
bishops unanimously propose a teaching on faith and morals as something "to be held definitively," their "ordinary universal magisterium"
teaches infallibly, as does the extraordinary magisterium. However,
the text says, "to be held," not "to be believed," since according to the
general view, not every doctrine taught unanimously is infallible.
"The text does not, of course, take up the difficult question, which
can be of practical consequence at times, of how this specially qualified unanimity is to be ascertained by the faithful who are bound to
believe."[16]

---

[15] "Synod of Bishops: The Final Report," *Origins* 15 (1985): 444–50.
[16] Rahner, "The Hierarchical Structure of the Church," 210–11.

Though the language is somewhat indirect, the faithful also are included in the exercise of the church's infallibility: "The assent of the church can never be lacking to such definitions on account of the same holy Spirit's influence, through which Christ's whole flock is maintained in the unity of the faith and makes progress in it" (LG 25). Or as the text says earlier, "The whole body of the faithful who have received an anointing which comes from the holy one (see 1 Jn 2:20 and 27) cannot be mistaken in belief. It shows this characteristic ... when, 'from the bishops to the last of the faithful,' it manifests a universal consensus in matters of faith and morals" (LG 12). In other words, the magisterium teaches what the whole church believes. The International Theological Commission spelled this out even more clearly in its 2014 text "The *Sensus Fidei* in the Life of the Church," as did Pope Francis as we shall see later.

INSTRUMENTS OF COLLEGIALITY

Charles Murphy attributes the phrase "instruments of collegiality" to Pope John Paul II. At the beginning of his pontificate John Paul spoke of "the adequate development of organisms, some of which will be entirely new, others updated, to ensure a better union of minds, intentions, and initiatives in the work of building up the Body of Christ which is the Church," referring to national episcopal conferences and the synod of bishops as "two new instruments of collegiality."[17]

Episcopal Conferences

Episcopal conferences are national or international associations of the bishops of a country or region who gather for pastoral planning and action for their churches. *Christus Dominus*, the council's Decree on the Pastoral Office of Bishops in the Church, affirmed the existence of episcopal conferences from the earliest ages of the church and called for them to flourish with renewed vigor to more effectively serve the growth and discipline of their churches (36). During the debate over the Constitution on the Sacred Liturgy, *Sacrosanctum Concilium*, a key question was whether episcopal conferences had the right to determine (*statuere*) or propose (*proponere*) liturgical issues, including the use of the vernacular. The result was that "the decision lay with

---

[17] Murphy, "Collegiality: An Essay," 41.

the bishops' conferences and Rome reserved the right of scrutinizing and confirming it."[18]

There is some controversy as to whether their decisions are truly collegial or merely collective actions of the conference. Some theologians, among them Henri de Lubac, Jerome Hamer, and Joseph Ratzinger, see their actions as collective rather than truly collegial events. De Lubac argues that they may be considered "partial realizations" of collegiality, but episcopal collegiality like that of the Twelve is universal or it isn't collegiality.[19] Joseph Ratzinger, in his long interview with Vittorio Messori, was reported as saying, "We must not forget that the episcopal conferences have no theological basis, they do not belong to the structure of the Church, as willed by Christ, that cannot be eliminated; they have only a practical, concrete function."[20] In 1998, Pope John Paul II issued a *motu proprio, Apostolos Suos,* on the teaching authority of episcopal conferences, saying that they could make doctrinal statements only if by a unanimous vote of all the members, or by at least two thirds of the members, provided that it would not be published without first receiving the *recognitio* of the Holy See.[21] Pope Francis suggests that episcopal conferences may have a greater authority, as we shall see.

Synod of Bishops

The synod of bishops was another new instrument of collegiality. The council fathers had hoped to establish a representative collegial body to assist the pope in his teaching office and government of the church, but before they could outline its structures, Pope Paul VI established the synod himself by a *motu propio* issued on September 15, 1965. In his 1965 report on the theological highlights of the council, Joseph Ratzinger noted that many of the bishops were disappointed with the difference between the synod as established and that desired by the council fathers. Rather than describing it in terms of collegiality, the *motu proprio* said that the synod would be "directly and immediately subordinated to the authority of the bishop of Rome," the only one who had the right "to convoke the synod, whenever it appears to him opportune,

---

[18] Josef Andreas Jungmann, "General Principles for the Restoration and Promotion of the Sacred Liturgy," in *Commentary on the Documents of Vatican II,* vol. 1, 26.

[19] Ibid., 44; Francis A. Sullivan reviews this controversy in "The Teaching Authority of Episcopal Conferences," *Theological Studies* 62 (2002): 476–78.

[20] Vittorio Messori, *The Ratzinger Report: An Exclusive Interview on the State of the Church* (San Francisco: Ignatius, 1985), 59.

[21] Pope John Paul II, *Apostolos Suos,* §21, July 23, 1998, in *Origins* 28 (July 30, 1998): 152–58.

and also to appoint the place of its deliberations." For these fathers, "[a] collegial organ had been turned into an instrument of the primate to use as he wished."[22] Ratzinger's somewhat optimistic conclusion was that whether the synod appears "under the aegis of collegiality or as an aid to the primatial office" will make little difference; "The primatial office will in any case take on a new aspect, if the pope's brother-bishops are included in his own ministry."[23]

However, prior to Francis's papacy, the synod had generally proved to be a disappointment. Meeting every three or four years, the pope determined the agenda and control remained in the hands of Vatican staffers who prepared the *lineamenta* or questions to be discussed, appointing other staffers to collate the synod's work. There was little free discussion, except in the language group. As Michael Fahey wrote, "Each new synod attracts less and less attention; the structure of their sessions has become unwieldy, they have become rituals with little practical impact on the life of the Church."[24] Many of the bishops felt they were not worth their time and energy.

RECENT DEVELOPMENTS

Pope Francis' apostolic exhortation *Evangelii Gaudium* ("The Joy of the Gospel") was the official papal response to the 2012 Synod of Bishops on the new evangelization, but in many ways it represents the pope's vision for the renewal of the church.[25] His remarks on episcopal conferences are interesting. While Pope Benedict argued that episcopal conferences had no magisterial authority, unless unanimous or approved by Rome as we have seen, the approach of Francis is different.

Strengthening Authority of Episcopal Conferences

In *Evangelii Gaudium*, Pope Francis writes that both the papacy and the central structures of the universal church need to hear the call to pastoral conversion. Then he turns to episcopal conferences. Citing Vatican II, he observes that, like the ancient patriarchal churches, episcopal conferences are in a position "to contribute in many and fruitful

---

[22] Joseph Ratzinger, *Theological Highlights of Vatican II* (New York: Paulist, 2009), 203; first published 1966.

[23] Ibid., 204.

[24] Michael Fahey, "The Synod of America: Reflections of a Nonparticipant," *Theological Studies* 59 (1998): 489.

[25] See Gerard Mannion, ed., *Pope Francis and the Future of Catholicism:* Evangelii Gaudium *and the Papal Agenda* (New York: Cambridge University Press, 2017).

ways to the concrete realization of the collegial spirit." However, "this desire has not been fully realized, since a juridical status of episcopal conferences which would see them as subjects of specific attributions, including genuine doctrinal authority, has not yet been sufficiently elaborated. Excessive centralization, rather than proving helpful, complicates the Church's life and her missionary outreach" (32).[26]

Francis also returned the authority over liturgical translations to episcopal conferences. In his *motu propio Magnum Principium* of September 2017, he modified canon law, granting episcopal conferences specific authority "to faithfully prepare . . . approve and publish the liturgical books for the regions for which they were responsible after confirmation by the apostolic see." When Cardinal Robert Sarah, prefect of the Congregation for Divine Worship, insisted in a "Commentary" on the ongoing validity of the congregation's 2001 instruction, *Liturgiam Authenticam*, the pope issued a public statement making clear that the Commentary "wrongly attributed" to the cardinal was incorrect. Instead of conformity to the norms of *Liturgiam Authenticam*, the changes in canon law take precedence to the congregation's instruction.[27] Finally, in February 2018 the pope and his council of cardinals began a process of rereading Pope John Paul II's *Apostolos Suos* in light of Francis' *Evangelii Gaudium*.

Reforming the Synod of Bishops

Francis has also sought to revitalize the synod of bishops. Shortly before the 2014 Extraordinary Synod on the Family, he addressed the 180 assembled synod members, encouraging them to speak openly and honestly, using the word *parrhesia*, which means "to speak freely" or "free speech." Synod members should not refrain from speaking honestly "out of respect for the pope" or concern that the pope thought differently: "This is not good, this is not *synodality*, because it is necessary to say all that, in the Lord, one feels the need to say: without polite deference, without hesitation. And at the same time, one must listen with humility and welcome, with an open heart, what your brothers say. *Synodality* is exercised with these two approaches."[28]

---

[26] A footnote references Pope John Paul II's *motu proprio Apostolos Suos*.

[27] Anne Kurian, "Liturgy: Pope's Letter to Cardinal Sarah, (Unabridged Translation)," *Zenit*, October 23, 2017, https://zenit.org/articles/liturgy-popes-letter-to-cardinal-sarah-unabridged-translation/.

[28] "Greetings of Pope Francis to the Synod Fathers during the First General Congregation of the Third General Assembly of the Synod of Bishops," October 6, 2014, https://w2.vatican.va/content/francesco/en/speeches/2014/october/documents/papa-francesco_20141006_padri-sinodali.html.

Also significant was a letter sent to all the bishops by Cardinal Lorenzo Baldisseri, secretary general of the synod, asking them in preparation for the synod to survey the faithful on questions of divorce and remarriage, rules for annulments, children in marriages not recognized by the church, contraception, and ministering to those in same-sex relations. While not all bishops included the faithful in their responses, the results were significant. A report released by the Vatican on June 26, 2014, found that "many Christians 'have difficulty' accepting church teaching on key issues such as birth control, divorce, homosexuality and cohabitation."[29] What was remarkable about the cardinal's survey was that it represented an unprecedented effort to consult the faithful on issues that touched them deeply.

Preparation for the October 2018 Synod on Young People, the Faith, and Vocational Discernment showed a similar openness. Preparation began with a 2017 online survey of young people that gathered 221,000 responses, with some 100,500 completing it. It included a meeting of youth and young adults in Rome in April 2017, and another week-long meeting with 300 young people in late March 2018. The working document or *instrumentum laboris* for the Synod drew on considerations from the bishops' conferences, the online survey, and a document prepared by young people in Rome at their March 2018 meeting. The text mentions that many young Catholics do not follow the church's teaching on sexuality, at one point referring to "LGBT youth" rather than "homosexuals" or "persons with homosexual tendencies," the more familiar language in church documents.[30]

Two papers appeared shortly before the Synod on Young People, designed to make the synods more effective. The apostolic constitution *Episcopalis Communio* states that even though the synod is essentially an episcopal body, article 18 acknowledges the possibility of the pope granting deliberative power to a synod assembly, which would mean that it would participate in the church's magisterium. The synod does not exist separately from the rest of the faithful; it is an instrument to give voice to the entire people of God. Thus the apostolic constitution outlines how the bishops in preparation for a synod assembly must submit the questions to be explored in the assembly to the priests,

[29] Josephine McKenna, "Vatican Confronts Shifting Landscape on Family Issues," *Religion News Service*, June 26, 2014, https://religionnews.com/2014/06/26/vatican-confronts-shifting-landscape-on-family-issues/.

[30] "Instrumentum Laboris," Fifteenth Ordinary General Assembly of Synod of Bishops, www.synod2018.va/content/dam/synod2018/documenti/instrumentum%20laboris%20in%20pdf/Instrumentum%20laboris_ENGLISH.pdf.

deacons, and lay faithful of their churches for their input. It provides also that the synod may be opened to certain invited guests: experts (*periti*) to help with the preparation of the documents, auditors (*auditores*) with special competence in the issues under discussion, and fraternal delegates from other churches and ecclesial communities.

The second paper was a study entitled "Synodality in the Life and Mission of the Church," prepared by the International Theological Commission. A broader concept than that of collegiality, synodality refers to the process for consulting the entire people of God (65–66), citing Pope Francis to the effect that "a synodal Church is a Church which listens ... The faithful People, the College of Bishops, the Bishop of Rome: all listening to each other; and all listening to the Holy Spirit" (110).

Reclaiming the *Sensus Fidei*

Finally, for Francis, Ignatius of Loyola's principle of "thinking with the church" does not mean simply thinking with the hierarchy, as is so often supposed. When asked by Father Antonio Spadaro in his famous interview how he understood Ignatius' principle, Francis spoke of the "holy, faithful people of God" as itself constituting a subject; he described it as that "complex web of relationships that take place in the human community" into which God enters. "And all the faithful, considered as a whole, are infallible in matters of belief, and the people display this *infallibilitas in credendo*, this infallibility in believing, through a supernatural sense of the faith of all the people walking together." He adds, "We should not even think, therefore, that 'thinking with the church' means only thinking with the hierarchy of the church."

He concludes, "This is what I understand as the 'thinking with the church' ... When the dialogue among the people and the bishops and the pope goes down this road and is genuine, then it is assisted by the Holy Spirit."[31] Richard Gaillardetz comments: "Let us not overlook the audacity of this claim. Francis is saying that we can be confident of an assistance of the Holy Spirit to the bishops on the condition that they are open to listening to others. This perspective stands in startling contrast to the almost mechanistic notions of the assistance of the Holy Spirit often invoked by church leaders."[32]

---

[31] Pope Francis, "A Big Heart Open to God: The Exclusive Interview with Pope Francis," *America* 209, no. 8 (September 30, 2013): 22.

[32] Richard R. Gaillardetz, "The Francis Moment: A 'Kairos' for Catholic Ecclesiology," *Proceedings of the Catholic Theological Society of America* 69 (2014): 72.

With his ecclesiological emphasis on the people of God as a subject, assisted by the Spirit, Francis is reclaiming the doctrine of the *sensus fidei*, a doctrine Cardinal Walter Kasper describes as well established in the biblical and theological tradition but often neglected.[33] In June 2014, the International Theological Commission (ITC) published an important text entitled "*Sensus Fidei* in the Life of the Church." The document cites Francis several times.

Like Francis, the ITC text argues that the faithful "are not merely passive recipients of what the hierarchy teaches and theologians explain: rather, they are living and active subjects within the Church" (67). They play a role in the development of doctrine, sometimes when bishops and theologians have been divided on an issue (72) and in the development of the church's moral teaching (73). If this is so, it follows "that the magisterium needs means by which to consult the faithful" (74). As the *sensus fidelium* is not simply identical with the majority opinion of the baptized, theology needs to provide principles and criteria for discernment (83), echoing what Francis had said in his address to the ITC the previous December. The text also argues that there is an ecumenical dimension to the *sensus fidei*; the text asks if separated Christians can be understood as participating in the *sensus fidelium* in some manner, answering in the affirmative (no. 86).

Most importantly, the ITC document suggests that the old distinction between the church teaching (*ecclesia docens*) and the church learning (*ecclesia discens*), where church teaching was identified exclusively with the hierarchy, is no longer theologically appropriate. "Banishing the caricature of an active hierarchy and a passive laity, and in particular the notion of a strict separation between the teaching Church (*Ecclesia docens*) and the learning Church (*Ecclesia discens*), the council taught that all the baptised participate in their own proper way in the three offices of Christ as prophet, priest and king" (4). The text credits Yves Congar for developing the doctrine of the *sensus fidei fidelis* and the *sensus fidei fidelium*, showing the organic unity between the *ecclesia docens*, "the teaching church," and the *ecclesia discens*, "the learning church": "The Church loving and believing, that is, the body of the faithful, is infallible in the living possession of the faith, not in a particular act or judgment" (43).

Toward the end, the ITC text notes that sometimes the majority of the faithful remain indifferent to doctrinal or moral decisions of the

---

[33] Walter Kasper, "Open House: How Pope Francis Sees the Church," *Commonweal* 142, no. 7 (April 10, 2015): 13.

magisterium, or reject them, perhaps from weak faith or an uncritical embrace of contemporary culture. However, it also points out that "it may indicate that certain decisions have been taken by those in authority without due consideration of the experience and the *sensus fidei* of the faithful, or without sufficient consultation of the faithful by the magisterium" (123).

CONCLUSION

Foundational to Pope Francis' ecclesiology is the image of the church as the people of God, rooted in the theology of his Argentine mentors, Lucia Gera with his emphasis on the *sensus fidei* in all the baptized and Rafael Tello's stress on the church as the faithful people of God. His preferred image is the church as "the holy, faithful people of God," a communion of diverse peoples and cultures, men and women, lay and ordained, guided by the Spirit.[34] He has taken specific steps to move beyond an overly hierarchical, clerical approach to church that tended to reduce the faithful to passive recipients. In virtue of their baptism, all members of the church are called to be missionary disciples (EG 120).

He has sought to elevate the status of episcopal conferences, raising the question of their juridical status, including a genuine teaching authority. In his apostolic exhortations and his encyclical *Laudato Si'* he frequently cites the teachings of episcopal conferences around the world, six times in *Evangelii Gaudium*, thirteen in *Laudato Si'*, nine in *Amoris Laetitia*, and seven in *Gaudete et Exsultate*. He does not want his to be a solitary voice, but one drawing on the wisdom of his brother bishops.

Similarly, he has sought to bring new life to the international synod of bishops, calling for two assemblies to deal with the family, seeking input from the faithful by means of surveys and allowing an unprecedented discussion in which real differences were aired. The two assemblies of the synod on the family were remarkable for the honest conversations and indeed disagreements that surfaced, with cardinals and bishops openly differing with each other, sometimes in the media. An episcopal assembly had not seen such transparency since the Second Vatican Council. Francis has also given new prominence to the doctrine of the *sensus fidei*, helping all the faithful to discern what is of God (EG 119). It is clear that this pope wants to include the voices of the faithful in the government of the church.

---

[34] See *Evangelii Gaudium*, nos. 111–34.

FURTHER READING

Buckley, Michael J. *Papal Primacy and the Episcopate: Towards a Relational Understanding.* New York: Crossroad, 1998.

Congar, Yves. *True and False Reform in the Church.* Translated with an Introduction by Paul Philibert. Collegeville, MN: Liturgical Press, 2010.

Gaillardetz, Richard R. *By What Authority? Foundations for Understanding Authority in the Church,* revised and expanded edition. Collegeville, MN: Liturgical Press, 2018.

Hinze, Bradford E. and Peter C. Phan, eds. *Learning from All the Faithful: A Contemporary Theology of the Sensus Fidei.* Eugene, OR: Pickwick Publications, 2016.

International Theological Commission. Sensus Fidei *in the Life of the Church.* 2014.

Mannion, Gerard. *Ecclesiology and Postmodernity: Questions for the Church in Our Time.* Collegeville, MN: Liturgical Press, 2007.

Oakley, Francis and Bruce Russett, eds. *Governance, Accountability, and the Future of the Catholic Church.* New York: Continuum, 2004.

Quinn, John R. *The Reform of the Papacy: The Costly Call to Christian Unity.* New York: Crossroad, 1999.

Rausch, Thomas P. and Richard R. Gaillardetz, eds. *Go into the Streets! The Welcoming Church of Pope Francis.* New York: Paulist Press, 2016.

Sullivan, Francis A. *Creative Fidelity: Weighing and Interpreting Documents of the Magisterium.* New York: Paulist Press, 1996.

14 Ministry in the Church

RICHARD LENNAN

Three interwoven features distinguished the landscape of ministry in the Catholic Church prior to the Second Vatican Council. First, "priest" came more easily to Catholics than did "minister;" the ordained priest was the norm for ministry, especially in parishes. Second, the theology of the priesthood centered on the role of the priest in offering the Eucharist; the discipline and goals of seminary life fostered this focus. Third, lay Catholics had access to few opportunities for training or recognition as ministers; non-ordained women and men, including vowed religious, contributed significantly to ecclesial life, but were peripheral to the church's structured ministry.

Both official teaching and popular perception classified priests principally as actors in the drama of the Eucharist, more than as preachers or pastors. When Pope Pius XI declared in 1935 that "the ineffable greatness of the human priest stands forth in all its splendour; for he has power over the very Body of Jesus Christ, and makes It present upon our altars," he was not only affirming a conviction that his contemporaries shared, but echoing a theology that stretched back for a millennium.[1] Medieval sacramental theology, endorsed at the Council of Trent (1545–63), showcased the "character" that ordination conferred, the gift of grace that marked the priest as "another Christ" empowered to confect the Eucharist.[2] Consequently, the "handing-over of the instruments," the chalice and paten used in the eucharistic liturgy, was regarded as the key element of priestly ordination; this perspective

---

[1] Pope Pius XI, *Ad Catholici Sacerdotii* (1935), article 16; the text can be found at: http://w2.vatican.va/content/pius-xi/en/encyclicals/documents/hf_p-xi_enc_193512 20_ad-catholici-sacerdotii.html.

[2] Hervé-Marie Legrand, "The 'Indelible' Character and the Theology of Ministry," in *The Plurality of Ministries*, ed. Hans Küng and Walter Kasper, *Concilium* 74 (1972): 54–62.

continued until 1947, when Pope Pius XII ruled that only the biblically warranted laying-on of hands was constitutive of a valid ordination.[3]

Predictably, the characterization of priests as participants in sacred events exerted an overriding influence on seminary training. In order to prepare candidates worthy to receive the sacramental character of ordination and become ministers of the Eucharist, seminaries functioned as "'total institutions' in the sociological sense of the word, designed to build character, obedience, spirituality, and camaraderie."[4] The fact that seminaries were largely self-contained bodies, removed even from the ecclesial community, furthered the notion that priests were "an order of men separated from the world to bear witness to the transcendent."[5]

The dominance of priestly and sacral interpretations of ministry ensured "that all not under orders or vows remained in the secular sphere capable not of ministry, but of a vague witness ... derived from minor shares in the episcopal office."[6] The split between ordained and lay Catholics mirrored and reinforced the split between the church and the world: "spiritual things belonged to the clergy and religious while worldly or profane things pertained to the laity. The laity therefore had no role, responsibility, or power in the inner life of the church."[7]

Against the backdrop of this three-paneled sketch of ministry in the Catholic community prior to Vatican II, this chapter will assemble its own three panels to represent the work of the council. These panels will review the evolution of Vatican II's approach to ecclesial ministry, detail its specific teaching and the relationships between the various strands of its vision for ministry in the church, and sketch the council's legacy on the unfolding of ecclesial ministry.

[3] See Yves Congar, "Reception as an Ecclesiological Reality," in *Election and Consensus in the Church*, ed. Giuseppe Alberigo and Anton Weiler, *Concilium* 77 (1972): 55–56; see also Edward Kilmartin, "Reception in History: An Ecclesiological Phenomenon and Its Significance," *Journal of Ecumenical Studies* 21 (1984): 43.

[4] Dean Hoge and Jacqueline Wenger, *Evolving Visions of Priesthood: Changes from Vatican II to the Turn of the New Century* (Collegeville, MN: 2003), 10; see also Thomas Dubay, *The Seminary Rule* (Dublin: Mercier Press, 1953).

[5] William Burrows, *New Ministries: The Global Context* (Maryknoll, NY: Orbis, 1980), 107.

[6] Thomas O'Meara, "Ministry in the Catholic Church Today: The Gift of Some Historical Trajectories," in *Together in God's Service: Towards a Theology of Ecclesial Lay Ministry* (Washington, DC: United States Catholic Conference, 1998), 79–80.

[7] Aurelie Hagstrom, *The Emerging Laity: Vocation, Mission, and Spirituality* (Mahwah, NJ: Paulist Press, 2010), 22–23.

VATICAN II ON THE ORDAINED PRIESTHOOD

The Background to the Council's Decree

Since the bishops who gathered for Vatican II were products of the long period of stability in the theology and practice of the priesthood, there was little expectation that the priesthood would require much of the council's time and energy. That expectation was confirmed when a comprehensive draft for a document on the priesthood reached the full assembly of bishops only in October 1965, two months before the end of Vatican II; the promulgation of the final decree occurred on the council's penultimate day.[8]

The first draft for a document dedicated to the priesthood – "On Clerics" (De Clericis) – was little more than "summary statements of papal proclamations and of prevailing Roman theology and pastoral practice."[9] The text was juridical in tone, while offering neither a thoroughgoing theology of the priesthood nor any acknowledgment that changing circumstances in the world and the church would be likely to affect priestly ministry. Those limitations sufficed to make the text unappealing to the majority of bishops who submitted opinions on it; the first draft, then, failed without reaching the floor of the council.

The second draft – "On Priests" (De Sacerdotibus) – followed the first in eschewing a detailed theology of the priesthood; in place of an expansive theology, the text identified ten key principles about the priesthood.[10] Those principles affirmed the obligations proper to priests and the particularity of priestly spirituality, which derived largely from the priest's sacramental ministry. After the episcopal responses subjected the text to extensive critical comments, the second draft went the way of its predecessor. Nonetheless, it became the nucleus for a third draft – "On the Life and Ministry of the Priest" (De Vita et Ministerio Sacerdotali) – that increased its guiding principles from ten to twelve.[11]

The full council discussed the third draft in October 1964, but the text did not achieve majority support. While the third draft advanced further than its two predecessors, it was subject to scathing criticism –

---

[8] Joseph Lécuyer, "History of the Decree," in *Commentary on the Documents of Vatican II* Vol. 4, ed. Herbert Vorgrimler (New York: Crossroad, 1969), 183–209; Maryanne Confoy, *Religious Life and Priesthood:* Perfectae Caritatis, Optatam Totius, Presbyterorum Ordinis (Mahwah, NJ: Paulist Press, 2008), 8–26.

[9] Confoy, *Religious Life and Priesthood*, 9.

[10] For a list of the principles see, Lécuyer, "History of the Decree," 189–90.

[11] Ibid., 191–92.

Yves Congar, for example, dismissed the draft as "weak, moralising, paternalistic, without vision, inspiration, or prophetic spirit."[12] The rejection of the third draft marked the final break with what Peter Hünermann identifies as the attitude that had undergirded all earlier efforts: "to deal with the discipline of the clergy and the Christian people without getting into the question of an appropriate theological description of the ministry of priests."[13] The failure of the third draft laid the path for a text that was more than a schematic overview of the priesthood, while also aligning reflection on the priesthood with the council's other endeavors.

A wider perspective on the priesthood was evident even in the title of the next draft – "On the Ministry and Life of Priests" (De Ministerio et Vita Presbyterorum). The priority of "ministry" over "life" show-cased pastoral activity, rather than the status derived from priestly "character," as integral to the priesthood. The adoption of presbyter ("elder") as the term for "priest" marked a deliberate departure from sacerdos, the preferred option in earlier drafts. Where sacerdos conveyed the distinctiveness of the principal figure in a cultic action, presbyter echoed both the setting for leadership evident in the various ecclesial bodies of the New Testament and the communal practices characteristic of the faith of Israel.

Although the council's sitting in November 1964 sought numerous changes to the text, the bishops did not press for another root-and-branch revision. Only a few days before the next draft came up for review by the full council in October 1965, Pope Paul VI denied permission for the bishops to debate the law on priestly celibacy, a topic that bishops from South America had sought to raise.[14] The October session voted to advance the revised draft toward a final vote, but the bishops pressed for more emendations on a number of issues – among them were the differences in spirituality between diocesan and religious priests, the witness of married priests, ministry as a means of sanctification, and the virtue of poverty in the life of priests. On December 7, 1965, the council

---

[12] Yves Congar, My Journal of the Council, trans. ed. D. Minns (Collegeville, MN: Liturgical Press, 2012), 624.

[13] Peter Hünermann, "A Half-Hearted Reform: The Decree on the Ministry and Life of Priests," in History of Vatican II, Vol. 5: The Council and the Transition. The Fourth Period and the End of the Council, September 1965–December 1965, ed. Giuseppe Alberigo and Joseph A. Komonchak, trans. M. O'Connell (Maryknoll, NY: Orbis, 2006), 457.

[14] See Confoy, Religious Life and Priesthood, 22–24.

gave all-but-unanimous assent to the Decree on the Ministry and Life of Priests, referred to usually as *Presbyterorum Ordinis* (PO).[15]

The Council's Teaching on the Priesthood

A comparison of the opening statements of the Council of Trent and Vatican II on the priesthood captures how the latter diverged from the long-prevailing tridentine pattern. Trent, faithful to its medieval inheritance and anxious to underscore that Catholics diverged from Protestants on the issue of the priesthood as on all else, affirmed that "since in the new covenant the catholic church has received the visible sacrifice of the eucharist from the Lord's institution, it is also bound to profess that there is a new, visible and external priesthood into which the old has been changed."[16] Vatican II's text, on the other hand, stressed that "through the sacred ordination and mission which they receive from the bishops, priests are promoted to the service of Christ the teacher, priest and king"; through thus sharing in Christ's ministry, priests were at the service of the church, which "is being unceasingly built up into the people of God, Christ's body and the temple of the Spirit" (PO 1).

Although the absence of any reference to the Eucharist in the initial article of Vatican II's decree is striking, no less significant are the features it does include: a trinitarian formula; an ecclesial framework, captured by both the reference to "the people of God" and the highlighting of the priest's relationship to the bishop; a mission-based vision for priestly ministry, one modeled on Christ as "teacher, priest, and king"; and a reminder of the eschatological orientation of the church, an orientation inseparable from Christ and the Holy Spirit. For this framing of the priesthood, the council drew on concepts that it had refined in its already-completed documents, especially the Dogmatic Constitution on the Church *Lumen Gentium*, which the council promulgated in November 1964.

Lumen Gentium sidesteps the usual clergy–laity division by referring to the whole church as "a holy priesthood," one anointed by the Holy Spirit and enabled through baptism to offer "spiritual sacrifices" that bear witness to the hope that comes from Christ (LG 10). In a text that has been the locus of much contention in the decades since the

---

[15] Lécuyer, "History of the Decree," 200–8. The vote to confirm the text was 2,390 in favor, with 4 against.

[16] The Council of Trent, "The true and catholic doctrine of the sacrament of order, to condemn the errors of our time" (session 23, July 15, 1563); the text can be found in *Decrees of the Ecumenical Councils*, vol. 2, ed. Norman Tanner (Washington, DC: Georgetown University Press, 1990), 742.

council, *Lumen Gentium* identifies two forms of priesthood, acknowledging both the distinction and the relationship between them: "Though they differ essentially and not only in degree, the common priesthood of the faithful and the ministerial or hierarchical priesthood are none the less interrelated: each in its own way shares in the one priesthood of Christ." The text stipulates that "the ministerial priest" exercises "sacred power" in governance and especially in offering the Eucharist, but it states too that "the faithful indeed, by virtue of their royal priesthood, share in the offering of the Eucharist" (LG 10). Consistent with the council's overarching ecclesiology, the constitution presents the two modes of priesthood as expressions of the one priesthood of the church, serving the communion and mission of the one people of God.

In another move that embodied the council's key emphases, *Lumen Gentium* channels much of its presentation of the priesthood through the relationship between the priest and the bishop. In stating that ordained priests "are consecrated in the image of Christ, the supreme and eternal priest," the constitution affirms the traditional notion of the divine vocation of priests, but it also determines that priests "depend on the bishops for the exercise of their power" (LG 28). The basis for this dependency lay in the identification of bishops as alone exercising "the fullness of the sacrament of Orders" (LG 21). In a similar vein, the Decree on the Pastoral Office of Bishops in the Church *Christus Dominus*, which appeared in October 1965, declares that bishops, because they "enjoy" this fullness of orders, are "the principal dispensers of the mysteries of God" at the heart of the church's liturgy (CD 15).

Both the document on the church and that on the bishops make plain that priests as ministers of God's word, of sanctification, and of pastoral leadership are not private contractors, but linked inextricably to the bishop. Together with the bishop, priests are part of a "presbyterate," a body in which they are to be "prudent cooperators of the episcopal college and its support and instrument" (LG 28; CD 15). As envisaged by the documents, the ordering of the relationship between bishops and priests aims at more than administrative efficiency: its goal is unity in service directed toward "building up the whole body of Christ" (LG 28; CD 28–31).

Presbyterorum Ordinis likewise illuminates the ecclesial nature of the priesthood. It does so initially by acknowledging that the sacraments of initiation precede ordination, a point not always evident in earlier theologies of the priesthood (PO 2). *Presbyterorum Ordinis* follows *Lumen Gentium* in elucidating the ecclesial identity of priests principally by presenting the link between the priest and the bishop as integral to priestly ministry. Indeed, the decree interweaves the priest's ministry with his relationship to both Christ and the bishop: "Because it is joined with the episcopal order the priesthood shares in the authority by which Christ himself builds up, sanctifies and rules his body"; priests, then, are to be "co-workers" with the bishops (PO 2).

The decree explores the specifics of priestly ministry by elaborating on each aspect of the tripartite formula that identifies the ordained as teacher, priest, and king after the manner of Christ. In detailing this threefold activity of the priest, *Presbyterorum Ordinis* ascribes priority (*primum officium*) to the ministry of the word, a ministry that involves not only preaching but also embodying the word (PO 4). Accordingly, the Dogmatic Constitution on Divine Revelation *Dei Verbum*, promulgated in November 1965, extends to priests the council's insistence that engagement with Scripture must be "the church's support and strength ... a pure and unfailing fount of spiritual life (DV 21)"; it also encourages priests to undertake "constant spiritual reading and diligent study" of Scripture (DV 25).

The decree on the priesthood unites the ministry of the word with the priest's ministry of sanctification and pastoral leadership of the Christian community. Thus, the priest's preaching is to nurture the faith that is central to celebration of the sacraments, including the Eucharist, in which is contained "the entire spiritual wealth of the Church" (PO 5). This integration of the elements of priestly ministry notwithstanding, the spotlighting of the ministry of the word was a departure from the long practice of centering the priesthood on the action of the Eucharist. One implication of this new emphasis, an implication that affected the training of priests, is the obligation on priests to be aware of the "concrete circumstances of life" that constitute the environment of those who would hear their preaching (PO 4).

When the decree on the priesthood turns to the particularly "priestly" element of presbyteral ministry, the notion of "sanctification" comes to the fore. The sanctification offered through the priest's actions, especially in the liturgy of the sacraments, was the direct product of their ordination, which the document describes in familiar terms: "the anointing of the holy Spirit, puts a special stamp on them and so conforms them to Christ the priest in such a way that they are able to act in the person of Christ the head" (PO 2). Both *Lumen*

Gentium and *Presbyterorum Ordinis* echo the theological and magisterial tradition that showcases the Eucharist as the paradigmatic means through which priests sanctify God's people. *Lumen Gentium* reaffirms of priests that "it is above all in the Eucharistic worship or assembly of the faithful that they exercise their sacred functions" (LG 28); similarly, *Presbyterorum Ordinis* describes "the eucharistic celebration [as] the center of the assembly of the faithful over which the priest presides" (PO 5).

Even though the role of the priest in the Eucharist had long been a vehicle for distinguishing priests from the wider community of the baptized, Vatican II's texts seek explicitly to connect the priest's presidency of the liturgical assembly to the responsibility that the priest was to exercise for the formation in faith of the worshipping community. Consequently, the council in various reflections on the Eucharistic liturgy interlaces the "kingly" or pastoral role of the ordained with their service as teacher and priest. The thread of this connection runs from the Constitution on the Sacred Liturgy, *Sacrosanctum Concilium* – "[Pastors] must also ensure that the faithful take part fully aware of what they are doing, actively engaged in the rite and enriched by it" (SC 11) – to the document on the priesthood – "[Priests] teach [the faithful] to take part in the celebrations of the sacred liturgy in such a way as to achieve sincere prayer in them also" (PO 5).

Beyond ending the exclusive concentration on the sanctifying office, *Presbyterorum Ordinis* offers an alternative to depictions of the priesthood that insulated priests from history. The decree acknowledges that the complexity endemic to the modern world, no less than the challenges that priests themselves faced, confronted the church's ordained ministers with the task of unifying "their interior life and their program of external activity" (PO 14). As a means to foster this unity, the decree encourages priests to follow the example of Christ, finding "in the practise of pastoral charity itself the bond of priestly perfection which will harmonise their lives and activity" (PO 14). Among the aids that the text endorses as means to growth of pastoral charity, the Eucharist and relationship to the wider community of the church are prominent, but so too are humility, obedience, discernment of God's will, a positive relationship to the bishop and other ministers, and a willing embrace of both celibacy and voluntary poverty, all of which require the ongoing conversion inseparable from prayer and study (PO 14–19).

Assessments of the Decree on Priests

Peter Hünermann describes *Presbyterorum Ordinis* as "one of the Council's stepchildren."[17] In pronouncing that verdict, Hünermann draws attention not merely to the pre-history of the text, but to what he judges to be the document's lack of consistency: "While the text does offer an abundance of positive approaches and aspects, these are not thought through in depth and are offset by a lot of statements that set a traditional sacerdotal image of the priest over against a theologically up-to-date understanding of ministry."[18]

On the positive side of the document's ledger, Christian Duquoc argues that the concentration of *Presbyterorum Ordinis* on the three-fold ministry of the priest, rather than solely on the cultic dimension, was a watershed in the history of the priesthood: "[the priest's] manner of life no longer flows from the sacrality of the liturgical action, but instead from the mission assigned him of preaching the gospel of Jesus Christ in a way that will make it intelligible to both believers and nonbelievers."[19] On the other hand, the biblical scholar James Dunn castigates *Presbyterorum Ordinis* for applying uncritically to the church's sacramental priesthood the description of priests of the old covenant in the Letter to the Hebrews: "Priests, while being chosen from the midst of humanity and appointed to act on its behalf in what pertains [to] God, to offer gifts and sacrifices for sins (see Heb 5:1), live with the rest of humanity as with brothers and sisters" (PO 3). Dunn dismisses this use of Hebrews by the council as "a form of eisegesis which ranks more as abuse than as correct use of Scripture."[20]

Beyond such inconsistences, there are key aspects of the decree in need of fuller explanation; one of these is the relationship between the priest and the bishop. While the documents insist on the dependence of priests on bishops, they offer no exegesis of "the fullness of orders," the quality that accounts for the dominance of bishops. This silence prompts Anthony Barratt to ask a series of questions: "Is fullness a qualitative or quantitative term or both? Does fullness imply that the presbyterate (and the diaconate) are simply a sharing in the bishop's own

---

[17] Hünermann, "A Half-Hearted Reform," 457.

[18] Ibid., 457–58.

[19] Christian Duquoc, "Clerical Reform," in *The Reception of Vatican II*, ed. Giuseppe Alberigo, Jean Pierre Jossua, Joseph Komonchak, and Matthew O'Connell, trans. M. O'Connell (Washington, DC: Catholic University of America Press, 1987), 303.

[20] James Dunn, "Another Test Case," in James Dunn and James Mackey, *New Testament Theology in Dialogue: Christology and Ministry* (London: SPCK,1987), 125–26.

ministry, since, for example, the bishop cannot be everywhere and do everything? Is fullness primarily a term connected with function, or does it have a more ontological, or relational meaning?"[21] Barratt's response to his questions presents "fullness" not as a quantity, but a quality tied to the bishop's representation of the church as the sacrament of Christ; this connects the relationship between the bishop and priests to the unity and catholicity of the church, rather than to a more juridical concern with power and authority.[22] Although Barratt's approach is helpful, the absence from the documents themselves of a guiding interpretation of "fullness" has ensured that debate continues concerning whether priestly ministry is more than a subordinate service to the bishops.

If *Presbyterorum Ordinis* seems to disadvantage priests in relation to bishops, the fact that the document concentrates on the threefold ministry of ordained priests, rather than only the priest's representation of Christ in the Eucharist, while also stressing the priesthood of all the baptized, can also appear to be a diminishment of the priest. On this score, Edward Pfnausch articulates a twofold critique: The decree "does not completely or adequately separate presbyteral spirituality from the spirituality of all believers";[23] the stress on the priest sharing in the mission of all believers "can lead to a loss of appreciation for the distinctive ministry of the presbyter or lead to the danger of activism," to priests in search of a specific role.[24] Brian Daley too points to the danger of "activism" if the priesthood lacks a center of gravity akin to what the absolute link to the Eucharist had long provided: "it is possible to read *Presbyterorum ordinis* as inviting a kind of clerical activism, as representing priesthood more as a profession than as a role within the sacramental Body, where God is the principal actor; emphasis on the ministry of the word can be taken as an excuse for turning liturgy into a kind of talk-show."[25]

---

[21] Anthony Barratt, "The Sacrament of Order and the Second Vatican Council: The Presbyter-Bishop Relationship Revisited," *International Journal for the Study of the Christian Church* 2 (2002): 12.

[22] Ibid., 21–26.

[23] Edward Pfnausch, "The Conciliar Documents and the 1983 Code," in *The Spirituality of the Diocesan Priest*, ed. Donald Cozzens (Collegeville, MN: Liturgical Press, 1997), 161.

[24] Ibid.

[25] Brian Daley, "John Paul II and the Jesuit Vocation to the Priesthood," in *John Paul II on the Body: Human-Eucharistic-Ecclesial*, ed. John McDermott and John Gavin (Philadelphia: Saint Joseph's University Press, 2007), 228.

While it is debatable whether *Presbyterorum ordinis* occasioned greater "activism" and a more functional interpretation of the priesthood, it is undeniable that the focus on the priest as minister of word and pastoral leadership, not simply of sanctification, moved priestly spirituality, and the preparation of candidates for ordination, into unchartered territory. Prior to the council, the standard model of seminary education had not focused on proclamation of the word or on pastoral ministry, outside of administration of the sacraments and one-to-one pastoral care.[26] Now, however, the priest's growth in holiness and his relationship with the community of believers required a different perspective, one for which seminaries had not prepared him.

In his evaluation of *Presbyterorum Ordinis*, the historian John O'Malley points to a different lacuna: a lack of attention to ordination and ministry in the context of religious life, including monastic priesthood. O'Malley's critique finds support in the document's opening paragraph, which specifies its focus on those priests "who are engaged in the care of souls [and] to religious priests insofar as its provisions suit their circumstances" (PO 1). O'Malley concludes that Vatican II's understanding of the difference between diocesan and religious priests "seems to be at most one of emphasis or consists simply in the juridical fact of public vows or perhaps life in community."[27] Ironically, in light of O'Malley's analysis, Pfnausch claims that the decree's failure to develop "a distinctive spirituality" for either diocesan or religious priests disadvantaged the former in particular since religious could draw on the evangelical counsels, as well as their communal charisms.[28]

David Power faults *Presbyterorum Ordinis* for failing to account for the historical and cultural influences affecting the present and future of the priesthood. For Power, "there is a sense in which [*Presbyterorum Ordinis*] is anachronistic inasmuch as it takes for granted a community in which there is an ample supply of priests ... Nor therefore was it foreseen how the structures that supposed a clear differentiation between the ordained and baptized would no longer satisfy."[29] Clearly, the two issues that Power nominates have expanded exponentially in the decades since Vatican II.

---

[26] See David Walker, "Models of Spirituality for Ordained Ministers," in *Priesthood: The Hard Questions*, ed. Gerald Gleeson (Newtown, NSW: E.J. Dwyer, 1992), 14.

[27] John O'Malley, "Priesthood, Ministry, and Religious Life: Some Historical and Historiographical Considerations," *Theological Studies* 49 (1988): 223.

[28] Pfnausch, "The Conciliar Documents," 161.

[29] David Power, *Mission, Ministry, Order: Reading the Tradition in the Present* (New York: Continuum, 2008), 88.

THE DECREE ON THE TRAINING OF PRIESTS

Since the Council of Trent used the canons of its decree on the sacrament of order as the venue to mandate seminaries, Vatican II's Decree on Priestly Formation, *Optatam Totius*, can lay claim to producing the first conciliar document in the church's history dedicated to this topic.[30] *Optatam Totius*, which the council promulgated in October 1965, begins discussion of preparation for the priesthood by acknowledging both the present – "the changed conditions of our time" require "new elements" in the training of priests – and the past – "the experience of centuries" must continue to guide the church's preparation of its future ordained ministers (OT preface).

As the text progressed through various drafts to its final acceptance, the awareness of "changed conditions" expressed itself in anxiety about a decline in the number of vocations, as well as a desire to ensure that priests could be effective in the midst of the flux affecting social and cultural norms, including the place of religion in the modern world (OT 6). The commitment to "the experience of centuries" revolved around the disciplines of seminary life and the place that the thought of St Thomas Aquinas ought to have in seminary studies.

While not highly regarded – "poor and destined to be forgotten"[31] – *Optatam Totius* makes two noteworthy contributions to the development of ecclesial ministry after Vatican II. First, it recognizes that local churches must shape formation programs for their context, rather than relying on a "one-size-fits-all" model across the whole church; second, it promotes priesthood as a ministry, rather than a means to status in the church. In relation to the first point, the decree encourages local episcopal conferences, in light of "the great diversity of peoples and countries," to draw up their own program for the preparation of candidates for ordination (OT 1). That recommendation represented an application of *Lumen Gentium*'s teaching on episcopal collegiality and on the local church (LG 26–27).

---

[30] Confoy, *Religious Life and Priesthood*, 77–173; Mathijs Lamberigts, "*Optatam Totius* The Decree on Priestly Formation: A Short Survey of Its History at the Second Vatican Council," *Louvain Studies* 30 (2005): 25–48; Josef Neuner, "Decree on Priestly Formation," *Commentary on the Documents of Vatican II*, vol. 2, ed. Herbert Vorgrimler (New York: Crossroad, 1968), 371–404.

[31] Giuseppe Alberigo, "The Conclusion of the Council and the Initial Reception," in *History of Vatican II Vol. 5: The Council and the Transition. The Fourth Period and the End of the Council, September 1965–December 1965*, ed. Giuseppe Alberigo and Joseph A. Komonchak, trans. M. O'Connell (Maryknoll, NY: Orbis, 2006), 551.

In underscoring the priority of priestly ministry over priestly dignity, *Optatam Totius* insisted that candidates for ordination ought to realize "that they are not destined for a life of power and honors, but are destined to be totally dedicated to the service of God and pastoral ministry" (OT 9). To that end, the document accords with *Presbyterorum Ordinis* in the emphasis it gives to the ministry of word, worship, and pastoral leadership (OT 4). On the other hand, *Optatam Totius*, although finalized only six weeks before the decree on the priesthood, prefers *sacerdos* to *presbyter*, a choice indicative of an approach to the priesthood that was more cautious than innovative.

Paul VI's decision to prohibit any discussion of the requirement for celibacy meant that *Optatam Totius* does little more than repeat the standard affirmation of the superiority of celibacy over marriage (OT 10). The fact that the "human person" as the subject of formation appears only within the discussion of the spiritual development of seminarians left little room for the human sciences to play a role in the processes of formation. More positively, there is encouragement for psychology to inform the classroom education of seminarians (OT 11); for students to understand "the present age" by openness to various forms of philosophical thinking (OT 15); and for pastoral ministry to employ "the various aids provided by pedagogy, psychology and sociology" (OT 20). Those emphases opened possibilities for the seminary curriculum to move beyond the traditional reliance on Thomistic studies.

MINISTRY BEYOND THE PRIESTHOOD

The Diaconate

Vatican II's consideration of ministry in the church enabled the diaconate to become more than a step on the way to priestly ordination. This step had long been a canonical requirement, but conveyed no expectations of a sustained or comprehensive diaconal ministry. The council opened the way for legislation enabling the diaconate to be "permanent," a status that had ended in the first millennium, to have a theological underpinning that recognized it as an ordained ministry distinct from that of priests, and to be open to married men.

Unlike the lack of preconciliar discussion about the ordained priesthood, the revival of the diaconate had aroused considerable interest before the council. Theologians in Europe, especially Germany, argued that the church's threefold ordained ministry required an authentic practice of the diaconate, which could also aid the church's obligation to meet pastoral needs untouched by the ministry of priests.[32] Despite this groundwork, enthusiasm for the diaconate among the bishops was muted in the early stages of the council, especially since deacons were not an obvious solution to a reduced number of priests.[33] Ultimately, the bishops made some major recommendations about deacons, albeit within only three paragraphs of the council's entire corpus.

The diaconate appears in the final article of the chapter in *Lumen Gentium* dedicated to the hierarchical nature of the church; the inclusion of deacons alongside bishops and priests underscored their place within the church's threefold ordained ministry. The article, drawing on patristic texts, classifies the diaconate as being "dedicated to the people of God, in communion with the bishop and his presbyterate, in the service of the liturgy, of the word and of charity" (LG 29). This inventory of the deacon's activities suggests that the bishops envisaged deacons as able to supplement the ministry of the priest.

Since a description of diaconal ministry is not the same as having deacons available to fulfill that ministry, the council acknowledges the need to "restore" the diaconate as a permanent ministry. Rather than mandate this restoration, *Lumen Gentium* cedes any decision about restoration to "local episcopal conferences" in dialogue with the pope (LG 29). The text also envisages the possibility that married men might become deacons, a concession that it allows while also stressing the importance of celibacy (LG 29).

The freedom of an episcopal conference to decide about the diaconate was prominent in the other text that mentions the diaconate, the Decree on the Church's Missionary Activity, *Ad Gentes*. Here, the underlying concern was less with the integrity of the church's threefold ministry than with the grace of sacramental ordination for "those men who carry out the ministry of the diaconate" (AG 16). Since the context for this document was the church's work in countries where priests were in short supply, the decree recognizes the likelihood of deacons "governing scattered christian communities in the name of the bishop or parish priest" (AG 16). The document does not elaborate on the relationship between this "governing" activity of deacons and other forms of ministry proper to deacons.

---

[32] Tim O'Donnell, "How the Ecclesiological Visions of Vatican II Framed the Ministry of Deacons," *Worship* 85 (2011): 427–32.

[33] O'Donnell, "The Ecclesiological Visions of Vatican II," 432–41.

Openings to Lay Ministry

In the decades since the close of Vatican II, Catholics in various parts of the world have become familiar with the "lay ecclesial minister." It seems reasonable, therefore, to conclude that this phenomenon was a product of the council. In fact, not only is such a concept absent from the conciliar documents, but only a handful of instances among the council's uses of "minister" and "ministry" are applicable to lay members of the church.[34] Still, the council's texts provide a foundation for later developments in lay ministry.

Even though the opening sentiments of the chapter on the laity in *Lumen Gentium* may sound today somewhat patronizing, or at least reflective of the supremacy of the ordained – "The sacred pastors, indeed, know well how much the laity contribute to the well-being of the whole church. For they know that they were not established by Christ to undertake by themselves the entire saving mission of the church to the world" (LG 30) – the chapter homes in positively on the implications of baptism. Accordingly, "the laity" designates all the faithful "who by Baptism are incorporated into Christ, are constituted the people of God, who have been made sharers in their own way in the priestly, prophetic and kingly office of Christ and play their part in carrying out the mission of the whole christian people in the Church and in the world" (LG 31).

Lumen Gentium recognizes likewise that "all are called to holiness and have obtained an equal privilege of faith through the justice of God" (LG 32). The document does portray "the rest of the faithful" primarily as people who "should eagerly collaborate with the pastors and teachers," but the fact that lay people share in the offices of Christ identifies them as other than passive recipients of clerical initiatives (LG 32).

While the council emphasizes the equality of all the baptized, it specifies "the world," rather than "the church," as the principal venue for the laity's exercise of the three offices of Christ: "to be secular is the special characteristic of the laity" (LG 31). *Lumen Gentium* presents the secular character of the laity as an uncontroversial conclusion of a sociological fact: the laity are engaged "in each and every one of the world's occupations and callings and in the ordinary circumstances of social and family life" (LG 31). Consequently, *Lumen Gentium*,

---

[34] See Elissa Rinere, "Conciliar and Canonical Applications of 'Ministry' to the Laity," *The Jurist* 47 (1987): 204–27; only nineteen of the council's two hundred uses of "ministry/minister" apply to lay people.

together with other documents of Vatican II that refer explicitly to the laity, depicts the particular mission of the laity as the call "to the sanctification of the world" (LG 31; AA 2).

The emergence of lay ecclesial ministers, people embodying the council's teaching on the implications of baptism, offers the possibility of interpreting more broadly the laity's role in sanctifying the world. In other words, when lay people exercise leadership in the church, when they build up the church in order that all of its members, lay and ordained, might be more attuned to their mission in the world, they also fulfil their baptismal call to sanctify the world.

THE CHURCH'S MINISTRY SINCE VATICAN II

Vatican II opened the door to an unknown future for the church's ministry. It did so principally through its presentation of the priesthood in pastoral terms and its acknowledgment of the baptismal priesthood of the faithful. Although both emphases had a strong foundation in the most ancient layers of the church's tradition, the period immediately following Vatican II witnessed a dramatic, and unanticipated, upheaval in the church's ministry.

Emblematic of that upheaval were widespread resignations from priestly ministry and a corresponding drop in the number of seminarians. Those developments generated a high level of anxiety among priests, anxiety that the Synod of Bishops in 1971 distilled into questions about the future of priestly ministry: "Does the priestly ministry have any specific nature? Is this ministry necessary? Is the priesthood incapable of being lost? What does being a priest mean today? Would it not be enough to have for the service of the Christian communities presidents designated for the preservation of the common good, without sacramental ordination, and exercising their office for a fixed period?"[35] That such questions came to the fore only a few years after the council testifies to the breadth and depth of change in the landscape of ecclesial ministry.

In the decades since the 1960s crises of various forms have stalked the church's ordained priesthood. Concern about the number of priests remains, but mandatory celibacy and the ongoing exclusion of women from the possibility of priestly ordination also generate controversy.

[35] "The Ministerial Priesthood" (*Ultimis Temporibus*), article 4; the text can be found in *Vatican Council II: More Postconciliar Documents*, ed. Austin Flannery (Northport, NY: Costello Publishing Co., 1982), 674.

Most recently, and most tragically, the revelations of clerical sexual abuse of minors and vulnerable adults have deeply damaged the priesthood.

Crises affecting the ordained priesthood have an impact on issues of ministerial identity and role for both deacons and lay ministers. The growth of the diaconate in many countries has brought into sharper relief the challenge of presenting deacons as other than a "junior priest" compensating for a lack of priests. Since the diaconate is another ordained ministry inaccessible to women, the reception of deacons at a time of expanding lay ministry has become difficult. The exponential multiplication of lay ecclesial ministers is in sharp contrast to the history of ordained priests since Vatican II. That multiplication represents a strong appropriation of the council's promotion of the gifts of all the baptized. Still lingering, however, are questions about collaboration between ordained and lay ministers, as well as many practical concerns about just employment conditions.

The contours of ecclesial ministry in the early decades of the twenty-first century differ radically from those evident when the council closed in 1965. Most of the changes that have taken place are best described as indirect effects of Vatican II. The council did not fashion a blueprint for the future of ministry, but its repeated insistence that all the baptized, each in a particular way, share in the priestly, prophetic, and pastoral presence of Christ has been the catalyst for a reordering of ministry. It is unlikely that this catalyst is now exhausted.

FURTHER READING

Bevans, Stephen and Robin Ryan, eds. *Priesthood in Religious Life: Searching for New Ways Forward*. Collegeville, MN: Liturgical Press, 2018.

Conway, Eamonn, ed. *Priesthood Today: Ministry in a Changing Church*. Dublin: Veritas, 2013.

Ditewig, William and Michael Tkacik, eds. *Forming Deacons: Ministers of Soul and Leaven*. Mahwah, NJ: Paulist Press, 2010.

Fox, Zeni, ed. *Lay Ecclesial Ministry: Pathways toward the Future*. Lanham, MD: Rowman & Littlefield, 2010.

Hagstrom, Aurelie. *The Emerging Laity: Vocation, Mission, and Spirituality*. Mahwah, NJ: Paulist Press, 2010.

Hahnenberg, Edward. *Theology of Ministry: An Introduction for Lay Ministers*. Collegeville, MN: Liturgical Press, 2014.

O'Collins, Gerald and Michael Keenan Jones. *Jesus Our Priest: A Christian Approach to the Priesthood of Christ*. Oxford: Oxford University Press, 2010.

Power, David. *Mission, Ministry, Order: Reading the Tradition in the Present.* New York: Continuum, 2008.

Schuth, Katarina. *Seminary Formation: Recent History, Current Challenges, New Directions.* Collegeville, MN: Liturgical Press, 2016.

Wood, Susan, ed. *Ordering the Baptismal Priesthood: Theologies of Lay and Ordained Ministry.* Collegeville, MN: Liturgical Press, 2003.

15 Professed Religious Life

GEMMA SIMMONDS

The Decree on the Up-To-Date Renewal of Religious Life, *Perfectae Caritatis*, was proclaimed on October 28, 1965. In comparison with the council's four constitutions, it appears a brief and largely juridical piece. It bears the hallmarks of the fatigue, division, and compromise that accompanied its creation as council fathers argued over the nature of religious life and its place within the church. Yet hidden behind its brevity lie the rich and complex theologies and ecclesiologies within the Dogmatic Constitution on the Church *Lumen Gentium* and the Pastoral Constitution on the Church in the Modern World *Gaudium et Spes*, as well as the pastoral wisdom of the Decree on the Church's Missionary Activity *Ad Gentes*.[1] The decree cannot be properly understood without reference to these documents. It urged the more than one million women and three hundred thousand men living under religious vows at the time to undertake a comprehensive program of renewal and adaptation of their life in the light of both their founding charism and the contemporary context.[2] The energy with which they did so would have an impact on religious themselves, and thus on the wider church, which few at the time could have foreseen. Not only did the decree on renewal provoke monumental practical upheavals but it also initiated theological shifts that to this day continue to provoke profound disagreement on how it should be interpreted.

---

[1] See Maryanne Confoy, *Religious Life and Priesthood:* Perfectae Caritatis, Optatam Totius and Presbyterorum Ordinis (Mahwah, NJ: Paulist Press, 2008) and Friedrich Wulf, "Decree on the Appropriate Renewal of the Religious Life," in *Commentary on the Documents of Vatican II*, vol. 2, ed. Herbert Vorgrimler (London: Burns & Oates, 1968), 301–70.

[2] Norman Tanner, "The Church in the World," in *History of Vatican II, Vol. 4: Church as Communion: Third Period and Intersession, September 1964–September 1965*, ed. Giuseppe Alberigo and Joseph A. Komonchak (Maryknoll, NY: Orbis Press, 2003), 269–386, at 367.

RELIGIOUS LIFE BEFORE THE COUNCIL

Vatican II did not invent or discover the need for the reform of religious life. Pope Pius XII and the Congregation for Religious in Rome had already made vigorous attempts to introduce the change and renewal they saw as urgently necessary.[3] At the time of the council the style of life of many religious, particularly of women, was considered by council fathers like Cardinal Léon Suenens of Brussels to be damagingly anachronistic and far removed from that desired and imagined by the founders of their orders.[4] The principles of *ressourcement* and *aggiornamento* were therefore seen as vital in the reform of religious life, as they were in other aspects of the church's life. *Ressourcement* would enable religious to sort the wheat of their founding charism and rule from the chaff of historical developments, not all of which were in tune with their founding spirit. *Aggiornamento* would respond to Suenens' conviction that religious could only serve the church as the Spirit had originally inspired them to do if they were freed from oppressive and unnecessary structures.

Many congregations of women and some of the brotherhoods struggled to find their identity between the apostolic charism received from their founders and the mainly monastic model imposed on them by a church that had not shifted its thinking from earlier forms of consecration. While this was partially addressed by Leo XIII's Apostolic Constitution *Conditae a Christo* of 1900, Cardinal Suenens raised concerns some fifty years later regarding the tensions for women religious struggling to maintain apostolic ministries in the modern world while stifled by rigid rules, which he saw as part of the church's complicity with the "ideologies and deficiencies of their epoch."[5] By this he meant above all misogynistic attitudes embedded within society but also reflected within the church, which suppressed sisters' potential for leadership and gave rise to anachronisms in religious life based on social norms of bygone ages.[6] The ban on sisters practicing medicine as doctors or midwives (the latter profession considered a potential threat to their vow of chastity), while lifted in 1936, is a particular example.

---

[3] Friedrich Wulf, "Decree on the Appropriate Renewal of the Religious Life," 301–2.

[4] Tanner, "The Church in the World," 367; Léon Joseph Suenens, *The Nun in the World: New Dimensions in the Modern Apostolate* (London: Burns & Oates, 1962).

[5] Gérard Huyghe, *Tensions and Change: The Problems of Religious Orders Today* (London: Chapman, 1965), 6 and Suenens, *Nun in the World*, 42.

[6] Confoy, *Religious Life and Priesthood*, 201–2.

At the time of the council women constituted the majority of religious by a ratio of 4:1, but they were not permitted to participate in meetings of the Commission for Religious. Some commentators deplored this state of affairs, which was justified by reference to I Cor. 14:34 ("women should be silent in the churches. For they are not permitted to speak, but should be subordinate, as the law also says"). This exclusion should be read in the context of the broader exclusion of women from the council's preparatory and conciliar commissions as official experts. They were also excluded as communicants at Masses celebrated for wider council participants.[7] In time, Pope Paul VI acceded to the many requests to permit some participation in the council by women "so that women will know how much the Church honors them in the dignity of their existence and their human and Christian mission."[8]

Like numerous groups of apostolic women, many religious brotherhoods had emerged from groups of men living the evangelical counsels but without formal vows, committed to humble service in imitation of Christ. In time these brotherhoods transmuted into religious congregations, modeled on monastic lines alien to their origins. Frequently, they found themselves urged to accept ordination when bishops saw in them potentially useful additions to priestly numbers, but there was strong resistance to this pressure. The distinctiveness of their vocation received renewed impetus with Vatican II's call for religious to return to their historical roots, but it took the brothers themselves several decades to clarify their particular role within the church.[9]

These issues offer a context within which to consider the changes called for at the council and their implementation in its aftermath.

THE NATURE OF THE DEBATE

The renewal of religious life by the council was not a straightforward matter. It produced much heated debate, changes of key personnel, and multiple revisions both of documents and schemes of work during the council.[10] Critics of the unnecessary historical accretions smothering

---

[7] Wulf, "Decree on the Appropriate Renewal of the Religious Life," 4, 20–27.

[8] Confoy, Religious Life and Priesthood, 199.

[9] Benedict Foy, "Some Reflections on the Religious Brothers' Vocation since Vatican II: Its Present and Future," in A Future Built on Faith: Religious Life and the Legacy of Vatican II, ed. Gemma Simmonds (Dublin: The Columba Press, 2014), 63–80.

[10] Confoy, Religious Life and Priesthood, 177–271 and Denis Minns, ed., Yves Congar, OP: My Journal of the Council (Collegeville, MN: Liturgical Press, 2012), 670–71, 674.

original charisms called for a bringing up to date of lifestyles and customs. Others feared a watering down of vital tradition, leading to a fatal assimilation of religious life to secular influences. Much of the debate centered on where religious belong within the church, since this points to the nature and purpose of this ecclesial phenomenon, which has no direct roots in scripture.

In the popular mind and in much traditional treatment of the subject, the people of God was thought of according to a three-tiered order, moving from the priority of the clergy to religious with the laity coming last. One of the seismic shifts stemming from the council's first session was the re-prioritization of the Christian faithful as a whole, thus effectively doing away with this three-tiered conceptual framework.[11] *Lumen Gentium* declared that:

> This state of life, from the point of view of the divine and hierarchical nature of the church, is not to be seen as a middle way between the clerical and lay states of life (43).

Lumen Gentium describes religious life as an ancient tradition following the evangelical counsels of chastity, poverty, and obedience in imitation of Christ himself. This notion of the origin of religious life lying in the *sequela Christi* (imitation or following of Christ) is also repeated in *Perfectae Caritatis*:

> In the constitution, *Lumen Gentium*, the holy synod has already shown that the quest for perfect charity by means of the evangelical counsels traces its origin to the teaching and example of the Divine Master, and that it is a very clear symbol of the heavenly kingdom (1).

Thus, while not being directly founded by Christ, religious life's symbolic significance for the church as a whole is emphasized. The Decree on Religious Life places religious life within the charismatic rather than the hierarchical realm. But while *Lumen Gentium* 44 refers to the special way in which the evangelical counsels join their followers to the church and its mystery, it does not make clear wherein this specialness lies. This overall lack of precision concerning the nature and function of religious life would prove one of the major weaknesses of the council's teaching. The inclusion of secular institutes in the document on religious life (PC 5) only added to the confusion. It might be

---

[11] Wulf, vol. 1: 253ff.

thought that a conciliar theological definition claiming divine origin for the charismatic nature of religious life would be sufficient to settle any questions of its distinct source and purpose. But the desire of some postconciliar commentators to continue to distinguish hierarchies of value among the faithful still makes this a vexed question. Widely differing interpretations have failed to yield a satisfactory resolution.[12]

Prior to the council, when one spoke of someone having a vocation, this was universally understood to refer to a priestly or religious vocation. *Lumen Gentium* argued differently:

> Strengthened by so many and such great means of salvation, all the faithful, whatever their condition or state are called by the Lord – each in his or her own way – to that perfect holiness by which the Father Himself is perfect (11).

This theology of the primordial baptismal vocation made clear that every member of the people of God is invited to share in the life of Jesus as prophet, priest, and king, constituting the holy nation claimed by 1 Pt. 2:9–10 (LG 10). Those seeking a radical life of dedication to God were encouraged for centuries to believe that this was principally found in the priesthood or religious life. The radical self-emptying required for successful married life and parenthood was very rarely considered in comparison with the exaltation of the asceticism of religious life, despite the fact that it often entailed sacrifices as great, if not greater, than those made in the name of poverty, chastity, and obedience.[13]

For a clear reading of the council's teaching on religious life it is important to understand how it saw the principal motive for undertaking this vocation and its significance to the church as a whole. If the council presented the *sequela Christi* as the dominant motive for joining a religious order, there was also a long tradition of connecting it with the *fuga mundi*, the flight from the world typical of the desert fathers and mothers of the third and fourth centuries, from which religious life is generally held to have evolved. A desire to resist the lures of worldly values and to live a more radical life of self-giving was common to most founders of religious congregations, but many of the apostolic congregations also called their members to respond to Christ

---

[12] See Sandra M. Schneiders, *Prophets in their Own Country: Women Religious Bearing Witness to the Gospel in a Troubled Church* (Maryknoll, NY: Orbis, 2011) and Sara Butler, "*Perfectae Caritatis*," in *The Reception of Vatican II*, ed. Matthew Lamb and Matthew Levering (Oxford: Oxford University Press, 2017), 208–33.

[13] Confoy, *Religious Life and Priesthood*, 192.

found at the margins of society in the poor and suffering. The challenge to engage with the secular world in all its "joys and hopes, griefs and anxieties" found within *Gaudium et Spes* led many religious to question the unreflective assumptions regarding the *fuga mundi* in their lifestyle which were alien to their founding charism.

Some commentators have attributed the alarming and steady drop in the number of religious in the global north to misinterpretations of the council's teaching, though it had begun before the council.[14] Social scientists suggest that factors within history and society impacting women have in fact been the predominant reason behind it. This is also emerging as a pattern in areas of the global south that have hitherto been rich in vocations to the religious life.[15] The Religious Life Futures Project, undertaken in the United States, suggests that the confusion and lack of clarity resulting from the council had a negative effect on religious life in many cases.[16] Others suggest that *Lumen Gentium's* teaching on the universal call to holiness cut the ground from beneath the feet of religious as the spiritual *virtuosi* among the faithful.[17] Some forms of postconciliar experimentation undoubtedly proved ill-advised, and the desire to update and experiment was not always accompanied by theological depth and clarity. Nevertheless, one can also read the postconciliar changes in religious life in light of wider theological and social trends and take a more positive view. Major cultural and social shifts were happening within the world at the same time as the council, such as the women's movement, different anti-colonial and political liberation movements, and a general shift in previous claims to authority based on class, age, race, and social privilege. Religious life has always been strongly attuned to prevailing cultural movements, and these shifts had a profound impact on a renewed understanding of its nature and purpose. The council makes clear that the capacity to read and respond to the signs of the times is a grace of the Holy Spirit. Many

[14] See Butler, "*Perfectae Caritatis,*" 218.

[15] See Patricia Wittberg, *The Rise and Fall of Catholic Religious Orders: A Social Movement Perspective* (Albany, NY: SUNY Press, 1994).

[16] David Nygren and Miriam D. Ukeritis, "The Religious Life Futures Project: Executive Summary," *Review for Religious* 52, no. 1 (January–February 1993): 6–55, 47–48.

[17] Friedrich Wulf, "Introductory Remarks on Chapters V and VI," in *Commentary on the Documents of Vatican II,* ed. Herbert Vorgrimler (London: Burns & Oates, 1967), 1:259–60 and Patricia Wittberg, *From Piety to Professionalism – and Back?: Transformations of Organized Religious Virtuosity* (Lanham, MD: Lexington Books, 2006).

religious saw their interrogation of their life in light of these shifts as part of that same prophetic and charismatic exercise.

RELIGIOUS LIFE: A VOCATION TO HOLINESS

Religious life has traditionally been considered a higher calling than that of lay life, a "state of evangelical perfection" among the baptized. Thomas Aquinas, himself a friar, considered those who deal in temporal goods as less perfect than those who renounce material possessions.[18] His teaching on the evangelical counsels offered theological legitimation for many of the claims regarding the superiority of religious life still circulating at the beginning of the council. The preparatory schema on the church included a chapter on religious life that referred to "the states of evangelical perfection to be acquired." This was contradicted, however, by John XXIII's encyclical of 1961, *Mater et Magistra*, which robustly states,

> In His solemn prayer for the Church's unity, Christ Our Lord did not ask His Father to remove His disciples from the world ... Let no one therefore imagine that a life of activity in the world is incompatible with spiritual perfection. The two can very well be harmonized. It is a gross error to suppose that a person cannot reach perfection except by putting aside all temporal activity (255).

The preparatory schema's reference to the "states of perfection" was eventually eliminated in favor of a consideration of those who bound themselves to the evangelical counsels. Even this revision proved controversial, since it too implied that religious were a spiritual elite within the church and that following the evangelical counsels led to a higher state of perfection than that attained by following the commandments.[19]

While religious life generally commanded respect within the church at the time of the council, nevertheless certain hierarchies of value were still operative. Mary of Bethany was often held up in contrast to her sister Martha, as having "chosen the better part" (Luke 10:38–42). This comparison exalted the enclosed life of the cloistered contemplative above both that of lay women in the secular world and that of religious women in simple vows living the "active" life. *Lumen Gentium* contradicts this and *Perfectae Caritatis* also makes clear that contemplation is the proper activity of all religious, irrespective of their form of

---

[18] *Summa Theologiae* (ST) II–II q. 184, a. 3, but see also ST II–II q. 186, a. 2. ad. 3.
[19] Wulf, "Introductory Remarks," 254ff.

life (PC 5–8).[20] Despite recent claims to the contrary, the majority of religious have not, in an uninformed manner, viewed *Lumen Gentium's* theology of the universal baptismal call to holiness as a signal that religious life was simply a human construct entirely the same as any other form of life.[21] Professed religious in the postconciliar period have recognized *Lumen Gentium's* teaching that religious are marked by a particular relationship to holiness even within the universal call. The distinctiveness of that relationship remains broadly clear to religious, even if it does not provide the basis for a sense of objective superiority.

How to witness to that distinctiveness without appearing to claim a "higher" calling has proved challenging. The whole tone of *Lumen Gentium*, particularly of chapter 5, lays emphasis on the potential for the baptized life of the laity to lead them to the highest degree of union with God within their distinct daily labors and relationships. Paragraph 39 underlines the evangelical counsels as the "perfection of charity," while paragraph 41 insists that the perfection of charity is the call of every Christian, since all are called to sanctity. "The forms and tasks of life are many but there is one holiness, which is cultivated by all who are led by God's Spirit and, obeying the Father's voice and adoring God the Father in spirit and in truth, follow Christ" (LG 41).

If Aquinas' understanding of religious consecration as a "higher" form of life within the church had not entirely been displaced, it was certainly put into a very different context by this emphasis. Paragraph 42 again speaks of the special way in which the holiness of the church is fostered through the observance of the evangelical counsels and stresses the eminence and particular honor in which virginity, celibacy, and continency are held.

Although *Lumen Gentium* weakens notions of religious life as a "state of evangelical perfection" objectively superior to the life of the laity, it does claim that religious life offers particular testimony to the life chosen by Christ and his Mother. It also claims that religious life manifests the reign of God, showing forth the power of the Spirit at work in the church. The document hints at the existence of temporal "hindrances that could hold them back from loving God ardently and worshipping him wholeheartedly" (LG 44), the inference being that those who withdraw from these "hindrances" are more likely to be distinguished in holiness. Such assertions can appear confusingly close

---

[20] Gregory Baum, "Commentary," in *The Decree on the Renewal of Religious Life of Vatican Council II* (Mahwah, NJ: Paulist Press, 1966), 16.

[21] See Butler, *"Perfectae Caritatis,"* 213–14.

to traditional claims of superiority, yet religious life can be understood as a distinct and particular vocation while not down-playing the universal call to holiness. The preface of the Mass for religious profession shows the theological understanding of a link between the way Jesus himself chose to live his human life and religious life in the present day.

> He is the unblemished flower who sprang from the root of the Virgin and declared the pure in heart blessed, teaching by his way of life the surpassing worth of chastity. He chose always to hold fast to what is pleasing to you and, becoming obedient for our sake even until death, he willingly offered himself to you as a perfect and a fragrant sacrifice. He consecrated to a fuller service of your majesty those who for love of you leave all earthly things and promised they would find treasure in heaven.[22]

Holiness is one of the four marks of the church, deriving from God, rather than from any personal religious virtuosity. Religious life nevertheless has particular sign value in the realms of incarnation, *kenosis*, and eschatology. By offering themselves to God in both body and soul in celibate chastity and by ministering to God's people in a life of prayer and apostolic service, religious are seen as incarnating in their own flesh the life of Christ the Suffering Servant. His self-emptying *kenosis* is also embodied in religious poverty and obedience. The council teaches that all religious vows have an eschatological function, pointing to a life beyond that of this world but also to the reign of God at work here and now (LG 43–44). This is as true of the contemplative as the apostolic way of life, and it was a particular spiritual insight of St. Thérèse of Lisieux to see her life enclosed within Carmel as a missionary life in and of itself. While this makes the vocation to religious life necessarily distinctive, and fundamentally of divine rather than human origin, it does not necessarily imply a hierarchy of value.

Perfectae Caritatis

The Decree on Religious Life begins by identifying religious life with the evangelical counsels, referring to the "special consecration" of religious, which is "deeply rooted in their baptismal consecration and is a fuller expression of it" (PC 5). This appears to be a compromise expression, neither entirely advocating the idea of a "superior" way of life to that of the laity nor entirely avoiding it.

---

[22] Bishops' Conference of England and Wales, *Roman Missal* (Catholic Truth Society, London, 2011), 1271.

Following *Lumen Gentium* 44, *Perfectae Caritatis* identifies religious life as an ecclesial vocation of public witness through the following of Christ. It identifies, within the different forms of religious life, the essential components of life in community, prayer, and consecration by public vows and evangelical mission, with common life as an eschatological sign and a source of apostolic energy (PC 15). The decree's recommendation to bring constitutions up to date led to a renewal in the interpretation of the vows of chastity and obedience with the help of contemporary disciplines such as the psychology of human development (PC 12, 14), while also urging a more evident life of evangelical poverty in light of local conditions. The decree also recommends a deepening in the life of prayer through closer contact with the "authentic sources of Christian spirituality" (PC 6), warning that a renewal of spirit must take precedence even over the demands of ministry.

The distinction of grades between choir and lay brothers or sisters is called into question and, in the case of women religious, done away with altogether (PC 15). As this distinction was an anachronistic source of frequent injustice, the suppression of these categories was widely welcomed. Obsolete forms of papal enclosure of women are also suppressed (PC 16). One of the most obvious signs of adaptation of religious life in the aftermath of the council lay in changes to the habit. *Perfectae Caritatis* did away with the more bizarre and unwieldy forms of religious dress that had arisen over time. It required habits to meet the requirements of health and to be suited to circumstances of time and place and the needs of ministry (PC 17). These instructions were perhaps easier to gain consensus on than the recommendation that they be simple, modest, poor, and at the same time becoming. When some congregations took the overall recommendation in conjunction with that of returning to their sources, they found that their (usually female) founders never wanted them to wear monastic style dress. This precipitated an often fraught struggle. Guided by an understanding of *Lumen Gentium* in which theirs was a form of lay life, this generally ended in sisters reverting to lay dress, a decision that is being questioned today, both by "traditionalists" but also by those seeking to proclaim the distinctiveness of a life wholly given over to the gospel.

Perfectae Caritatis' recommendation to found conferences of religious and corporate bodies to facilitate governance for groups of smaller institutes and houses also encountered difficulties, with the United States having two separate juridical bodies of women religious, representing different poles of theological and ecclesial perspective. Article

18 also urges a greater measure of education in "the behavior patterns, the emotional attitudes, and the thought processes of modern society" as the best source of renewal and adaptation. Overall, there was agreement that these adaptations were necessary, though few envisaged at the time where they would lead.

HIERARCHY AND CHARISM: AN UNEASY ALLIANCE

Left unresolved at the council was the sometimes uneasy relationship between religious and the hierarchy. The church in its hierarchical body ratifies and approves the rules by which founders and their followers live under the guidance of the Holy Spirit. The testing of spirits has been a legitimate office of leaders within the community of the faithful since the early church. It cannot rightly be claimed, therefore, that the church's hierarchy has no jurisdiction within religious life.[23] In the present day the role of CICLSAL, the Roman Congregation for Institutes of Consecrated Life and Societies of Apostolic Life, provides necessary boundaries to the needless proliferation of diocesan congregations in the global south. At the same time the tragic revelation of systemic child abuse in institutions run by religious illustrates what happens when they build their own self-referential worlds and ignore proper and necessary dialogue with episcopal bodies attempting to respond to stringent safeguarding laws demanded by the state. But history shows that this office of oversight and discernment of spirits has not always been practiced by the hierarchy with sensitivity to the responsibility of religious to read the changing signs of the times, as witnessed by the experience of the medieval Béguines and Béghards, Mary McKillop and Mary Ward.[24]

Part of the historical trajectory of religious life has been that its emergence was not only a flight from the power structures and values of the world but also an alternative path into a more challenging and liminal form of life within a church whose own power structures were seen to reflect those of the world too closely. Religious life has at its heart vows that opt in the most radical way against the fundamental human drives toward mastery and possession through power, sex, and

---

[23] Compare Sandra M. Schneiders, "The Ongoing Challenge of Renewal in Contemporary Religious Life," working paper, CORI Conference, "Religious Life Evolving: Faithful and Free," Malahide, Dublin, 2014.

[24] Gemma Simmonds, "Women Jesuits?" in *The Cambridge Companion to the Jesuits*, ed. Thomas Worcester (Cambridge: Cambridge University Press, 2008), 120–35.

money. Although religious have not been immune to corruption within their history, that sense of offering an alternative to what is happening even within the church has been a perennial pattern. One has only to look at the early reception by church authorities of the vocations of Francis and Clare of Assisi to understand this.

Religious life attracts many who are radically inclined, and radicals do not always sit happily within hierarchical systems. Among women religious there is considerable evidence across the world of tensions in their relations with priests, bishops, and male religious. Among religious brothers there are centuries of experience of being belittled or ignored by those rejoicing in the power conferred by priestly ordination. Among missionaries there is a history of struggling on behalf of the poor, sometimes at the cost of their very lives, in the face of a church that has made alliances with the wealthy and powerful that it is anxious to defend. To see the charismatic and hierarchical elements of the church as inevitably locked into an "us" and "them" duality is a false dichotomy that can easily lead to its own idolatries and to a disengagement with the very source and context of the religious vows. Religious life is mandated by the church. Religious vows are made publicly, and there is a mutuality within the way they are lived in the wider community of the church and the world. Religious incarnate in ways seen and unseen the mystery of God's indwelling in human lives. In their own turn the people of God continue to respond to the ideals and purpose contained within a vowed life in community expressed in self-giving (and self-fulfilling) ministry. These tensions between hierarchy and charism were clearly present at the council and continued beyond it.

In March 1996, Pope John Paul II issued *Vita Consecrata*, the last of his post-synodal exhortations on the three "states of life" in the church. This exhortation aimed to interpret Vatican II and implement its documents "authentically." The synod from which the document emerged proved problematical, as some bishops made clear their hostility to the reforms religious had undertaken since Vatican II.[25] To the dismay of many religious, the English translation of *Vita Consecrata*, at variance with the overarching implications of *Lumen Gentium*, referred to the consecrated life as having an "objective superiority" over other forms of Christian life (VC 32). What emerged in synod debates were two different paradigms – a consecration paradigm, reflecting the concern of the

---

[25] James Sweeney, "Religious Life after Vatican II," in *English Catholics 1950–2000: Historical and Sociological Perspectives*, ed. Michael Hornsby-Smith (London: Cassell, 1999), 266–87, at 283.

magisterium to define consecrated life within the structure of the church, and the charism paradigm, reflecting the lived experience of many religious and their more flexible understanding of their place in the church.[26] The tension between these two paradigms was reflected with dramatic intensity by the Apostolic Visitation of female religious in the United States in 2008.[27] Whatever version of the history of this episode one relies on, the underlying question remains one of finding a middle ground between the tensions engendered by these two paradigms.

RENEWAL AND ADAPTATION: QUESTIONS REMAINING

While the profession of religious vows is not a sacrament, as are marriage and ordination, *Lumen Gentium* taught that "the state of life, then, which is constituted by the profession of the evangelical counsels, while not belonging to the hierarchical structure of the church, belongs absolutely to its life and holiness" (44). Over the centuries, some religious orders have spearheaded powerful spiritual reform movements within the church, and have won for themselves important exemptions from episcopal authority. *Lumen Gentium* calls for a re-emphasis on the importance of the local church and its bishop. But it also frames the important theological concept of the *sensus fidelium*, a recognition of the capacity for the faithful to follow the guidance of the Holy Spirit. Many religious took this as including their competence to make decisions about their own appropriate renewal.[28] Pope John Paul II's direct interventions in the general chapters of several major religious orders illustrate the tensions involved in deciding what was prudent and who was competent to enact these revisions and reforms.[29] The more than one thousand council fathers who were members of religious orders did their best to defend the principles of legitimate self-governance within religious life.[30]

---

[26] James Sweeney, "The Synod and Theology," *Religious Life Review* 34 (1995): 75–85.

[27] See www.usccb.org/beliefs-and-teachings/vocations/consecrated-life/apostolic-visitation-final-report.cfm and http://elephantsinthelivingroom.org/Resources/Women_Religious_and_the_Apostolic_Visitation.pdf.

[28] *Catechism of the Catholic Church*, §§91–94 and John J. Burkhard, "The *Sensus Fidelium*," in *The Routledge Companion to the Christian Church*, ed. Gerard Mannion and Lewis S. Mudge (London: Routledge, 2008), 560–75.

[29] Gemma Simmonds, "John Paul II and Religious," in *A Companion to John Paul II*, ed. Gerard Mannion (Collegeville, MN: Liturgical Press, 2009).

[30] Alberto Melloni, "The Beginning of the Second Period: The Great Debate on the Church," in *History of Vatican II, Vol. 3: The Mature Council. Second Period and*

While the majority of religious since the council have rejected the notion of any moral or spiritual hierarchy within the community of the lay baptized, a new generation of religious, some in newer congregations founded on what are perceived to be "traditional" lines, has challenged this understanding. The adaptation to the changed conditions of the times is especially important within mission territories, where cultural and socioeconomic factors are to be taken seriously into account. This "inculturation," together with a greater sensitivity to sociopolitically accented forms of theology, brought about changes in mission and community structures that did not always subsequently prove popular in Rome.

Some of these structures, especially regarding the common life, would come to take forms so divergent from what was customary that they appeared to casual observers to have disappeared completely. While a more nuanced view accepts that a strong sense of community can exist among religious living separately, recent research makes clear that newer generations of religious are attracted to community life and have a stronger sense of ecclesial vocation than many of those who have lived through the decades subsequent to the council. Fifty years on, this calls for a review of structures and attitudes adopted in opposition to rigidities that no longer generally exist.

As with the reform of the liturgy and the renewal of scriptural and patristic scholarship, the best theological method for renewal was thought to lie in *ressourcement*, a return *ad fontes* to the founding moment and charismatic vision from which the particular religious congregation had emerged. For many religious this would provoke a dramatic rediscovery of original charisms and intentions hidden by time, involving re-interpretations of their current way of life and, in some instances, a crisis of identity that was to have long-lasting consequences.[31] The ancient rules of monasticism have long been honored within the church. The imposition of the monastic form as the principal model of religious life proved problematic, however, since it left little room for social change, the birth of new charisms, or new ways of living religious consecration. In time it would raise difficulties for religious

---

Intersession, September 1963–September 1964, ed. Giuseppe Alberigo and Joseph A. Komonchak (Maryknoll, NY: Orbis Press, 2000), 3, 91 n. 356, and 92–93.

[31] Mary Finbarr Coffey, "The Complexities and Difficulties of a Return *ad fontes*," in *A Future Full of Hope?* ed. Gemma Simmonds (Dublin: The Columba Press, 2012), 38–51.

women and men responding to an apostolic vocation that required a very different form of life.[32]

These tensions were not necessarily the product of the council, but its call for renewal and adaptation often revealed fault lines within religious life that had lain semi-dormant for many years. The Second Vatican Council's call to religious to adapt and renew *their life* was as sure a sign of the Spirit as any other within its overall achievement. While *Perfectae Caritatis* is a weak document read alone, together with *Lumen Gentium* and *Gaudium et Spes* it provided a charismatic and prophetic impetus for religious to break free from outdated and sterile restrictions. The holiness of religious life is and must always be seen as distinctive from that of lay life, while sharing in a call to holiness that is universal to the entire church. While the conflicts provoked within religious life by the council are by no means over, the witness of martyred religious like the beatified martyrs of Algeria and Ita Ford and her companions in El Salvador, as well as the example of countless faithful religious pursuing their life in obscurity, together embody the holiness to which the evangelical counsels have continued to inspire women and men since the council.[33]

FURTHER READING

Brueggemann, Walter. *The Prophetic Imagination*. 2nd ed. Minneapolis: Fortress Press, 2001.

Butler, Sara. "*Perfectae Caritatis*." In *The Reception of Vatican II*, edited by Matthew Lamb and Matthew Levering, 208–33. Oxford: Oxford University Press, 2017.

Confoy, Maryanne. *Religious Life and Priesthood:* Perfectae Caritatis, Optatam Totius *and* Presbyterorum Ordinis. Mahwah, NJ: Paulist Press, 2008.

Council of Major Superiors of Women Religious. *The Foundations of Religious Life: Revisiting the Vision*. Notre Dame, IN: Ave Maria Press, 2009.

---

[32] Elizabeth M. Makowski, *Canon Law and Cloistered Women: Periculoso and Its Commentators 1298–1545* (Washington, DC: The Catholic University of America Press, 1997), 40, 46; Walter Simons, "In Praise of Faithful Women: Count Robert of Flanders's Defense of Beguines against the Clementine Decree *Cum de quibusdam mulieribus* (ca. 1318–1320)," in *Christianity and Culture in the Middle Ages*, ed. David C. Mengel and Lisa Wolverton (Notre Dame, IN: University of Notre Dame Press, 2015), 331–57.

[33] See Robert Royal, *The Catholic Martyrs of the Twentieth Century: A Comprehensive World History* (New York: The Crossroad Publishing Company, 2000) and Jon Kiser, *The Monks of Tibhirine: Faith, Love, and Terror in Algeria* (New York: St. Martin's Press, 2003).

Johnson, Mary, Patricia Wittberg, and Mary L. Gautier. *New Generations of Catholic Sisters: The Challenge of Diversity*. New York: Oxford University Press, 2014.

Pinto, Philip. "Out of Darkness Breaks," Conference address given at CORI Conference, Dublin, Ireland, May 7, 2011. https://psgedmundrice.files.word press.com/2017/03/out-of-darkness-breaks.pdf.

Schneiders, Sandra M. *Buying the Field: Catholic Religious Life in Mission to the World*. Mahwah, NJ: Paulist Press, 2013.

Simmonds, Gemma, ed. *A Future Built on Faith: Religious Life and the Legacy of Vatican II*. Dublin: The Columba Press, 2014.

Sweeney, James. "Religious Life after Vatican II." In *Catholics in England 1950–2000: Historical and Sociological Perspectives*, edited by Michael P. Hornsby-Smith, 266–87. London: Cassell, 1999.

Wittberg, Patricia. *The Rise and Fall of Catholic Religious Orders: A Social Movement Perspective*. Albany, NY: State University of New York Press, 1994.

Wulf, Friedrich. "Decree on the Appropriate Renewal of the Religious Life." In *Commentary on the Documents of Vatican II*, vol. 2, edited by Herbert Vorgrimler, 301–70. London: Burns & Oates, 1968.

16 Ecumenism

SUSAN K. WOOD

ORIGINS OF CATHOLIC PARTICIPATION IN ECUMENISM

The contemporary ecumenical movement is generally dated as beginning with the 1910 World Missionary Conference in Edinburgh, where Protestant pastors addressed the challenges posed to evangelization by competing Christian claims in the mission fields. This meeting was followed by the first Life and Work conference in 1925 and the first world conference on Faith and Order in 1927. These two groups eventually merged into the World Council of Churches (WCC) in 1948. While the Catholic Church has been a member of the Faith and Order Commission, it has never been a member of the WCC, largely because of its overwhelming size, its global organization, and its international nature and diplomatic status.

The beginning of the twentieth century witnessed the origins of Catholic involvement in the ecumenical movement. The Anglican Society of the Atonement was founded in 1898 with the purpose of working for Christian unity and continued its ecumenical mission when it obtained recognition as a Roman Catholic community in 1909. On a personal level, there were informal conversations between Roman Catholics and other Christians exploring the possibility of reunion, especially the Malines Conversations (1921–25) between Catholics and Anglicans. One of the earliest influential Catholic studies was Yves M.-J. Congar's *Chrétiens désunis: principes d'un "oecuménisme" catholique* (1937).

Nevertheless, despite these early efforts, the period immediately prior to Vatican II witnessed a deep suspicion of the ecumenical movement, as reflected in Pope Pius XI's encyclical, *Mortalium Animos* (1928). Pius XI prohibited Catholics from taking part in assemblies of non-Catholics and stated that "the union of Christians can only be promoted by promoting the return to the one true Church of Christ of those who are separated from it" (MA 10). This is a "return ecumenism," which presupposes a monolithic uniformity and which is not ecumenism at all. Pius XI also condemned indifferentism to the unique claim of the Roman Catholic Church to be the one, true church of Jesus Christ here on earth and identified the Roman Catholic Church with Christ's mystical body, holding that separation from the first prevented incorporation in the latter: "For since the mystical body of Christ, in the same manner as His physical body, is one, compacted and fitly joined together, it were foolish and out of place to say that the mystical body is made up of members which are disunited and scattered abroad: whosoever therefore is not united with the body is no member of it, neither is he in communion with Christ its head" (MA 10).

Pope Pius XII's encyclical *Mystici Corporis* (1943) reiterated this identification of the Church of Christ with the Roman Catholic Church: "This true Church of Jesus Christ – which is [*est*] the One, Holy, Catholic, Apostolic and Roman Church" (MC 13). Such an identification did not allow for degrees of incorporation within the Church of Christ or for elements of the Church of Christ to exist beyond the boundaries of the Roman Catholic Church. Pius XII did advance beyond the thought of Pius XI when he admitted that non-Catholic Christians are in "a certain relationship with the Mystical Body of the Redeemer" by an "unconscious desire and longing" (MC 103), but still advocated a return ecumenism, saying "may they enter into Catholic unity ... joined with Us in the one, organic Body of Jesus Christ" (MC 103).

Finally, yet another ecumenical setback occurred in 1948 and in 1954 when Catholic observers were forbidden to participate in the assemblies of the World Council of Churches in Amsterdam and in Evanston, Illinois.

VATICAN II

The official foundations for the Catholic Church's entry into the contemporary ecumenical movement were laid before the council in the 1950s when a letter from the Holy Office referred to the ecumenical movement as inspired by the Holy Spirit and Catholic theologians were allowed to participate in some dialogue under strict conditions. However, the Second Vatican Council marked the formal entrance of the Catholic Church into the ecumenical movement, and ecumenism was a principal concern of the council. In his apostolic constitution *Humanae Salutis* (December 25, 1961), with which he solemnly convoked the council, Pope John XXIII spoke of his desire for the forthcoming council to "provide the premises of doctrinal clarity and of mutual charity that will make more alive in our separated brethren the desire for the hoped-for return to unity and will smooth the way to it."[1] His successor, Pope Paul VI, in his address to the opening of the second session of the council, spoke of his "deep sadness" at the "prolonged separation" of the communities of the non-Catholic observers. He asked for forgiveness if Catholics were in any way to blame for that separation and extended forgiveness for the injuries that the Catholic Church has suffered. In his enumeration of objectives of the council, the third was the bringing together of all Christians in unity. For both John XXIII and Paul VI, the ecumenical agenda was intrinsic to the council. The opening paragraph of the first document issued by the council, the Dogmatic Constitution on the Sacred Liturgy *Sacrosanctum Concilium*, cites ecumenical unity as one of the goals of the council, saying that one of the council's intentions is "to encourage whatever can promote the union of all who believe in Christ" (SC 1). The council's Decree on Ecumenism, *Unitatis Redintegratio* (UR), begins, "The restoration of unity among all Christians is one of the principal concerns of the Second Vatican Council" (UR 1).

Vatican II represents a turn to a much more positive understanding of ecumenical dialogue and a more positive appraisal of that which is of value in other Christian traditions. The Dogmatic Constitution on the Church *Lumen Gentium* really paved the way for the entry of the Catholic Church into the ecumenical movement by articulating a theology of the church that allowed for a positive assessment of other Christian communities. It did this by recognizing "that it is joined to the baptized who are honored by the name of Christian, but do not profess the faith in its entirety or have not preserved unity of communion under the successor of Peter" (LG 15) and by recognizing that the church of Christ includes many elements of sanctification and of truth outside the structure of the Catholic Church (LG 8).

In contrast to a "return" ecumenism, Vatican II advocated a unity of "the corporate groups in which they [Christians] have heard the Gospel, and which each regards as his or her church and indeed, God's" (UR 1). This is a full, visible unity that does not erase the unique history of various traditions or their particular identities, but is a unity in essentials at the same time through which "all, according to the office

---

[1] Translation by Joseph Komonchak, https://jakomonchak.files.wordpress.com/2011/12/humanae-salutis.pdf. The official Latin text may be found in *Acta Apostolicae Sedis* 54 (1962): 5–13.

entrusted to them, preserve a proper freedom in the various forms of spiritual life and discipline, in the variety of liturgical rites, and even in the theological elaborating of revealed truth" (UR 4). In all things charity should prevail.

The presence of ecumenical observers – numbering from fifty-four during the first period to over one hundred during the final period – throughout the four sessions of the Council exerted an ecumenical influence on the proceedings of the entire council, albeit in an indirect way. The observers were seated in a special section within the *aula* (discussion hall) and mixed freely with the council fathers during the breaks. The Secretariat for Promoting Christian Unity (SPCU) asked for their opinions and made their positions known to the pertinent commissions. Edward Iris Cardinal Cassidy, appointed president of the Pontifical Council for Promoting Christian Unity in 1989, cites as one example of this influence the introduction of the notion of the "hierarchy of truths" in *Unitatis Redintegratio* 11 by Archbishop Andrea Pangrazio of Gorizia, who had been given a text by his friend Johannes Feiner.[2] Lutheran theologian Oscar Cullmann (1902–99) regarded the passage as "the most revolutionary to be found, not only in the ecumenism schema but in any of the schema."[3]

Initially, three different draft documents touched on ecumenism: (1) a document on Eastern Orthodoxy written by the Commission for Eastern Churches, (2) a chapter on ecumenism in the document on the church written by Cardinal Ottaviani's Theological Commission, and (3) a draft on general ecumenical principles written by the Secretariat for Christian Unity under the direction of Cardinal Bea. At the first session of the council, only the first document was discussed. It was heavily criticized for its authoritative tone, its emphasis on a "return" ecumenism, and for its Latin bias. Patriarch Maximos IV Sayegh, representing the Melkite churches in union with Rome, asked that the three separate documents be combined into one. The council accepted Cardinal Bea's proposal that his secretariat prepare a single document drawing on the three drafts. This document was ready for the beginning of the second session and consisted of five chapters: (1) principles of Catholic ecumenism, (2) practical aspects of ecumenism, (3) Christian communities separated from the Catholic Church, (4) non-Christians, especially Jews, and (5) religious liberty. Chapters four and five were set aside, eventually to

---

[2] Edward Idris Cardinal Cassidy, *Ecumenism and Interreligious Dialogue:* Unitatis Redintegratio, Nostra Aetate (New York: Paulist, 2005), 10.

[3] Cited by ibid.

become two separate documents, the Declaration on Religious Freedom *Dignitatis Humanae* and the Declaration on the Relation of the Church to Non-Christian Religions *Nostra Aetate*, respectively. With the change of the first section to read "Catholic principles of ecumenism" and other revisions, *Unitatis Redintegratio* was approved 2,137 to 11. In the end, three documents of the council directly contributed to Catholic ecumenical engagement: The Dogmatic Constitution on the Church *Lumen Gentium* (November 21, 2964), the Declaration on Religious Freedom *Dignitatis Humanae* (December 7, 1965), and the Decree on Ecumenism *Unitatis Redintegratio* (November 21, 1964).

LUMEN GENTIUM: A NEW CONTEXT FOR CONSIDERING THE BOUNDARIES OF THE CHURCH

From the Protestant Reformation up to the Second Vatican Council, the church had often been interpreted in juridical terms as a sociologically determined corporation. Robert Bellarmine (1542–1621) refuted certain ecclesiological themes in Protestant theology, such as its emphasis on the notion of a hidden church, by emphasizing the institutional church as a society visible through the profession of faith, communion of the sacraments, and governance by legitimate pastors.[4] Aware that institutional models of church, and therefore criteria for church membership, cannot be exhaustive, Vatican II entitled the first chapter of the Constitution on the Church "The Mystery of the Church." *Lumen Gentium* 8 tackled the problem of the relationship between the institutional church and its spiritual dimension by situating the church within a new context. It addressed the problem of identity and difference between the church on earth and the body of Christ through an analogy with the incarnate Word; the visible assembly and the spiritual community were compared to the human and divine natures of the divine Word.

The concept of the people of God also served as a new perspective that allowed for relocating the church within the history of salvation and in the midst of humanity. It retrieved a comprehensive view of the church by describing its pilgrimage "from the beginning of the world" and waiting for the end of time when "all the just from the time of Adam, 'from Abel, the just one, to the last of the elect,' will be gathered together with the Father in the universal church" (LG 2). Structuring its thought around the theme of the people of God, the council chose a new

---

[4] Robert Bellarmine, *Of Controversies of Christian Faith against Heretics of Today* (1582), III, ii.

approach for dealing with the topic of *membership* in the church. Instead of the binary category of membership, i.e., being a member or not, it employed the more elastic language of belonging to the people of God (being "related to the people of God in various ways" (LG 16); "*plene ... incorporantur*" [fully incorporated] instead of "*reapse et simpliciter ... incorporantur*" [actually and simply incorporated] (LG 14). The first expression allows for varying degrees of association with the church, while the second makes belonging to the church a matter of yes or no. This groundwork in *Lumen Gentium* bore fruit in *Unitatis Redintegratio* 3, which speaks of the necessity of all who "belong in any way to the people of God" being fully incorporated (*plene incorporantur*) into the one body of Christ. *Unitatis Redintegratio* similarly eschews the category of membership and introduces instead the category of communion, distinguishing "full communion" from "imperfect communion" (3). This difference in degrees of relationship with the Catholic Church may result from differences in doctrine, discipline, or church structures. The council not only allowed for degrees of belonging to the people of God or to the society of the church but it also affirmed an ecclesial reality beyond the borders of the Catholic Church.

Lumen Gentium does not exclusively identify the Catholic Church with the Mystical Body of Christ, but instead recognizes outside the visible structure of the church many elements of sanctification and truth that impel toward catholic unity (LG 8), a significant development from the position of both *Mortalium Animos* and *Mystici Corporis*. While affirming that the Church of Christ "subsists" in the Catholic Church, meaning that the Church of Christ continues to exist in the Catholic Church, which has all those elements necessary for salvation and to be Christ's Church, the council also acknowledges that "many elements of sanctification and of truth are found outside its visible confines. Since these are gifts belonging to the church of Christ, they are forces impelling towards catholic unity" (LG 8). *Unitatis Redintegratio* 3 clarifies that these are "significant elements and endowments which together go to build up and give life to the church itself." When the commission responsible for the text explained *Lumen Gentium* 8, it stated that the former *est* [is] was replaced by *subsistit* [exists, subsists in] in order to correspond to the affirmation of the "elements" outside the visible boundaries of the Catholic Church.[5]

---

[5] *Acta Synodalia* 3/1, 177. See also Congregation for the Doctrine of the Faith, "Responses to Some Questions Regarding Certain Aspects of the Doctrine of the Church," *Origins* 37 (2007): 134–36.

Other suggestions had been to use the verbs *invenire* [to be found] or *adesse* [to be present]. Furthermore, the council rejected the proposal by some council fathers who wanted to state that the church confessed in the creed *subsistit integro modo in Ecclesia catholica* [subsists completely in the Catholic Church].[6]

Furthermore, within *Lumen Gentium* the concept of the body of Christ is reinterpreted pneumatologically in such a way that "the visible social structure of the Church" is not itself the body of Christ but serves "the Spirit of Christ who vivifies it in the building up of the body" (LG 8). This is a further indication that the body of Christ extends beyond the visible structure of the church. The existence of the elements of the Church of Christ outside the structures of the Catholic Church is the basis for the Catholic Church's affirmation that other traditions are also truly ecclesial.

DIGNITATIS HUMANAE: RELIGIOUS FREEDOM FOR ALL

The Declaration on Religious Freedom *Dignitatis Humanae* represents a watershed moment in the history of the church in terms of its articulation of the relationship between church and state and its affirmation of pluralism as a consequence of religious tolerance, freedom of conscience, and religious freedom. For the first millennium and a half, unity in religion was considered necessary for public order. For example, at the time of the sixteenth-century Reformation, only the Anabaptists promoted religious freedom and separation between church and state. These values surfaced during the Enlightenment and at the time of the political revolutions in Europe and the United States beginning in the eighteenth century but were not infrequently accompanied by antireligious or anti-Catholic sentiments. Within this context, Pius IX (1846–78) published the encyclical *Quanta Cura* (1864) and a Syllabus of Errors, which condemned as erroneous propositions asserting religious freedom, the possibility of salvation in the observance of any religion whatsoever, separation of church and state, or that it is no longer expedient that the Catholic religion should be the only religion of the state to the exclusion of others. After the Second World War, "religious liberty," where interpreted as a suppression of religious expression, was seen as a threat in a laicist France and in anticlerical

---

[6] AS 3/6, 81.

revolutionary governments such as those in Mexico and Spain. Freedom *of* religion often meant freedom *from* religion in these contexts. For the church, the ideal was the Catholic Church as the one true church in a Catholic state. Where Catholicism was a minority religion in pluralist societies, however, toleration of other religions was possible.

On the eve of the Council, the founding of the World Council of Churches (WCC) in 1948 was an impetus for religious freedom and influenced Catholics like Johannes Willebrands (1909–2006), Gustav Weigel, SJ (1906–64), Yves Congar, OP (1904–95), and Jérôme Hamer, OP (1916–96), who closely followed the work of the WCC. The French philosopher Jacques Maritain (1882–1973), who favored religious freedom, was consulted by Pope Paul VI. Despite these positive influences, the silencing of Yves Congar and John Courtney Murray (1904–67) prevented open discussion of the topics of religious freedom and the relations between church and state.

At its first plenary meeting in November 1960, the SPCU established a subcommission chaired by Bishop Émile de Smedt, who remained the SPCU's spokesperson on religious freedom and was a key contributor to the text. Work on a draft on religious freedom, completed in 1961, was seen as a step forward in establishing a foundation for ecumenical work. Another influence on the text was Pope John XXIII's encyclical *Pacem in Terris* (April 11, 1963), composed right after the 1962 Cuban missile crisis, in which the pope stated, "Also among one's rights is that of being able to worship God in accordance with the right dictates of a person's own conscience and to profess his or her religion both in private and in public" (14).

A minority of bishops at the council supported the classical position, promulgated for more than a century, that error has no rights and that everyone is bound to seek the truth, which exists fully only in the Catholic Church, with the consequence that the state has an obligation to support the Catholic Church. Nevertheless, it became clear that an affirmation of religious freedom would be necessary if the Catholic Church were to enter into the modern ecumenical movement. Furthermore, for the church to witness to the world in matters of human dignity, justice, and peace, it would need to affirm the civil right of the human person and of human communities to freedom in matters of religion.[7]

---

[7] Stephen B. Bevans, SVD, and Jeffrey Gros, FSC, *Evangelization and Religious Freedom: Ad Gentes, Dignitatis Humanae* (New York: Paulist, 2009), 168.

Between the second and third sessions of the council, John Courtney Murray and Pietro Pavan worked with the SPCU on the second draft
of the text, which at that point was an appendix to the Decree on
Ecumenism. The focus of the text in the third draft (November 1964),
having now become a free-standing document, had changed from a
focus on church–state relations to a discussion of religion and society.
The text does not address freedom of Catholics within the church, but
social relations in the public sphere. The final text received a vote of
2,208 in favor and 70 opposed on December 7, 1965.

The Declaration on Religious Freedom elicited new confidence in
ecumenical relationships by developing three points: "The ethical doctrine of religious freedom as a human right (personal and collective); a
political doctrine with regard to the functions and limits of government
in matters religious; and the theological doctrine of the freedom of the
Church as the fundamental principle in what concerns the relations
between the Church and the socio-political order."[8] This teaching elim-
inates the situation in which the church enjoys freedom when it is a
minority and exercise intolerance when it is a majority.

UNITATIS REDINTEGRATIO: CATHOLIC
PRINCIPLES OF ECUMENISM

Unitatis Redintegratio is the conciliar document that describes the
church's position on ecumenism most comprehensively. After conciliar
debate, the title of the first section of *Unitatis Redintegratio* became
"Catholic Principles of Ecumenism" rather than "Principles of Catholic
Ecumenism," indicating that there are not two different concepts of
ecumenism, one Catholic and the other non-Catholic. The preface
acknowledges the origin of the ecumenical movement outside the Catholic Church on the basis of the invocation of the triune God and confession of Jesus Christ as Lord and Savior by separated Christians, not only
as individuals, but as members of corporate bodies, and states that the
council now wishes to "set before all Catholics guidelines, helps and
methods, by which they too can respond to the grace of this divine call"
to unity (1). The decree develops its teaching on ecumenism in three
chapters. Chapter one gives the Catholic principles of ecumenism;
chapter two discusses the practice of ecumenism; and chapter three
examines the two chief types of division in terms of Eastern churches

---

[8] John Courtney Murray, "Religious Freedom," in *The Documents of Vatican II*, ed.
Walter M. Abbott (New York: America Press, 1966), 672–73.

and ecclesial communities in the West separated from the Roman Apostolic See.

Major Catholic principles of ecumenism include acknowledgment that the model and source of unity is founded on the unity of the persons of the Trinity, a unity of one God in the person of the Father, Son, and Spirit. Unity among Christians is the will of God, and the Spirit brings about the communion of the faithful in Christ and so is "the principle of the church's unity" (2). The Eucharist is the sacrament that effects and signifies unity. The successors of Peter and the apostles through their administration of the sacraments and governance perfect the unity of the people in their common confession of faith, their worship in common, and harmony.

Current members of separated communities are not guilty of the sin involved in the separation and are considered to be brothers and sisters, have the right to be called Christian, and are members of Christ's body since "those who believe in Christ and have been properly baptized are put in some, though imperfect, communion with the Catholic Church" (3). The chapter reiterates the teaching of *Lumen Gentium* 8 that significant elements that build up and give life to the church can exist outside the boundaries of the Catholic Church. It acknowledges the salvific contribution of many sacred actions of these communities.

The final section urges the avoidance of expressions, judgments, and actions that do not accurately represent separated brothers and sisters. Indeed, the Catholic Church is itself edified by the witness of other Christians. Although unity "subsists in the Catholic Church," its own catholicity is not fully realized in the present situation of separated Christians. The section distinguishes the desire for full communion with the Catholic Church on the part of individuals, which results in these individual becoming Catholics, from ecumenical action, which is the effort to achieve full, visible unity between faith communities. Finally, the principle of ecumenical action is unity in essentials; freedom in various forms of spiritual life, discipline, liturgical rites, and theological expressions of revealed truth; but charity in all things.

THE PRACTICE OF ECUMENISM: ITS SPIRITUAL CENTER

Unitatis Redintegratio addresses the practice of ecumenism in chapter two with a discussion of spiritual ecumenism, which entails continual reformation of the Catholic Church, an increase of fidelity to the church's own calling, a change of heart, prayer, self-denial, and effort to live holier lives (6–8). The ringing challenge is, "There can be no ecumenism worthy of the name without interior conversion" (7). All efforts toward internal renewal of the Catholic Church – such as the biblical and liturgical movements, a renewed emphasis on preaching the word of God, and new approaches to catechetics, the recognition of the baptismal foundation of the apostolate of the laity, new forms of religious life, a renewed spirituality of married life, and the church's social activity and teaching – "should be considered as promises and guarantees for the future progress of ecumenism" (UR 6). Deficiencies in moral conduct or church discipline as well as in the formulation of church doctrine are to be set right. In other words, ecumenism begins at home with the Catholic Church setting its own house in order. Ecumenism is a spiritual undertaking before all else.

A key to ecumenical work is found in *Unitatis Redintegratio* 9, which states, "We must become familiar with the outlook (*animum*) [literally "spirit"] of the separated churches and communities." This means getting to know their doctrines, history, spiritual and liturgical life, their religious psychology, and their culture. In other words, Catholics need to learn to view the world and Christianity through the lens and perspective of their ecumenical partner in order to understand why there may be a divergence in doctrine or practice and how their partner is attempting to be faithful to the gospel. This requires a displacement of self and fusion of horizons so that the Catholic is no longer the reference point for all difference. *Unitatis Redintegratio* does not completely achieve this, but does represent a major step forward from *Mortalium Animos*, especially with the introduction of the notion of the hierarchy of truths: "When comparing doctrines with one another, they should remember that in catholic doctrine there exists an order or 'hierarchy' of truths, since they vary in their relation to the foundation of the christian faith" (UR 11). Ecumenical dialogue is to be pursued "with love for the truth, with charity, and with humility" even as theologians stand fast by the teachings of the church (UR 11).

CHURCHES AND ECCLESIAL COMMUNITIES

Chapter three of *Unitatis Redintegratio* distinguishes between churches and ecclesial communities. Communities that have maintained ministry in apostolic succession are designated as churches in the proper sense, while communities issuing from the Reformation are called ecclesial communities. This distinction has been the cause of much angst on the part of communities issuing from the Reformation,

who consider themselves deprived of the designation "church" by Catholics. The distinction was reiterated in *Dominus Iesus*, the document of
the Congregation of the Doctrine and the Faith (2000), although it has
been contested by some theologians who maintain that Vatican II was
being inclusive of communities that do not self-designate as churches,
such as the Salvation Army. Nevertheless, today the distinction is
firmly in place and provides a major agenda topic for postconciliar
ecumenical dialogue.

Chapter three privileges the Eastern churches, inclusive of the
Orthodox churches that came into being since 1054 and the non-
Chalcedonian churches, describing their position as "special" and
emphasizing what is held in common: the existence of patriarchates,
ministry in apostolic succession and related sacramental validity, and
emphasis on the Eucharist. The discussion of these Eastern churches
refers to Orthodox churches not in communion with Rome and are to be
distinguished from the Eastern Catholic Churches, which are in communion with Rome. The latter are sometimes referred to as "Uniate
churches," although the term is now considered to be derogatory. The
relationship between Orthodox churches and the Eastern Catholic
Churches is painful since some of the latter resulted from an effort to
proselytize Eastern Orthodox Christians. Others, such as the Maronite
Catholic Church and the Syro-Malabar Catholic Church, trace their
origins to the earliest centuries of Christianity. Because these churches
are already in full, visible communion with Rome, they are not considered to be the object of Rome's ecumenical activity. Nevertheless,
the great contribution of a consideration of these churches to ecumenism lies in the recognition that a diversity in liturgical rite, canon law,
and spirituality is compatible with full, visible unity. Ecumenical unity
does not mean uniformity, but a reconciled diversity. The Decree on the
Eastern Catholic Churches (*Orientalium Ecclesiarum*) addresses the
relationship with these churches.

The spirituality, liturgy, monastic tradition, and trinitarian and
Christological doctrines developed in the East are the source for an
evident respect and affection extended to these churches. The reason
for the schism between the Catholic Church and these Eastern churches
is cited as a failure in mutual understanding and charity, in addition to
external causes (14), suggesting that both sides were responsible for the
division.

The major point of division with the Eastern Orthodox churches is
their rejection of the primacy of the bishop of Rome, although differences also exist in the theology and practice of conciliarity, synodality,

and in understandings of the nature of the church. While church-dividing issues require resolution, the relationship with these Eastern churches shows that a legitimate diversity in discipline, spirituality, doctrine, law, and liturgy can coexist within ecclesial communion. Examples of these differences include the doctrines of purgatory, the reservation and adoration of the Eucharist outside of the Divine Liturgy, clerical celibacy for priests, age for reception of the Eucharist, etc. Doctrine continued to develop in the Catholic Church after 1054, most notably with the two Marian definitions in 1856 and 1954, the Immaculate Conception and the Assumption, respectively, as well as the definition of papal infallibility in 1870. The Second Vatican Council repeated the declaration of previous councils and Roman pontiffs, "that in order to restore communion and unity or preserve them, one must 'impose no burden beyond what is indispensable (Acts 15, 28)" (UR 18). While determining what that burden would be requires discernment, uniformity is not the goal of ecumenism. In relationships with ecclesial communities issuing from the Reformation, it is helpful to note which doctrines are not considered essential to communion with the East and to ask whether they must be imposed on ecclesial communities in the West.

With respect to ecclesial communities in the West, *Unitatis Redintegratio* comments that the diversity among these communities, including historical, sociological, psychological, and cultural factors, makes generalization difficult. These communities diverge from the Catholic Church in their interpretation of revealed truth with respect to such doctrines as the work of redemption, the nature and ministry of the church, the role of Mary, moral teaching, and the relationship between scripture and the church, particularly in the role of the teaching office in the interpretation of scripture and in preaching. Only after listing a number of differences between these communities and the Catholic Church does *Unitatis Redintegratio* identify a number of positive characteristics of these communities such as private prayer, meditation on the Bible, Christian family life, and communal worship.

Not until §22 does *Unitatis Redintegratio* discuss baptism as the sacramental bond of unity that unites all those who have been reborn by it. Here the difference in the approach to unity with the Eastern churches from the approach toward separated ecclesial communities in the West becomes apparent. Where the discussion on the special position of the churches begins positively with the union in faith and sacramental life shared by the church of the east and the west and the spiritual treasury from which the western church has drawn extensively, the discussion of separated western communities begins by focusing on differences rather than the sacramental bond of unity shared with these communities in baptism. Even though the Orthodox do not admit Catholics to communion, the Eucharist is identified as the bond of unity between Eastern churches and the Catholic Church.

The difference, of course, is that the Catholic Church recognizes the apostolic succession of the ministry of Eastern churches and consequently the substantial real presence of Christ in their liturgies, which does not apply to Western communities. Even though baptism is cited as the sacramental bond of unity with these communities, the unity achieved in baptism is one that is oriented toward "a complete integration into eucharistic communion" (22). These communities are considered not to have the full substance (*integrum substatiam*) of the Eucharist because their sacrament of orders is "*defectum*" (commonly translated as "lacking," although recent ecumenical documents call for a translation of it as "deficient").[9] The Catholic doctrine is that the sacramental sign of ordination is not fully present, not only because the ministry is not individually in apostolic succession but also because those who ordain do not act in communion with the Catholic episcopal college.[10]

CRITIQUE IN RETROSPECT AND FUTURE POSSIBILITIES

Precisely because of the achievements of *Lumen Gentium* and *Unitatis Redintegratio*, more than fifty years of subsequent ecumenical dialogue suggest areas of critique as well as further developments possible today that were underexplored at the time, even though the seeds for these developments were planted at the council. One area of criticism concerns an underdeveloped baptismal theology. Another area inviting further development is a reevaluation of the sacramental celebrations of separated Christians. Finally, while there has always been a tight connection between recognition of ministry and recognition of eucharistic reality in another tradition, ecumenical progress can be made when other doctrines are not considered in isolation, but in correlation to

---

[9] See, for example, the Agreed Statement of the U.S. Lutheran-Roman Catholic Dialogue, *The Church as Koinonia of Salvation: Its Structures and Ministries*, Lutheran and Catholics in Dialogue, vol. X, (Washington, DC: United States Conference of Catholic Bishops, 2005), §109.

[10] Study Document of the Lutheran–Roman Catholic Commission on Unity, *The Apostolicity of the Church* (Minneapolis: Lutheran University Press, 2006), §283.

other doctrines. The correlation of the recognition of churches and ministry suggests further possibilities for ecumenical progress

A COMPARATIVELY UNDERDEVELOPED
BAPTISMAL THEOLOGY

The sacramental center of an analysis of the relationship between Catholics and other traditions has generally been the Eucharist despite the fact that Christians who baptize with water in the name of the Father, Son, and Spirit claim baptism as the source of their unity. This is most likely due to the fact that division among Christians is most acutely experienced by their inability to share the Eucharist and that Catholics consider fullness of unity to be effected and expressed by the Eucharist. Ministry is often the second most contested topic in terms of questions concerning apostolicity and how both are tied to a valid Eucharist. Yet, rarely has baptism been explored for the implications of what a shared baptism can contribute to growth in ecclesial communion, although the International Lutheran-Roman Catholic Commission on Unity launched such a study in 2009 and completed its document, *Baptism and Growth in Communion*, in 2019, more than fifty years after the Council.

This pattern of prioritizing the Eucharist as a point of reference is replicated in *Unitatis Redintegratio*. Chapter 1, which provides the Catholic principles of ecumenism, begins with the Eucharist, not baptism, as the sacrament by which "the unity of the church is both signified and brought about" (2). The chapter only mentions baptism twice and not until the third article, which states that "all who have been justified by faith in baptism are incorporated into Christ; they therefore have a right to be called Christians," and so are deservedly considered as brothers and sisters of Catholics. The primary baptismal text is found in §22, which takes up the baptismal theology of Rom 6:4 and Col 2:12, speaking of baptism as incorporation into the crucified and glorified Christ and as constituting the sacramental bond of unity existing among all who through it are reborn. The text insists, however, that baptism is only a beginning, an inauguration, which is oriented toward the complete professions of faith, complete incorporation into the institution of salvation, and the completeness of unity that eucharistic communion gives.

Four observations are in order. First, unity in *Unitatis Redintegratio* exists in reference to the Catholic Church. The text speaks of how other ecclesial communities are in (imperfect) communion with the Roman

Catholic Church rather than how they and Roman Catholicism are in communion with each other within the church of Christ. Even accounting for the fact that the church of Christ subsists in the Catholic Church (LG 8), and that the Catholic Church possesses the fullness of the means of salvation, the point of reference in ecumenical unity is the degree of communion with the Catholic Church. Second, the emphasis is soteriological rather than ecclesial. The text says that we are incorporated into Christ in baptism, not that we are incorporated into the church. Third, unity is not found absolutely in baptism since the unity achieved is only an "imperfect" one and baptism is only a "point of departure" for full unity. This is due to the fact that within this document lies a tension between two forms of communion, a communion envisioned between churches as institutions and a Christological communion that transcends, but does not bypass, the churches as institutions. This tension mirrors the distinction between visible and invisible elements of communion. What baptism is ordered toward, but cannot contain within itself, belongs to the visible elements of unity: *profession* of faith, a *system* of salvation, and *participation* in eucharistic communion (see LG 14). Yet, the unity achieved in baptism is deeper than the divisions among Christians and is what makes the divisions among Christian churches scandalous. The fundamental problem that the ecumenical movement seeks to resolve is primarily ecclesial, not sacramental or soteriological. Fourth, the missing element in all this analysis is the pneumatological dimension of baptism, i.e., the gift of the Spirit. The entire analysis is predominantly Christological with reference to incorporation into and communion with the body of Christ. There is nothing about discerning the presence of the Spirit within the other community and what that presence means for ecumenical unity.

A RE-EVALUATION OF THE SACRAMENTAL CELEBRATIONS OF SEPARATED CHRISTIANS

Prior to Vatican II, it was commonly held that ministry was lacking (the usual translation of *defectus*) to those groups who had broken apostolic succession at the time of the Reformation. Leo XIII had declared in 1896 that Anglican orders were null and void on account of a deficient sacramental form in the ordination rite (*Apostolicae Curae*). Because ordination was considered null for these reasons, the conclusion was that these communities do not possess a valid Eucharist. In contrast, the sacraments of the churches of the Christian East have been affirmed as possessing "true sacraments" (UR 15).

Unitatis Redintegratio's evaluation of the liturgical life of the separated communities begins with an affirmation of the sacramental bond
of unity existing among those who have been reborn by baptism, but the
document adds that "baptism, of itself, is only a beginning," an inauguration directed toward the fullness of life in Christ and the "complete
integration into eucharistic communion" (UR 22). Nevertheless,
although *Unitatis Redintegratio* 22 states that these communities
"have not preserved the proper reality of the eucharistic mystery in its
fullness, especially because of the absence of the sacrament of orders
(*propter sacamenti ordinis defectum*) [because of the defect/lack of the
sacrament of orders]," it goes on to affirm that these communities
"when they commemorate the Lord's death and resurrection in the holy
supper, they profess that it signifies life in communion with Christ"
(UR 22). This must be read in connection with article 3, which states,
"Our separated brothers and sisters also carry out many liturgical
actions of the christian religion. In ways that vary according to the
condition of each church or community, these liturgical actions most
certainly can truly engender a life of grace, and, one must say, are
capable of giving access to that communion in which is salvation."
Moreover, *Unitatis Redintegratio* 3 concludes that the Spirit uses these
communities as means of salvation "which derive their efficacy from
the very fullness of grace and truth entrusted to the Catholic Church."

Several conclusions can be drawn from these remarkable texts,
which opened promising paths for ecumenical dialogue after the Council. First, as a number of ecumenical texts after the council have pointed
out, *defectus* should no longer be translated as "lack," but rather as
"deficient." That which is deficient within the logic of the council lies
within the category of "communion" rather than within a juridical
category of validity. In a situation of ecumenical separation, ministry
not in communion is deficient in its catholicity, but one can no longer
say that ministry is simply absent or lacking. If there were not efficacy
in preaching the gospel, the Catholic Church could never have arrived
at a consensus statement, *The Joint Declaration on the Doctrine of
Justification*, with the Lutheran World Federation in 1999.

Furthermore, it is important to note that in *Unitatis Redintegratio*
22's statement that although the ecclesial communities separated from
the Catholic Church "have not preserved the proper reality of the
eucharistic mystery in its fullness," it refrains from using juridical
language, opting instead for language of fullness, which admits of
degrees rather than a binary presence or lack of presence. Neither the
Eucharist nor ministry can be simply lacking because they both

function as a means of grace within these communities in keeping these communities in the faith of the gospel, in engendering a life of grace, and giving access to that communion in which is salvation. Theological reflection has yet to grapple sufficiently with the implications of a shift from the metaphysical categories of traditional sacramental theology with its accompanying juridical category of "validity" to a perspective that discerns a sacramental reality through its efficacy rather than vice versa. Yet, Joseph Cardinal Ratzinger, when prefect of the Congregation of the Faith, wrote in 1993 to the Bavarian Lutheran Bishop Johananes Hanselmann, "I count among the most important results of the ecumenical dialogues the insight that the issue of the eucharist cannot be narrowed to the problem of 'validity.' Even a theology oriented to the concept of succession, such as that which holds in the Catholic and in the Orthodox Church, need not in any way deny the salvation-granting presence of the Lord in a Lutheran Lord's Supper."[11] Much ecumenical work remains to be done on these sacramental and ministerial issues.

CORRELATION OF THE RECOGNITION OF CHURCH AND THE RECOGNITION OF MINISTRY

The Catholic Church explicitly recognizes some separated groups as churches in the proper sense, especially those in the Christian East whose episcopacy is in apostolic succession. Those communities issuing from the Reformation whose ministry is not in apostolic succession are termed "ecclesial communities." Although some theologians have maintained that the intention of the council in using the term "ecclesial communities" was to be inclusive of those communities that do not self-identify as churches, since the council this distinction based on apostolic succession of ministry has been the dominant interpretation.

Recognition of ministry has up to the present been in terms of "all or nothing." Either ministry is recognized as valid or invalid. The present official line of the church is that valid ministry confers the identity of "church" on an ecclesial body. In its absence, one is left with an "ecclesial community." The question of the mutual recognition of ministry raises the question of whether recognition of ministry should in some measure follow on from recognition of churches rather than

---

[11] Joseph Ratzinger, "Briefwechsel von Landesbischof Johananes Hanselmann und Joseph Kardinal Ratzinger über das Communio-Schreiben der Römischen Glaubenskongregation," *Una Sancta* 48 (1993): 348. Cited in US Lutheran-Catholic Dialogue statement, *Church as Koinonia of Salvation*, §107.

precede it. An imperfect communion among churches would correlate with an imperfect recognition of ministry consonant with a translation of *defectus* as deficient, rather than "lacking." Ecumenically, this would mean that the recognition of ministry would depend on the recognition of the churchly character of that ministry's community and not vice versa. This would lead to a discernment of the elements of the Church of Christ outside the visible boundaries of the Catholic Church. There would, no doubt, be additional criteria for the recognition of ministry in terms of understanding its function with respect to proclamation of the gospel, to its role in the sacraments, and to its service to the apostolicity of the church. Nevertheless, the recognition of the churchly character of the community would play a much larger role in the recognition of ministry than it presently does.

RECEPTION AND FRUIT OF THE COUNCIL

The first fruit of the work of the council on ecumenism occurred in December 1965 when the Roman Catholic and Orthodox churches issued a declaration removing "from memory and the midst of the Church the sentences of excommunication that had been leveled against each other in 1054." Pope John Paul II reiterated the ecumenical orientation and mandate given by Vatican II in his encyclical *Ut Unum Sint* (May 25, 1995) where he states that at the council "the Catholic Church committed herself irrevocably to following the path of the ecumenical venture" (3). Commenting on the "elements of sanctification and truth" in other communities, he said, "To the extent that these elements are found in other Christian Communities, the one Church of Christ is effectively present in them," (10) and that "these are by their nature a force for the re-establishment of unity" (49).

The major ecumenical advance with western ecclesial communities was the *Joint Declaration on the Doctrine of Justification* (JDDJ) signed by representatives of the Catholic Church and the Lutheran World Federation on October 31, 1999. The genius of the "Common Understanding" of the *Joint Declaration* lies in the trinitarian framework of the agreement on justification, which situates justification within the relations of Father, Son, and Spirit and their attributed works. By situating justification within a trinitarian framework with Christ at the center, the *Joint Declaration* is able to distinguish justification and sanctification without separating them. Catholics can affirm that justification is the *ground*, not the *goal* of sanctification, and Lutheran confidence in the Father's favor is inseparable from renewed life as the work of the Spirit. The "Common Understanding" in part three of the *Joint Declaration* thus provides the theological framework for Catholics to distinguish justification and sanctification and for Lutherans to connect them.[12]

Originally a bilateral ecumenical consensus, the JDDJ now expresses a shared understanding of justification on the part of five Christian world communions. The World Methodist Council adopted it in July 2006, as did the World Communion of Reformed Churches in July 2017. The Anglican Consultative Council adopted Resolution 16.17 on the *Joint Declaration on the Doctrine of Justification* and presented the text to the Rev. Dr. Martin Junge, General Secretary of the Lutheran World Federation, and Bishop Brian Farrell on October 31, 2017. Reception of this bilateral document by three additional communions shows how reception is shaped by the particularity of the receiving church communions. Succinctly put, the Methodists receive it through the lens of sanctification, the World Communion of Reformed Churches through the lens of justice, and the Anglican Communion through the lens of ecclesiology. Consequently, the consensus articulated in the JDDJ has far-reaching implications in the areas of ethics, sanctification, justice, ecclesiology, and ministry insofar as these topics touch on justification and sanctification.

Principles shaping this relationship were identified at a meeting of representatives of the five communions at the University of Notre Dame on March 26–28, 2019. Chief among them was the imperative articulated at the Joint Catholic-Lutheran Commemoration of the Reformation October 31, 2016 in Lund, Sweden: "Catholics and Lutherans should always begin from the perspective of unity and not from the point of view of division in order to strengthen what is held in common even though the differences are more easily seen and experienced." This principle, as well as the methodology of the JDDJ – a differentiating consensus, which enables dialogue partners to affirm what is held in common while acknowledging differences – provides a promising basis for further ecumenical progress.

FURTHER READING

Becker, Werner. "Decree on Ecumenism: History of the Decree." In *Commentary on the Documents of Vatican II*, Vol. 2, edited by Herbert Vorgrimler, 1–164. New York: Herder and Herder, 1968.

[12] Ibid., 458.

Bevans, Stephen B., SVD, and Jeffrey Gros, FSC. *Evangelization and Religious Freedom:* Ad Gentes, Dignitatis Humanae. New York: Paulist Press, 2009.

Cassidy, Edward Idris. *Ecumenism and Interreligious Dialogue:* Unitatis Redintegratio, Nostra Aetate. New York: Paulist Press, 2005.

Congar, Yves M.-J., OP. *Chrétiens désunis: principes d'un "oecuméisme" catholique.* Unam Sanctam 1. Paris: Cerf, 1937.

Gaillardetz, Richard R. *The Church in the Making:* Lumen Gentium, Christus Dominus, Orientalium Ecclesiarum. New York: Paulist Press, 2006.

Kasper, Walter. *Harvesting the Fruits: Basic Aspects of Christian Faith in Ecumenical Dialogue.* New York: Continuum, 2009.

Kasper, Walter. *That They May All Be One: The Call to Unity Today.* London: Burns & Oates, 2004.

Radano, John, ed. *Celebrating a Century of Ecumenism: Exploring the Achievements of International Dialogue.* Grand Rapids, MI: Eerdmans, 2012.

Radano, John A. *Lutheran and Catholic Reconciliation on Justification.* Grand Rapids, MI: Eerdmans, 2009.

Wicks, Jared, SJ. *Investigating Vatican II: Its Theologians, Ecumenical Turn, and Biblical Commitment.* Washington, DC: The Catholic University of America Press, 2018.

Wood, Susan K., SCL. *One Baptism: Ecumenical Dimensions of the Doctrine of Baptism.* Collegeville, MN: Liturgical Press, 2009.

Wood, Susan K., SCL, and Timothy J. Wengert. *A Shared Spiritual Journey: Lutherans and Catholic Traveling toward Unity.* New York: Paulist Press, 2016.

17 The Church and Other Religions

EDMUND KEE-FOOK CHIA

INTRODUCTION

That it was the Holy Spirit who inspired the convocation of the Second Vatican Council needs no further discussion. However, one of the more provocative fruits of the work of the Spirit at Vatican II is evident in the council's groundbreaking treatment of the Catholic Church's relationship with other religions.

To better appreciate why this development is so significant, this chapter begins with a quick overview of the history of the church's relationship with other religions. It then examines what was initially referred to at the council as "the Jewish question." The concern for the church's relationship toward Judaism eventually broadened to include other religious traditions. The council's tumultuous debates ultimately led to the council's landmark document *Nostra Aetate*, "On The Relation of the Church to Non-Christian Religions," a declaration on the church's relationship with the other religions in general. This declaration will have to be considered in concert with the other documents of Vatican II and its own postconciliar reception.

HISTORY OF CHRISTIAN ATTITUDES TOWARD OTHER RELIGIONS

As Christianity evolved from the Jewish faith, it inherited many Jewish beliefs and practices. Nevertheless, the early biblical community often found it necessary to affirm an exclusive salvific value to faith in Jesus Christ. For example, the highly theologized account of the origins of Christianity in the Acts of the Apostles has Peter preaching an early version of Christian exclusivism: "There is salvation in no one else, for there is no other name under heaven given among mortals by which we must be saved" (Acts 4:12). Likewise, the apostle Paul affirms "For there is one God; there is also one mediator between God and humankind, Christ

Jesus, himself human, who gave himself as ransom for all" (1 Tim 2:5–6). Along the same lines John's Gospel has Jesus claiming at the Last Supper, "I am the way, and the truth, and the life. No one comes to the Father except through me" (John 14:6). These exclusivist claims, used initially to nurture the early disciples' faith in Jesus, later played a role in shaping the church's attitude toward those who were outside of the church.

By intensifying their absolute claims about the lordship of Jesus Christ and triumph of Christian salvation, the early Christians were able to ensure the survival of their vulnerable faith even in the light of persistent persecution. The teaching of *extra ecclesiam nulla salus* (outside the church, no salvation), for example, which came into ascendancy during the time of St. Cyprian in the early third century, served to discourage Christians facing difficulties from leaving the church. That teaching was primarily concerned, however, with the salvific status of schismatic Christian communities. With the decriminalization of Christianity by Emperor Constantine in the early fourth century and subsequent declaration of it as the official religion, the judgment of "no salvation outside the church" became lethal. It was now no longer applied only to those who were abandoning their faith but also to indict the Jews and pagans and those who did not become Christian under the Roman imperial government. Christianity advanced significantly – as being Christian was advantageous – but also rather arrogantly and aggressively. Christians no longer regarded the Jewish people (and later the Muslims) as belonging to the one people of God. This gave rise to sentiments of anti-Semitism, and the rhetoric that Jews were Christ-killers or God-killers (deicide) became more pronounced and was used to incite violence against the Jews.

This exclusivist strand of Christian thought emerged alongside other currents that offered a more capacious account of God's saving work being offered beyond the boundaries of formal Christian faith. Justin Martyr in the second century and Clement of Alexandria in the late second and early third centuries both affirmed in their distinct ways a more universal scope of God's salvific activity. Yet it must be said that this remained a minority position within Christianity.

In the medieval period Christianity became associated with militancy, the peak of which was expressed in the Crusades. In 1302 the papal bull *Unam Sanctam* insisted that even kings and heads of states were subject to papal authority:

> That there is only one, holy, catholic and apostolic Church we are compelled by faith to believe and hold, and we firmly believe in her

and sincerely confess her, outside of whom there is no salvation, nor remission of sins ... Furthermore, we declare, state and define that it is absolutely necessary for the salvation of all people that they submit to the Roman Pontiff.[1]

Along similar lines the 1442 Bull of Union with the Copts proclaimed:

[The Holy Roman Church] ... firmly believes, professes and preaches that 'no one remaining outside the Catholic Church, not only pagans,' but also Jews, heretics and schismatics, can become partakers of eternal life; but they will go to the 'eternal fire prepared for the devil and its angels' [Mt 25:41], unless before the end of their life they are joined (aggregati) to it.[2]

These sentiments by and large shaped much of the church's dealings with those falling outside of the Christian fold. It provided the theological justification for the Christian mission that accompanied European colonization beginning in the fifteenth and sixteenth centuries. Anthropologies that regarded the aboriginal natives in the Americas, Africa, and Asia as less than human or at least inferior to the European race provided the intellectual and theological justification for the conquest. The unbelief of the "infidel" natives constituted their sin or even crime against Christianity. The Christian missionaries, therefore, "often adopted the attitude that non-Christian religions were simply the work of Satan and the missionaries' task was to convert from error to knowledge of the truth."[3] This represented the general mindset of Catholics toward those outside of the church for centuries, even up until the eve of the Second Vatican Council.

POPE JOHN XXIII AND "THE JEWISH QUESTION"

When Pope John XXIII announced his intention to convoke the Second Vatican Council on January 25, 1959, no one, probably not even the saintly pope himself, could have imagined that the council would address the question of the relationship of the church to religions other

---

[1] As cited in Jacques Dupuis, *Toward a Christian Theology of Pluralism* (Maryknoll, NY: Orbis Books, 1997), 94.

[2] Ibid., 95.

[3] This quote is from footnote 11 of the commentary on Vatican II's Declaration on the Relationship of the Church to Non-Christian Religions, *Nostra Aetate*. See *The Documents of Vatican II: With Notes and Comments by Catholic, Protestant, and Orthodox Authorities*, ed. Walter M. Abbott (London: Geoffrey Chapman, 1967), 662.

than Christianity. John XXIII had only the church's relationship with other Christian denominations in mind as he made the quest for Christian unity one of the council's objectives. The June 13, 1960, visit of the Holocaust survivor and Jewish historian Dr. Jules Isaac to Pope John XXIII, however, changed the scenario.[4] Isaac, who had researched extensively and published on the topic of *The Teaching of Contempt: Christian Roots of Anti-Semitism*, presented the pope with an overview of the Catholic teachings that have fueled violence against the Jews and implored John XXIII to correct that at the council.[5]

According to Thomas Stransky, until that time the dominant Christian tradition had held that:

> God continues to punish the Jewish people for its rejection and killing of Jesus, the Son of God, Messiah and Savior of all. By this deicide Jews have forsaken all rights to God's promise in the Old Covenant, which has been completely replaced by the New, identified as the Catholic Church (supercessionism). Like sinful Cain, Jews should continue to wander the earth as vagabonds without a homeland. God sustains their dispersed existence to remind Catholics of the divine blessings of the New Covenant and Jews of their true calling to share the same by converting.[6]

Pope John XXIII needed little convincing by Isaac on the issue. Prior to his election to the papacy, "John XXIII served as an apostolic delegate in Turkey from 1935–1944. During that time he saw not only the effects of the Nazis' genocidal policies, but also personally saved thousands of Jews by providing them with citizenship and ersatz baptismal papers. He also provided food to needy Jewish communities."[7] It is clear that he was sympathetic to the Jewish cause. This became evident in his first celebration of Holy Week as pope, in March 1959, when he asked that the Latin word *perfidis* (faithless), which had been used for centuries to

---

[4] See John Borelli, "*Nostra Aetate*: Origins, History, and Vatican II Context," in *The Future of Interreligious Dialogue: A Multireligious Conversation on Nostra Aetate*, ed. Charles L. Cohen, Paul F. Knitter, and Ulrich Rosenhagen (Maryknoll, NY: Orbis Books, 2017), 23.

[5] Jules Isaac, *The Christian Roots of Anti-Semitism* (New York: Holt, Rinehart and Winston, 1964).

[6] Thomas Stransky, "The Genesis of *Nostra Aetate*: Surprises, Setbacks and Blessings," *America* 193, no. 12 (Oct. 24, 2005): 8.

[7] Elena Procario-Foley, "Heir or Orphan? Theological Evolution and Devolution before and after *Nostra Aetate*," in *Vatican II: Forty Years Later*, ed. William Madges (Maryknoll, NY: Orbis Books, 2006), 309.

describe the Jews, be erased from the Roman Missal in its Good Friday prayer for the conversion of the Jews.

The pope quickly arranged for Isaac to meet with Cardinal Bea whom Pope John had appointed to head the newly established Secretariat for Christian Unity. The secretariat was charged with preparing discussion topics for the council. On Bea's recommendation, Pope John XXIII mandated that "the Jewish question" be officially addressed by the preparatory commissions for the Second Vatican Council. Thus, a brief schema entitled De Judaeis ("On the Jews") was prepared. The inclusion of this topic was indeed the work of the Holy Spirit: "Until that day it had not occurred to John XXIII that the council had to deal also with the Jewish question and antisemitism. But from that day on he was completely taken by it."[8]

When word got out that the council was preparing a positive statement about the Jews, the Muslim world feared it was a mere preparation to the Vatican establishing diplomatic relations with the State of Israel: "When the Arab governments learned of the bare fact that the Secretariat for Promoting Christian Unity had a portfolio on 'the Jewish question,' their diplomats rushed alarmist inquiries to the Vatican Secretariat of State."[9] This led Cardinal Bea, in his first presentation of a draft of the text for discussion on November 18, 1963, to make clear the following: "The decree is very brief, but the material treated in it is not easy ... There is no national or political question here. In particular, there is no question of recognition of the State of Israel by the Holy See."[10] Anyway, to allay the fears of the bishops serving in Muslim-majority countries, the decision was made by the preparatory commissions to include a brief statement of respect for the religion of Islam as well.

Aside from the Arab-Muslim concerns, the bishops of Asia and Africa also raised concerns, but theirs were with regard to the non-Abrahamic religions. Consequently, the decision was made to include

---

[8] Memorandum of then-Monsignor Loris Capovilla who had served as private secretary to John XXIII, as quoted in John Borelli, "Nostra Aetate: Origins, History, and Vatican II Context," 22.

[9] Thomas Stransky, "The Genesis of Nostra Aetate," 9.

[10] Augustin Cardinal Bea, SJ, The Church and the Jewish People: A Commentary on the Second Vatican Council's Declaration on the Relation of the Church to Non-Christian Religions, trans. Philip Loretz, SJ (London: Geoffrey Chapman, 1966), 154–72, as cited in John Borelli, "Nostra Aetate: Origins, History, and Vatican II Context," 33.

positive statements in the document concerning the non-Abrahamic religions, particularly the traditions native to Asia and Africa.

NOSTRA AETATE ON OTHER RELIGIONS

The declaration *Nostra Aetate* ("In Our Time," from the first three words of the Latin text) is the shortest document produced by the Second Vatican Council. It consists of 1,141 words that make up the forty-one sentences in five articles of the document. The document had a long history marked by numerous debates and five major drafts spread over a period of three years. The text was finally approved by the council fathers on October 28, 1965, with 2,221 voting in its favor and only 88 voting against. *Nostra Aetate*, the full title of which is "The Declaration on the Relation of the Church to Non-Christian Religions," radically changed the way the Catholic Church regarded the other religions of the world. The statement was unambiguous in its assertion that Catholicism does not reject the truths found in the other religions. This document marked the first time in which an ecumenical council mentioned something positive about non-Christian religions.

In the document's first article, written in an era when the phenomenon of globalization was just dawning on human consciousness, the council notes that the world is becoming a global village. This fact invites us to pursue the unity and oneness of humanity, both in its origins and final goal. Furthermore, since people "look to different religions for an answer to the unsolved riddles of human existence," the council invites "the church [to examine] more carefully its relations with non-christian religions" (NA 1).

In the second article the council identifies by name the religions of Hinduism and Buddhism, spelling out the essential dimensions of each of these traditions. It also acknowledges the "other religions which are found throughout the world," stating unequivocally that "the Catholic Church rejects nothing of what is true and holy in these religions. It has a high regard for the manner of life and conduct, the precepts and doctrines which, although differing in many ways from its own teaching, nevertheless often reflect a ray of that truth which enlightens all men and women" (NA 2).

It is in the third article that the council explicitly addresses Islam, stating that "the church has also a high regard for the Muslims" (NA 3). It then singles out areas in Islam's teachings and practices that coincide with the Christian faith, including its worship of the one Creator God who reveals through the prophets and in whom all will be judged at the time of death. The council acknowledges the centuries of hostilities between the two religions, but "pleads with all to forget the past, and urges that a sincere effort be made to achieve mutual understanding; for the benefit of all, let them together preserve and promote peace, liberty, social justice and moral values" (NA 3).

Article four attends explicitly to Judaism. It was disproportionately longer than all the other articles as it was the original impetus for the declaration. The declaration reminds the faithful of the intrinsic connectedness between Christianity and the Jewish religion and states that the church "cannot forget that it received the revelation of the Old Testament by way of that people with whom God in his inexpressible mercy established the ancient covenant" (NA 4). It is not possible, therefore, to understand Jesus and Christianity independent of Judaism. Even as the majority of the Jews did not accept Jesus and the gospel, God continues to hold "that the Jews remain very dear to God, for the sake of the patriarchs, since God does not take back the gifts he bestowed or the choice he made" (NA 4). *Nostra Aetate* quotes Romans 9–11, a biblical text rarely cited in this regard prior to Vatican II, indicating that the church is now taking up where Saint Paul left off in his insistence that the Jewish people continue to remain part of the covenant even after the coming of Christ and his Resurrection. The council insists that "neither all Jews indiscriminately at that time, nor Jews today, can be charged with the crimes committed during [Christ's] passion" (NA 4). There is, therefore, absolutely no basis for the centuries-old charge of deicide that had been levelled against the Jews as a community. Thus, *Nostra Aetate* asserts, "the church reproves every form of persecution against whomsoever it may be directed" (NA 4).

In the document's concluding article the council calls on all Christians to adhere to the commandment of love for God and love for neighbor. Although rather tame when measured against the state of Catholic theology in the present moment, when the council promulgated *Nostra Aetate* it was considered a groundbreaking contribution toward a thorough re-imagination of the Catholic Church's relationship to other religious traditions.

OTHER VATICAN II DOCUMENTS ON OTHER RELIGIONS

Nostra Aetate was by no means the only conciliar text to address issues relating to practitioners of other religions. Of particular import was the conciliar teaching developed in *Lumen Gentium*, the Dogmatic Constitution on the Church, which was approved on November 21, 1964, a year earlier than *Nostra Aetate*. After considering the place of Catholics who are "fully incorporated" into the life of the church (*plene incorporantur*) in article 14, the council then attended to non-Catholic Christians who are "joined to" the Church (*coniunctum esse*). This led the council, in article 16, to consider the relationship of non-Christians to the church. These persons are in some way "related to the people of God" (*ordinantur*). The text explicitly mentions Jews and Muslims, spelling out ways in which they are intimately related to Christianity, and also makes mention of "those who in shadows and images seek the unknown God" (LG 16). By citing Acts 17: 25–28 for this last group of believers, the text seems to be referring to persons of all other religions, akin to the way in which Paul referred to those at the Areopagus who were praying to unknown gods. This led the council to a central doctrinal affirmation:

> Those who, through no fault of their own, do not know the Gospel of Christ or his church, but who nevertheless seek God with a sincere heart, and, moved by grace, try in their actions to do his will as they know it through the dictates of their conscience – these too may attain eternal salvation. Nor will divine providence deny the assistance necessary for salvation to those who, without any fault of theirs, have not yet arrived at an explicit knowledge of God, and who, not without grace, strive to lead a good life. Whatever of good or truth is found amongst them is considered by the church to be a preparation for the Gospel and given by him who enlightens all men and women that they may at length have life. (LG 16)

Some bishops were concerned that this remarkable assertion in fact undercut the Christian imperative to evangelize. Consequently, *Lumen Gentium*'s treatment of non-Christians concludes with article 17, which highlighted the importance of proclaiming the Gospel, especially to those who have not had a chance to hear it. Yet the constitution on the church will anticipate one of *Nostra Aetate*'s most important assertions, confirming that "whatever good is found sown in people's hearts and minds, or in the rites and customs of peoples, is not only saved from destruction, but is purified, raised up, and perfected for the glory of God, the confusion of the devil, and the happiness of humanity" (LG 17). While the council obviously held firm to the finality and superiority of the Gospel of Christ over other religions, what is important to note here is the acknowledgment that even before receiving the Good News, members of other religions are already in possession of goodness and truth, suggesting that in some way there may be salvific import to the religious convictions and practices of other traditions.

Another council document of significance for our topic is *Ad Gentes*, the Decree on the Church's Missionary Activity, promulgated near the end of the council. This decree not only reaffirms the possibility of salvation for non-Christians but it is the first text to explicitly attribute faith to them: "In ways known to himself God can lead those who, through no fault of their own are ignorant of the gospel, *to that faith* without which it is impossible to please him" (AG 7).[11] Since there can be no faith except as a response to what God has revealed, by attributing a genuine faith to those outside Christianity, this is the closest the council would come to admitting that those persons might be recipients of a genuine revelation.

The missionary decree repeats the teachings of *Lumen Gentium* 17 regarding the good found "in the particular customs and cultures of peoples" (AG 9), and then exhorts Catholics in different parts of the world to honor their own "national and religious traditions" (AG 11). It encourages them to "uncover with gladness and respect those seeds of the word which lie hidden among them" (AG 11). Here the council seems to be recalling that ancient tradition associated with Justin Martyr and Clement of Alexandria affirming the *logos spermatikoi*, "the seminal word" embedded in other religious traditions. This recognition, indeed, should spur Christians to dialogue with the practitioners of these other faiths.

The document mentions "seeds" again in article 18, inviting Christian missionaries to "consider how traditions of asceticism and contemplation, whose seeds have been sown by God in certain ancient cultures before the preaching of the gospel, might be incorporated into the christian religious life" (AG 18). This statement appears to refer to the Eastern religions, known for their contemplation and asceticism. Thus, Vatican II is again asserting that the God whom Christians believe in also planted those mystical seeds of truth and goodness in the other religious traditions and, more importantly, that it would do well for Christians to incorporate some of these elements in order to enrich their very own religious practice.

A final document to be considered is *Gaudium et Spes*, the longest document of Vatican II and the last to be approved. Known as the Pastoral

---

[11] Emphasis is mine.

Constitution on the Church in the Modern World, its emphasis is on the dignity of the human person, focusing on universal rights and responsibilities and the role of conscience in decision-making. It was a document that addresses "not only the daughters and sons of the church and all who call upon the name of Christ, but the whole of humanity as well" (GS 2). Three themes of relevance to our topic should be noted: First, the pastoral constitution refers to peoples of other religions as "people of good will in whose hearts grace is active invisibly" (GS 22). Second, it acknowledges the value of "the spiritual qualities and endowments of every age and nation" (GS 58). Third, it states unequivocally that social transformation needs to take into account the traditions of each culture: "Every branch of the human race possesses in itself and in its nobler traditions some part of the spiritual treasure which God has entrusted to humanity, even though many do not know its source" (GS 86).

POSTCONCILIAR PAPAL TEACHING AND INTERRELIGIOUS DIALOGUE

While Vatican II was still in session, Pope Paul VI, who succeeded Pope John XXIII in 1963, issued his first encyclical, *Ecclesiam Suam* (ES), in which he developed an ecclesiology of dialogue. Remarkably, his consideration of dialogue with the world at large occupied more than half the length of the document. The word "dialogue," in fact, appears eighty-one times. In the encyclical Paul VI differentiated this dialogue according to four concentric circles. He began with the outermost, dialogue with the entire human race, the world, including those who profess no religion (ES 97–106). Moving inward, he then considers dialogue with worshippers of the one God, the Jews, the Muslims, and followers of the great Afro-Asiatic religions (ES 107–8). Then he considered dialogue with other Christians before concluding with a reflection on dialogue within the Catholic Church. Paul VI's contributions to inter-religious dialogue go well beyond this groundbreaking encyclical. The pope who brought the council to its conclusion also established a special department of the Roman Curia for relations with peoples of other religions, known first as the Secretariat for non-Christians (1964) and later renamed the Pontifical Council for Interreligious Dialogue (1988).

If Paul VI is identified as the pope who first introduced dialogue into the vocabulary of the church, John Paul II was something of a trailblazer in the actual practice of interreligious dialogue. Whenever he visited a country where the majority of the population adhered to a religion other than Christianity, he would include in his itinerary not only a meeting with the religious leaders but also a visit to a place of worship of that religion. Thus, he became the first pope to visit a Buddhist temple in Thailand (1984), to enter Rome's Great Synagogue (1986), to wear the Hindu *tilaka* (sacred sign on one's forehead) in India (1986), to pray at the Western Wall of Jerusalem (2000), and to enter a Muslim mosque in Syria (2001). He was also the first pope to call for an assembly of the world's religious leaders to pray for peace. This World Day of Prayer for Peace was held in Assisi on October 27, 1986, and saw the participation of more than 120 representatives of different religions and Christian denominations who spent the day in fasting and prayer. These activities speak to John Paul II's respect for the other religions.

In his long reign as pope, John Paul II's commitment to inter-religious dialogue was reflected as well in his magisterial teaching. His inaugural papal encyclical *Redemptor Homin* (RH) offers a glimpse of his attitude toward religions other than Christianity:

> "Does it not sometimes happen that the firm belief of the followers of the non-Christian religions – a belief that is also an effect of the Spirit of truth operating outside the visible confines of the Mystical Body – can make Christians ashamed at being often themselves so disposed to doubt concerning the truths revealed by God and proclaimed by the Church and so prone to relax moral principles and open the way to ethical permissiveness" (RH 6).[12]

We must also note the appearance during his pontificate of two significant Vatican documents pertaining to our topic: first, the 1984 document "Reflections and Orientations on Dialogue and Mission: The Attitude of the Church towards the Followers of Other Religions" (referred to as "Dialogue & Mission" [DM][13]) and second, the 1991 document "Dialogue and Proclamation: Reflection and Orientations on Interreligious Dialogue and the Proclamation of the Gospel of Jesus Christ" (referred to as "Dialogue & Proclamation" [DP])[14]. However, it is in his 1990 encyclical *Redemptoris Missio* that his teaching on those belonging to other religious traditions finds its most

---

[12] Pope John Paul II, *Redemptoris Hominis* (March 4, 1979), http://w2.vatican.va/content/john-paul-ii/en/encyclicals/documents/hf_jp-ii_enc_04031979_redemptor-hominis.html.

[13] Secretariat for Non-Christians, "The Attitude of the Church towards the Followers of Other Religions: Reflections and Orientations on Dialogue and Mission" (May 10, 1984), www.pcinterreligious.org/dialogue-and-mission_75.html.

[14] Pontifical Council for Inter-religious Dialogue, "Dialogue and Proclamation: Reflection and Orientations on Interreligious Dialogue and the Proclamation of the Gospel of Jesus Christ" (May 19, 1991), www.vatican.va/roman_curia/pontifical_councils/interelg/documents/rc_pc_interelg_doc_19051991_dialogue-and-proclamatio_en.html.

mature form.[15] A synthetic consideration of these three documents yields three highlights. First, there is a positive evaluation of other religious traditions: "They command our respect because over the centuries they have borne witness to the efforts to find answers 'to those profound mysteries of the human condition' (NA 1) and have given expression to the religious experience and they continue to do so today" (DP 14). Note that this positive evaluation is not just about peoples of other religions but about the religions themselves, affirming that they share, together with the Christian religion, a place in God's divine economy of salvation. Second, *Redemptoris Missio* posits that "inter-religious dialogue is a part of the Church's evangelizing mission" (RM 55) while *Dialogue & Proclamation* contends that "the foundation of the Church's commitment to dialogue is not merely anthropological but primarily theological" (DP 38). In other words, dialogue is not just a human or social activity but part of God's calling for Christians to discover more fully God's plan of salvation. Finally, *Redemptoris Missio* affirms that the praxis of dialogue is "a method and means of mutual knowledge and enrichment" (RM 55) while *Dialogue & Proclamation* suggests that the ultimate aim of dialogue is "a deeper conversion of all towards God . . . In this process of conversion 'the decision may be made to leave one's previous spiritual or religious situation in order to direct oneself towards another'" (DP 41). This papal teaching makes it clear that Christians must also see dialogue as an occasion for mutual enrichment, where both parties witness to one another and where both are led to a deeper conversion, including the possibility of leaving one's religious situation.

Prior to becoming Pope Benedict XVI, Cardinal Joseph Ratzinger served as Prefect of the Sacred Congregation for the Doctrine of the Faith. He was thus the guardian of Catholic teachings and in that capacity presented the "Declaration *Dominus Iesus*: On the Unicity and Salvific Universality of Jesus Christ and the Church" in September 2000.[16] The aim of *Dominus Iesus*, according to Ratzinger, was to clarify certain aspects of church teachings in light of the debate on the relationship of Christianity to other religions. The document singled

[15] Pope John Paul II, *Redemptoris Missio: On the Permanent Validity of the Church's Missionary Mandate* (December 7, 1990), http://w2.vatican.va/content/john-paul-ii/en/encyclicals/documents/hf_jp-ii_enc_07121990_redemptoris-missio.html.

[16] Congregation for the Doctrine of the Faith, *Dominus Iesus: On the Unicity and Salvific Universality of Jesus Christ and the Church* (August 6, 2000), www.vatican.va/roman_curia/congregations/cfaith/documents/rc_con_cfaith_doc_20000806_dominus-iesus_en.html.

out for mention the dangerous influence of what it alleged were "relativistic" theories advanced to address the phenomenon and fact of religious pluralism. To counter them, *Dominus Iesus* insisted that other religious traditions were "gravely deficient," reaffirmed the doctrines of the uniqueness and universality of Jesus Christ and the church, and asserted that these doctrines must be upheld in the church's dialogue with other religions.

Although we cannot examine the document in detail, it suffices to say that *Dominus Iesus* was quite controversial and not well received either within or beyond the Catholic Church.[17] But the theological exclusivity of the document could help shed light on why, when Pope John Paul II hosted the Assisi World Day of Prayer for Peace in 1986, Cardinal Ratzinger did not support the event for fear that it would give the impression that the Catholic Church promotes relativism. Interestingly, as pope, Benedict XVI did participate in the twenty-fifth anniversary of the Assisi event on October 27, 2011, by conducting a pilgrimage of leaders of the other religions and Christian denominations, as well as secularists and humanists, on a train journey from Rome to Assisi, where the interreligious encounter took place. A year after becoming pope, Benedict XVI visited the Istanbul Blue Mosque in Turkey, where he was pictured standing alongside an imam, facing toward Mecca in silent prayer. He did this respectfully and, following the demeanor of the imam, had his hands crossed on his stomach in classical Muslim style. While the gesture touched many a Muslim heart, some conservative Catholic groups condemned the pope's actions as heretical and scandalous.

Cardinal Jorge Bergoglio adopted the name Francis, thereby evoking an attitude of humility, simplicity, openness, and a radical commitment to the poor. In a book coauthored with his Argentine compatriot Rabbi Abraham Skorka, *On Heaven and Earth*, the future pope had this to say:

> Dialogue is born from a respectful attitude toward the other person, from a conviction that the other person has something good to say. It supposes that we can make room in our heart for their point of view, their opinion and their proposals. Dialogue entails a warm reception and not a preemptive condemnation. To dialogue, one

---

[17] See, for example, Stephen J. Pope and Charles Hefling, eds., *Sic et Non: Encountering Dominus Iesus* (Maryknoll, NY: Orbis Books, 2002).

must know how to lower the defenses, to open the doors of one's home and to offer warmth.[18]

This attitude of respect for other religious traditions is also evident in his first apostolic exhortation *Evangelii Gaudium* (EG).[19] In the context of religiously plural societies, *Evangelii Gaudium* teaches that "an attitude of openness in truth and in love must characterize the dialogue with the followers of non-Christian religions, in spite of various obstacles and difficulties, especially forms of fundamentalism on both sides. Interreligious dialogue is a necessary condition for peace in the world, and so it is a duty for Christians as well as other religious communities" (EG 250). Francis has modeled this respect for the religious other quite concretely. One example suffices. Shortly after his election, Francis celebrated the Holy Thursday Mass of the Lord's Supper at a juvenile detention center in Rome where he washed the feet of twelve young detainees of different nationalities and faiths, including at least two Muslims and two women. This ritual act can be regarded as a concrete manifestation of radical Christian hospitality toward the religious other.

CONCLUSION

The Catholic Church has come a long way in its relations with religions other than Christianity, thanks to the renewal inaugurated by the Second Vatican Council. The positive effects of its teachings are quite tangible. The fact that so many interreligious commissions have been established at the levels of parishes, dioceses, and regional episcopal conferences throughout the world is one example of this development. That Catholics feel at ease visiting places of worship of other religions is another, as is their participation in interreligious prayers and comparative theological discussions. The study of the world religions has become a given in many Catholic schools and colleges and even seminaries.

All of this would have been unthinkable in the years prior to the Second Vatican Council. The Jesuit theologian Gerald O'Collins

---

[18] Jorge Mario Bergoglio and Abraham Skorka, *On Heaven and Earth: Pope Francis on Faith, Family and the Church in the 21st Century* (New York: Bloomsbury Publishing, 2013), xiv.

[19] Pope Francis, *Evangelii Gaudium* (November 24, 2013), http://w2.vatican.va/content/francesco/en/apost_exhortations/documents/papa-francesco_esortazione-ap_20131124_evangelii-gaudium.html.

contends that "Vatican II brought such a remarkable change in teaching about other religions and in subsequent church practice that it represents considerable discontinuity, if not reversal."[20] The council transformed centuries-old attitudes and even official church teaching. Its consideration of the church's relationship to other religious traditions can only be characterized as revolutionary.

FURTHER READING

Amaladoss, Michael. *Interreligious Encounters: Opportunities and Challenges.* Edited by Jonathan Y. Tan. Maryknoll, NY: Orbis Books, 2017.

Becker, Karl Josef, and Ilaria Morali, eds. *Catholic Engagement with World Religions: A Comprehensive Study.* Maryknoll, NY: Orbis Books, 2010.

Chia, Edmund Kee-Fook. *World Christianity Encounters World Religions.* Collegeville, MN: Liturgical Press, 2018.

D'Costa, Gavin, ed. *The Catholic Church and the World Religions: A Theological and Phenomenological Account.* London: T & T Clark, 2011.

Dupuis, Jacques, SJ. *Christianity and the Religions: From Confrontation to Dialogue.* Maryknoll, NY: Orbis Books, 2002.

Fitzgerald, Michael L. and John Borelli. *Interfaith Dialogue: A Catholic View.* London: SPCK, 2006.

Kärkkäinen, Veli-Matti. *An Introduction to the Theology of Religions: Biblical, Historical & Contemporary Perspectives.* Downers Grove, IL: InterVarsity Press, 2003.

O'Collins, Gerald, SJ. *The Second Vatican Council on Other Religions.* Oxford: Oxford University Press, 2013.

---

[20] Gerald O'Collins, *The Second Vatican Council on Other Religions* (Oxford: Oxford University Press, 2013), 197.

18 The Renewal of Moral Theology

JAMES KEENAN

A survey of the vast literature on the Second Vatican Council reveals a surprising lacuna in the treatment of moral theology.[1] Ecclesiologists and church historians have tended to convey at best a modest assumption about the relationship between theological ethics and the council. At the same time, many theological ethicists writing more recently have emphasized either *Gaudium et Spes*' ("The Pastoral Constitution on the Church in the Modern World") anthropological assumptions, embrace of human dignity, affirmation of conscience and personal freedom, together with its wide array of urgent concerns, or *Dignitatis Humanae*'s ("The Declaration on Religious Liberty") own defense of the conscience and religious freedom. The council has clearly had a profound effect on the contemporary work of theological ethicists. Many ethicists today find in the council extensive and fundamental resources and, most of all, mandates for the work we do today.

That being said, Western European moral theologians were much more participative in the preparation of, and more importantly in the early reception of, the council than were those from English-speaking countries of the industrialized north. As I will argue in this chapter, moral theology before World War II was a regulatory field that guided priests in their confessional duties to their fairly compliant penitents. Most of the subject matter of the confessional dealt with the fairly self-centered sins of the modest penitent. After the war, the confessional and its practices were strongly critiqued in Western Europe, though in the English-speaking industrialized world (United States, United Kingdom, Ireland, Australia, New Zealand, and to some small extent Canada) the regulatory function of moral theology only increased. One part of the church in the north was waiting for the council and its renewal; another side was actively disinterested.

---

[1] James F. Keenan, "Vatican II and Theological Ethics," *Theological Studies* 74, no. 1 (2013): 162–90.

I divide this essay into three parts: European moral theology before the council; the council and its impact on the renewal of moral theology; and, the English-speaking world of moral theology from before the council to the 1968 encyclical on birth control, *Humanae Vitae* ("On Human Life").[2]

EUROPEAN MORAL THEOLOGY BEFORE THE COUNCIL

In the mid-sixteenth century, moral theology began as a separate field of theology in the aftermath of the Council of Trent as seminaries for the training of priests developed and textbooks were produced. In these texts, the "moral manuals" as they came to be called, moral theologians wrote singularly for the priest who heard confessions. They were designed to help the confessor fulfill his work in keeping penitents from being lost to eternal damnation and therefore were singularly focused on sin.

In 1906, for instance, the leading English-speaking moralist Thomas Slater, SJ, wrote in the introduction to his work an unapologetic description of the singular aim of the manual:

> The manuals of moral theology are technical works intended to help the confessor and the parish priest in the discharge of their duties. They are as technical as the text-books of the lawyer and the doctor. They are not intended for edification, nor do they hold up a high ideal of Christian perfection for the imitation of the faithful. They deal with what is of obligation under the pain of sin, they are books of moral pathology.[3]

For the most part, during these centuries penitents confessed sins that the church provided for their review: these were mostly infractions of the fifth, sixth, seventh, and eighth commandments, that is, any harms against a neighbor, any sexual impropriety, and any form of theft or lying; and any violations of the commandments of the church which required attendance at mass on Sundays and certain feasts and/or observance of particular fasting practices. Significantly, because Rome insisted that there was no parvity of matter on the sixth

---

[2] James F. Keenan, *A History of Catholic Moral Theology in the Twentieth Century: From Confessing Sins to Liberating Consciences* (New York: Continuum, 2010).

[3] Thomas Slater, *A Manual of Moral Theology for English-Speaking Countries* (London: Benziger Brothers, 1906), 5–6.

commandment,[4] the confessor and penitent often focused on sexual matters like impure thoughts, masturbation, and, significantly, birth control. This was especially the case after the papal encyclical *Casti Connubii* (1930), which not only reiterated the condemnation on birth control but insisted that the teaching is unchangeable and that the distinctive nature of Catholic moral theology is that its teachings are eternally unchangeable because they are from God.

Needless to say, there was little innovation in the moral manuals during the twentieth century except in determining how culpable the penitents were. This involved the appropriation of scientific literature that focused on psychological impediments to genuine human freedom. Significantly, the penitent rarely was encouraged to think in any way of the social order, or for that matter, of the formation of a conscience that pursued the good. The anthropology of the preconciliar, twentieth-century penitent was one concerned about having broken any church teaching, not whether one was adequately responsive to the neighbor's needs.[5]

In order to appreciate how radically a-social the mid-twentieth century confessional was, we should consider that, internationally, one of the most popular moral manuals was by Heribert Jone, a German Capuchin. His *Moral Theology*, first published in 1929, guided the confessor and penitent, regardless of whether they were in the confessional in Franco's Spain, Hitler's Germany, Churchill's England, or Roosevelt's America.[6] Preconciliar sinful matter rarely touched on the social order.

As it emerged from the rubble of World War II, European moral theology had a radical reorientation. If the Council of Trent is the locus for the birth of moral theology as a specific science, then the savagery of World War II wherein 47 million people died marks the most critical moment in its modern history. Moral theology would either shrivel and die from its complete incapacity to speak to the now-haunted conscience of the post-war, modern world or it would need to reconstitute itself completely, repudiating what the moral manual had become and offering an entirely new framework, method, and vision for the moral formation of conscientious Christian communities.[7]

---

[4] Patrick Boyle, Parvitas materiae in sexto *in Contemporary Catholic Thought* (Washington, DC: University Press of America, 1987).

[5] Keenan, *A History*, 9–34.

[6] Heribert Jone, *Moral Theology* (Charlotte, NC: Tan Books, 2009).

[7] Stephen Schloesser, "Against Forgetting: Memory, History, Vatican II," *Theological Studies* 67, no. 2 (2006): 275–314.

The seeds for the development of a new framework were sown before the war. In 1912, a Scripture scholar, Fritz Tillmann (1874–1953), was censured for a work he edited and was ordered by the Vatican to leave Scripture studies, but was given the option to enter another field of theology. He chose moral theology.[8] In 1934, he wrote a groundbreaking work, *Die Idee der Nachfolge Christi* and effectively proposed "discipleship" as the primary identity for the Christian, a fundamental concept not in theological use before this work.[9]

In 1937, he published his own moral manual not about sin, but rather discipleship. *Der Meister Ruft*, translated into English in 1960 as *The Master Calls*, was written not for the confessor but for the lay Catholic and is a more accessible text with practical explications of charity as the love of God, self, and neighbor. Throughout, he highlights the grandeur of the Christian vocation: "The goal of the following of Christ is none other than the attainment of the status of a child of God."[10] The language, vision, and agenda of Tillmann's handbook marked a major, remarkable alternative to the works of moral pathology.

In 1947, Gérard Gilleman defended his dissertation on the role of charity in moral theology in Paris under the guidance of René Carpentier. After defending his dissertation, Gilleman was assigned to teach in India and Carpentier published Gilleman's *The Primacy of Charity*.[11] It is hard to over-estimate the influence of Gilleman's work. His charity gave Tillmann's discipleship the interior virtue that would make it possible for moral theologians to see the field not primarily as a study of how to avoid sin, but rather about how to follow in love of neighbor as a disciple of Christ. Together they began to change the field of moral theology in Europe on the eve of the council.

After the war, Dom Odon Lottin (1880–1965) led the critical repudiation of the moral manuals. In 1946, he published his first moral theological synthesis, *Principes de Morale*. Rather than being a manual for hearing confessions, it was a theological foundation for anyone interested in the formation of conscience.[12] Later, in 1954, he published his

---

[8] Keenan, *A History*, 59–69.

[9] Fritz Tillmann, *Die Idee der Nachfolge Christi* (Dusseldorf: Patmos, 1934).

[10] Fritz Tillmann, *Der Meister Ruft* (Düsseldorf: Patmos Verlag, 1937); *The Master Calls: A Handbook of Morals for the Layman* (Baltimore: Helicon Press, 1960) 4–5.

[11] Gérard Gilleman, *Le primat de la charité en théologie morale: essai méthodologique* (Paris: Desclée de Brower, 1952); *The Primacy of Charity in Moral Theology* (Westminster, MD: Newman Press, 1959).

[12] Odon Lottin, *Principes de Morale* (Louvain: Abbaye du Mont César, 1946).

revolutionary *Morale Fondamentale*, where he critiqued the wretched past of moral theology, blaming the priest confessor's singular focus on sin as the principal cause for moral theology's failure.[13] He attacked recent developments wherein canon law had come to dominate moral theology, forcing it to focus exclusively on external acts, when in fact, historically speaking, moral theology had been primarily interested in the internal life. Overtaken by canon law, moral theology had lost its moorings in dogmatic theology and in the biblical and patristic sources of theology; not only had it abandoned its pursuit of the Christian vocation, but it had lost its deep connection to ascetical and mystical theology.[14] In this work Lottin, like his predecessors, turned to the conscience as foundational to the moral life and argued that priests are called to help the members of the church lead conscientious lives.[15] Lottin wrote at length on the virtuous life and "formation" of both the conscience and the prudential judgment. By turning to prudence, Lottin liberated the Christian conscience from its singular docility to the confessor priest. He instructed church members to become mature self-governing Christians, insisting that they have a life-long task, a progressive one, as he called it, toward growing in virtue.[16] By turning to conscience, Lottin urged his readers to find within themselves, their community, their faith, the church's tradition and its Scriptures, the mode and the practical wisdom for determining themselves as better Christian disciples.

Finally, in *Au Coeur de la Morale Chrétienne*, he commented on the "poor manuals *ad usum confessariorum*" wherein not a trace of biblical inspiration can be found. He returned to the question of why the moral manuals were so singularly interested in sin, and this time blames the very numerous mediocre Christians who asked their confessors to give them minimalist expectations for the moral life.[17] Lottin cleared the space for further innovation.

In 1936 the young Redemptorist Bernard Häring was asked by his superiors to prepare to teach moral theology. "I told my superior that this was my very last choice because I found the teaching of moral theology an absolutely crushing bore."[18] Häring realized that if he finds

---

[13] Odon Lottin, *Morale Fondamentale* (Tournai: Desclée, 1954).

[14] Ibid., 23–25. He entitles this section, "Causes de l'inferiorité actuelle de la théologie morale."

[15] Ibid., 297–339.

[16] Ibid., 54ff.

[17] Odon Lottin, *Au Coeur de la Morale Chrétienne* (Tournai: Desclée, 1957), 6.

[18] Bernard Häring, *My Witness for the Church* (Mahwah, NJ: Paulist Press, 1992), 19

little benefit in its study, so do the laity. But his own experience of the war intervened and shaped the breadth and depth of his project. "During the Second World War I stood before a military court four times. Twice it was a case of life and death. At that time I felt honored because I was accused by the enemies of God. The accusations then were to a large extent true, because I was not submissive to that regime."[19]

Häring witnessed to how many Christians recognized the truth, were convicted by it, and stood firm with it. There he understood moral truth not primarily in what persons say, but in how they act and live. The war experiences irretrievably disposed him to the agenda of developing a moral theology that aims for the bravery, solidarity, and truthfulness of those committed Christians he met in the war.[20] At the same time, he also witnessed to "the most absurd obedience by Christians toward a criminal regime. And that too radically affected my thinking and acting as a moral theologian. After the war, I returned to moral theology with the firm decision to teach it so that the core concept would not be obedience but responsibility, the courage to be responsible."[21] He saw the manualists as being responsible for this conforming, obediential moral theology, one that was worried solely about following Church rules; instead, he summoned conscientious Christians to a responsive and responsible life of discipleship.

In the same year that *Morale Fondamentale* was published, Bernard Häring published in German the sixteen-hundred page, three-volume magisterial manual *Das Gesetz Christi* (English: *The Law of Christ: Moral Theology for Priests and Laity*).[22] Of his 104 published books, this was his landmark contribution. The opening words of the foreword were decisive: ""The principle, the norm, the center, and the goal of Christian moral theology is Christ."[23] Christ surrounded by his disciples, and not sin, became the subject of moral theology. Among its innumerable contributions are five central themes: an entirely positive orientation in the pursuit of the good; an emphasis on history and tradition; human freedom as the basis on Christian morality; the formation of the conscience; and the relevance of worship for the moral life. These themes later appeared especially in *Gaudium et Spes*. Häring's

---

[19] Ibid., 132.

[20] Bernard Häring, *Embattled Witness: Memories of a Time of War* (New York: Seabury Press, 1976).

[21] Ibid., 23–24.

[22] Bernard Häring, *Das Gesetz Christi* (Freiburg: Verlag Wewel, 1954); *The Law of Christ* (Paramus, NJ: The Newman Press, 1961).

[23] Häring, *The Law of Christ*, vii.

work is a complete contradiction of the pathology-focus of the moral manuals. What Tillmann, Carpentier, and Gilleman passed on, Lottin and Häring took up and reshaped.

THE COUNCIL AND ITS IMPACT ON THE RENEWAL OF MORAL THEOLOGY

After 1946 those men who eventually became the council fathers from Western Europe were now trained in a very new moral theology, a moral theology certainly distinct from the moral manuals. In these new manuals, charity, the Scriptures, Christ, conscience, and discipleship were the watchwords of the great innovators of moral theology: Tillmann, Gilleman, Carpentier, Lottin, and Häring. They would teach this in all their major seminaries and at their universities. Others like Émile Mersch, Phillippe Delhaye, Josef Fuchs, and Louis Janssens also entered the classroom and took this new moral theology further forward. In their classrooms were the future council fathers, influenced not by the rigidity and self-centered moral theology of the manuals but by the other-directed moral manuals of the post-war world.

When *Optatam Totius* ("The Decree on the Training of Priests") was promulgated, it offered a simple two-sentence statement on moral theology. This comment not only validated the work of the reformers but it also gave a directive to the syllabus and style of moral theology. Häring was its draftsman and, as simple as it was, its emphases on scripture, on charity, and the exalted vocation of discipleship captured the synthesis of the type of moral theology that Europeans were developing to replace manualism. "Special care should be given to the perfecting of moral theology. Its scientific presentation should draw more fully on the teaching of holy Scripture and should throw light upon the exalted vocation of the faithful in Christ and their obligation to bring forth fruit in charity for the life of the world (OT 16)."

Among others, Josef Fuchs made this directive the key to understanding Vatican II's mandate to moral theologians.[24] In a fifty-page article penned in 1966, Fuchs unpacked the document on a variety of levels, noting first that the summons of "perfecting" moral theology should be understood as being that the "Council requires, above all, that

---

[24] Josef Fuchs, "Theologia moralis perficienda: Votum Concilii Vaticani II," *Periodica de re morali, canonica, litugica* 55 (1966): 499–548. In English, "Moral Theology According to Vatican II," *Human Values and Christian Morality* (Dublin: Gill and Macmillan, 1970), 1–55.

moral theology – and other theological disciplines – shall be renewed."[25] In five parts he laid out the implicit agenda of the two-sentence summons for renewal. The first part is the most fundamental and the most relevant for us: "The Basic Truth: The Exalted Vocation of the Faithful in Christ." Here Fuchs writes: "The Council requires that moral theology shall be taught not only and not primarily as a code of moral principles and precepts. It must be presented as an unfolding, a revelation and explanation, of the joyful message, the good news, of Christ's call to us, the vocation of believers in Christ." He adds: "the fundamental characteristic of Christian morality is a call, a vocation, rather than a law; Christian morality is therefore responsive in character."[26] Later in his article, Fuchs underlines the closing words of the conciliar mandate, "for the life of the world," and writes: "moral theology must stress the importance of every individual's moral life for the true life of the world. Beyond all doubt, personal morality has social significance."[27] *Optatam Totius* invites us to consider moral theology as "a genuine theological discipline."[28]

The conciliar summons in *Optatam Totius* was repeatedly investigated in basic texts of moral theology around the world. Universally, *Optatam Totius* is the first of all reference points for moralists' reception of the council. Rightly so, as Richard Gula writes: It is the "only explicit statement of the council on moral theology."[29]

The reformers recognized their innovative work as now validated and eventually this renewal movement in moral theology was identified as "revisionism," after the summons to renew the discipline.[30] The revisionism will be a complete one, as Kenneth Melchin notes, in "totally reassessing the nature and object of moral knowing."[31] The revisionism project has Christ at the center and the conscientious agent as his disciple. It wants its own rational investigation into responsive living to be rooted in the coupling of Scripture with the gift of charity, bringing us into union with God, neighbor, and self. As such, it calls for a complete rebuilding of the theological project, bringing the disciple into engagement with the world. With such "personalist" or subjective

[25] Fuchs, "Moral Theology," 2.
[26] Ibid., 3.
[27] Ibid., 20.
[28] Ibid., 3.
[29] Richard Gula, *Reason Informed by Faith* (Mahwah, NJ: Paulist Press, 1989), 29.
[30] Kenneth Melchin, "Revisionists, Deontologists, and the Structure of Moral Understanding," *Theological Studies* 51, no. 3 (1990): 389–426.
[31] Ibid., 392.

claims as the call, the response, and the primacy of conscience as negotiating that response in charity, invariably the disciple's own experience is brought into relief. How then to construct a moral theology that adheres to the fundamental presupposition that the pursuit of morally right living is about moral objectivity?

Importantly, the council's address to moral theology was modest: only two sentences. These two sentences, however, were leveraged by Häring, Fuchs, Janssens, Delhaye, Auer, and others to give the revisionist project uncontested legitimacy. Here then we see the unalterable legacy of the council on the renewal of moral theology, which impacted significantly, as we will see later, what I call, the "conscientious" reception of *Humanae Vitae*.

We need to appreciate, nonetheless, that the early revisionists (Carpentier, Gilleman, Mersch, Lottin, Häring, and Janssens) had already helped form a European episcopacy, especially in France and Belgium and to some extent in Germany, that would shape the ethical vision for the church, especially in *Gaudium et Spes*. While Häring was involved in its writing, this time as the secretary of the editorial committee that drafted it, and was referred to as its "quasi-father,"[32] his actual draftsmanship was eclipsed by the influence of others, noticeably Archbishop Gabriel Garrone and Cardinals Leo Joseph Suenens and Paul-Émile Léger as well as theologians like Marie Dominique Chenu, Yves Congar, Josef Ratzinger, Karl Rahner, and the social scientist Louis Lebret. None of these were moral theologians but each of them knew and were influenced by the emergent work of the revisionists, such that Joseph Selling calls *Gaudium et Spes* the "manifesto" of the revisionists.[33]

Revisionism is replete in the document: The anthropological vision is based on the human as a social being (GS 23–25). Moral issues are not treated as primarily individual, but rather as communal and even global. Even though the reality of sin is consistently acknowledged in the document (GS 10, 13–14, 22, 25, 37, 40–41, 58, 78), the vision is fundamentally positive as the church stands with the world in joy and hope (GS 1). A new moral theological foundation is emerging: Here the church conveys a deep sympathy for the human condition, especially in all its anxieties, and stands in confident solidarity with the world.

---

[32] Charles Curran, "Bernard Häring: A Moral Theologian Whose Soul Matched His Scholarship," *National Catholic Reporter* 34 (17 July 1998): 11.

[33] Joseph Selling, "*Gaudium et Spes*: A Manifesto for Contemporary Moral Theology," in *Vatican II and Its Legacy*, eds. Mathijs Lamberigts and Leo Kenis (Leuven: Peter, 2002), 145–62.

The entire experience of ambivalence that so affected the world in its tumultuous changes of the 1960s is positively, but realistically, engaged.[34] Finally, in looking at contemporary moral challenges, the church encourages an interdisciplinary approach in understanding and promoting a globalized vision of modernity (GS 77–78). In a manner of speaking, *Gaudium et Spes* lays the ecclesial context for the revisionist agenda and this has enormous influence on the renewal of moral theology.

Four particular dimensions of *Gaudium et Spes* bear mentioning. First, the theology of marriage is remarkably different from *Casti Connubii*: Marriage is a "communion of love" (GS 47), an "intimate partnership" (GS 48); it is no longer seen as a contract, but as a covenant (GS 48). Rather than asserting procreation as the singular end of marriage, the council fathers argued: "Marriage was not instituted solely for the procreation of children" (GS 50). Such positive, non-legalistic, deeply affirming language is a new phenomenon for Vatican teaching on marriage. In a way, these elements on marriage influence *Humanae Vitae* as well as its "conscientious" reception.

Second, out of this same framework the council shaped its teaching on conscience, evidently indebted to Carpentier, Gilleman, Lottin, and Häring's extensive work.[35] Their work anticipated, inspired, and formed the now-famous conciliar definition of conscience in paragraph 16, which is, I think, the emblematic expression of the hopeful expectations raised by the revisionists and affirmed by Vatican II.

Deep within their conscience men and women discover a law which they have not laid upon themselves and which they must obey. Its voice, ever calling them to love and to do what is good and to avoid evil, tells them inwardly at the right moment: do this, shun that. For they have in their hearts a law inscribed by God. Their dignity rests in observing this law, and by this they will be judged. Their conscience is people's most secret core, and their sanctuary. There they are alone with God whose voice echoes in their depths. Through loyalty to conscience, Christians are joined to others in the search for truth and for the right solution to so many moral problems which arise both in the life of individuals and from social relationships. Hence, the more a correct conscience

---

[34] Philippe Bordeyne, *L'homme et son angoisse: la theologie morale de 'Gaudium et Spes'* (Paris: Cerf, 2004).

[35] See, for instance, Häring, *Law of Christ*, 1:135–89.

prevails, the more do persons and groups turn aside from blind choice and endeavor to conform to the objective standards of conduct. Yet it often happens that conscience goes astray through ignorance which it is unable to avoid, without thereby losing its dignity. This cannot be said of the person who takes little trouble to find out what is true and good, or when conscience is gradually almost blinded through the habit of committing sin. (GS 16)

Significantly, *Gaudium et Spes* roots the possibility of conscience in freedom (GS 17). There are many reasons for the turn to freedom: the Fascist and Nazi movements that imprisoned millions across the European continent; the subsequent developments in the philosophy of existentialism; the incredibly obsessive control of the manualists and the ever encroaching dictates from the Vatican; and Soviet expansionism into Eastern Europe. But this freedom is rooted in Pauline theology, which teaches us that our freedom is secured by Christ and the Spirit. This freedom that guarantees that one can follow conscience's dictates[36] becomes the very opening salvo of *Dignitatis Humanae*:

> People nowadays are becoming increasingly conscious of the dignity of the human person; a growing number demand that people should exercise fully their own judgment and a responsible freedom in their actions, and should not be subject to external pressure or coercion, but inspired by a sense of duty. At the same time, to present excessive restrictions of the rightful freedom of individuals and associations, they demand the constitutional limitations of the powers of government. This demand for freedom in human society is concerned chiefly with the affairs of the human spirit, and especially with what concerns the free practice of religion in society. (DH 1)

Just as the earlier revisionists influenced these texts, the texts themselves became enormous catalysts for moral theology's ongoing renewal. The German Josef Fuchs, the Australian Terence Kennedy, and the American Charles Curran each published collected essays on the topic.[37] Full-length books were written by Eric D'Arcy from

---

[36] John W. O'Malley, *What Happened at Vatican II* (Cambridge, MA: Harvard University Press, 2008), 308–9.

[37] Josef Fuchs, ed., *Das Gewissen* (Düsseldorf: Patmos Verlag, 1979);Marian Nalepa and Terence Kennedy, eds., *La Coscienza morale oggi* (Rome: Editiones Academicae Alphonsianae, 1987); Charles E. Curran, ed., *Readings in Moral Theology No. 14: Conscience* (Mahwah, NJ: Paulist Press, 2004).

Australia, Linda Hogan from Ireland, Kevin Kelly from England, Ann Patrick from the United States, Osamu Takeuchi from Japan, and Paul Valadier from France.[38] Conscience became the locus for developing moral judgment, which itself sets the standard of moral objectivity.

Third, in providing the ecclesial context in which the renewal of moral theology could flourish, *Gaudium ets Spes* prompted moral theology and social ethics to take down the wall that let them be two autonomous fields. As we will see later, John Courtney Murray, who influenced *Dignitatis Humanae*, was never considered a moral theologian; social ethics, like social encyclicals, had their own ambit distinct from moral theology and the moral magisterium. Still, the revisionists' move toward the social meant that their anthropological core could not remain individualistic and solitary. The moral virtues could no longer be solely about chastity, temperance, fortitude, obedience, a cautious prudence, and fear of the Lord; charity demanded justice, mercy, and solidarity. Nonetheless, though the revisionists insisted on the social, it was not until the council that the fields were forced to engage each other. *Gaudium et Spes* is written in such a way that the lines that demarcated them are no longer acceptable, or for that matter, visible. It is for this reason today that few self-identify as moral theologians or as social ethicists, but are more at home with the appellation of theological ethicist.

Fourth, while there was little instruction about ethics (natural law, moral principles, and virtues are referred to as dependable, but with no appreciation for revisionists' radical rethinking of each of the three areas), still the council was deeply concerned about discourse between the world and the church. Upholding repeatedly the conscience, particularly of the laity (conscience is cited twenty-eight times in *Gaudium et Spes*), the council fathers argued that no one can "indulge in a merely individualistic morality" but "must consider it their sacred duty to count social obligations among their chief duties today" (GS 30). Together through discourse the foundations of good order depend on the well-formed consciences (GS 43, see also 16, 26, 41). Moreover, as the laity pursue solutions they need to be mindful "that their pastors will not always be so expert as to have ready answer to every problem,

[38] Eric D'Arcy, *Conscience and Its Right to Freedom* (London: Sheed and Ward, 1961); Linda Hogan, *Confronting the Truth: Conscience in the Catholic Tradition* (New York: Paulist Press, 2001); Kevin Kelly, *Conscience: Dictator or Guide* (London: Geoffrey Chapman, 1967); Anne Patrick, *Liberating Consciences* (New York: Continuum, 1997); Osamu Takeuchi, *Conscience and Personality* (Chiba, Japan: Kyoyusha, 2003); Paul Valadier, *Éloge de la conscience* (Paris: Seuil, 1994).

even every grave problem" (GS 43) and that in differing opinions, "no
one is permitted to identify the authority of the church exclusively with
her or his opinion" (GS 43).

A new humility was being proposed about Catholic discourse. "The
church is guardian of the deposit of God's word and draws religious and
moral principles from it, but it does not always have a ready answer to
every question" (GS 33). Now theologians are being asked to develop
more efficient ways of communicating church teaching, "for the deposit
and truths of faith are one thing, the manner of expressing them –
provided their sense and meaning are retained – is quite another"
(GS 62). Now the church attends to boundaries: "The political community and the church are autonomous and independent of each other in
their own fields" (76). This does not endorse, however, the "pernicious
opposition between professional and social activity on the one hand and
religious life on the other" (GS 43). Still, it does mean that the church
must heed the variety of competencies that are needed, that theology
must keep pace with scientific findings, and that "the faithful, both
clerical and lay, should be accorded a lawful freedom of inquiry, of
thought, and of expression, tempered by humility and courage in whatever branch they have specialized" (GS 62).

This description of discourse empowers theological ethical inquiry
to be conducted in the public square where a new tolerance for conscientious pursuit of the truth is promoted. Nothing like this had ever
been given to theological ethics.

But then came *Humanae Vitae*.

MORAL THEOLOGY IN THE ENGLISH-SPEAKING
WORLD FROM BEFORE THE COUNCIL TO
HUMANAE VITAE

Unlike in Europe, the end of World War II did not prompt in the United
States or in other English-speaking lands a repudiation of the manuals.
That repudiation came in 1968, in the wake of *Humanae Vitae*. Until
then, most American moral theologians were actively disinterested in
the council.

The developing role of the moral theologian as primarily the interpreter and parser of the church's laws for the sake of the confessor,
rejected in 1946 by the Europeans and replaced by a revisionist agenda,
had an extended life span in the United States, giving this development
a chilling maturity that is with us today. Charles Curran, in his compel-
ling *Catholic Moral Theology in the United States: A History*, makes a

similar point. As opposed to the newer approaches from Europe, "Catholic moral theology in the United States continued to use the manuals as the textbook for the discipline and followed existing approaches in sexual and medical ethics. As a result, theologians in this country were not prepared for the new perspectives ushered in by the Second Vatican Council."[39] While Europeans anticipated the renewal of moral theology by nearly twenty years before the promulgation of conciliar documents, in the United States, for instance, the council was long over before it had any impact on the field.

From 1940 onward, moral theologians writing the "Moral Notes" in *Theological Studies* vetted the European developments. John Lynch and then John Ford and Gerald Kelly were the gate-keepers of acceptable innovation, and they were parsimonious in granting entrance. While a survey of the works of the journal's first twenty-five years (1940–65) shows substantive innovations in the field of social ethics, whether from John Ryan, Paul Furfey, John LaFarge, or John Courtney Murray,[40] hardly any innovation can be found in the moral theology by Lynch, Ford, and Kelly. The divide between the fields remained until roughly the end of the twentieth century. Thus Ford's much cited essay on "Obliteration Bombing" is the exception.[41] As Eric Genilo shows us, these moralists often resisted innovation, unless the magisterium had not *yet* declared on a matter.[42]

In fact, they were in some ways more rigid, authoritative, and intolerant than even their predecessors like Slater and Jone. For instance, Ford and Kelly inverted the order of authority that the early manualists used, acknowledging the authority of the papacy and of Roman dicasteries *before* and, in fact, sometimes *without* considering the authority of the argument itself. A magisterial claim is, for Ford and Kelly, itself the guarantor of its truthfulness. "It is only through conformity with the teaching of the Church that the individual conscience can have security from error. The 'autonomy of the individual conscience' cannot be reconciled with the plan of Christ and can produce only 'poisonous fruit'."[43]

---

[39] Charles Curran, *Catholic Moral Theology in the United States: A History* (Washington, DC: Georgetown University Press, 2008), 59.

[40] Curran, 63–82.

[41] John Ford, "The Morality of Obliteration Bombing," *Theological Studies* 5, no. 3 (1944): 261–309.

[42] Eric Genilo, *John Cuthbert Ford: Moral Theologian at the End of the Manualist Era* (Washington, DC: Georgetown University Press, 2007).

[43] John Ford and Gerald Kelly, *Contemporary Moral Theology I: Questions in Fundamental Moral Theology* and *Contemporary Moral Theology II: Marriage*

Their intolerance of European innovation is palpable. Ford and Kelly ridiculed Gilleman for his work on the primacy of charity.[44] Farraher derided Bernard Häring for *Das Gesetz Christi*: "In much of his complaining, Haring, like many who make similar complaints, seems to confuse moral theology with ascetical and pastoral theology."[45] The divide became more frequent and regular when Europeans entertained the legitimacy of oral contraceptives. Lynch developed an entire note to refute and dismiss the now-famous groundbreaking articles by W. Van der Marck and Louis Janssens on the topic.[46]

Theologians are singularly the mediators of magisterial teaching as Ford and Kelly write:

> An earnest student of papal pronouncements, Vincent A. Yzermans, estimated that during the first fifteen years of his pontificate Pius XII gave almost one thousand pubic addresses and radio messages. If we add to these the apostolic constitutions, the encyclicals and so forth, during the same period of fifteen years, and add furthermore all the papal statements during the subsequent years, we have well over a thousand papal documents ... Merely from the point of view of volume, therefore, one can readily appreciate that it was not mere facetiousness that led a theologian to remark, that even if the Holy See were to remain silent for ten years, the theologians would have plenty to do in classifying and evaluating the theological significance of Pius XII's public statements.[47]

Ford and Kelly's approach was eventually critiqued by their peers. Daniel Callahan described the authors as "loyal civil servants" and "faithful party workers" and dismissed their work "as years behind

Questions (Westminster, MD: Newman Press, 1964), 1:111. They refer to a radio address by Pope Pius XII, *"De Conscientia Christiana in Iuvenibus Recte Efformanda,"* Acta Apostolica Sedis 44 (12–28 April 1952): 271.

[44] John Ford and Gerald Kelly, "Notes on Moral Theology, 1953," *Theological Studies* 15, no. 1 (1954): 52–102, at 53; see also Gerald Kelly, "Notes on Moral Theology, 1952," *Theological Studies* 14, no. 1 (1953): 31–72.

[45] John Farraher, "Notes on Moral Theology," *Theological Studies* 21, no. 4 (1960): 581–625, at 581.

[46] W. van der Marck, O.P., "Vruchtbaarheidsregeling: poging tot antwoord op een nog open vraag," *Tijdsckrift voor théologie* 3 (1963): 378–413; L. Janssens, "Morale conjugale et progestogènes," *Ephemerides theologicae Lovanienses* 39 (Oct–Dec 1963): 787–826. John Lynch, "Notes in Moral Theology," *Theological Studies* 25, no. 2 (1964): 232–53, at 246.

[47] Ford and Gerald Kelly, *Contemporary Moral Theology I*, 20–21.

the (theological) revolution now in progress."[48] Later, in a significant study of Catholic medical ethics in the United States in the twentieth century, David Kelly identified the period from 1940–68 as "ecclesiastical positivism."[49]

The demise of the manualist theology in the United States was caused by its greatest success: the encyclical *Humanae Vitae*. In 1960, Dr. John Rock, an American Catholic, developed the birth control pill and did so precisely to provide Catholics with a "natural" recourse to acceptable birth control, that did not use "barrier methods" or "obstacles to conception" like intrauterine devices or the prophylactics. This Catholic invention became the subject of considerable debate and, in 1963, Pope John XXIII decided to take birth control out of the deliberations of the council by establishing a "Pontifical Commission for the Study of Population, Family, and Births."[50]

Still, at the council, the hopes of developing church teaching on the topic hit an enormous impasse during a week of tumultuous debate over birth control in the final stages of the preparation of *Gaudium et Spes*.[51] Eventually, the council fathers wrote: "In questions of birth regulation the daughters and sons of the church ... are forbidden to use methods disapproved of by the teaching authority of the church in its interpretation of divine law" (GS 51). For all the joy and hope that the council fathers offered to married couples, when it came to the issue of responsible parenthood they were not ready to substantiate their theology of marriage with the teaching of conscience that they had repeatedly endorsed. Instead, they reiterated the teaching of *Casti Connubii*. The divides between theology and norm and between teaching and conscience became all too apparent and, in a word, foreboding.

Meanwhile the commission was meeting. On it sat, among others, Ford and Häring and later Fuchs. Earlier, in 1955, Fuchs had written on the natural law. There he claimed that the magisterium's "duty within the actual order of salvation is to form the consciences of all men,

---

[48] Daniel Callahan, "Authority and the Theologian," *Commonweal* 30, no. 11 (June 5, 1964): 319–23.

[49] David Kelly, *The Emergence of Roman Catholic Medical Ethics in North America* (New York: The Edwin Mellen Press, 1979): 231.

[50] Mark S. Massa, *The Structures of Theological Revolutions: How the Fight over Birth Control Transformed American Catholicism* (New York: Oxford University Press, 2018): 56–60.

[51] O'Malley, *What Happened at Vatican II?* 284–89; Jan Grootaers and Jan Jans, *La régulation des naissances à Vatican II: Une semaine de crise* (Leuven: Peeters, 2002).

primarily those in charge of public life."[52] During the first meetings of
the papal commission, Häring and others were thought to be tending
toward reform of the teaching on birth control. Purportedly, in an effort
to counterbalance their attempts, the new Pope Paul VI appointed a
number of more conservative archbishops, bishops, and theologians to
the commission, among them Fuchs. Many believed that it was Ford
who suggested his fellow Jesuit Fuchs to the pope, believing that the
man who wrote in 1955 would continue to think the same way. On the
commission, however, already disposed to the revisionists, Fuchs began
listening to the testimony of married couples and eventually abandoned
his conviction that moral truth is founded necessarily and primarily in
long-held norms articulated by the magisterium.

By listening to others, Fuchs slowly recognized that his original
supposition was inadequate, and began to critically explore a key question: whether the method of directly applying a norm to a case is also
adequate for determining moral truth. If that question were posed to
Josef Fuchs in 1955, his answer would have been a resounding yes; by
1968, it was an equally decisive no. For Fuchs, *Optatam Totius* was a
foundational experience.

To Ford's surprise, Fuchs became the author of the commission's
majority report that essentially advocated that decisions on birth control be made in conscience.[53] There he wrote that the competency of a
moral decision depends on the ability to consider adequately the various
claims on an agent (*Gaudium et Spes* 26). From the testimonies of the
married couples, he saw that their understanding of the various claims
on them is more comprehensive and more adequate than the general
teachings of Rome and acknowledged that the Christian finds moral
truth through the discernment of an informed conscience confronting
reality. The majority report is effectively the first revisionist church
document after the council.[54]

Still, in the interim between the report and the publication of
Humanae Vitae, Ford became indomitable both in convincing Pope
Paul VI that he cannot change *Casti Connubii* nor accept the majority
report of the birth control commission. He also authored the commission's minority rebuttal.[55]

---

[52] Ibid., 12.

[53] Keenan, *A History*, 120–34.

[54] The Majority Report was never published, though copies of it can be found through a
variety of sources. The document can be found here: www.ldysinger.com/@magist/
1963_Paul6/o68_hum_vitae/majority%20report.pdf.

[55] See Genilo, 63–65.

Much can be said about *Humanae Vitae*. For our purposes, we should simply see that it is the first papal rejection of the revisionists' innovative approach and the first significant papal endorsement of neo-manualism after Vatican II. Nonetheless, the two tracks that we have been following determined very much the reception of the encyclical when it appeared in 1968. Just as the council fathers from Western Europe gave us the conciliar teachings that led to the renewal of moral theology, similarly we find that their episcopal conferences (the French, German, Canadian, Scandinavian, and Dutch) provided a variety of responses that reminded the laity to follow their consciences as they read the encyclical. On the other hand, the United States' episcopal conference along with other English-speaking ones stood univocally with the reception of the encyclical, with hardly a word on conscience.[56]

Still, as clergy and laity in the United States heard from bishops overseas, they finally turned away from the manuals of Ford, Kelly, and company and looked for leadership elsewhere. In the United States, two major movements developed after *Humanae vitae* that made the reception of Vatican II much more significant. The first was the critical evaluation of the encyclical, and the second was the renewed engagement with the Europeans. Two people led the way on both matters: Charles Curran and Richard McCormick. This essay cannot go into the intricacies or the skills that each conveyed but the council's call to renewal in the United States was heard by moral theologians and their students almost singularly because of these two men.[57] While their styles are very different, together they made possible the indisputable reception of the council for the renewal of moral theology. Similarly, in Ireland, Enda McDonagh and Vincent MacNamara, and in the United Kingdom, John Mahoney and Kevin Kelly led their theologians into the renewal process of theological ethics in light of the council.

By the mid-1980s the revisionist project continued growing on both sides of the Atlantic. Ironically, the repudiation of the neo-scholastic manuals led to the conciliar summons to return to the sources of moral theology and that led the revisionists to provide a renaissance in the studies of Thomas Aquinas. These investigations led in turn to two other expansive developments on the nature of natural law and the virtues.

---

[56] John Horgan, Humanae Vitae *and the Bishops* (Dublin: Irish University Press, 1972).

[57] On McCormick, see James F. Keenan, "Making Sense of Eighty Years of Theological Ethics," *Theological Studies* 80, no. 1 (2019); on Curran see, Massa, *The Structure of Theological Revolutions*, 79–105.

CONCLUSION

This chapter cannot go into further detail about the ongoing renewal of moral theology but it must note two extraordinary developments in conclusion. First, throughout the world church, contextual moral theology has been emerging on each continent. Now being catholic captures both the universal and the local. The Europeans continued to lead with a conscientious or autonomous ethics that is constitutively relational; then, from Latin America there emerged liberation theology, first as a matter of systematic theology, but eventually in theological ethics as well. Later there developed another theology, the theology of the people. The North Americans were prompted by the Latin Americans and developed a series of liberative models, first feminism and then black theology, but later strands like womanist and *mujerista* theologies also emerged, and now more recently queer theology. In Africa, a strong contextual theology, inculturationism, emerged immediately after the council that sought to retrieve the long-held native African values that were oppressed by colonizers' evangelism; later a liberationist critique of African inculturationism developed as well; and finally, in Asia, a respect for inter-religious dialogue developed, much in the spirit of *Dignitatis Humanae*.[58]

Second, in all these localities, moral theologians turn to an enormous array of methods that today highlight the rich contextual complexity of local but catholic theological ethics. Still an interesting development, quite apart from the methodological differences, is how many new efforts in a biblical virtue ethics are emerging.[59] But that story is only now beginning.

FURTHER READING

Cahill, Lisa Sowle. *Global Justice, Christology and Christian Ethics*. New York: Cambridge University Press, 2013.

Chan, Lúcás. *Biblical Ethics in the 21st Century: Developments, Emerging Consensus, and Future Directions*. New York: Paulist Press, 2013.

Curran, Charles E. *Tradition and Church Reform: Perspectives on Catholic Moral Teaching*. Maryknoll, NY: Orbis Books, 2016.

Fuchs, Josef. *Human Values and Christian Morality*. Dublin: Gill and Macmillan, 1970.

---

[58] Keenan, *A History*, 173–242.

[59] Yiu Sing Lúcás Chan, James. F. Keenan, and Ronaldo Zacharias, eds., *The Bible and Catholic Theological Ethics* (Maryknoll, NY: Orbis Press, 2017).

Himes, Kenneth, ed. *Modern Catholic Social Teaching: Commentaries and Interpretations*. 2nd ed. Washington, DC: Georgetown University Press, 2018.

Hogan, Linda. *Confronting the Truth: Conscience in the Catholic Tradition*. New York: Paulist Press, 2001.

Keenan, James F. *A History of Catholic Moral Theology in the Twentieth Century: From Confessing Sins to Liberating Consciences*. New York: Continuum, 2010.

Kelly, Kevin. *50 Years Receiving Vatican II: A Personal Odyssey*. Dublin: Columba Press, 2012.

Mahoney, John. *The Making of Moral Theology: A Study of the Roman Catholic Tradition*. New York: Oxford University Press, 1987.

Massa, Mark S. *The Structures of Theological Revolutions: How the Fight over Birth Control Transformed American Catholicism*. New York: Oxford University Press, 2018.

McCormick, Richard A. *Notes on Moral Theology: 1965 through 1980*. Washington, DC: University Press of America, 1981.

McDonagh, Enda and Vincent MacNamara. *The Irish Reader in Moral Theology: The Legacy of the Last Fifty Years: The Foundations*. Dublin: Columba Press, 2009.

Appendix: Sources for the Study of Vatican II

CATHERINE CLIFFORD

The Second Vatican Council stands as one of the most extensively documented conciliar events in the history of the church. In addition, the council texts themselves are more extensive than any other body of conciliar teaching in the history of Christianity. These facts, to say nothing of the vast reservoir of secondary and tertiary sources, can make the prospect of critical research on any aspect of Vatican II a daunting one.

This chapter provides the reader with an initiation into the sources for a critical study of the Second Vatican Council. First, it considers the documentary sources of the council's teaching. A brief presentation of the various editions of the sixteen conciliar documents is followed by a consideration of available commentaries that merit consultation for a sound interpretation. Next, an introduction to the complex apparatus of the official "Acts" of the council and to the various synopses available for scholarly research urges researchers to go behind the documents to the council debate, properly speaking. The second section explores the variety of sources left behind by participants of the council: bishops, theologians, auditors, and observers. These provide a unique and unprecedented window into daily events and encounters both within and outside of official meetings. The third section considers the available sources for a general history of the council including chronicles of the conciliar period and later histories, works that explain the role and function of the various conciliar commissions and meetings in the conciliar process, and finally works that introduce council participants. The final section provides a brief overview of bibliographical instruments intended to support the historical and textual study of the conciliar event and its teaching. In this short space it is only possible to provide a thumbnail sketch of the vast array of sources at hand. While this survey is not intended to be exhaustive, it suggests a number of representative works.

DOCUMENTATION

The Sixteen Conciliar Documents

English-speaking students of the Second Vatican Council are likely familiar with two major translations of the sixteen council documents, both of which were prepared in the wake of the council. Latin was the official language of discourse of the council fathers in the four sessions that met each fall in Rome from 1962 to 1965. It was the language of the preliminary drafts or *schemata* and of the official version of the final council documents – four constitutions, nine decrees, and three declarations. The first English translation was prepared under the editorship of Walter Abbott (*The Documents of Vatican II* [New York: America Press/London: Geoffrey Chapman, 1966]), and included brief introductions to each of the documents by Catholic authors with responses by Protestant and Orthodox scholars. This translation relied on the earliest versions of the council documents that appeared in the *Acta Apostolica Sedis* and the publication of the Vatican news service, *L'Osservatore Romano*.

A second English translation was prepared a decade later, this one based on the official Latin collection of council documents, which by then was published by the General Secretariat of the council in *Sacrosanctum Oecumenicum Concilium Vaticanum II: Constitutiones, Decreta, Declarationes* (*Vatican Council II: The Conciliar and Postconciliar Documents*, ed. Austin Flannery [New York: Costello Publications/Dublin: Dominican Publications, 1975]). The Flannery edition was revised and updated in 1992 and incorporated gender-inclusive language. Translators of this edition were able to consult other existing editions including the Abbott edition and those appearing in French and Italian.

A critical edition with a new translation of the documents of Vatican II appeared in 1990 in the two-volume *Decrees of the Ecumenical Councils* (Washington, DC: Georgetown University Press/London: Sheed & Ward, 1990). The English version of this compendium, originally compiled under the direction of Giuseppe Alberigo, was edited by the British Jesuit Norman P. Tanner.[1] It has the merit of providing the reader with side-by-side versions of the Latin original and an excellent rendering in English, also employing gender-inclusive language. This

---

[1] G. Alberigo, et al., ed. *Conciliorum Oecumenicorum Decreta*, 3rd ed. (Bologna: Istituto per le Scienze Religiose, 1973).

edition also includes helpful indices of references to scriptural, patristic, and conciliar sources.

Commentaries on the Council Documents

The earliest commentaries on the documents of Vatican II make for essential reading as they were written by many participants at the council, often with first-hand knowledge of the elaboration of the conciliar texts. Among the most significant is the five-volume *Commentary on the Documents of Vatican II*, ed. Herbert Vorgrimler (Burns and Oates / Herder and Herder, 1967–69). This collection, which first appeared in German as a supplement to the *Lexikon für Theologie und Kirche* (Freiburg: Herder, 1966–68), provides a brief historiography and detailed commentary for each of the sixteen documents.

The postconciliar period also saw the publication of commentaries on individual council documents by theologians who had collaborated in their redaction. Among these, one might consider: Gérard Philips, *L'Église et son mystère au IIe concile du Vatican: Histoire, texte et commentaire*, 2 vols. (Desclée: 1967–68); Y. Congar, M. Peuchmaurd, and P. Delhaye, eds., *L'Église dans le monde de ce temps: Constitution pastorale* Gaudium et Spes, 3 vols., Unam Sanctam 65 (Paris: Cerf, 1967); George A, Tavard, *De Divina Revelatione: The Dogmatic Constitution on Divine Revelation of Vatican Council II* (Glen Rock, NJ: Paulist Press, 1966); Gustav Thils, *Le décret sur l'œcuménisme: commentaire doctrinal* (Paris: Desclée de Brouwer, 1965); Pietro Pavan, *La dichiarazione conciliare Dignitatis Humanae a 20 anni della pubblicazione* (Cassale Monferrato: Piemme, 1986).

More recently, scholars have begun to produce new commentaries that take some account of the postconciliar reception: *Herders theologische Kommentar zum Zweiten Vatikanischen Konzil*, ed. P. Hünermann, J. Hilberath, G. Bausenhart (Freiburg: Herder, 2009); *Commentario ai documenti del Vaticano II*, 6 vols., ed. S. Noceti and R. Repole (Bologna: EDB, 2014–18); and the *Rediscovering Vatican II* series published by Paulist Press, 2005–9.

Navigating the *Acta Synodalia*

Anyone interested in the critical study of the development of the council's teaching will benefit greatly from putting to use those skills acquired in their study of ecclesiastical Latin and consulting the official council proceedings, or the *Acta Synodalia*. Somewhat like the Congressional Record – the official record of the proceedings of the US Congress, or the Acts of Parliament in other democratic systems of government – the *Acta Synodalia* are the official record of the proceedings of the council, a legislative event by the most important governing body in the church. It includes procedural rules, the names of those in attendance, the composition of commissions, the various drafts of conciliar documents, speeches, written remarks, reports, and records of voting. Published over the span of three decades from 1960 to 1991 and filling over fifty volumes, this mass of material is sometimes poorly indexed and can be a challenge to navigate.[2]

The *Acta* are organized into three series. Each series is divided into several volumes, and each volume has several parts, which fill separate folios or bound volumes of material. The first series, *Acta et documenta Concilio Vaticano II apparando. Series I: Antepraeparatoria*, is a compilation of materials from the antepreparatory period from May 1959 to June 1960. It includes the *vota* (hopes, expectations, and suggested items for the conciliar agenda) of bishops from each continent, from faculties of theology and seminaries, and from the offices of the Roman Curia. These were submitted in response to a consultation on the conciliar agenda initiated by Pope John XXIII and intended to orient the work of the various preparatory commissions.

The second series, *Acta et documenta Concilio Vaticano II apparando, Series II: Praeparatoria*, covers the official preparatory phase of the council from June 1960 to September 1962, and is organized into three volumes. The first contains the official acts of Pope John XXIII in this period; the second, the mandates of the ten preparatory commissions – each of which corresponded roughly to existing congregations of the Roman Curia and to two new secretariats – one for Social Communications, the other for the Promotion of Christian Unity; finally, a third volume comprising the proceedings of the Central Commission established to ensure the smooth conduct of the conciliar process under the guidance of the council's Secretary General, Archbishop Pericle Felici.

The third and most comprehensive series, the *Acta synodalia sacrosancti concilii oecumenici Vaticani II*, covers the council proceedings properly speaking from October 11, 1962 to December 8, 1965. Materials in these volumes are presented in chronological order, somewhat like a series of minutes for the council meetings of each day, known as "General Congregations." The council met in 168 General Congregations over four years. The proceedings for each year are found in separate volumes, one for each "session," which ranged over the months

---

[2] For a more detailed presentation, consult G. Lefeuvre, "Les actes du concile Vatican II, I et II," *Revue théologique de Louvain* 11, nos. 2–3 (1980): 186–200; 325–51.

from September to December 1962 to 1965: Vol. I: First Session, 1962, 4 parts (*AS* I/ I–IV); Vol. II: Second Session, 1963, 6 parts (*AS* II/I–VI); Vol. III: Third Session, 1964, 8 parts (*AS* III/I–VIII); Vol. IV: Fourth Session, 1965, 7 parts (*AS* IV/I–VII).

These four volumes of the *Acta Synodalia* fill twenty-five folios and contain different forms of documentation. Most common among them are the *orationes* – the text of the oral interventions or speeches made by the council fathers in favor of a given argument or perspective in their own name, and often on behalf of a group of conciliar bishops. Other significant forms of intervention were the *relationes* (*relatio* in the singular) or reports of the conciliar commissions. Presented by bishops designated as *relators* (reporters) by the various conciliar commissions, these reports present the draft documents for debate or deliberation and provide the rationale for the general orientation of each one. Other reports explain the reason for the various revisions made in response to the requests for modifications (*modi*) made by the bishops. Detailed lists of the amendments (*emendationes*) made in response to the written remarks (*animadversiones*) and requests for revision submitted by the council fathers are found in Volumes I and II. Each speech and written request for amendment is attributed to the bishop concerned and given a protocol number. The volume of indices for this series contains a list of the General Congregations and their corresponding dates, a useful piece of information to have at hand.

The three series of *Acta* are generally abbreviated as *ADA*, *ADP*, and *AS*, respectively. References to the *Acta Synodalia* include the volume number – a reference to one of the four council sessions – and the "part" or bound folio. By way of example: *AS* I/III refers to the first session (*periodus prima*), part III (*pars* III), and contains material from General Congregations XIX–XXX (14–30 November 1962). The *Acta* are now available in a searchable digital format at archive.org.

A valuable instrument for exploring the development of the council documents is found in a series of synopses prepared by Francisco Gil Hellin. These place the various draft schemas side by side. A useful set of notations refers the reader to the speeches and written remarks made by the conciliar bishops that inspired the various revisions of each draft. The full text of these interventions is compiled in the same volume with the protocol numbers that appear in the official *Acta*. Six volumes have appeared to date, including: *Synopsis: Constitutio Dogmatica de Divina Revelatione "Dei Verbum"* (1993); *Synopsis: Constitutio Dogmatica de Ecclesia "Lumen Gentium"* (1995); *Synopsis: Decretum de Presbyterorum Ministerio et Vita "Prebyterorum Ordinis."* (1996);

Synopsis: Constitutio Pastoralis "Gaudium et Spes" (2003); *Synopsis: Constitutio de Sacra Liturgia "Sacrosanctam Concilium"* (2005); and *Synopsis: Decretum de Oecumenismo "Unitatis Redintegratio"* (2006) (all published by Libreria editrice vaticani, Vatican City). These synopses have the advantage of enabling the reader to find all pertinent documentation in a single volume, rather than having to consult multiple volumes of the *Acta*.

Archival Sources and Inventories

A still under-utilized source of primary data is the archival material held in the official Archives of Vatican II located in the Vatican Apostolic Archives in Rome. In 1966 to 1967 the documentation of the various Conciliar Commissions and Secretariats, with the exception of the Secretariat for the Promotion of Christian Unity, were gathered together into a single archive in the Vatican. Since then the long process of cataloguing these materials has resulted in an inventory of seventeen volumes. While the work of cataloguing continues, the archive is now open to scholars and researchers. Piero Doria, chief archivist of this special collection, has helpfully described in detail the development of the Archives of Vatican II and their significance.[3]

EYE-WITNESS ACCOUNTS OF THE CONCILIAR EVENT

Around the world the conciliar papers, notes, and diaries of individual bishops and theologians await the attention of knowledgeable investigators in research centers, diocesan, and personal archives. Massimo Faggioli and Giovanni Turbanti have helpfully taken stock of many existing archives in *Il concilio inedito: Fonti del Vaticano II* (Bologna: Il Mulino, 2001). In the case of the more significant collections, scholars may consult published inventories containing catalogues and brief descriptions of available archival materials. By way of example, complete inventories can be found in *Carnets conciliares de Mgr Gérard Philips, secrétaire adjoint de la commission doctrinale*, eds. L. Declerck and Cl. Soetens (Leuven: Peeters, 2006), and P. Fontaine, *Inventaire des archives conciliaires du Fonds Paul-Émile Léger* (Outremont: Editions des Partenaires, 1995). Both of these figures played important roles in the leadership of the council. With the passing of the generation of

---

[3] Piero Doria, "L'Archivio del Concilio Vaticano II: Storia e Sviluppo [The Archives of Vatican II: History and Development]," *Annuario de Historia de la Iglesia* 21 (2012): 135–55.

eye-witnesses to Vatican II, more archival materials have become available. The work of cataloguing these materials and the preparation of new inventories is proceeding apace.

A full telling of the story of Vatican II is enriched by the personal accounts of the protagonists. Alberto Melloni has written on the significance of personal journals as a source for scholarly research on Vatican II and provides a helpful typology of personal journals, diaries, and memoirs.[4] While personal notes and journals are admittedly subjective, they nonetheless provide important insights into the complexity and the humanity of the conciliar process. Their accounts of meetings, conversations, and encounters in the wings of the conciliar assembly can help to clarify the chronology of events, shed light on the dynamics of personal interactions, and illuminate the clash and convergence of theological and pastoral concerns. Today we have access to the personal journals of many council fathers, of theologians who served as expert advisors to the various commissions and to individual bishops, and of lay and religious auditors. Ecumenical observers kept personal diaries and produced official reports following each session for their delegating church bodies.

Council Fathers

While a good number of council fathers have left behind important personal journals and notes, many remain in archival form and have yet to be published. Some have been inventoried. Recent publications include the memoirs of Cardinal Léon-Joseph Suenens, Archbishop of Mechelen-Brussels, *Mémoires sur le Concile Vatican II*, ed. Werner van Laer (Leuven: Peeters, 2014), and the council daybook and notes of Cardinal Julius Döpfner, Archbishop of Munich, *Konzilstagebücher, Briefe und Notizen zum Zweiten Vatikanischen Konzil*, Schriften des Archives des Erzbistums München und Freising, Band 9 (Schnell und Regensburg: Steiner, 2006). Both men served on the Central Preparatory Commission, the Coordinating Committee of the Council, the Secretariat for Extraordinary Affairs, and were two of the four Moderators appointed by Pope Paul VI in 1963 to guide the council proceedings.

Archival notes and personal diaries form the basis of a number of publications that provide insight into the role of other important protagonists, including Cardinal Alfredo Ottaviani, Secretary of the Holy

---

[4] Alberto Melloni, "Introduction: Private Journals in the History of Vatican II," in Marie-Dominique Chenu, *Vatican II Notebook*, trans. Paul Philibert (Adelaide: ATF Theology, 2015), 1–56.

Office and President of the council's Doctrinal Commission (E. Cava-
terra, *Il prefetto del Sant'Ufficio.* [Milan, Mursia, 1990]); Cardinal
Augustin Bea, President of the Secretariat for the Promotion of Christian Unity (S. Schmidt, *Augustin Bea: The Cardinal of Unity* [New
Rochelle, NY: New City, 1992]); and Cardinal Giuseppe Siri, a vocal
member of the conciliar minority (B. Lai, *Il papa non eletto: Giuseppe
Siri, cardinale di Santa Romana Chiesa* [Rome and Bari: Laterza, 1993]).

Conciliar Theologians[5]

Valuable resources for the background of the theological debates at the
council are the journals and diaries of the *periti*, consultants to the
conciliar commissions and to individual bishops. Many had a hand in
drafting portions of the council documents or in crafting the texts of the
oral and written interventions of the bishops. Perhaps the most detailed
daily account of the inner workings of the council is to be found in Yves
Congar's *My Journal of the Council* (Collegeville, MN: Liturgical Press,
2012) (original version: *Mon journal du concile* [Paris: Cerf, 2002]).
A remarkable document of over 900 pages, his penetrating insights
shine a light on the true character of the men around him and on the
crushing workload borne by the commission members in formal meetings, informal lectures, and working groups.

One finds a more sober and sparing outline of the business of the
council chronicled in Latin in the daybooks of Sebastian Tromp, Secretary of the Doctrinal Commission (*Konzilstagebuch Sebastian Tromp
mit Erläuterungen und Akten aus der Arbeit der Theologischen Kom-
mission: II Vatikanisches Konzil,* ed. A. von Teuffenbach, 3 vols. [Pon-
tificia Universita Gregoriana/Bautz Velag, 2006, 2011, 2014]). The
perspectives of Henri de Lubac fill two substantial volumes (*Vatican
Council Notebooks,* 2 vols. [San Francisco: Ignatius, 2015]; original
version: *Carnets du Concile,* 2 vols. [Paris: Cerf, 2007]), while the brief
notes of Marie-Dominique Chenu cover only the first two conciliar
sessions (*Vatican II Notebook* [Adelaide: ATF Theology, 2015]; original
version: *Notes quotidiennes au Concile* [Paris: Cerf, 1995]).

Ecumenical Observers

Over the span of four years no less than 174 official non-Catholic
observers and guests took part in the conciliar assembly. Their numbers

---

[5] For further reading on conciliar theologians and lay auditors, see Peter De Mey's essay
in this volume, "The Role of Non-voting Participants in the Preparation and Conduct
of the Council" (Chapter 5).

expanded with each successive session of the council, from fifty-four in the first session to 116 in the fourth. While not permitted to vote or to speak *in aula*, they followed each General Congregation closely with the help of simultaneous translation. On Tuesday afternoons they attended meetings organized by the Secretariat for Promoting Christian Unity, where bishops and theologians explained the significance of the draft texts under discussion. These meetings developed into a forum for frank exchanges with the observers, whose concerns were often relayed to the council floor by sympathetic bishops and members of the Secretariat. Many observers published personal accounts and relayed reports back to their churches and worldwide confessional families. Mauro Velati has drawn from many available archival sources to provide a balanced account of the significant contribution of the observers throughout the council.[6]

Among the more comprehensive accounts by the ecumenical observers, one might consider the reports provided to the Central Committee of the World Council of Churches and published in *The Ecumenical Review* (1962–66) by Lukas Vischer, a Swiss Reformed theologian and Director of the Faith and Order Commission, and by the Greek Orthodox theologian and director of the Ecumenical Institute of Bossey, Nikos Nissiotis. A significant delegation from the Anglican Communion was supported by the establishment of a new Anglican Centre in Rome. Their work is reflected in a volume, *Observing Vatican II: The Confidential Reports of the Archbishop of Canterbury's Representative, Bernard Pawley, 1961–1964* (Cambridge: Cambridge University Press, 2014). Others penned more personal accounts, including Edmund Schlink, representative of the Evangelical Lutheran Church of Germany, *Nach dem Konzil* (Göttingen: Vandenhoeck u. Ruprecht, 1966); Hébert Roux, representative of the World Alliance of Reformed Churches, in *Foi et Vie* (1963–65); and the American Albert Outler, representing the World Methodist Council, *Methodist Observer at Vatican II* (Westminster, MD: Newman Press, 1967), to name but a few.

Lay Auditors

The laity were represented from the second session of the council in 1963 by thirteen male auditors chosen for their experience in the leadership of international Catholic organizations, many of them connected to the Standing Committee of International Congresses for the Lay

---

[6] Mauro Velati, *Separati ma Fratelli: Gli osservatori non cattolici al Vaticano II (1962–1965)* (Bologna: Il Mulino, 2014).

Apostolate (COPECIAL) and the Conference of International Catholic Organizations. Twenty-nine men in all would participate in this or in subsequent sessions. Beginning with the third session they were joined by ten religious and thirteen lay women, also selected for their role in international organizations for the laity, the family, and for women religious. They contributed both directly and indirectly to commissions responsible for the drafting of the Decree on the Apostolate of the Laity, *Apostolicam Actuositatem*, and of schema XIII, the basis of the council's Pastoral Constitution on the Church in the Modern World, *Gaudium et Spes*. On six occasions laymen addressed the council fathers on matters pertaining to ecumenism, poverty, and the apostolate of the laity. First to address the council fathers were the French philosopher Jean Guitton[7] and the Italian President of COPECIAL, Vittorino Veronese, who spoke on December 3, 1963.[8]

Although they worked closely with their male counterparts, women auditors were not permitted to address the council. The full story of their participation and influence has yet to be told. The Australian Rosemary Goldie, a leading member of COPECIAL and one of the most active lay auditors, would be appointed as Undersecretary of the new Pontifical Council for the Laity in 1967.[9] Maria Pillar Bellosillo, president of the World Union of Catholic Women's Organizations and a leading proponent of Catholic Action in Spain, exercised considerable influence. Carmen McEnroy produced a first survey on the participation of women at Vatican II in the mid-nineties, *Guests in their Own House: The Women of Vatican II* (New York: Crossroad, 1996). More critical studies have begun to emerge, including the collections found in *"Tantum Aurore Est." Donne e Concilio Vaticano II*, eds. M. Perroni, A. Noceti, A. Melloni (Berlin: Lit Verlag 2012) and *Katholikinnen und die Zweite Vatikanischen Konzil: Petitionen, Briefe, Fotografien*, eds. Regina Heyder und Gisela Muschiol (Münster: Aschendorff, 2018).

---

[7] Jean Guitton, *Regard sur le concile* (Paris: Aubier, 1963); English translation: *Guitton at the Council: A Layman's Appraisal and Predictions* (Chicago: Franciscan Herald Press, 1964).

[8] F. Malgeri, C. Casula, R. Franch, et al., *Vittorino Veronese dal dopoguerra al Concilio: un laico nella Chiesa e nel mondo*. Atti del convegno di studi promosso dall'Istituto Internazionale J. Maritain, l'Istituto Luigi Sturzo e l'Istituto Paolo VI di Roma. Rome, May 7–8, 1993 (Rome: AVE, 1994).

[9] Rosemary Goldie, "La participation des laïcs aux travaux du concile Vatican II," *Revue des sciences religieuses* 62, no. 1 (1988): 54–73.

THE COUNCIL IN CONTEXT

Chronicles

The Second Vatican Council was a significant media event, capturing the world's attention at the very moment that satellite communications became possible and televisions had become affordable to middle-class families in the developed world. Religious and secular journals included regular chronicles, interviews, and journalistic accounts that traced the progress of conciliar debate. Among the most readable were the "Letters from Vatican City" that appeared in *New Yorker* magazine from the pen of the American Redemptorist, Francis Murphy (a.k.a. Xavier Rynne), now reprinted in *Vatican Council II* (Maryknoll, NY: Orbis Books, 1999), and R. M. Wiltgen's *The Rhine Flows into the Tiber* (New York: Hawthorne Books, 1967). Antoine Wenger, editor of the French Catholic journal *La Croix*, was among the only journalists permitted inside the council hall. From this unique perspective he produced a detailed weekly chronicle of events: *Vatican II*, 4 vols. (Paris: Centurion, 1963–66); English translation: *Vatican II* (Westminster, MD: Newman Press, 1966). M. von Galli and B. Moosbrugger contributed a series of "Briefe aus Rom" to the German review *Orientierung* (1963–1966). A collection of significant council speeches and texts was made available to American readers in *Council Daybook – Vatican II: Session 1-4*, ed. Floyd Anderson (Washington, DC: National Catholic Welfare Conference, 1965–66). In every local context one is likely to find newspaper coverage and commentary from religious and secular sources. These provide insight into the expectations of church and society and the initial reception of the council.

Historical Studies

A good place to begin the study of the council is with the reading of the highly accessible *What Happened at Vatican II* by the Jesuit historian John W. O'Malley (Cambridge, MA: Belknap Press, 2008). For a shorter introduction, one might consider Giuseppe Alberigo's *A Brief History of Vatican II*, trans. Matthew Sherry (Maryknoll, NY: Orbis, 2009). These well-researched volumes complement the perspectives reflected in the journalistic chronicles written for a wider audience from the conciliar period suggested previously.

Access to the *Acta* of the council has made it possible to re-examine the conciliar event and its teaching from a more critical perspective. The first comprehensive study of both the council itself and the development of the sixteen documents to draw consistently from the *Acta* and from many of the eye-witness accounts described here is found in the five-volume *History of Vatican II*, developed by an international team of scholars under the direction of Guiseppe Alberigo, and appearing in several languages: English edition, eds. Guiseppe Alberigo and Joseph A. Komonchak (Maryknoll, NY/Leuven: Peeters, 1996–2005). These provide a fuller picture of the council than the original detailed chronicle prepared in the immediate aftermath of the council by G. Caprile, *Il Concilio Vaticano II: cronache del Concilio Vaticano II*, 5 vols. (Rome: La Civiltà Cattolica, 1966). New studies on various aspects of the individual conciliar documents have begun to appear in recent years that draw from these same historical sources.

Also of interest are critical studies of the contribution to the council by protagonists from different regions and works exploring the regional reception of the conciliar teaching. Worth consulting, given the extraordinary influence of the Belgian bishops and theologians, is *The Belgian Contribution to the Second Vatican Council*, ed. Doris Donnelly (Leuven: Peeters, 2008). Other contextual studies include: *Vatican II: Reception and Implementation in the Australian Church*, eds. Neil Ormerod et al. (Strathfield: St Paul's, 2012); and *Vatican II: Expériences canadiennes – Canadian Experiences*, eds. G. Routhier, M. Attridge, C. Clifford (Ottawa: University of Ottawa Press, 2012). In many contexts, one is likely to find collected papers in special issues of local reviews to mark significant anniversaries. By way of example, we mention Kathleen Coyle, ed., "40 Years of Vatican II and the Churches of Asia and the Pacific: Looking Back and Moving Forward," *East Asian Pastoral Review* 41–42 (2005).

OTHER RESEARCH INSTRUMENTS

The Council at Work
A number of resources provide insight into the actual functioning of the council. Among the most useful is *Vatican II: The Complete History* (New York: Paulist Press, 2015), produced under the direction of Alberto Melloni (Italian edition: *Atlante Storico del Concilio Vaticano II* [Milan: Jaca Book, 2015]). Its chapters helpfully introduce readers to the history of the council session by session and include useful timelines, tables, comprehensive lists of council participants, commission members, and descriptions of their respective roles.

A more critical study of the contributions of the various conciliar commissions can be found in *Les commissions conciliaires à Vatican II*, eds. M. Lamberigts, C. Soetens, J. Grootaers (Leuven: Bibliotheek van de

Faculteit Godgeleerdheid, 1996). In a similar vein, readers will find it useful to consult *Experience, Organizations and Bodies at Vatican II,* Instrumenta Theologica 21, ed. Maria Teresa Fattori (Leuven: Bibliotheek van de Faculteit der Godgeleerdheid, 1999).

Yet another practical resource is the *Personenlexikon zum Zweiten Vatikanischen Konzil,* eds. Michael Quisinsky and Peter Walter (Freiburg: Herder, 2013), which provides biographical information on several hundred council participants, indications of their roles on various conciliar commissions, and bibliographical data. To complete this picture, one might consult the numerous biographical works pertaining to council participants, many of which are referenced here. An introduction into the theological themes of the council, with greater attention to the contributions to the council by Latin American and Spanish-speaking protagonists, is found in the *Diccionario Teológico del Concilio Vaticano II* (Pamplona: Ediciones Universidad de Navarra, 2015), prepared by Jose Ramon Saldana.

Bibliographical Surveys

Keeping up with the volume of literature treating the Second Vatican Council is a challenge. This is especially true since the fiftieth anniversary of the council (2009–15), which generated a renewed interest in conciliar studies. Philippe Roy-Lysencourt has produced a general bibliography in *Bibliographie du concile Vatican II,* Atti et Documenti 34 (Vatican City: Libreria Editrice Vaticana, 2012). While it makes no claim to be an exhaustive compilation, this volume can be a helpful starting point for anyone wishing to identify essential reading. Researchers will also find it informative to consult the occasional literature reviews published by Gilles Routhier, "Recherches et publications récentes autour de Vatican II," in *Laval théologique et philosophique* (1997, 1999, 2000, 2002, 2003, 2004, 2005, 2008, 2011, 2013), or the bibliographical surveys of Massimo Faggioli appearing in both Italian and English in *Cristianesimo nella storia* (2003, 2005, 2008, 2016).

CONCLUSION

From this brief survey it is clear that a wide array of tools exists to assist scholars and historians as they probe the history and theological developments of the Second Vatican Council. If the volume of documentation and the variety of existing publications is formidable, determined readers seeking to understand the events of the council will be rewarded by a broader and deeper understanding of the church in council – a drama in several acts, filled with thousands of players on a stage as wide as the world itself. Attentive readers will discover how God has made use of the most human of instruments to speak the gospel to a new age of human history and will witness how the church itself is formed in the processes of sustained prayer, study, encounter, and dialogue.

FURTHER READING

Acta Et Documenta Concilio Oecumenica Vaticano II Apparando. Vol. I–IV, 16 tomes, *Series I (Antepraeparatoria)*. Vatican City: Typis Polyglottis Vaticanis, 1960–61.

Acta Et Documenta Concilio Oecumenico Vaticano II. Vol. I–IV, 8 tomes, *Series II (Praeparatoria)*. Vatican City: Typis Polyglottis Vaticanis, 1964–88.

Acta Synodalia Sacrosancti Concilii Oecumenici Vaticani II. Vol. I–VI, 31 tomes. Vatican City: Typis Polyglottis Vaticanis, 1970–91.

Gil Hellin, Francisco. *Synopsis. Constitutio De Sacra Liturgia "Sacrosanctam Concilium."* Vatican City: Libreria Editrice Vaticana, 2005.

Gil Hellin, Francisco. *Synopsis. Constitutio Dogmatica De Divina Revelatione "Dei Verbum."* Vatican City: Editrice Libreria Vaticana, 1993.

Gil Hellin, Francisco. *Synopsis. Constitutio Dogmatica De Ecclesia "Lumen Gentium."* Vatican City: Editrice Libreria Vaticana, 1995.

Gil Hellin, Francisco. *Synopsis. Constitutio Pastoralis "Gaudium Et Spes."* Vatican City: Editrice Libreria Vaticana, 2003.

Gil Hellin, Francisco. *Synopsis. Decretum De Oecumenismo "Unitatis Redintegratio."* Vatican City: Editrice Libreria Vaticana, 2006.

Gil Hellin, Francisco. *Synopsis. Decretum De Presbyterorum Ministerio Et Vita "Prebyterorum Ordinis."* Vatican City: Editrice Libreria Vaticana, 1996.

Hünermann, Peter, and Jochen Hilberath. *Herders Theologische Kommentar Zum Zweiten Vatikanischen Konzil*. 5 vols. Freiburg: Herder, 2004–6.

Vorgrimler, Herbert, ed. *Commentary on the Documents of the Second Vatican Council*. Vol. 1–5. Freiburg: Herder and Herder, 1967–69.

Index of Names

Index of Subjects

Index of Conciliar References

CPSIA information can be obtained
at www.ICGtesting.com
Printed in the USA
LVHW052319081220
673656LV00016B/374